Anonymous

International Congress on the Prevention and Repression of Crime,

including penal and reformatory treatment

Anonymous

International Congress on the Prevention and Repression of Crime,
including penal and reformatory treatment

ISBN/EAN: 9783337297459

Printed in Europe, USA, Canada, Australia, Japan

Cover: Foto ©Suzi / pixelio.de

More available books at **www.hansebooks.com**

INTERNATIONAL CONGRESS

ON THE

PREVENTION AND REPRESSION OF CRIME,

INCLUDING

PENAL AND REFORMATORY TREATMENT:

PRELIMINARY REPORT OF THE COMMISSIONER

APPOINTED BY THE PRESIDENT TO REPRESENT THE UNITED STATES
IN THE CONGRESS, IN COMPLIANCE WITH A JOINT
RESOLUTION OF MARCH 7, 1871.

———⋘•⋗———

WASHINGTON:
GOVERNMENT PRINTING OFFICE.
1872.

<hr>

APPENDIX.

INTERNATIONAL PENITENTIARY CONGRESS.

MESSAGE FROM THE PRESIDENT OF THE UNITED STATES, COM-
MUNICATING THE PRELIMINARY REPORT OF THE COMMISSIONER
TO THE INTERNATIONAL PENITENTIARY CONGRESS OF LONDON,
IN COMPLIANCE WITH A JOINT RESOLUTION OF MARCH 7, 1871.

To the Senate of the United States:

I transmit herewith, for the consideration of the Senate, a preliminary
report of Dr. E. C. Wines, appointed, under a joint resolution of Congress of the 7th of March, 1871, as commissioner of the United States
to the international congress on the prevention and repression of
crime, including penal and reformatory treatment.

U. S. GRANT.

WASHINGTON, *February* 23, 1872.

PRELIMINARY REPORT TO THE PRESIDENT OF THE UNITED STATES
OF THE COMMISSIONER TO THE INTERNATIONAL PENITENTIARY
CONGRESS OF LONDON.

WASHINGTON, D. C., *February* 15, 1872.

As Commissioner of the United States to the "International Congress on the Prevention and Repression of Crime, including Penal and
Reformatory Treatment," I have the honor to submit to the President,
and to ask that he will lay before Congress, the following preliminary
report:

The first legislative act of the Forty-second Congress was the passage, on the 7th day of March, 1871, by a unanimous vote, of a joint
resolution authorizing the President to appoint a commissioner to represent the United States in the proposed congress. The President was
pleased to name the undersigned as such commissioner. The appointment was conferred nearly a year and a half in advance of the meeting
of the congress—much earlier, therefore, than would have been necessary if the intention had been simply to provide for representation in
the congress on the part of the Government. It was understood
(although the joint resolution did not in terms embody a declaration to
that effect) that my appointment included the further duty of arranging
the preliminaries of the congress, and made it necessary to open communications, either personally or by correspondence, with all the civilized nations of the earth. In this view, the honorable Secretary of
State kindly furnished me with a letter addressed to our diplomatic
and consular representatives abroad, requesting them to afford such aid
as they properly might in the prosecution of my mission.

As it would be obviously impossible for me, within the time at my
command, to communicate in person with the governments of all civil-

ized nations, I sought and obtained permission from the honorable Secretary of State to call upon the foreign ministers accredited to this Government, with a view to secure, if possible, their friendly co-operation. This was not found to be a difficult task. The ministers—I believe without exception—entered promptly and warmly into the project, and pledged such aid as they might be able to render toward its realization. Those from European countries gave me letters of personal introduction to the proper ministers in their respective cabinets, and all addressed notes to their governments explaining what was proposed, and commending it to a favorable consideration.

I sailed from New York on the 8th of July, and, returning, arrived at the same port on the 20th of November, spending thus a little more than four months in Europe, organizing the elements of the proposed international penitentiary congress. The governments with which I was able to open personal communications were those of Great Britain, France, Belgium, Netherlands, the North German Empire, Austria, Italy, and Switzerland.

The British government, without pledging itself to official representation, entertained the idea of the proposed congress with much favor, and promised co-operation in a variety of ways. With Englishmen, however, as with us, the method of voluntary action is much employed, both in the study of social problems and in the pursuit of social reforms. This characteristic was conspicuously displayed in the present case. Thus, at its annual meeting in Leeds, last October, the British Association for the Promotion of Social Science took decided action in favor of the congress; and Sir John Pakington, president of the meeting, in his closing address, gave emphatic expression to the general satisfaction occasioned (he averred) by the presence of the American commissioner among them. Thus, again, at a meeting held in London, on the 3d of November, in which several ex-cabinet officers and members of Parliament participated, a large and most respectable national committee was named, to be charged with whatever pertained to preparation for the congress in England.

From England I passed over to France. Here, by procurement of Colonel Hoffman, then in charge of the American legation, audiences were had of the ministers of foreign affairs and of the interior, MM. de Rémusat and Lambrecht. These gentlemen gave favorable entertainment to the idea of the congress; and by them I was brought into communication with M. Jaillant, supreme director of prisons for France, a gentleman of great intelligence, and intensely devoted to the problems of penitentiary reform. I was given to understand that a prison commission, created by Napoleon in 1869, would be revived and reorganized by the present government, and that it would be named by the government as the National Committee for France, and charged with the needful preparatory work in that country. That has since been done. M. de Rémusat further testified his interest in the congress and his desire to contribute to its success by procuring for me from the French Academy an invitation to read a discourse on the subject before that illustrious body; and the president of the Academy, in replying to my remarks, pledged its members to the use of their best efforts in aid of the proposed conference.

I may state here, in passing, that in my negotiations upon this subject with the different governments, three things were asked of each, viz: 1. That it would name commissioners to the congress of London. 2. That it would name a national committee for its own country. 3. That it would supply certain information relative to its prisons and prison administration.

From France I proceeded to Belgium, and thence to Holland. In both these countries the governments had already taken the first steps toward an active participation in the congress, moved to such action by communications on the subject received from their ministers at Washington. This greatly smoothed my path and facilitated my work. There were no prejudices to be overcome, no indifference to be removed. The official judgment had been gained and the sympathy of the authorities enlisted. In one, a national committee had been named; in the other, it had been determined upon. Little remained to be done, beyond conference and suggestion. My task here was, therefore, an easy one; and the progress made since my visits has been such that preparation may be said to be well-nigh completed in the two states. Both will be fully and ably represented in London by government members and others. A difficulty, peculiar in character and of considerable magnitude, has been surmounted. In continental countries a strict line of demarkation is drawn between governments and the public at large, to this effect: that where governments associate for international purposes, private participation is excluded; and, conversely, where assemblages of private citizens are convened, governments are not accustomed to send representatives. There is reason to believe that this usage will be widely if not universally disregarded in the present instance; and that governments, as such, will name delegates of their own to the congress, while national committees will designate others. Thus, for instance, Mr. Grevelink, chief superintendent of prisons and state police for Netherlands, and a member of the national committee for that country, informs me that the minister of justice has, on the nomination of the committee, named two of its members, and will probably name a third, to represent the government in the congress at the public expense, and that, at the proper time, the committee itself will invite such others as it may deem expedient, to attend the congress as delegates at their own expense.

On my arrival at Berlin, Prince Bismarck was not at the capital. Minister Bancroft therefore put me in communication with the honorable secretary of state, who replaces him in his absence, and by that gentleman I was introduced to Count Eulenburg, minister of the interior, who is charged with the oversight of the prisons and penal administration of the empire. After listening to an explanation of the nature and objects of my mission, the minister was pleased to express, in very emphatic terms, his approval of those objects, and to promise an earnest support of the congress, and the use of his best endeavors to secure participation therein by all the different states composing the North German Union. This pledge has since been amply redeemed. Count Eulenburg, under instruction from Prince Bismarck, took effective measures to have the interest not only of Prussia, but of all the other governments of the empire, directed to the approaching congress. He called to his aid for this work a distinguished councilor in his own ministry—Herr Steinmann—who is specially occupied with the prison question. Besides charging this officer with the preparation of a report in answer to the questions submitted relative to the condition of German prisons, he directed him to place himself in communication with persons in the several states of the empire, for the forming of committees, with whom he may confer, and through whom representation in the congress of London may be secured from all the different members of the Union.

My negotiations with the Austro-Hungarian government were prior to the late change in the ministry, and while Count Beust was still prime minister and chancellor of the empire. Mr. Jay, American minister at Vienna, whose zeal in the cause of the congress has been conspicuous, though scarcely exceptional, (for all our ministers have lent prompt and willing assistance,) honored me by a personal introduction to the chancellor, with whom our interview lasted more than half an hour. Count Beust received the idea of the proposed international reunion with much favor, gave his adhesion to it without hesitation, and, the minister of justice being absent at the time, placed me in communication with Dr. Eduard Ritter Von Liszt, attorney general (the highest law officer) of the empire. This gentleman from the first manifested the deepest interest in the movement, regarding it as one of the most important and most hopeful that had been or could be proposed. The crisis through which the government has passed since the date of my visit, resulting in a change of the ministry, has delayed the action confidently anticipated at that time; but it is believed to be only a postponement, and not a declension. Mr. Jay has not forgotten the object, nor been idle; and Dr. Von Liszt informs me that the present minister of justice has the most favorable disposition, and he feels confident that, through his interest and efforts, my wishes regarding the participation of Austria will have a perfect realization.

Mr. Lanza, president of the council of ministers, and minister of the interior, having in this latter capacity charge of the penal affairs of the kingdom of Italy, entered with all his heart into what he himself has designated "this great scientifico-social movement." In my interview with him, he unhesitatingly assured me that Italy should be behind no nation of the world in the support it would give to the congress of London, and in the efforts it would put forth to insure its success. And that promise he has nobly fulfilled. He addressed an elaborate and exhaustive report upon the subject to the King, submitting to him at the same time the draught of a royal decree, which His Majesty immediately promulgated, naming twenty-one eminent citizens as a royal commission, charged with the duty of studying and proposing the solution of the more important questions offered by modern penitentiary science. This commission has a special and most important work to do for Italy; but its labors are intended at the same time to aid the congress of London, and it has formed a sub-committee of its own members to act as the national committee of Italy. It is due to Minister Lanza, as showing at once his zeal in this movement and his friendship for our country, to state that he caused the commissioner, during his sojourn at Rome, to be entertained as the guest of the Italian government.

Switzerland was the last of the European governments with which personal communication was had. Though smallest in extent and population, the Swiss Confederation has not been behind any of the European states in the zeal and earnestness with which it has accepted the idea of the congress, and labored for its realization. President Schenk, to whom Minister Rublee personally introduced me, at once pledged the co-operation of his government, and the faith thus plighted has been kept to the letter. The council of the confederation has created a national committee; has named a commissioner to the congress, reserving the right of naming others if it see occasion; has answered the question submitted; and, in short, may be said to have already all but completed the work of preparation for Switzerland.

From most of the continental governments visited reports in answer to the questions submitted have been received touching their prisons and prison administrations; and from the others I have information that similar reports are on the way, and may be expected within a few days.

The undersigned was unable, within the time to which his mission abroad was necessarily restricted, to visit and open negotiations with the more distant of the European governments, viz: those of Sweden and Norway, Denmark, Russia, Turkey, Greece, Spain, and Portugal. These governments have been addressed through the American ministers accredited to them.

It is perhaps a little singular, and will be interesting to the President and the American people to be informed, that the Ottoman government, of those just enumerated, has, thus far, shown most interest in the congress, and taken action in regard to it in advance of all others. The Hon. Mr. Brown, American *chargé d'affaires ad interim* at Constantinople, has brought the ·proposition for the congress to the notice of the Turkish government, which at once responded favorably, and will be represented in the conference. He reports the minister of police as feeling so warm an interest in the matter that he has caused the proceedings of the public meeting in London relating to it to be translated into Turkish for circulation through the empire. The journals publish leaders on the subject, and urge that the various communities—Armenian, Greek, and Mussulman—as well as the government, send delegates to the congress, claiming that the country has of late made much progress in the principles of truth and justice, as well as in intellectual culture, and that this will be a good opportunity to show to the world how great the advance has been. Our ministers to Russia, Spain, Portugal, and Sweden and Norway have, at the instance of the undersigned, brought this subject before the governments of those countries; but as yet no decision has been reported, though the hope is expressed in reference to all, that the decision, when reached, will be favorable. Minister Cramer, accredited to Denmark, writes that, owing to the failure of certain documents to reach him, he had been unable to formally address the government on the subject, but would do so as soon as fresh copies of the said papers should come to hand, and would use his best endeavors to secure favorable action. I have some knowledge of the interest in prison reform which exists to-day in Denmark, and especially of the favor in which the proposition for the international congress is held by the able and accomplished gentleman at the head of the prison administration of that country; and judging from the facts thus within my knowledge, I have little doubt that Denmark will be present and will contribute her full share toward any useful results that may be reached. Greece is the only country in Europe from which no communication whatever has been received.*

In some, at least, of the numerous British colonies scattered over the face of the earth, interesting experiments in prison discipline are going on; questions of penitentiary reform are keenly studied; and substantial progress is making in the right direction. It is a pleasure to be able to report that a number of these are likely to be represented in the congress, and some, indeed, have already appointed their delegates.

Turning from the Old World to the New, we find the prospect for a successful conference scarcely less promising. The ministers of the Spanish-speaking republics of North and South America, as also of the Empire of Brazil, have taken a strong interest in this movement from the first, and have made active exertion to promote its success in their respective countries. Mexico, Brazil, the Argentine Republic, Chili, Colombia, and other South American states have decided to take part in the congress, and some of them have already named their commissioners. Japan and Hayti will be likely to be present by their repre-

---

* Since the date of this report information has been received from the Hon. Mr Francis, United States minister, that the government of Greece has taken the action asked, and has named a commissioner to represent it in the congress.

sentatives. Indeed, the strong probability is that there will be few, if any, of the civilized nations of the earth unrepresented in the approaching international congress of London, called for the study of all questions connected with the repression of crime and the reformation of criminals.

As regards the United States, little need be said. The General Government inaugurated this movement, and it is freely accorded by other nations the honor which belongs to that position. As the nation itself is to be officially represented in the congress, so, it is hoped, will be each of the States as well. The legislatures of several have already, by joint resolution, authorized the appointment of one or more commissioners. This has been done in New Hampshire, Rhode Island, Connecticut, New Jersey, Indiana, and, I think, Michigan; perhaps in some other States also. It is believed that most of the States will take similar action, and that all, or nearly all, might be induced to do so by the necessary effort to that end. The leading penal and reformatory institutions of the country, as well as their governing boards, are likely to send delegates to the congress; and so are the boards of State charities. It is believed, also, that the police organizations of our larger cities, and the more important criminal courts, will be in the conference by their representatives. It seems a thing much to be desired that the country which originated the congress should be largely represented in it; and the reverse of this would be proportionately humiliating.

I have thus endeavored to offer a truthful, though brief, sketch of the work done, and the progress made in organizing this great movement in the interest of civilization and humanity. Every day now witnesses an advance in some part of the field; every day brings fresh evidence that the movement is gaining strength, and taking on a fixed form; every day strengthens the hope of large and lasting benefits from a consummation which seems well nigh if not rather quite assured.

From the exacting nature of other duties I was unable to examine any great number of prisons and reformatories while abroad, though by great effort I managed to see between forty and fifty in the aggregate. What I have to say on these will be more fitly said in connection with the official reports on prisons, received from the governments of the countries visited; and I therefore forbear all reference to them in the present paper.

I beg to submit to the President, as a part of this report, the following documents, all of them bearing upon the congress, and all intended to aid the preparations for it, and to promote its success and usefulness, that is to say:

I. Sundry official reports of European governments on the prisons and prison administrations of their respective countries; in connection with which will be submitted a report of the commissioner's personal observations on foreign prisons and reformatories.

II. The principles of prison discipline as set forth in the works of Alexander Maconochie, one of the profoundest thinkers and most vigorous writers on penitentiary questions.

III. Reports by standing committees of the National Prison Association of the United States on criminal law reform, prison discipline, juvenile delinquency, and the disposal of discharged prisoners.

IV. A review of the State prisons, jails, and juvenile reformatories of the United States for 1871.

All of which is respectfully submitted.

E. C. WINES,
Commissioner of the United States to the International
Penitentiary Congress of London.

ACCOMPANYING DOCUMENTS.

A.—OFFICIAL REPORTS OF EUROPEAN GOVERNMENTS ON THE PRISONS AND PRISON ADMINISTRATIONS OF THEIR RESPECTIVE COUNTRIES, FURNISHED IN REPLY TO QUESTIONS SUBMITTED BY THE COMMISSIONER OF THE UNITED STATES.

[Want of time for such a purpose has been an absolute bar to the preparation by the commissioner of any report on the penal and reformatory institutions visited and examined by him during his European tour of last year. He hopes to supply this lack in his final report, to be made after the International Penitentiary Congress shall have completed and closed its labors. The following is the series of questions submitted to the different governments, in reply to which the reports printed below have been furnished.]

QUESTIONS.

I. Are all the prisons in your country placed under the control of a central authority? If so, does this authority absorb all the powers of administration, or does it share them with local authorities, and in what proportions?

II. What is the classification of your prisons?

III. In what proportions are the cellular and associated systems of imprisonment applied in your country?

IV. What results have been obtained, severally, from these two systems? Which of them do you prefer, and what are the grounds of your preference?

V. From whence are the funds for the support of the prisons obtained? What proportion of these funds are yielded by the labor of the prisoners?

VI. Who appoints the directors and other officers of the prisons, and what is their tenure of office?

VII. What special abilities and qualifications do you consider necessary in prison officers? Are the qualifications judged requisite actually possessed by the greater part of these officers in your country?

VIII. Have special schools been established in your country for the education of prison officers? If such institutions do not exist, would you favor their establishment, and why?

IX. What pension is accorded to prison officers who have become incapacitated by age or otherwise to fulfill the duties of their office?

X. What is the exact difference between sentences to imprisonment, to reclusion, and to hard labor?

XI. Does there exist in your prisons a system of classification of the prisoners? If so, how is it applied, and what are its results?

XII. Can prisoners, by good conduct and industry, shorten their terms of imprisonment, and how is this reduction effected?

XIII. Do your prisoners share in the earnings of their labor? If so, in what proportion?

XIV. What other rewards, if any, are employed to stimulate the zeal of the prisoners?

XV. What prison regulations are most frequently violated?

XVI. What disciplinary punishments are employed in your prisons?

XVII. Is an exact record kept of these punishments?

XVIII. Are chaplains provided in all your prisons, and for prisoners of all the different religions?

XIX. What, in general, are the duties of the chaplains?

XX. What importance do you attach to religious instruction as a means of reforming prisoners?

XXI. Are persons of both sexes, apart from the administration of the prisons, permitted to labor for the moral amelioration of the prisoners?

XXII. Do Sunday-schools exist in your prisons?

XXIII. How often are your prisoners permitted to write and to receive letters?

XXIV. Is the correspondence of the prisoners with their friends found to produce, upon the former, a good or evil influence?

XXV. Are the prisoners allowed to receive visits from their friends?

XXVI. How are these visits regulated? Is there between the prisoner and the visitor an officer charged with listening to their conversations, or is such officer only employed to observe their persons without interfering with the privacy of the interview?

XXVII. Is the moral influence of these visits good or bad?

XXVIII. What is the proportion of prisoners who are able to read at their commitment?

XXIX. Do schools for secular instruction exist in your prisons?

XXX. On what conditions and in what proportions are prisoners permitted to attend these schools?

XXXI. What branches of learning are taught in the prison schools, and what progress is made therein?

XXXII. Are libraries found in your prisons? What is the general character of the books composing them?

XXXIII. Do prisoners read much? What books do they prefer? What influence does their reading exert upon them?

XXXIV. Are your prisons provided with a good system of sewerage?

XXXV. How is the water-supply as respects both quantity and quality?

XXXVI. Are your prisons well ventilated?

XXXVII. What means are provided to insure the cleanliness of the prisons?

XXXVIII. How is the cleanliness of the prisoners assured?

XXXIX. How are the water-closets arranged?

XL. What system is adopted for lighting the dormitories and cells?

XLI. How are your prisons heated?

XLII. Of what material are the prisoners' beds made?

XLIII. What bedding is provided for them?

XLIV. What are the hours of labor, of recreation, and of sleep?

XLV. Where and how are the diseases of prisoners treated?

XLVI. What diseases are most frequent?

XLVII. What is the average proportion of the sick?

XLVIII. What is the average death-rate?

XLIX. Is there a distinction made in your prisons between penal and industrial labor? What kinds of labor are adopted in the different prisons?

L. Is the deterrent effect of penal labor conspicuous, as shown by the diminished number of relapses?

LI. What is found to be the moral effect of penal labor upon the prisoners?

LII. What is the effect of penal labor upon the health of the prisoners?

LIII. Is industrial labor in your prisons conducted by contractors or directed by the administration itself?

LIV. Which of these two systems do you prefer?

LV. If there are different systems of contracting for the labor of the prisoners, which do you prefer?

LVI. What proportion of your prisoners are ignorant of a trade at the time of their committal?

LVII. Do the prisoners learn a trade while in prison?

LVIII. Is it regarded as important that the prisoner, during his incarceration, be taught the art of self-help, and how is this result sought to be attained?

LIX. Is the frequent repetition of short imprisonments for minor offenses found to produce a good effect?

LX. What is the proportion of recidivists?

LXI. Are recidivists sentenced to severer punishments than first offenders?

LXII. Does imprisonment for debt still exist in your country? If so, do imprisoned debtors receive the same treatment as imprisoned criminals?

LXIII. What, in your opinion, are the principal causes of crime in your country?

LXIV. In what proportion are the two sexes represented in your prisons?

LXV. Is the reformation of the prisoners made the primary aim in the prisons of your country?

LXVI. As a matter of fact, do your prisoners in general leave the prison better or worse than they entered it?

LXVII. Are efforts made to aid liberated prisoners in finding work, and thus saving them from a relapse? How is this done, and what results have been obtained?

LXVIII. Do prisoners' aid societies exist in your country? Are they numerous and active? What results have been accomplished by their labors?

LXIX. Are you satisfied with the penitentiary system of your country? What defects, if any, do you find in it? What changes or modifications would you wish to see introduced?

ANSWERS.

[N. B.—The Roman numerals, in all the reports which follow, refer to the questions printed above. It was not deemed necessary to repeat the questions in each individual report. The arrangement actually adopted was thought sufficiently convenient, and is a great economy of space.]

I.—FRANCE.

[Translation.]

I, The prisons of France, with exceptions to be indicated hereafter, depend upon a central power, which is represented by the minister of the interior, and, under his authority, by the director of the administration of prisons.

§1. CONTROL.

The central power exercises its control by means of general inspections, made by special functionaries, viz: inspectors general of prisons.

Besides this direct and most important control, there is a local control of the prefects for all the prisons and penitentiary establishments; of the mayors and commissions of supervision for the houses of arrest, of justice, and of correction; and, finally, of the council of supervision for the colonies of correctional education of juvenile delinquents. It is necessary further to mention the intervention, though to a very limited degree, of magistrates of the judicial order.

General inspections.

The inspectors general have two classes of functions, the one accomplished during their tours of inspection, and the other, as will be hereafter seen, in the interval of these tours. They are charged with visiting all the prisons and penitentiary establishments, and they give account to the minister of the observations made on these visits, in a special report relating to each establishment.

The prefects.

The prefect represents the central power in the department as regards the supervision and administration of prisons; and it is his duty to visit, at least once a year, the prisons of his department. (Article 611 *du Code d'Instruction criminelle.*)

Mayors.

It is the duty of the mayor of each commune, where there is a house of arrest, a house of justice, or a house of correction, to make, at least once a month, a visitation of these houses. (*Article 612, du Code d'Instruction criminelle.*) By virtue of article 613, of the same code, there is, besides the police of these prisons. As a prison is an establishment of general and not merely municipal interest, the authority which the mayor is called to exercise therein partakes essentially of the central administration. It is as its representative that he acts on such occasions.

Commissions of supervision.

The commission of supervision, which is established, in principle, near each departmental prison, exercises, as its name imports, a supervisory action over whatever relates to health, to supplies, to religious instruction, and to moral reform.

The function of this commission is limited to the control of the various services. Its members, having no responsibility, cannot perform any act of authority in the prisons, in which it is important, moreover, to maintain unity of command.

As regards the penitentiary colonies of juvenile delinquents, the act establishes (*article 8 de la loi du 5 août,* 1850) a council of supervision, charged with the same mission of control in these establishments as the commission of supervision in the houses of arrest, of justice, and of correction.

Intervention of the judicial authority.

The penitentiary and correctional colonies are, besides, subjected to the special supervision of the attorney general of the jurisdiction, whose duty it is to visit them every year.

But this is not the only case in which penitentiary establishments are subjected to the control of the judicial authority.

By the terms of the 611th article of the code of criminal procedure, the committing magistrate (*juge d'instruction*) is bound to visit, once a month at least, the persons confined in the house of arrest of his arrondissement, and the president of the court of assizes, at least once in the course of each session, must visit the persons confined in the house of justice.

§ 2. ADMINISTRATION.

Criminal legislation being the same for all throughout the entire territory of France, the same rules ought to control its application, without exception either of places or of persons. As regards prisoners under sentence, inequality of discipline is inequality of punishment. As regards prisoners awaiting trial, this inequality constitutes a grave abuse, because it subjects a man, innocent perhaps, to rigors and privations which could not be elsewhere imposed by the administration upon another man in the same condition.

To establish and maintain in the same prisons the application of the same principles and of a uniform system, two elements are indispensable, unity of direction and centralization of the financial means of execution.

Unity of direction.

The director of the administration of prisons is charged with administering, under the authority of the minister of the interior, the prisons and penitentiary establishments of every class in France. Under him, and as a deliberative consultative board, is found the council of inspectors general of prisons, which is called upon, in the interval of their tours of inspection, to give advice on the more important questions of the service. The instructions and regulations emanating from the central administration are addressed, through the intervention of the prefects, who represent the executive power in the departments, to the directors of the different establishments.

At the head of each central prison is found a director. His action extends to all parts of the service. He is specially charged with conducting the correspondence with the minister of the interior, to whom he addresses his reports on the financial, industrial, and disciplinary condition of the establishment, through the agency of the prefects, except in urgent and extraordinary cases.

Directors of the houses of arrest, of justice, and of correction are charged with the administration of those establishments in one or more departments. In the prisons situated at the place of their residence their action makes itself felt directly, like that of the director of a central prison, on all parts of the service, and in the other prisons indirectly, through the agency of the principal keepers, who receive their instructions and are required to address to them frequent reports.

An important part of their functions has reference to the economical administration of the prisons, to purchases, to the verification of expenses, to the control of the accounts, cash, and material; in short, to the preparation of the various financial documents which they send to the central administration.

The principal keepers are the agents charged with the care and supervision of the houses of arrest, of justice, and of correction.

The organization which has just been described is the same in all the departments of France, except in one only, that of the Seine, an exception which deranges the harmony of the system.

The directors of the public colonies of juvenile delinquents are assimilated by their functions to the directors of the central prisons. It is therefore the central power which conducts the administration by their hands.

It cannot be the same in the other colonies, which are private establishments. The director is only approved by the administration, and this latter exercises such control as it has only through the intermediate agency of the prefects and the inspectors general. The administration of these private establishments has been determined by a general regulation of recent date, which explains why they have not yet been able to attain that administrative uniformity which is remarked in the public establishments of the same kind.

The colonies are appropriated to children who have for the most part been acquitted, but have been sent by the tribunals into a house of correction, to be there trained under a severe discipline. There are establishments in which education is made more prominent than repression, and the duty of the central power is to see that the children are properly treated, and that they receive, conformably to law, a moral, religious, and industrial education.

Centralization of the financial means of execution.

A law of the 5th of May, 1855, which transferred to the budget of the state the ordinary expenses of the houses of arrest, of justice, and of correction, which had previously belonged to the departmental budgets, has accomplished, for all the degrees of imprisonment, the centralization of the financial means of execution; a centralization which till then existed only with regard to the central prisons. Nevertheless this is still a point where the central power is not completely independent of the local authorities, and where the vote of the general council of the department must lend its concurrence. The department has preserved since 1855 its property in the buildings used as houses of arrest, of justice, and of correction, and has been at the expense of all needed repairs.

Penal establishments not depending on the ministry of the interior.

Certain establishments for punishment do not depend on the direction of prisons in the ministry of the interior, to wit:

1. The establishments in which men are undergoing the punishment of hard labor.

2. The prisons appropriated to prisoners of the army and navy.

The administration of the bagnios, of the penal colonies, and of the prisons of ports and arsenals, is centralized in the ministry of the navy; that of the military penitentiaries in the ministry of war.

However the case stands with the central prisons, the houses of arrest, of justice, and of correction, and the establishments of correctional education for juvenile delinquents, the administration of prisons in the ministry of the interior has an importance which is computed by a budget of about 15,000,000 francs, by a *personnel* of 4,700 employés, and by an average population exceeding 50,000 prisoners.

II. The establishments which receive prisoners are:

Navy:

1. The penal colonies of Guiana and New Caledonia, and the bagnio of Toulon, for prisoners sentenced to hard labor.

Interior:

2. The central prisons of hard labor and correction.
3. The houses of arrest, of justice, and of correction.
4. The penitentiary establishments devoted to the education of juvenile delinquents.
5. The chambers and depots of safe-keeping.

War and Navy:

6. The prisons devoted to prisoners of the army and navy.

1. PENAL COLONIES.

Bagnio at Toulon.

(Establishments placed under the jurisdiction of the ministry of the navy and of the colonies.)

The punishment of hard labor has been for a long time undergone in France, as formerly that of the galleys, in certain ports and arsenals.

The execution of this punishment, with the open-air labor of the convicts, in sight of the free population and in contact with it, was characterized by defects of every species and by innumerable perils. The law of the 31st of May, 1854, relative to the execution of the punishment of hard labor, brought a remedy to this state of things by substituting for the former the punishment transportation with hard labor. Establishments devoted to transportation, on the territory of one or more of the French possessions, other than Algiers, can be created only in virtue of a legislative act. Nevertheless, in case of obstacles in the way of the transfer of convicts, and until such obstacles shall have ceased, this punishment is undergone provisionally in France.

As a consequence of the enactment of the law of 1854, the bagnios of Rochefort and Brest were suppressed. There remains, therefore, only that of Toulon as a depot for convicts sentenced to transportation. The most important establishment for prisoners sentenced to hard labor is the penal colony of Guiana. A second was created in 1864, in an island of Oceanica—New Caledonia—which offers, by the salubrity of its climate and the fertility of its soil, conditions propitious to transportation. The transportation of women is authorized by the law, in view of marriages to be contracted with the convicts after their provisional or definitive liberation. The administration selected, from among the female prisoners of every class, those who expressed a desire to profit by these arrangements. These women are placed, to undergo their punishment until their provisional or definitive liberation, in a special establishment at Maroni, under the supervision of the religious ladies of Cherry. There is found, already, a certain number of women at Cayenne; but the majority of females sentenced to hard labor still undergo their punishment in the central prisons of the continent, agreeably to the sixteenth article of the penal code.

2. CENTRAL PRISONS.

The central prisons of hard labor and corrections receive—1. Certain persons sentenced to hard labor, namely, women and old men of the age of sixty and upward; 2. Persons sentenced to reclusion; 3. Persons sentenced as correctionals to an imprisonment of more than one year.

The central prisons, whose origin dates back to the law of the constituent assembly of October 6, 1791, were constituted a general system, to extend over the whole country, by an imperial decree of June 16, 1808. Their existing organization dates from the royal ordinance of April 2, 1817, which gave them the name they still bear, of houses of hard labor and correction, a designation in harmony with the penal code promulgated in 1810.

3. HOUSES OF ARREST, OF JUSTICE, AND OF CORRECTION.

These prisons are also called departmental prisons, not only because they are devoted to the exclusive service of the department in which they are placed, but, above all, from considerations of property and of the budget. On one side, the property in them, though they belong to the State, was assigned to the departments by a decree of April 9, 1811, together with the charges thereupon, whether for repairs, enlargement, or the construction of new buildings; on the other side, the current expenses of these prisons were for a long time a charge of the departmental budgets.

These prisons receive—the arrested; the accused; the *correctionnels* sentenced to one year and less; persons sentenced to severer punishments, who are awaiting their transfer; police prisoners; persons imprisoned for debts in matters criminal, correctional, of simple police, and of *fisc;* juvenile prisoners, whether arrested, accused, or in the way of paternal correction; and civil and military prisoners *en route.*

Houses of arrest and of justice are indispensable to each jurisdiction; consequently they are found in each chief place of *arrondissement.* To answer to the intention of the law, (*article* 604 *Code d'Instruction criminelle,*) they ought to be entirely distinct from the prisons established for punishment. But the complications which would ensue upon this separation in the services, the increase of the *personnel,* which it would render necessary in the greater number of localities, in which a single chief keeper is sufficient for the three houses, and, finally, the difficulty of obtaining from the departments special places, have led to this result: that the three houses are, in general, but three distinct wards of the same prison.

4. ESTABLISHMENTS DEVOTED TO THE CORRECTIONAL EDUCATION OF JUVENILE DELINQUENTS.

These establishments receive minors, of sixteen years and under, of both sexes. They are divided, for young male prisoners, into penitentiary colonies and correctional colonies. In the first are placed—1. Young children acquitted in virtue of the 66th article of the penal code as having acted without knowledge, but who are not sent back to their parents; 2. Young prisoners sentenced to an imprisonment of more than six months and not exceeding two years. These establishments are public or private. Those are called public establishments which have been founded by the state, and of which the state names and pays the directors and employés; and those are called private establishments which are founded and directed by private persons, with the authorization of the state.

The correctional colonies receive—1. Young prisoners sentenced to an imprisonment of more than two years; 2. Young prisoners from the penitentiary colonies who have been declared insubordinate. The correctional colonies are all public establishments.

A similar classification has been established for young female prisoners. They are received either into a correctional ward directed by the state, or into penitentiary houses connected with religious establishments.

These various establishments were called into being by the law of the 5th of August, 1850. There are actually counted of them thirty-two, viz: three public colonies, four correctional wards, and twenty-five private colonies. Twenty establishments are devoted to young female prisoners. One of them is directed by the state.

5. CHAMBERS AND DEPOTS FOR SAFE-KEEPING.

The name of chambers for safe-keeping is given to places in which are received prisoners who are being conveyed from point to point in localities where there is no house of arrest, of justice, or of correction. These chambers and depots have the same destination as such houses, and are but places for the temporary confinement of prisoners *en route*. The chambers are under the care of the *gendarmes* of the locality; the depots under that of the agents of the administration of prisons. No punishment, however trivial, can be undergone in them. The number of this class of prisoners is about 2,400.

6. PRISONS DEVOTED TO PRISONERS OF THE ARMY AND NAVY.

(These establishments are placed under the care of the ministries of war and of the navy.)

§ 1. *Houses of arrest and prisons of ports and arsenals.*—These establishments receive—1. The sailors, soldiers, or laborers of the navy under disciplinary punishment; 2. Persons arrested for crimes or misdemeanors within the jurisdiction of the several tribunals of the navy; 3. Persons sentenced by these tribunals to correctional imprisonment of one year and under.

§ 2. *Military prisons.*—Every military prison, situated in a place which is the seat of a council of war, should be divided into three sections: 1. A military house of arrest, receiving soldiers of every grade sentenced to disciplinary punishment; 2. A house of justice, receiving soldiers who are being conveyed before a council of war, and convicts awaiting either the execution of their sentence or a commutation of punishment; 3. A house of correction, receiving officers sentenced to the punishment of imprisonment, and soldiers sentenced to less than a year of imprisonment.

§ 3. *Military penitentiaries.*—These contain persons sentenced to an imprisonment of at least one year. These are persons undergoing a 'punishment of a correctional nature—the only punishment that does not exclude from the ranks of the army. Painful and afflicting punishments, such as irons, hard labor, reclusion, involve military degradation and the remission of the convict to the civil authority for the execution of those punishments.

III. The question relating to the measure in which the cellular and associated systems are applied in France will be answered with reference to the several classes of prisons.

1. *Central prisons.*

The cellular system is not applied in any central prison. The discipline of these prisons is that of detention in common with the obligation of silence. Some of them, however, have cellular wards, in which may be confined certain classes of prisoners.

2. *Houses of arrest, of justice, and of correction.*

A certain number of these establishments is constructed on the cellular system. Out of four hundred in all, there are about fifty of this kind. The other departmental prisons have been constructed or arranged upon plans, the latest of which bears date the 7th of January, 1863, and which have had for their aim the moral advantages of cellular imprisonment, with economy in the means of execution. In these mixed prisons, then, the discipline is neither that of the cell nor that of imprisonment in common. It includes three kinds of imprisonment, that of wards designed for prisoners, whose isolation is required by no special circumstance, and who constitute the greatest number (with common yards, dormitories, and heaters;) that of common apartments which are capable of receiving certain classes of prisoners not very numerous; finally, that of individual apartments, designed to secure, in certain cases, private instruction, to protect against injurious or dangerous contacts young prisoners under arrest, who are shielded by a presumption of innocence, and also to separate individuals for whom, before or after their condemnation, exceptional precautions of discipline or safe-keeping are necessary.

3. *Juvenile delinquents.*

Among the establishments designed for youthful prisoners, the prison of la Roquette, situated in Paris, is the only one in which cellular imprisonment is applied day and night, but this prison receives only minors of sixteen years, arrested or accused, and persons sentenced to an imprisonment not exceeding six months.

IV. As regards the results of the two systems of separation and association, there can be no question in France, except as to houses of arrest, of justice, and of correction; the only ones, as we have just seen, which have been constructed partly on the cellular system and partly on a system of a different kind.

Nevertheless, it is impossible to establish, even for these prisons, a comparison of the results yielded by the two systems. On one side, in effect, the statistics do not make a distinction between prisoners in the cellular prisons and those confined in prisons of the other class; and, on the other, in a great number of the former, it is only the edifice which is cellular. The system followed is that of association by day, in workshops for labor, and in yards for the hours of rest. Cellular separation has place only at night. The cellular prison at Mazas, and a part of that called La Santé, both situated in Paris, form an exception to this state of things.

Preferences.—The successive tendencies of the administration as regards the system to be followed in the houses of arrest, of justice, and of correction, may be epitomized thus: 1. Exclusive adoption of the cellular system down to 1853; 2. Subsequently to 1853, abandonment of that system from motives of economy, and adoption of a mixed system; 3. Resumption of studies, commenced in 1840, on the application of individual imprisonment.

In the first period, the administration began by repelling every project of reconstruction and of repair of the houses of arrest, of justice, and of correction, not conformed to the rules of the cellular system. The expenses involved in this system, and the impossibility of any great number of departments providing the necessary funds from their own resources, arrested the favorable dispositions of the councils general; the administration then renounced, for the future, the cellular system, and entered upon a new path, by substituting the separation of classes for that of individuals. It is in this spirit that plans were prepared from 1853 and 1860 for the construction and arrangement of departmental prisons, which comprised, as we have already seen, wards, common apartments, and individual cells. These plans are still in vigor, only care has been taken, in building prisons during these later years, to multiply the number of individual cells.

But this system is not the last word of the administration in regard to the prisons of the departments. The results obtained by the system are far from being satisfactory. We shall see in effect, in the matter of relapses, that out of one hundred prisoners in the central prisons fifty-two men and thirty-one women had been previously confined as convicts in the departmental prisons.

The administration has, therefore, just resumed the studies commenced in 1840, on the application of individual imprisonment. This system, in effect, appears to be the only one capable of averting the dangers of promiscuous association, so formidable in prisons which receive prisoners of origins the most diverse—arrested, accused, persons sentenced for at least a year, convicts awaiting transfer, young prisoners, civil and military prisoner *en route*, &c., &c. Separation by classes presents no difficulties, but there is a selection to be made of persons for each class, which requires great discrimination and a special study of the cases and character of every prisoner to prevent a corrupting contact with others. The chief keepers of the prisons of *arrondissement*, who have to maintain the order and police of the prison and to watch over the general services of the house, cannot be required to engage in this minute study of prisoners. That is impossible, and it is what renders promiscuous association so dangerous.

Individual imprisonment, moreover, it would seem, ought to give to punishments of short duration a character of intimidation, which they now lack, the existing system too often producing only the sad effect of familiarizing the prisoner with the *régime* of the prison. The consideration of economy, which heretofore has been of controlling force, and whose reality has been placed in doubt by recent examples, no longer seems sufficient to balance the opposite considerations of public morality, which recommend the abandonment of the *régime* in common as far as the arrested, the accused, and persons sentenced to short imprisonments are concerned.

V. Provision for the cost of maintenance of the prisoners in most penitentiary establishments is made—1. By the payment by government of a sum for each day of imprisonment, fixed by contract, for a period, on agreement of the parties, generally of three, six, or nine years; 2. By the right conceded to the contractor, who has made the highest bid, to the product of the prison labor, on condition that he pay to the prisoners a portion of their earnings, the amount of which varies according to the penal class to which each prisoner belongs. The price of the labor is fixed by special tariffs, approved for each industry by the superior administration. In consideration of these conditions the contractor is obliged to provide for the board and maintenance of the prisoners, in health and sickness, as well as meet numerous obligations specified in a list of charges, which comprises not less than one hundred and sixteen articles.

Several important penitentiary establishments are administered, as regards their industries, directly by the State. This mode of administration admits of a practical comparison of the two systems, and affords also the possibility of utilizing the labor of the convicts under certain conditions which are quite incompatible with the management of the industries by way of contract; such, for example, as agricultural labors.

According to the latest statistics, the product of the labor in the central prisons, agricultural penitentiaries,* and kindred establishments, brought an average gain of 74.33 centimes (nearly 15 cents) for each day of *labor*, which was reduced to 53.90 centimes (nearly 11 cents) for each day of *detention*, or of presence in the establishment.

The average *peculium*,† assigned to each prisoner on the above-mentioned gain, was 33.48 centimes (nearly 7 cents) for each day of *labor*, and 24.68 centimes (nearly 5 cents) for each day of *detention*.

The contractor received, from the tenths conceded to him,‛25.73 centimes (nearly 6 cents) for each day of detention. This sum represents the part which the prisoners contribute toward their support by their labor. The proportion is the same for the two central prisons and the three agricultural colonies, whose industries are managed by the state.

In general, and with the exception of the establishments in Corsica, the cost of support (not including the expenses of supervision and of administration) may be set down at 50 centimes *per capita* for each day of imprisonment. Consequently, it may be claimed that the convict meets about one-half the cost of his maintenance. •

It is important to remark that in one of the female central prisons it has been possible entirely to withdraw the subsidy granted to the contractor, the earnings of the prisoners being sufficient for the support of the establishment. In another prison the contractor, instead of receiving anything from the state, pays to it a centime per day for each convict. It is permitted to hope from this example that the administration will at length attain the end which it has always sought in this regard, that of exempting the treasury from the personal expenses of the prisoners who are confined in its great prisons for punishment.

In the houses of arrest, of justice, and of correction, as in nearly all the central prisons, the contract system of labor is adopted. The system is worked upon the same principles in the departmental as in the central prisons.

The short stay of the prisoners in the greater part of these prisons, the difficulty of organizing workshops for groups of individuals, subdivided almost to infinitude, not only because of the small importance of the establishment, but also as a consequence of the necessity of classing them in distinct categories; and, in short, the difference in the number of tenths‡ assigned to the contractor make the departmental prison proportionally more costly to the state than the central prisons.

Since 1855, when the service of the houses of arrest, of justice, and of correction became centralized in the ministry of the interior, the product of the labor, which, outside of the prisons of the Seine, did not exceed 16,000 francs, rose in 1868 to 1,811,672 francs, (the earnings of about 14,000 laborers, out of a total number of prisoners amounting to 22,998.)

The average product of the labor, then, has been, in the departmental prisons, a little more than six centimes for each day of imprisonment, (8,267,764 days.)

In 1868 the average expenditure for maintenance of these establish-

---

* This name is given to the three central prisons established in the island of Corsica.
† The part of his earnings belonging to the prisoner.
‡ Persons under arrest and awaiting trial, who ask for work, are allowed seven tenths of their earnings.

ments was 50.30 centimes, (not including the expense of supervision and administration.)

To sum up, it results, from the preceding explanations, that the part contributed by the prisoner toward the cost of maintenance may be placed at 50 per cent. in the central prisons, and at about 17 per cent. only in the departmental prisons.

The state, in the public colonies for juvenile delinquents, and the director, in the private colonies, gets, in principle, the total product of the labor of the inmates. There is no exception to this rule, save a deduction to provide for certain rewards, under the title of encouragements to labor and good conduct, and in what relates to children placed, temporarily, with persons outside.

The directors of the private colonies receive a daily compensation for the labor of the *colons*, varying from 60 to 70 centimes, by means of which they ought to meet the expenses of the administration, the cost of maintenance, the expenses occasioned by their primary and religious instruction, as well as the redemption of the original cost of the establishment.

It is difficult to estimate with precision the product of the daily labor in the penal colonies. The juvenile prisoners are most commonly engaged in agricultural labors, or in improving the estate—labors whose value can be counted only in the increased value given to the domain which has been thereby improved.

The cost of maintaining the convicts in the bagnio of Toulon—abatement being made of some diminutions of expense—was estimated, for the year 1868, at 65.68 centimes per day for each prisoner.

At Guiana the cost per day amounted to not less than 1 franc and 71 centimes, including the proportional expense of transportation and return. There must, however, be deducted from this cost the value of the work done by the convicts, in regard to which it is impossible for the ministry of the interior to give sufficient indications.

VI. In regard to the appointment of officers and their tenure of office: The rules which govern the naming of the various agents who compose the *personnel* of the penitentiary establishments are different according as the question relates to—1. The central prisons, the agricultural penitentiaries, and the public colonies of juvenile delinquents; 2. The houses of arrest, of justice, and of correction; 3. The private colonies of juvenile delinquents.

In the central prisons and other similar establishments the functionaries, employés, and agents, to whichever service they may be attached, that is, where they are proposed for the administration, properly so called, or for special services, or for supervision, are named by the minister of the interior. An exception is made in the case of keepers called residentiary, (*stagiaires*,) who are admitted by the prefects on presentation by the directors. (Decree of the 24th December, 1869, articles 8 and 9.)

As regards the houses of arrest, of justice, and of correction, the functionaries and employés proposed for the administration are named by the minister, and the employés of the other services are named by the prefects, as also the agents of supervision, other than the chief keepers. Still, these appointments do not become definitive till they have received the ministerial approval. As regards the principal keepers, a recent decree of the chief of the executive power, under date of the 31st of May, 1871, reserves their appointment to the minister of the interior.

By the terms of the law of the 5th August, 1850, relative to the education of juvenile delinquents, every private penitentiary colony is governed by a responsible director, approved by the minister of the interior. The employés placed under the orders of the director must be, in like manner, approved by the prefect. (*Loi du 5 août* 1850; *Règlement général du* 10 *avril* 1869.)

In the department of the Seine, where the prisons are managed, in many of their relations, under authority of special provisions, the directors are named by the minister of the interior, on presentation by 'the prefect of police; the other employés are named by the prefect. In effect, it is the prefect of police who, in Paris, administers the penitentiary establishments.

The inspectors general of prisons and penitentiary establishments are named by the minister of the interior.

The duration of the functions of the different employés composing the *personnel* of the penitentiary service is not limited by any determinate time. The agents who have not been gravely derelict in the exercise of their functions continue in place till they have reached the age at least of sixty and have been in service thirty years.

VII. The seventh question relates to the necessary talents and qualifications of prison officers.

The management of penitentiary establishments requires technical and administrative knowledge of great breadth, and offers, besides, special difficulties, arising out of the complicated organization of the service. It demands, in truth, a profound knowledge of business, of ministerial regulations and details, and an unremitting application, a quality essentially requisite in all directors. The administrator who finds himself face to face with a contractor whose interests are directly antagonistic to those of the state, ought to unite an unceasing watchfulness with an intelligent control. The principal duties of the administrator of penitentiary establishments—such as the organization of the prison labor, the examination of tariffs of labor, the maintenance of discipline in the midst of a perverted population, the choice and employment of means to awaken in the prisoners thoughts of repentance and ideas of moral renovation—all these duties, and others analogous, demand a special aptitude, fortified by an experience more or less extended. Penetrated with the idea that the direction of the penitentiary establishments cannot be confided, without the gravest risks, to agents who do not offer the most,trustworthy guarantees, the superior administration has established rigid rules to guard against the bestowment of the elevated functions of the service upon agents whose aptitude and experience would leave the least room for doubt. In the same order of ideas, it exacts, in the case of all its agents, of whatever degree, the knowledge demanded by the positions which they are to fill, and makes their promotion dependent on conditions of time and experience, varying according to the importance of the trusts to which they aspire. *(Décret du 24 décembre* 1869, *titre III.)* In short, to keep out of the service of the prisons agents unable to offer the guarantees desired, a ministerial decree, under date of the 25th of March, 1867, instituted, in the ministry of the interior, a commission charged with the examination of candidates for employment in the active service of the central prisons and the houses of arrest, of justice, and of correction. The programme of the required examination comprises the following points: writing, grammar, arithmetic, the principles of accounts, history and geography, (principally of France,) general notions of the penal system and of criminal procedure, general ideas of civil law, the civil and judicial administration, and the most important provisions of the laws, decrees, and ordinances relating to the penitentiary *régime*. The examination includes, in addition, a written composition.

Thanks to these various measures, the *personnel* of the prison service is composed, for the most part, of agents, enlightened, capable, and up to the height of the duties with which they are charged. Many of the higher officers unite to all the aptitudes required in the director of a penitentiary establishment a rare administrative ability and an extensive knowledge of criminality. In the lower ranks of the *personnel*, a majority of the agents are upright, zealous, and earnestly devoted to their duties.

VIII. There do not exist in France schools specially devoted to the education of the directors and employés of prisons, and the necessity for establishing them has not been made apparent. The best school, in matters of this kind, appears to be that of practice and experience, and the prescriptions of the decree of the 26th December, 1869, constitute, certainly, sufficient guarantees that positions in the prison service will not be confided to incapable and inexperienced agents.

IX. As has been said in the answer to a previous question, prison officers whose commissions have not been revoked, continue the exercise of their functions until the day of their retirement from the service. The different agents of the penitentiary administration are subject, as regards their retirement and the pension that may be granted them, to the rules embodied in the law of the 9th of June, 1853, relating to civil pensions. The principle laid down by this law is, that every public functionary, paid directly from the funds of the state, has a legal claim to a retiring pension, when he fulfills the required conditions of age and of continuance in the service, that is to say, when he has attained the age of sixty, and has accomplished a service of twenty years. It is important to remark that account is made of military services, when there are superadded to them twelve years, at least, of civil services. Moreover, a pension can be granted at fifty years of age, and after twenty years of service, to those who have become incapacitated from a longer discharge of official duty by grave infirmities resulting from the exercise of their functions. In short, this same law relieves from every condition of age and continued service, 1. Those who may have been disabled from continuing their service, whether as the result of an act of devotion in some public interest, or in exposing their own life to save the life of one of their fellow-citizens, or as the result of a struggle or combat encountered in the discharge of their duties; 2. Those to whom a grave accident, resulting, notoriously, from the exercise of their functions, shall have made it impossible to continue them.

X. The tenth question calls for an explanation of the difference between sentences to simple imprisonment, to reclusion, and to hard labor.

Simple imprisonment is a correctional punishment; its duration is for six days at least, and for five years at farthest. The individual sentenced to simple imprisonment may be deprived, wholly or in part, of his civil and his family rights. In case of relapse, the duration of the punishment may be doubled.

The punishment of simple imprisonment is undergone in the departmental houses of correction, in case it is not for more than a year.

Sentences to simple imprisonment for more than a year are undergone in the central prisons of hard labor and correction.

The convict is employed at some one of the labors carried on in the establishment. (*Articles* 40, 41 *du Code pénal.*)

Reclusion is a punishment afflictive and infamous. Every person sentenced to reclusion is confined in a central prison, and employed in labors which are carried on in the prison. The duration of this punishment is for five years at least, and for ten years at the utmost.

A sentence to the punishment of reclusion implies, moreover, the loss of civic rights.

Hard labor is an afflictive and infamous punishment.

The actual mode of application of this punishment is regulated by the law of the 30th of May and 1st of June, of which mention has already been made.

The sentence to hard labor for life implies civic degradation and civil death. A sentence to hard labor for a limited term draws after it civic degradation. The person so sentenced is, during the continuance of his punishment, in a state of civil death. A guardian and subrogate guardian are appointed for him to manage and administer his goods.

The sentence which imposes the punishment of hard labor is printed and posted in the central city of the department, in the city where the sentence was pronounced, in the *commune* where the crime was committed, and in that of the domicile of the convict.

Criminals sentenced to hard labor for a limited term are, at the expiration of their sentence and during their whole life, legally under the supervision of the police.

XI. In the departmental prisons the prisoners are, as much as possible, divided into classes.

Adults and juveniles under arrest and civil and military prisoners *en route* occupy separate places in a ward which takes the name of house of arrest.

The accused, and persons sentenced by the court of assizes, awaiting their transfer, occupy distinct places in a ward which takes the name of house of justice.

Persons sentenced to simple police punishments, and those sentenced correctionally to punishments whose duration does not exceed a year, are confined in a special ward, which takes the name of house of correction.

In the female wards, the arrested, the accused, the sentenced, young girls, and prisoners *en route*, form distinct classes, and occupy separate apartments, as far as the prison buildings permit.

In what concerns the classes of sentenced prisoners forming the populations of the central prisons, the second article of the royal ordinance of April 2, 1817, directs that persons sentenced by courts of assizes and by correctional tribunals shall be confined in distinct and separate places.

Hitherto it has not been possible to apply this rule, but the central administration has for some time had under consideration a project which will enable it soon to give effect to the terms of the above-mentioned ordinance.

Conformably to this project, certain central prisons will be exclusively devoted, some to reclusionaries, others to correctionals.

The male and female prisoners undergo their punishments in distinct central prisons. Special wards in the central prisons of Clairvaux and of Nîmes are reserved for persons sentenced to simple imprisonment.

Juveniles from sixteen to twenty-one years of age, who from their age are exposed to certain dangers from which it is necessary to withdraw them, are placed in the agricultural penitentiary of Castelluccio, Corsica, or in special wards.

For a long time the French administration has felt the necessity of creating in the prisons classes based, above all, upon the degree of perversity of the convicts confined in them.

Thus, on the one side, the dangerous prisoners, those who, before their conviction, had a character which would be likely to expose them to the outrages of their fellow-prisoners, or who might be a cause of disorder and insubordination, are placed in special cellular wards, called wards of isolation.

Wards to which has been given the name of wards of preservation and amendment, have, on the other side, been established in various central prisons and appropriated to persons sentenced for a first offense committed under the influence of a sudden impulse, or of some violent and momentary passion.

This experiment is still so recent that it would be rash to pronounce upon its results; but the conditions under which it has been thus far conducted are of a nature to encourage the administration to persevere in the path on which it has entered. It can be affirmed that the prisoners placed in these wards have shown themselves sensible to the distinction of which they have been made the object, and have exerted themselves to justify it by their good conduct. They have been remarkable for their industrious application to work, and the local administration has rarely been under the necessity of putting them back into the common ward.

XII. It is asked whether prisoners, by their good conduct and industry, may shorten their punishment, and, if so, in what way? To this we reply:

Prisoners may be restored, by pardon, to free life; they can also obtain commutations or reductions of punishment. An ordinance of February 6, 1818, fixes the rules to be followed in applications for clemency, which is generally exercised in concert with the administrative and judicial authorities.

The admission of prisoners on the registers of preservation is not exclusively the result of their good conduct in prison. Regard is also had to their antecedents and the causes of their conviction. Greater severity and circumspection are shown in regard to recidivists and to convicts whose crimes point them out as specially dangerous, as well as in regard to those who, from their criminal connections, would seem almost sure to fall back into crime after their liberation.

As a general thing, prisoners placed on the lists of preservation must have previously undergone one-half of their punishment; still, this condition is not indispensable.

Finally, what is to be said relating to military prisoners will be introduced under a special head.

XIII. The products of the labor of persons sentenced correctionally, who undergo their punishment in a departmental house of correction, are shared in moieties between the administration and the prisoners, the administration surrendering its share to the contractors, who, by the terms of their contract, are charged with the entire expense of the economic services. The state pays to the contractors, in addition, a fixed sum for each day of imprisonment.

Labor is obligatory only for those who have been sentenced. The arrested and the accused can work when they desire it, and when it is possible to place tools in their hands without having to fear suicides or escapes.

The labor of the arrested and the accused, who have a right to the whole of the product, is the object of special agreements. To indemnify the contractor, who has to furnish material and tools, there is made, in his favor, from the sum total of their earnings, a deduction of three-tenths. In the central prisons the product of the labor is divided into tenths. A portion of these tenths is assigned to the convicts, and takes the name of *peculium*. The quota of tenths granted to the convicts is determined by the nature of the punishments and the number of convictions incurred. The assignment is adjusted between the three classes thus: correctionals, five-tenths; reclusionaries, four-tenths; those sentenced to hard labor, three-tenths.

The part assigned to prisoners sentenced on relapse is reduced from one to two-tenths for each previous conviction, down to the limit of the last tenth, which is, under all circumstances, paid to the convict.

The *peculium* is divided by moieties into *peculium* disposable and *peculium* reserved. The first is at the disposition of the convicts during their imprisonment for certain authorized uses, and especially for the purchase of supplementary provisions and supplies, for the relief of their families, and for voluntary restitutions. It also furnishes reserves, to the profit of the treasury, for fines, punishments, breaking prison, or damages to the prejudice of the state or the contractor. The *peculium* reserved was established in view of securing to liberated prisoners some resources for their first necessities on their discharge from the penitentiary.

The number of tenths, allowed to convicts by the ordinance of 1843, may be increased on account of their good conduct and their diligence. There may be granted to them, in consideration of these qualities, even six-tenths, conformably to a decree of 1854. The disposable *peculium* may be increased by gratuities granted by the treasury, the manufacturers, or the contractors, under the title of recompense and encouragement; and it may also be augmented by the transfer, under the same title, of portions of the *peculium* reserved to the *peculium* disposable.

Finally, as regards juvenile prisoners, the general regulation of the 10th of April, 1869, directs that the chiefs of colonies shall submit to the minister the dispositions having in view the rewarding, by a pecuniary payment drawn from the product of their labor, those youths who shall have distinguished themselves by their industry, their religious sentiments, or their obedience.

The same regulation authorizes the directors of the colonies to hire or confide, temporarily, the juvenile prisoners to private persons for agricultural labors, with the sanction of the minister of the interior, and under certain conditions.

Juveniles thus farmed out have a right to a moiety of the wages paid for their labor. These sums are given to them at the time of their liberation.

XIV. Other rewards, accorded to convicts, are: Designation for employment as foreman of a workshop, monitor in the school, overseer of a dormitory, and other positions of trust, such as hospital attendants, store-keepers, secretaries, &c.

In the colonies of juvenile prisoners the rewards are: the gift of playthings, public commendation, prizes at the time of the general distribution, positions of trust, grades, badges, (ribbons for the young girls,) good marks, additional food, the table of honor, inscriptions on the roll of honor, provisional liberation, or placing at apprenticeship outside of the colony, military enlistments, and the gift of little books, with credits in the savings-bank.

XV. The moral offenses most frequently exhibited are theft, assaults, indecencies. As regards the infractions of disciplinary rules, more than half the cases in the central prisons consist of violations of the law of silence.

In most of the penitentiary establishments, next to that just named, the most frequent infractions are: refusal to work, the secret use of tobacco, gambling, trafficking, and the unlawful possession of money.

The men sentenced to simple imprisonment are those who commit the greatest number of moral offenses, as well as infractions of the rules of discipline.

In the female prisons a comparison of the whole number of offenses and infractions yields, in like manner, a result unfavorable to those who are sentenced to simple imprisonment.

XVI. Order and discipline are, in general, well maintained in all establishments dependent upon the penitentiary administration, without the necessity of a recourse to coercive measures of an excessive severity.

Acts of rebellion and violence take place to only a limited extent; thanks to the vigorous enforcement of the rules intended to insure a strict but equitable distribution of disciplinary justice.

The punishments authorized by the regulation of the 10th May, 1839, so far as the central prisons are concerned, and those sanctioned by the regulation of the 30th of October, 1841, applicable to the houses of arrest, of justice, and of correction, are: confinement in a cell, with or without irons, the hall of discipline, dry bread for three days or more, deprivation of the *cantine*, or of other food, the reduction of the tenths, fines, privation of correspondence and of visits, and sometimes the loss of an honorable position, such as that of foreman, overseer of a dormitory, monitor in school, &c.

The convict who has incurred disciplinary punishments cannot be placed on the roll of honor.

Corporal punishments are expressly forbidden.

The punishments authorized in the colonies of juvenile prisoners are: privation of recreation, of correspondence, and of visits, the picket, kneeling, cleaning prison, the wearing of a disciplinary dress, the loss of grades, badges, and positions of trust, bad marks, reproof administered in private or in public, isolation at meals, erasure from the roll of honor, and confinement in the punishment cell.

Escape from prison involves the loss of the *peculium* of the juvenile prisoner, and prevents his being proposed as a candidate for provisional liberty.

Confinement in a punishment cell can be inflicted only for offenses of the gravest character.

XVII. Every day (Sundays and feast-days excepted) the director of a central prison, assisted by his assessors, holds a tribunal of disciplinary justice, at which are required to appear prisoners, reported on the previous evening as having committed some infraction.

The chief keeper inscribes, at the same moment, upon his register the decisions of the director.

Minutes are kept of the proceedings of each session.

The punishments adjudged are inscribed by the schoolmaster on the bulletin of the moral statistics of the convict.

In the houses of arrest, of justice, and of correction, the punishments are inflicted by the director or the chief keeper, and are inscribed on a special register, which is subject to the inspection of the prefect and the mayor.

In the colonies of juvenile delinquents the director alone has the right of inflicting punishments; these must be inscribed on a special register, and on the bulletin of moral statistics, which is attached to the papers (*dossier*) of each inmate.

XVIII. In the houses of arrest, of justice, and of correction, a chap-

lain, chosen ordinarily from among the priests attached to a parish of
the city, is charged with the moral and religious service. In each of the
central prisons, and of the more important houses of arrest, of justice,
and of correction, a special chaplain is exclusively devoted to the religious service, and is considered a regular employé of the establishment.

Liberty of conscience is guaranteed to convicts of all religions. Every
prisoner, on his entrance into the prison, is required to declare to what
religion he adheres, a declaration whose truth is verified by an administrative information, and in case he does not belong to the Catholic religion he is transferred, whenever it is possible, to an establishment designed to receive prisoners of the same religion with himself.

In the houses of arrest, of justice, and of correction, every non-Catholic
prisoner under arrest or accusation, whether Protestant or Israelite, is
interrogated as soon as he enters the prison, to ascertain whether he
wished to be visited by a minister of his religion, and, upon his affirmative response, the minister least distant from the establishment is written
to and informed of his wish.

As regards the convicts, the regulations are formal; they are required
to be present at all the exercises of their religion in the prison where
they are undergoing their punishment.

XIX. In the houses of arrest, of justice, and of correction, which in
general—save in the chief places of the departments—have but a moderate population, the duties of the chaplain are limited to celebrating
divine service on Sundays and feast-days, to giving to the prisoners, at
least once a week, a religious discourse, to visiting the dungeons, cells,
and infirmaries, to being present with those condemned to death at their
last moments, to visiting the sick when they desire it, and to teaching
the catechism to the young prisoners who have not made their first communion. His visits in the prison must be made at least twice a week.

These obligations are common to the ministers of dissenting religions
in everything which is applicable to them.

In the large penitentiary establishments, the chaplains consult with
the directors in determining upon the various religious offices and services. They visit the infirmaries, the sick, the places of punishment,
and the solitary cells. In the sessions of the tribunals at the *pretorium*
of disciplinary justice, they are entitled to a place among the assessors
of the director. To prisoners who are prevented, by their age or infirmities, from taking part in the labors of the evening, they give moral,
religious, or instructive readings. They are called upon to give their
advice on propositions for the exercise of executive clemency.

XX. Religious instruction cannot have a great importance in the
houses of arrest, of justice, and of correction, as their population is
renewed almost daily, more particularly in the houses of arrest of *arrondissement.*

The chaplains of these establishments, being at the same time parish
priests, have not generally the time necessary to discharge their ministry
with success.

In establishments situated in the chief place of the department, where
the sojourn of the prisoners is more prolonged, the chaplain is often
exclusively attached to the prison. He can then devote more time to
the reformation of the prisoners.

In the central prisons for women, where, over and above the aid of the
chaplain, there is that of religious communities, to whose care is confided
the service of supervision, it is no uncommon thing to see prisoners come
to themselves, and to renounce a past which they strive to forget.

Prison reform has found an active co-operation in the devotion and piety of the sisters.* .

Religious instruction does not yield, in the central prisons for men, as good results as in those for women, whatever may be the efforts of the chaplains.

Recent statistical studies have informed us that, generally, convicts coming from the country are more accessible to religious sentiments, and the precepts of morality, than those from great cities, that is to say, from important manufacturing cities, where corruption is more advanced and where the principles of religion are often ignored or denied.

XXI. No person is admitted into prisons to labor for the reformation of the prisoners, without a special authorization from the minister of the interior.

In the houses of arrest, of justice, and of correction, commissions of supervision, composed of men held in the highest esteem in each department, have been formed, whose mission is to watch over all the services of the prison, and, in particular, over everything that relates to the moral reformation of the prisoners.

These commissions are called, above all, to give their services in the prisons of *arrondissement*, where the action of the director, whose residence is at the chief place of the department, is not immediately felt.

Commissions of supervision have not, as yet, performed any services in the central prisons.

XXII. There is not in our prisons any Sunday-schools, properly so-called. The administration aims to have the repose of the Sabbath strictly observed, and the day consecrated to religious offices and to the reading of moral and instructive works. Yet a number of the chiefs of penitentiary establishments, with a view to avert the dangers of a protracted idleness, have thought it their duty to organize an hour of school on Sunday. The superior administration has generalized this innovation.

In the penitentiary colonies, where, at a certain period of the year, the exigencies of agricultural labor puts an end to the work of the class-room, the juvenile prisoners find compensation in the instruction given them, for two hours, on the Sabbath.

XXIII. A special regulation of the administration determines, in each house of arrest, of justice, or of correction, the days and hours on which attention must be given to correspondence.

In the central prisons, ordinarily the prisoner can, once a month, on a Sunday or a feast-day, write to his family. He can correspond only with his nearer relatives, and with the guardian appointed for him, in execution of the nineteenth article of the penal code, save in exceptional cases, of which it belongs to the director to judge.

All relation with convicts, confined in other prisons, and even with persons arrested or accused, is forbidden him, unless, at least, there exist ties of consanguinity between them and the prisoner. The same prohibition exists in regard to liberated prisoners—no communication being permitted with them. In a word, the administration permits to the convict correspondence only with his family, and such as is absolutely required by attention to positive interests.

The letters which prisoners may have occasion to address to the administrative authorities, and letters relating to disclosures to be made

---

* A special religious order—the order Marie-Joseph—was founded thirty years ago, for the service of supervision of female prisons.

to the judicial authority, go sealed to their destination, without having undergone the inspection of the chief of the establishment. In this regard any facility is accorded to the prisoners.

The directors of prisons are charged with examining the correspondence of the prisoners on their arrival and at their departure. This duty is confided to the chief keepers in the houses of arrest, of justice, and of correction. The letters retained by these last must be sent to the mayor or the sub-prefect, who considers whether there is any occasion to deprive the prisoner of his correspondence.

With regard to permission to receive letters from outside, the prison regulation determines still the conditions of the correspondence. In the central prisons it is the duty of the directors to arrest all letters which contain communications in violation of the rules of the service. In such cases extracts are made which are imparted to the convict.

• XXIV. Correspondence with friends other than relations is not allowed. The prisoner can write only to the members of his family most nearly related to him. If appearances may be trusted, if account is taken of the sacrifices which the prisoner imposes on himself in sending to his family pecuniary aid, we are compelled to recognize the fact that the ties of relationship are still very strong.

XXV. The reasons which have led to the prohibition of all correspondence with their friends, equally forbid that they should receive the visits of these latter.

Beyond the cases of special authorization by the prefects and sub-prefects, convicts can receive no visits. There are, nevertheless, 'excepted from this rule the father, mother, wife, husband, brother, sister, uncle, aunt, and guardian, for whom, in the departmental prisons, the written authorization of the sub-prefect suffices, and in the central prisons that of the director of the establishment or the prefect.

As regards the visits made necessary by higher considerations, such as those of advocates, notaries, magistrates, or ministerial officers, a special authorization is necessary, and is generally accorded.

Prisoners arrested or accused can receive the visits of their relatives, or carry on correspondence with them, only so far as the committing magistrate or the attorney general of the republic shall not have forbidden it.

XXVI. The special rule of each establishment determines the days and hours at which it is permitted to relatives to visit the prisons. Permits of communication are given—on work days, only for the hours of recreation; on feast-days and Sundays, only at times not consecrated to religious offices.

During the visit, the duration of which is fixed by rule, and does not ordinarily exceed twenty or twenty-five minutes, an agent of the service of supervision is present for the purpose of preventing all communication other than that by word of mouth, and to overlook the parties and prevent whatever might give occasion to abuses or to infractions of the discipline. Yet the directors accord to the prisoner, under certain circumstances, greater facility and more liberty to communicate with the members of his family than is indicated above.

XXVII. The moral effect of these visits is, in general, rather good than bad.

XXVIII. The number of prisoners who are able to read at the time of their commitment may be determined thus:

During the three years 1867 to 1869, when the average number of prisoners under arrest and accusation rose to 444,133, 1,939 persons (men and women) were able to read, that is 43.7 per cent.

During the years 1866 to 1868, the average number of convicts rose to 18,463; of this number 2,348 were able to read, which gives an average of 12.72 per cent. per annum.

Finally, during the same three years, out of a mean population of juvenile prisoners to the number of 8,139, 1,532 were able to read, which is an average of 18.86 per cent.

XXIX. The organization of primary instruction in the penitentiary establishments of France dates really from 1819. In virtue of a decree of the 26th of December of that year, primary instruction, embracing reading and the first elements of calculation, was required to be given to prisoners, following, as far as their number permitted, the method of mutual instruction.

Since that time the administration has established schools in all the important prisons.

In 1866, the minister of the interior ordered that a greater extension be given to primary instruction, and required that almost the entire prison population should be made to share in it, with the exception of old men, invalids, and those whose perversity requires their exclusion. The greater part of the departmental prisons are necessarily without schools on account of the very brief sojourn of the prisoners in them, and the obligation which exists of separating the different classes; but the administration has succeeded in organizing schools in the prisons of the chief places of departments, in which the greater number of prisoners permits the employment of a clerk, who is charged at the same time with the keeping of the school.

In the establishments of correctional education primary instruction is required to be given to all the juvenile prisoners. It comprises reading, writing, the first four rules of arithmetic, and the legal system of weights and measures. To this list of branches may be added mental calculation, surveying, linear drawing, and general notions on the geography and history of France. It is in like manner recommended that, in the establishments appropriated to young girls, elementary instruction be carefully imparted.

XXX. The penitentiary administration has not been able, thus far, to allow all the prisoners to participate in the benefits of primary instruction. While striving to give a stronger impulse to instruction, it has been obliged to discriminate in admitting prisoners to the school, by receiving first the youngest, afterward adults, and among the latter those whose conduct is the most satisfactory.

In most of the male prisons the number of prisoners admitted to the school varies from 12 to 15 per cent. of the total population. In the female prisons, it is from 5 to 8 per cent.

Attendance at school is obligatory on all the juvenile prisoners. Several hours of each day must be spent in school, except when the exigencies of agricultural labor, at the time of harvest, compels a restriction of the schooling to Sundays.

XXXI. The instruction given in the prison schools consists of reading, writing, calculation, a little orthography and geography, and the metric system.

As regards the methods followed the systems are different; they vary according to the judgment and taste of the teachers.

In the more important houses of arrest, of justice, and of correction, and in the male central prisons, the school is presided over by a lay teacher, to whom the chaplain lends, from time to time, his co-operation, in order to give to the instruction the moral and religious character which the administration seeks always to impress upon it. Monitors are selected from among the more intelligent and better educated prisoners.

In the female central prisons the school is confided to the care of religious sisters. They are aided by monitresses chosen from among the prison population.

The progress made by the prisoners of both sexes is generally rather slow, owing to the little aptitude of the greater part of the scholars. Many of the prisoners who entered wholly illiterate leave the prison knowing how to read, to write passably well, and to perform the simpler operations of arithmetic; but a complete elementary education is rare. The administration has not been, thus far, as well satisfied as it could have wished with the results of the instruction given in the prisons.

It is at this moment engaged in seeking new methods of instruction, and the council of general inspection is charged with the study of measures to be adopted for a better organization of the schools in the penitentiary establishments.

The teachers are required to make each year the reports necessary to inform the superior administration as to the progress of instruction. They must state the degree of education possessed by the young prisoners at the time of their entrance into the establishment. Mention of this, and of the date of admission to the school, are written on the copybook of each scholar, under his name, to which is added a statement of his age. The copy-books are shown to the inspectors general at the time of their visits, so that they may personally assure themselves of the progress of each juvenile prisoner, and particularly of those who are soon to be liberated.

XXXII. At the end of successive studies on the subject of libraries, the minister of the interior addressed, in 1864, to all the heads of penitentiary establishments, a catalogue comprising the books which were thereafter required to be distributed for the reading of the prisoners.

This catalogue includes works for Catholics, Protestants, and Israelites, which are intended to serve for their moral and religious instruction; also books of history, accounts of voyages, literary works, treatises on ordinary and technical science, novels, and miscellaneous works. These books are examined with care by the council of general inspection of the prisons. The works of piety admitted by each religion are designated only on the recommendation of the ministers of the different religions. The catalogue contains special indication of the books more particularly adapted to men, to women, and to children.

At this moment the superior administration is engaged in organizing libraries in all the penitentiary establishments. This measure, which is on the point of realization, will involve in the purchase of books an expenditure of about 30,000 francs.

XXXIII. The prisoners are generally fond of reading. Those who have a knowledge of this art nearly always profit from the practice of it. They have their Sundays for reading, and on week-days they read during the hours of rest, and at meals.

In some establishments there are readings in common to convicts who are unoccupied, and to others during the intervals of labor. Sometimes such readings are given during meal-time in the refectory. The prisoners listen to them with interest, but those who know how prefer to read to themselves.

The distribution of books takes place under the superintendence of an agent of the administration, viz, either the instructor or the chaplain, who, in his selection of books, has regard to the antecedents, the aptitudes, and the conduct of each prisoner, and the officers charged with this duty perform it in such manner as to cultivate a taste for reading, by all the means which are consistent with the exigencies of the service. The obligation of silence imposed on the prisoners by the regulation of the 10th of May, 1839, has greatly contributed to a love for reading on their part.

Books specially written for prisoners are not those which they prefer. They read with greater pleasure books of history, voyages, novels, and narratives which have touches of the marvelous, of elevated sentiment, and of renowned actions.

Reading exerts a happy moral influence upon the prisoners. Those who contract a taste for it during their imprisonment are generally well behaved. Properly directed, reading effects a salutary revolution in the soul and imagination of the prisoner. Hence, the choice of books is a matter of great importance. Works which amuse by the interest of the drama and the charm of the style, and those which have in them an element of instruction, contribute to enlighten and to inform the prisoner, at the same time that they afford to him diversion and consolation. They serve to awaken in him the love of home, and sometimes predispose him to the duties of religion.

XXXIV. The central administration attaches great importance to the hygiene of the prisons, and it takes special pains to free them from every cause of humidity. Even where the buildings which serve for imprisonment are not its own property, it reserves to itself an absolute right of control, as well as of preliminary approval, of all constructions and repairs appertaining to them. It has the power to insure, and it does insure effectively, that sanitary precautions are never neglected.

The projects, plans, and estimates prepared either by the architects of the central prisons, or by the architects of the departments, or by other professional men, are, agreeably to the 12th and 14th articles of a decree of the chief of the executive power, under date of the 25th November, 1848, submitted to the examination of the inspectors-general of prisons, assembled in council, to whom are added, whenever the question relates to sanitary science, the medical inspectors general attached to the sanitary service of the prisons.

To understand thoroughly the spirit in which this examination is made, especially as regards drainage, it is sufficient to glance over a circular of the 7th January, 1863, to which is subjoined a plan for the construction or alteration of houses of arrest, of justice, and of correction.

There are found in this plan the following rules:

The foundations and lower portions of the ground floor should be made in such manner as to completely exclude the humidity of the soil.

The soil of the ground floor should, as a general thing, be raised a half meter at least above the exterior soil, by means of materials adapted to exclude humidity, and in cases where it is absolutely necessary to construct dormitories on this floor, this elevation should be carried to not less than one meter.

At the foundation of the buildings there should be placed reverses or foot-pavements, to carry off the humidity.

For carrying off the water, there should be gutters or sewers, but no draining wells.

If these regulations cannot be applied, in all their details, to old constructions, they serve, at least, as a base or term of comparison, and act as a motive leading to alterations, by means of which the administration has succeeded in securing, almost everywhere, a satisfactory sanitary condition of the prisons.

XXXV. No prescribed rule determines the quantity of water to be provided for the necessities of the prisons. The plan above mentioned limits itself to recommending in all prison constructions, as an indispensable prerequisite, a good supply of water, and, with rare exceptions, it is with abundance rather than parsimony that water is brought into all our prisons.

As regards the quality, prisoners are generally treated like the free population of the localities in which they are incarcerated. Among the' establishments destined to their use, a great number are supplied with the same water which the neighboring cities or villages procure for their public fountains. The administration knows too well the influence which the water habitually drunk exercises upon the health of the prisoners not to take care that it be pure and healthful.

XXXVI. The ventilation of the prisons is made the object of a very special attention. The plan indicated below contains formal rules to this effect, among which are found the following:

The windows should have at least 1.2 meters in height to 1 meter in width on the ground floor, and 1 meter in height to .8 of a meter in width on the first floor.

The dormitories, workshops, and common apartments should be conveniently arranged and well lighted, and aired on two sides if possible, and should give at least 15 to 20 cubic meters of space to each prisoner, in addition to the special means of ventilation.

As regards these special means, those which are most effective consist of draught-chimneys, (cheminées d'appel,) placed at the top of the rooms to be ventilated, and working by means of small openings of some centimeters square made in the wall, so as to cause the miasms to escape and facilitate the renewal of the air.

For all the old constructions, in which the rules laid down in the above plan would be too difficult or too expensive to reduce to practice, the inspectors general carefully indicate, at the conclusion of their visitations, the improvements which they regard as necessary to a good ventilation. Almost all the observations hitherto made tend to show that in order most surely to attain this end, it is indispensable that openings be placed in the two parallel walls of each apartment destined to receive a large number of individuals. Thus it is sought as much as possible to make little openings, called barbacans, in the top of the wall facing the windows, which give light to each apartment. The results obtained by this simple arrangement, already almost everywhere adopted, are highly satisfactory.

XXXVII. The plan for the construction of departmental prisons, decreed in 1863, recommends corridors and stairs well lighted and airy, and the suppression of the dark subterranean passages. It prescribes that the floors of the several stories, especially for apartments in common, except the infirmary, be, as far as possible, covered with cement or stucco, in preference to flagging, tiles, or planks. The walls and ceilings are required to be carefully plastered and painted with oil, or at least washed with lime. These precautions, whose aim is to facilitate the maintenance of cleanliness, are completed by official measures, whose daily or periodical execution is placed in charge of the contractor of each establishment where the industries are managed by contract. These measures are specified in the contract. They consist principally in frequent and repeated sweepings, washings, and cleanings, as well as in fumigations, and in the annual whitewashing of all the buildings.

XXXVIII. The means of securing the personal cleanliness of the prisoners are of two kinds. The one, as the daily toilet, the bath, the washing of the feet, and the removal of the beard and long hair of the men, is applied directly to the individual. The other has for its object the linen and the clothing provided for the prisoners' use. They are both as extensive as possible, and are made the subject of numerous and detailed rules in the conditions of the contract and the regulations of the prisons. The same rules are applied in general to the female prisons and educational colonies for young girls, with the exception of the obligation to wear the hair short. Entire liberty of action is left with them in this respect.

The arrested and accused are subjected to no other obligations than those which are indispensable to the maintenance of good discipline, of general cleanliness, and of the health of their fellow-prisoners. They are permitted to keep their beard and their hair.

XXXIX. The central administration has long been impressed with the grave inconveniences occasioned by water-closets placed adjacent to the dormitories or other apartments occupied by the prisoners. As early as 1819 a decree of the minister of the interior, under date of the 25th December, bears traces of his attention to this matter. The fifteenth article decides, in effect, that measures shall be taken to protect the dormitories, and especially the infirmaries, from the infection of the gases emanating from the privies. He adds, that the *latrines* placed within the interior of the dormitories and cells shall be removed, and their places supplied by buckets, which are emptied and washed twice a day. The several essays, made since that period, have shown that whatever may be the precautions taken, whatever the system adopted, the privies are always an unhealthy neighborhood, and that the best plan is to have none at all, or at least to place them outside of the buildings; for example, in the space between the two encircling walls of the prison. These rules, which have been closely followed in the prisons recently constructed, have not yet been fully applied to the old prison buildings. The displacement of the privies involves considerable expense, from which, hitherto, many of the old establishments have recoiled. They have also, in considerable numbers, been retained in the exercise yards. But, as regards the introduction of buckets into the dormitories and workshops, the measure is now general, and is applied with satisfactory results in all the penitentiary establishments.

The removal of the privies, which still existed in the exercise yards in a certain number of establishments, is constantly going on, and a ministerial circular of the 20th of March, 1868, recalls the considerations of salubrity and security, as well as of decency, which recommend the suppression of the latrines in those courts.

XL. In the interest of good morals, as well as for the purpose of rendering supervision more easy, sundry regulations have prescribed the lighting, during the night, if not of the cells, at least of the common dormitories. This rule is applied to all of the penitentiary establishments. No particular mode of lighting is fixed upon absolutely. The administration reserves to itself the power of regulating it in each individual case, and it permits, indifferently, the use of tapers or lamps, either of oil or petroleum, or mineral essences. Gas is also sometimes used. However, according to the terms of the contract made for the central prisons, the contractor can use the mineral oils only on condition of conforming to such measures of precaution as may be prescribed to him. The necessary material must be furnished by him, and the supply renewed when necessary; and he is required to place in the dormitories small sheet-iron chimneys to carry outside the smoke of the lamps.

XLI. The heating of the prisons of every class is generally effected by means of stoves placed in the rooms which are to be heated. Some establishments, and those among the most important, are well furnished with heating apparatus, placed in the cellars or basements, which is designed to diffuse the heat throughout the several parts of the building; but serious inconveniences, as well in regard to the expense as to the distribution of the heat, have caused an abandonment of the system.

A note which accompanies the plan already referred to resolves this question thus: "The hot-air furnaces have not hitherto yielded satisfactory results. The workshops and other places where the prisoners are in association can be more readily heated by simple stoves. It is the same with individual cells." The administration aims only to prevent the effects of excessive-cold; in other words, to spare the prisoners the physical suffering which might react injuriously upon their health.

The contract for the service of the central prisons recalls, in articles 54, 55, and 56, the obligations which, in this regard, rest upon the contractor. The contract for the services of the departmental prisons contains the same enumeration in article 46. Finally, as regards the colonies of juvenile delinquents, the regulation of the 10th April, 1869, contains the following provisions:

ARTICLE 21. The schools and workshops shall be heated during six months of the year, viz, from the 15th October to the 15th April.

ARTICLE 22. The infirmaries and bath-rooms shall be heated for a longer period if the physician think it necessary.

XLII. Experience has shown that iron bedsteads are preferable to all others, and for many years they are the only ones whose purchase has been authorized by the administration for the departmental prisons, as well as for the central prisons, and the colonies of juvenile delinquents belonging to the state.

The bedstead, thus uniformly adopted for the whole of France, and which is to-day the only one recognized in the official regulations, is decreed in a note accompanying the ministerial circular of the 26th September, 1867, with this reservation, that the bottom in wire-cloth, designed to receive the mattress, must be replaced by an iron or sheet-iron lattice in prisons where paillasses were formerly in use. At the same time, in adopting definitively the model of a uniform bed for all the prisons, the administration did not intend that the then existing beds, of whatever style they might be, should be immediately displaced. On the contrary, it took pains to state, in a circular of the 20th of May, 1868, that this expensive change should be made gradually, and only as cases of absolute necessity for some change arose.

It follows from this that there are still found, in some prisons, traces of different kinds of beds, authorized prior to 1867, particularly by the general regulation of 1841, which had permitted, indifferently, the hammock, the bunk, and the iron bedstead. The work of transformation, pursued by the administration with prudence and economy, is already far advanced.

In the infirmaries the iron bedstead has long since been everywhere introduced. Larger dimensions are given to the hospital than to the ordinary bedstead.

XLIII. After having, formerly, consisted of loose straw, spread either on the floor or on camp bedsteads, the bedding of the prisoners has undergone, since the commencement of the century, successive ameliorations, which have brought it to the satisfactory state in which it is found to-day.

The complete bed of each able-bodied prisoner is composed of an iron bedstead, a mattress, or paillasse, a bolster, two sheets, and one coverlet in summer, and two in winter.

While the above-enumerated articles are of somewhat larger dimensions and a better quality for the sick than for those in health, there are added for the former a pillow and curtains. Moreover, they ought to have, and they have, both a mattress and a paillasse. These various articles, which are specified, with all the necessary details, in the contract, are supplied to the prisons of every class, with this single difference: .that, in the central prisons, the mattress constitutes the bed required by administrative regulation, and is found everywhere; whereas in the other establishments the mattress or the paillasse is indifferently supplied; and, as a consequence, the paillasse is generally used in the houses of arrest, of justice, and of correction.

This lack of uniformity is owing, in great part, to the fact that the service in the central prisons has been, for a long time, in the charge of the state, while it has been only à few years since the charge of the houses of arrest, of justice, and of correction, has passed from the hands of the department into those of the state. Other reforms were pressing, and all that were needed could not be undertaken at the same time. Moreover, aside from the fact that sleeping upon the paillasse is sufficiently comfortable, if the straw is frequently renewed, it is perhaps the mode best suited to the constant changes occurring in the population of 'these establishments. It is readily seen how much easier it is to increase, at short notice, the number of paillasses, and how the care and preservation of the mattresses would add to the embarrassment at times when the greater part of .the beds remain unoccupied.

XLIV. The hours of labor, of recreation, and of sleep are determined, for each establishment, by a special regulation, made by the prefect. But if the duty of regulating, in detail, the division of time in the different prisons, situated in each department, belongs to the departmental authority, the central administration does not any the less take care that differences of too material a character be not permitted to exist. Above all, it insists that the hours of labor imposed upon prisoners shall not exceed those of free laborers, viz, twelve to thirteen. In the case of juveniles, it is prescribed that the hours of work are never to exceed ten.

As a general thing, from twelve to thirteen hours are given to labor, from two to two and a half hours to meals and repose, and nine hours to sleep.

[N. B.—A question relating to prison dietaries was accidentally omitted from the list of interrogatories. The answer to such a question has been considerately introduced at this point, under the enumeration XLIV, bis, and is as follows :] The dietary of prisons for punishment is regulated on the following principle :

1. The food, gratuitously furnished to able-bodied prisoners, is limited to what is strictly necessary for the support of the vital forces. The renewal of the forces expended in labor is effected by means of supplementary food, furnished to the convicts out of the funds deposited to their credit, and principally out of the part which, according to the penal class to which they are severally assigned by their sentences, comes to them as the product of their labor.

2. The dietary ought, as far as possible, to have a certain repressive character, effected by the absolute exclusion of luxurious dishes and drinks, such as wines, spirits, &c.

Nevertheless, the food forming the usual dietary having given rise to some strictures, modifications were introduced into, in 1868, this part of the service.

The number of rations of soup furnished each day has been increased from one to two, with a view to facilitate the consumption of the bread ration. A greater variety of provisions has been supplied, and the number of meat rations has been advanced from one to two per week.

The savings, realized in the making of soup-bread, have been such that the expenses resulting from the above-specified ameliorations have been increased only to a very moderate degree; that is to say, about one and a half centimes for each day of imprisonment.

The sanitary state of the central prisons has been essentially improved under the influence of the new dietary. This *régime* has proved highly satisfactory.

The distribution of bread is regulated as follows:

For each day when meat is furnished, (Sunday and Thursday,) 775 grammes for the men; 725 grammes for the women.

For the five days when meat is not furnished, 840 grammes for the men; 790 grammes for the women.

In addition to this, supplementary bread is furnished to those convicts who have no resources from their disposable *peculium*.

The bread for able-bodied prisoners is, in general, composed of two-thirds of bolted wheat flour containing one-eighth of bran, and one-third of bolted rye or barley flour containing one-fifth of bran.

On Sunday and Thursday there is a meat-ration consisting, in the morning, of a bowl of soup containing five deciliters (nearly a pint) of broth, and, in the evening, 75 grammes on Sunday and 60 grammes on Thursday, of cooked meat without bone, together with a small quantity of (at least) three deciliters of rice or potatoes.

On each of the other days of the week, the ration consists of two bowls of soup, without meat, containing four deciliters, with the addition, at the evening meal, of at least three deciliters of potatoes, peas, lentils, or beans.

The expenditures for supplementary provisions purchased by the prisoners amounted, in 1867, to 692,181 francs, being an average of about ten centimes a day.

The supplementary provisions delivered gratuitously by the administration or the contractors, represent, in addition, another expediture of 57,980 francs, equal to 1.094 centimes for each day of imprisonment.

During the summer, there is distributed to the prisoners a hygienic drink, made after a formula laid down in the contract.

The dietary of the houses of arrest, of justice, and of correction is regulated agreeably to the principles above set forth in relation to the central prisons; but some modifications are made in the details on account of the small number of the prisoners.

In the colonies of juvenile delinquents, bread is given *ad libitum*. The number of meals in these establishments is three a day, and even four in time of harvest, during which rations of wine, beer, and cider are given.

The principal exceptions to the dietary arrangements just described relate—

1. To the prisons of the Seine, where, in respect as well of the quality of the bread as the quantity of the meat and other commodities, the rations differ not a little from those of the central and departmental prisons.

2. To the agricultural colonies of Corsica, where we have had to contend with climatic influences by toning up the dietary with supplementary additions of meat, and with rations of coffee, and even of alcoholic drinks.

It belongs to the ministry of the navy and the colonies to give exact instructions on the subject of the dietary of the prisoners sentenced to the bagnios.

XLV. In the great prisons for punishment, the sick prisoners are al-

ways treated in the establishment, whatever may be the nature or gravity of their disease. Exception, however, is made of the epileptics
and the insane, who are sent to special establishments.

In the houses of arrest, of justice, and of correction, sick prisoners are,
as far as possible, treated in the prison. There is a special apartment
designed to serve as an infirmary. A physician belonging to the town
is employed for the prison, and is required to make one visit daily for
the purpose of giving attention to the sick. To these a better dietary is
allowed. The prescriptions of the doctors, limited, it is true, in a certain degree, are always carried into effect. In prisons of less importance,
only the lighter ailments are treated. As soon as a prisoner becomes
seriously ill and has need of special care, he is conveyed to the hospital
of the town. The expenses of his treatment there are reimbursed to the
establishment by the state or the contractor.

The sanitary system of the central prisons is organized in a manner
the most complete. A physician, often resident in the establishment,
is attached to each. The infirmaries are arranged in the best possible
manner. A special dietary is accorded to the sick, agreeably to the prescriptions of the physician and the conditions of the contract. A dispensary, provided with all necessary medicines, is organized in each
central prison, and an apothecary is charged with preparing the prescriptions.

In the public colonies of juvenile delinquents, the sanitary service is
organized, in the main, as it is in the central prisons.

There are also infirmaries in the private colonies, and a physician attached to the establisement must make at least three visits a week.

XLVI. In the houses of arrest, of justice, and of correction, the stay is
too short for the imprisonment to produce any appreciable influence on
the sanitary state of the prisoners. The pathological condition of the
prisoners, before their incarceration, is the principal cause of the diseases
which are developed after their imprisonment. It may, therefore, be
said, as regards these prisons, that the diseases most common are the
same as those which affect the free population of the locality from which
the prison population is recruited.

A certain number of diseases developed in the central prisons are in
like manner due to the sanitary state of the prisoners, who, at the time
of their commitment, have already felt the effects of debauchery and
misery. It is, nevertheless, possible to perceive, in a certain measure,
the inevitable influence of the privations undergone during incarceration. It is affections of the digestive and respiratory organs and fevers
which furnish half, and often two-thirds, of the inmates of the infirmaries in the penitentiary establishments for both sexes.

It is certain that imprisonment very generally produces a lack of
blood, and this favors the development or the gravity of certain affections, such as phthisis and scrofula. As regards ailments which, without
being of a grave character, still render necessary the intervention of the
physician, it may be said that gastric complaints most frequently require treatment in the infirmary. In establishments designed for juvenile delinquents the most frequent affection, brought generally from
without, is scrofula. That which produces the greatest ravages is pulmonary consumption. Fevers come next.

XLVII. The average number of prisoners in the infirmaries compared
with the total prison population was, in 1868, in the central prisons, 4.05
per cent. of men and 5.16 per cent. of women; and in the establishments
of correctional education, 1.61 per cent. of boys and 2.23 per cent. of
girls.

XLVIII. In comparing in the various penitentiary establishments the average annual population with the number of deaths for the same time, the following percentages are obtained :

Houses of arrest, of justice, and of correction.—Men and boys, 3.79 per cent. ; women and girls, 4.91 per cent.

Central prisons.—Men, 3.65 per cent. ; women, 3.80 per cent.

Establishments of correctional education.—Boys, 1.67 per cent. ; girls, 2.20 per cent.

XLIX. Penal labor, properly so called, does not exist in the prisons of France. The penal system is no longer founded, as formerly, on suffering and terror. Corporal punishments have disappeared from the penal system. What is desired at present is to punish the criminal; what is sought as the end of that punishment is his reformation. Therefore, industrial labor alone is found in the prisons, obligatory in the case of those under sentence, permitted in the case of the arrested and the accused. This character of *obligation* may well be considered as a punishment to the convict, and a means of lessening the expenses caused by him to society ; but it is thereby sought, above all, to prevent the dangers of idleness and to form the taste and the habit of labor.

In the smaller houses of arrest, of justice, and of correction, there is difficulty in organizing the labor. The prisoners are engaged only in temporary occupations. A few, when that is possible, follow the trade by which they obtained a living outside. It is only in the larger departmental prisons that it has been possible to establish workshops of any importance.

In the central prisons the labor is thoroughly organized ; if any are without occupation, it is the exception and not the rule. Large industrial workshops in these establishments continually present a scene of busy toil. Different industries, to the number of fifty or sixty, have been introduced into the male central prisons. The principal are shoemaking, the manufacture of hosiery, weaving, button-making, cabinet-work, lock-smithing, the manufacture of hardware, tanning, &c., &c.

There are, besides, three establishments in Corsica, and one in Belle Isle, in which the prisoners are engaged in agricultural labors.

Sewing, which can be applied to very different kinds of work, is almost the only industry pursued in the female central prisons.

Remuneration by the day is the exception, and is applied only to the interior services of the prisons. Piece-work is the general rule. With a view to avoid the competition of prison-labor with free labor, the rates of payment for the work done have to be studied and regulated by the administration, which carefully considers before-hand the different interests involved. The rates must be the same as those paid to free industry for the same kinds of labor ; only there is made to the contractor a remission of 20 per cent., or one-fifth, to indemnify him for special expenses, which manufacturers outside do not have to incur. As regards minors of both sexes, subjected to the system of correctional education, they are required to be principally employed in agricultural labors.

L, LI, and LII. Penal labor does not exist in France.

LIII. In all the houses of arrest, of justice and of correction, in France, except those of Paris, the supplies of food and of other current necessities are confided, by way of contract, for three, six, or nine years, to a distinct contractor for each department, and on conditions mutually agreed upon. This contractor has the sole right to make the prisoners work; his interest compels him to that, since he shares about one-half of the product of their labor. This product comes in to lighten his expenses ;

but as the labor of these prisons cannot be so well organized as that in establishments for long punishments, and is, consequently, in them less productive, the cost of each day's imprisonment is greater than in the central prisons.

In the central prisons of the continent, with the exception of that of Belle Isle, which is administered by the state, the right of employing the labor of the prisoners is, in like manner, conceded to the general contractor of the services.

The administration reserves the right of utilizing the labor of the prisoners if the contractor leaves them unoccupied.

The directors of the private colonies employ, in industrial labors, without the intervention of contractors, those juveniles whom they have not been able to employ in agriculture.

The product of the labor of the young girls applied to field-labor or sewing is received by the religious communities charged with their penitentiary education.

LIV. The system which consists in awarding to contractors the profits of the industrial labor of the prisons appears to be the preferable one. If the state can produce more, it produces, in general, at greater cost. Personal interest and the desire of making money are powerful motives with the contractor; besides which, an officer of the government has not the same freedom of action nor so much practical knowledge of commercial affairs as a business man. Moreover, by giving to the same person the charge of the maintenance of the prisoners and a part in the product of their labor, the administration has realized a progress promotive of the interests of all. In proportion as the contractors have become familiar with the working of their contracts, they have learned that the surest benefits to be realized from them consisted rather in the impulse to and extension of industrial labor, than in the culpable profits to be obtained by the imperfect execution of the obligations which they had assumed. The labor being constant and becoming more and more productive, the profits of the contractor and those of the prisoners increase *pari passu*. The part of the product of the labor belonging to the contractor represents a profit more considerable in proportion as such product increases. The sum, then, to be paid by the state toward the maintenance of the prisoners becomes so much less when a new contract is to be made. The contractors have been made to comprehend that the sum total of the product of the labor is augmented, as the result of the general good care extended to the prisoners. This last result, conducive alike to the well-being of the prisoners and the interest of the treasury, is remarkable and immediate when the contractor directly utilizes the forces of the prisoners.

LV. Under reserve of the exception previously pointed out in what concerns the prisons of Paris, there is but one system of contracting the labor of the prisoners. The contractor, charged with the service of maintaining and feeding the prisoners, possesses the exclusive right to the labor of the convicts. The contractors in the departmental and central prisons themselves utilize directly the labor of the prisoners; those in the prisons of Paris do it through sub-contractors, for whom they become responsible to the administration.

The procedure which consists in the direct utilizing of the labor by the contractors has its advantages, which have been pointed out in the preceding paragraphs; but if it is, in certain respects, advantageous to the prisoners that the contractor be directly interested in the greater or less production of the labor, this state of things may be attended with some disadvantages. In effect, if the contractor is, at the same time, a manufacturer, it is probable that the greater part, if not all of the prisoners, will be placed upon a single industry, viz, that which he carries on outside.

When, in these conditions, a suspension of work happens, almost the entire prison population may have to suffer from this interruption of labor. If, on the contrary, the contractor has sub-letters for the various industries, any partial suspension will affect only a small number of prisoners, and, on the other side, the prisoners belonging to a shop which has suspended labor may pass, temporarily, into another shop, where they will be occupied.

LVI. Of the inmates of the central prisons, the men who had no regular calling or business prior to commitment were 4.78 per cent.; the women, 11.76 per cent.

In the establishments of correctional education, where the children are often placed, before having exercised any regular calling, either because of their youth or the indifference of their family, the proportion not having any regular business is about 65.61 per cent.

XVII. All the convicts are under obligation to labor. Each one is put, as far as possible, to the business which he followed before his imprisonment; and, when he is placed in a workshop, account is always taken of his aptitudes and tastes.

The prisoners of rural origin are, in general, sent into the agricultural establishments of Corsica, when the state of their health and the length of their sentence justify so expensive a transfer.

In the establishments of juvenile delinquents it is sought, above all, from considerations of health, and in the hope of teaching·them a business which may keep them away from the cities, to employ them in agricultural labors. Yet those who will be able to return to their family, and who are of city origin, are employed in industrial occupations, which they may exercise after their liberation.

LVIII. As has just been said, the administration exerts itself, as far as possible, to cause to be taught to the prisoners, previously without regular business, some calling, which will enable them, after their liberation, to gain an honest living. But, during their incarceration, they may already aid themselves by work. Not to repeat what was said in No. XIII, on the share accorded to prisoners of the product of their labor, it is sufficient to recall the fact that they can, during their imprisonment, avail themselves of their disposable *peculium* to ameliorate their condition, in respect of food or clothing, and to procure for themselves certain objects, the use of which is authorized by the regulations.

As regards the second part of their possession, the reserved *peculium*, which they can diminish during their imprisonment only on certain conditions, and to a limited degree, it is a kind of savings, designed to meet the first necessities of the liberated prisoner, if he does not find work immediately on his discharge from the establishment.

This resource is thus a means, prepared by his own efforts, during his incarceration, to aid himself. The administration, not limiting itself to this forecast, has still further taken means to prevent this reserved fund from being expended as soon as it comes into the possession of the prisoner. It has conceived that, on emerging from a prolonged state of affliction and restraint, the prisoner, finding himself in the possession of a sum relatively considerable, would be disposed to waste it immediately in debauchery. It therefore places at the disposal of the liberated prisoner only such sum as may be necessary for the expenses of his journey, and he can touch the rest of his possessions only after arriving at the residence which he has chosen, or which has been assigned him. As regards juvenile delinquents, whose labor is not remunerated so long as they have not been restored to freedom, except in case of being placed with farmers,* they receive, on their discharge, a complete outfit, and money enough for their journey.

LIX. The English and Anglo-American legislations are so unlike ours that it would be difficult to say, precisely, to what infractions in penal matters the words "minor offenses," employed in the question, are to be understood. Besides, certain infractions which are made the objects of prohibitions by foreign laws have no penal sanction in France, such, for example, as the observance of the Sabbath, public drunkenness, &c.

Nevertheless, in order to enter as much as possible into the sense of the question proposed, it would seem that it must refer to criminal acts of but a moderate gravity, which, according to the provisions of the fourth book of the French penal code, may be punished either by a fine of fifteen francs or less, or by an imprisonment of fifteen days. These acts are those which, in the exposition of "incentives" in the code of 1810, the reporter designated "violations of police regulations," and which the first article of the penal code has denominated "contraventions."

The contraventions are numerous, and it is certain that the penalties attached to them do not, from their very triviality, prevent a return to the offenses against which they are directed, whenever their authors find in them any profit, the gratification of some grudge, or even a passing diversion. These transgressions, often committed by the same persons, are no doubt vexatious, and it must certainly be admitted that respect for law is less profound in France than in England, for example; but if the trivial faults, denoting in those who commit them a certain levity of character, are often repeated, in spite of the punishment with which they are visited, it cannot, on the other side, be alleged with truth that graver offenses, constituting a misdemeanor or a crime, are more numerous in France than in other countries.

It is presumed that, in the thought of the author of the questions, the words "minor offenses" ought to correspond, in France, to those of "contraventions," which are punished with a light imprisonment.

If, on the contrary, they answer to misdemeanors of no considerable gravity, and are visited, consequently, with a trifling penalty, it might be said that, in this matter as in that of contraventions, though in a much less proportion, the first strokes of the penal law do not prevent a return to the criminal acts. Thus, in the year 1870, out of 160,129 previously convicted offenders, arraigned before the correctional tribunals, 46,441, that is, 25.23 per cent., had been previously punished, to wit: 7,858 by fines, and 38,783 by an imprisonment of one year and under. The relative smallness of the first punishments had not, therefore, in this case, had the salutary effect of preventing new offenses.

LX. In respect to the percentage of recidivists: In order to reply more fully to the spirit of the question upon this point, it will be necessary to take into view both the prosecution and the conviction.

According to the last official report on criminal justice, out of 4,189 individuals prosecuted for crimes, the recidivists are in the proportion (including men and women) of 1,780, that is to say, 42.49 per cent. Of this number of recidivists prosecuted, 272 were acquitted, being 11.91 per cent. only.

On the other hand, of 160,079 individuals of both sexes prosecuted for misdemeanors, the recidivists are to the number of 60,129, or 37.56

---

* They have a right in that case to the moiety of their earnings.

per cent. Of this number of 60,129 recidivists prosecuted in matters of misdemeanor, 1,725 only were acquitted, being 2.26 per cent.

LXI. A relapse, in the legal sense of the word, is the commission, after a penal sentence, of a new criminal act. It receives little favor from the French law. The circumstance of a prior conviction, and the greater perversity shown by a repetition of the offense, seems, in effect, to demand from the legislator an increase of punishment. Doubtless, neither theft nor homicide changes its nature because committed a second time; but a crime has two elements, the substance of the act and the criminality of its author. The legislator has thought it a duty to take both these circumstances into consideration in measuring the punishment.

Article 56 of the penal code lays down rules in regard to relapses in matters of crime. The punishment awarded is *generally* that which is placed above the first sentence in the scale of penalties.

Article 58 relates to relapses in matters of misdemeanor. It ordains that misdemeanants, who had been punished correctionally by an imprisonment of more than a year, be sentenced, in case of a second offense, to the maximum of the punishment permitted by the law, and declares that this punishment *may* be doubled, besides subjecting the offender to the supervision of the police during a period of five years at least, to ten years at most.

The effect of a second or third conviction in diminishing the share accorded to the prisoners of the product of their labor has already been stated.

LXII. The law of the 22d of July, 1867, put an end to imprisonment for debt in commercial and civil matters, and in those in which foreigners are concerned. The restraint of the body exists no longer, except in matters criminal, correctional, and of simple police. The usage has just been re-established as regards the payment of moneys due to the State.

The ordinary creditor who, under the empire of the old legislation, caused his debtor to be imprisoned, (in the exceptional case of which mention will be made further on,) was bound to deposit in advance, for each period of thirty days, the sum of 45 francs in Paris, and of 40 francs in other cities, in the hands of the prison-keeper, to provide subsistence for the imprisoned debtor.

This consignment of the means of support was not, and is not now, necessary, when the debtor is arrested and detained on account of debts due to the State for the public administrations. This expense is, in such cases, included in the number of expenses necessitated by the service of the prisons, agreeably to the terms of the decree of the 4th of March, 1808, article 2, which was not abrogated by the subsequent laws of 1832 and 1867 touching the restraint of the body. In this case, the public minister is bound to take care that persons imprisoned for debts to the State or the administrations receive the same rations as the other prisoners who are in the charge of the State.

It is a special case, that in which the unfulfilled engagements of a citizen toward others may also draw after it his incarceration, agreeably to the terms of article 460 of the Code of Commerce. The decree of bankruptcy may order the placing of the person of the bankrupt in a debtor prison, and, if there is no such prison, in a part of the house of arrest reserved for that purpose. This is a measure which prudence almost always dictates. If the debtor is simply unfortunate, a safe conduct soon restores him to his family and to liberty; if the examination of his conduct justifies rigorous measures, it will be impossible for him to liberate himself by flight.

The arrest and imprisonment of the bankrupt should be preceded by the consignment on the part of the commissioners of bankruptcy of the means of living, and, in case of insufficient means for this purpose, the advance of the moneys to be consigned is made from the public treasure, on the order of the commissioner, given at the request of the public ministry. (*Code de Commerce, article* 461.)

The French law, as is thus seen, places the incarcerated bankrupt in a situation altogether different from that of ordinary prisoners.

LXIII. This question asks for an opinion as to the principal sources of crime in this country. The absolute terms of this question render a categorical reply impossible, but there is reason to believe that in France, as in many other countries, the insufficiency of moral education, the general defect of intellectual culture, and the want of an industrial calling, not opposing to the appetites and instincts a barrier sufficiently strong, leave an open road to crimes and misdemeanors. These offenses are afterward modified and perpetrated under influences springing from the circumstances by which their authors are habitually surrounded.

It is thus that, on the frontiers, the populations, seeing in the code of fiscal laws only an enemy of natural right, have little hesitation, for the purpose of avoiding the payment of taxes, to sacrifice the lives of the agents charged with collecting them. In the cities the laborer, seduced by ideas of a luxury which his labor does not and ought not to give him, suffers himself to be drawn on to attempts against property, and, too often, against social order. The inhabitant of the country, who has under his eyes only the spectacle of a productive soil parceled out to infinity by the law of inheritance, demands violently, sometimes even at the cost of his neighbor's life, the enlargement of the patch that belongs to himself.

To these evils, of which France has no monopoly, does there exist a remedy which will prove absolute and complete? It may be doubted; but it is certain that, in elevating morality, in fortifying the heart, in enlarging the boundaries of knowledge, the practical ability of men would be increased, and the effects of these evils would be diminished by lessening their causes.

Certain humanitarian or economic writers have, in these latter times, seen in misery the supreme cause of criminality. They have rested their theory upon this statistical consideration, that the years most prolific in violations of law were precisely those in which the harvests were least abundant. We might say as much of the periods which correspond to the interruption of the great industries of the country, and, in a sense more restricted, of the effects of legal supervision over the persons who are subjected to it. But these are only accidents or influences which, at most, are but intermediate causes, subordinating themselves, in a manner little short of absolute, to the generic causes set forth above.

LXIV. As regards the proportion in which the sexes are represented in our prisons: On the 31st September, 1868, a point at which were arrested the indications of the statistical documents, recently published, on the subject of the movement of the population in the central prisons and the houses of arrest, of justice, and of correction, there were counted in all the different establishments: 33,978 men, being about 81 per cent. of the total population; and 7,993 women, being about 19 per cent., subdivided in the following manner:

S. Ex. 39——4

Central prisons.

Men sentenced to reclusion and to an imprisonment of more than one year, 15,467, or about 82 per cent. of the population of the central prisons.* Women sentenced to hard labor, to reclusion, and to an imprisonment of more than one year, 3,506, or about 18 per cent. of the population of the central prisons.

Houses of arrest, of justice, and of correction.

The arrested, the accused, and those sentenced, for the most part, to an imprisonment of one year, and less: Men, 18,511, or about 80 per cent. of the population of the departmental of prisons; women, 4,487, or about 20 per cent. of the population of the same prisons.

In recapitulating the statements relative to persons imprisoned under whatever title in the prisons, in the penitentiaries, in the public and private colonies, as well as at the bagnio and in the countries devoted to transportation, the following is the grand total for the year 1848 : 69,469 men, (adults and juveniles,) or 87 per cent. of the total of population ; 9,612 women, (adults and juveniles,) or 13 per cent. of the total population.

It is proper to remark, in regard to the classification of the prisoners in respect to the sexes, that the women commit in prison, as in free life, fewer moral offenses and breaches of discipline. They observe better and more readily the requirements laid down in the regulations. The proportional number of recidivists is also very sensibly less for the women.

LXV. The studies prosecuted in France with a view to organize a penitentiary system, as well as the modifications more recently introduced into the great prisons for punishment, have generally for their object, besides the reformation of the prisoners, the intimidation of criminals and the gradual repression of crime.

It could not, indeed, be otherwise. The doctrines of penal law are based upon the necessity of protecting society and of inflicting on criminals a punishment proportioned to the gravity of their offense, at the same time having regard, as far as possible, to certain principles of humanity.

The moral regeneration of the convicts is, therefore, considered in rance as one of the means of action which the state can and ought to employ to diminish the dangers of relapse, but not as the principal aim of the penitentiary system.

LXVI. It is asked whether, as a matter of fact, the prisoners leave the prison-house better or worse than they came in. It is very difficult to obtain favorable results in the case of prisoners sentenced to a short term in prisons where the associated system prevails.

Whoever has been imprisoned in these circumstances becomes sensibly deteriorated : on the one side, by contact with criminality; on the other, by the very influence of a punishment of which he no longer fears, in the future, the physical and moral consequences. In regard to the greater part of the prisoners of this class, the danger to society and to the individual is greater after than before his imprisonment. It would be desirable to modify, on this point, the sanction given to the awards of justice.

---

* Certain men sentenced to hard labor are exceptionally retained in these establishments.

It should be remarked, in support of this view, that the number of relapses is in inverse ratio to the duration of punishments. After the lapse of a certain period the prolonged action of a sojourn in the prisons makes itself advantageously felt.

LXVII. There are not yet, in France, institutions specially created to aid liberated prisoners in finding work, and in this manner to save them from falling back into crime. We can only cite, as exceptions to this, certain establishments whose creation is due to the private initiative of members of the clergy and of the Sisters of the Order of Mary-Joseph.

The Abbé Coural, founded in 1842, near Montpelier, under the title of Solitude of Nazareth, a refuge designed for the liberated females of the south. The Sisters of Mary-Joseph, in imitation of this example, have founded seven other refuges, near the central prisons, for women. To the present time there is only one establishment of this kind for men—the Asylum of Saint Leonard, at Couzon, (Rhone.)*

The administration is earnestly engaged in seeking the means to increase the number of institutions similar to those of which we have just spoken.

A commission, of which we shall speak further on, relating to the patronage of liberated prisoners, was organized by a decree of the 6th of October, 1869.

The labors of this commission were interrupted by the political events of last year. The inquiry conducted under its direction has, however, gathered very important information, which will soon be published. This commission is about to be re-organized.

A reform of considerable importance has already been effected in one of the points indicated by the commission, as creating an obstacle to the return of liberated prisoners to normal conditions of existence. A circular of the minister of justice has just re-established, in the case of persons subjected to legal supervision, the system in vogue prior to the year 1851. Henceforth liberated prisoners of this class will be known only to the administration, and, with the exception of certain great cities in which they are forbidden to reside, they are at liberty to choose the place of their abode. They are now able to escape the difficulties resulting especially from prejudices, salutary perhaps as far as public morality is concerned, but very prejudicial to them—prejudices which oppose their admission into workshops, or their employment on farms, and, consequently, their return to well-doing by the path of labor.

LXVIII. Besides the houses of refuge mentioned above, and the two patronage societies for liberated Protestants of the two sexes, there are not, in France, special patronage societies for liberated adults.

The liberated juveniles of the department of the Seine are placed under the patronage of a society which facilitates their admission to provisional liberty, and aids them in acquiring a trade.

A commission instituted, in virtue of a decree of the 6th October, 1869, was charged with studying all the questions relating to patronage, and with determining the measures adopted to facilitate the return of discharged prisoners to free life.

It seemed necessary to inquire especially: 1. Whether there are differences to be made between classes of prisoners, (correctionals, reclusionaries, and those sentenced to hard labor.) 2. Whether the commissions of supervisions of the prisons ought to be placed over the work of patronage, and, if so, whether it would be proper to leave to them the

---

* The results of the refuges devoted to women are good. Those obtained at the asylum at Saint Leonard are relatively less satisfactory.

free use of the *peculium* accumulated as a reserve for the prisoner during his imprisonment. 3. Whether the action of patronage can be fortified by the adoption and vigorous use of arrangements analogous to the system of preparatory liberations.

It is placed out of all doubt that the organizations of patronage will present, in certain cases, great difficulties; but they cannot be insurmountable. The various objections raised, hitherto, to this eminently social creation ought not to arrest the efforts of the administration. The inquiries made by the commission on this subject have shown that, with the co-operation pledged, from various quarters, toward the accomplishment of this work, a patronage, widely extended, ought to offer more advantages than disadvantages.

LXIX. The punishment of imprisonment in association, in different degrees, is applied in France under different conditions, on which account it has been found necessary to give attention to the nature and condition of the buildings which have been successively placed at the disposal of the administration of prisons.

The system of cellular imprisonment has not been practiced to any very great extent, except in certain establishments devoted to the treatment of prisoners awaiting trial.

France was on the point of adopting a penitentiary system homogeneous in all its parts and based, in principle, on the processes employed in America to secure personal separation, but, at the same time, softening the rigors inherent in this mode of imprisonment, and under the reserve of a proportional reduction of the duration of the punishments.

The legislation which had been directed to this end, and was upon the point of realizing it, was interrupted by the revolution of 1848. Since that time the cellular system has been made the occasion of very severe strictures, at least as regards punishments of a certain duration; and it is consequently probable that there would have been, on this point, important modifications in the details, whenever the system should have been definitively adopted.

To sum up, France has not yet adopted a well-defined penitentiary system.

The administration, shut up to its own resources, has been able to devote itself to reforms, certainly of great importance, relating to the economic *régime* and the organization of labor, order, and discipline. In these respects, the central prisons and the greater part of the houses of arrest, of justice, and of correction, may be placed in the first rank.

It seems difficult to secure greater regularity in the mode of administering these various services; but it is certain that the results obtained are not such as they ought to be, if the question is received in relation to moral reformation. It is impossible, then, to declare ourselves satisfied with institutions which, upon the whole, fail to secure the gradual repression of crimes and misdemeanors, and whose results are unsatisfactory in regard to the number of relapses, which is, to say the least, always far from inconsiderable.

To state with precision the defects of the penitentiary system in France would require explanations far beyond the plan of the present report. For the rest, these defects are similar to those which exist in all countries where imprisonment has been substituted for the various penalties previously in vogue. A complete examination of the question would, moreover, necessitate a scheme for the revision of the penal laws. Under the reserve implied in these observations, we will confine ourselves to pointing out the reforms and the ameliorations to be intro duced in France, into the penitentiary system, that is to say:

1. The abolition of the punishment of imprisonment for offenses of little gravity, in place of which should be substituted, as far as possible, pecuniary penalties, the temporary privation of certain civil rights, &c.

2. The definitive choice of a system of imprisonment for prisoners awaiting examination or trial, and for those sentenced to punishments of a duration of at least two years. The system of personal isolation, mitigated by labor, reading, visits, &c., and above all a proportionate diminution, more or less considerable, of the duration of the punishments, ought of themselves, it would seem, to be efficacious and salutary for the prisoners belonging to these classes.

3. The adoption of a penitentiary system, applicable under different degrees of severity, to—1. Correctional convicts sentenced to a punishment of two years and over—2. Reclusionaries—3. Persons sentenced to hard labor.

A large number of publicists and specialists recommend, for punishments of a long duration, and above all in the case of recidevists, the adoption, on a large scale, of the system of transportation, and in all cases, the progressive substitution of agricultural for industrial labors.

It is important to remark, nevertheless, that hitherto transportation has always occasioned excessive expenses, and that most frequently the punishment of hard labor, thus applied, has a less intimidating effect upon criminals than an imprisonment of long duration in the central prisons.

[N. B.—The agricultural colonies, established in Corsica, present similar inconveniences.]

4. The organization of patronage societies, to which liberated prisoners may have recourse on their discharge from the penitentiaries.

II.—BELGIUM.

[Translation.]

I. All the prisons of Belgium are under the jurisdiction of the minister of justice.

The penitentiary of Louvain has a commission charged with the inspection and suspervision of that establishment. There are also commissions charged with the general supervision of the other prisons, and constituting administrative boards, invested with the right of investigating and redressing abuses, of proposing and introducing reforms to the advantage of the service, of granting to the employés leave of absence for five days, and of imposing upon them certain disciplinary punishments.

II. Near the tribunals of primary jurisdiction are houses of arrest for prisoners awaiting examination; near the courts of justice for prisoners awaiting trial; near every court-martial there is a provostal prison for military prisoners awaiting examination or trial. In all the houses of arrest are found apartments for the punishment of convicts not sentenced to the central prisons.

Juveniles of both sexes acquitted as having acted without knowledge, and placed under the care of the government for a definite period, are sent to houses of refuge.

III. Of the twenty-six prisons in the kingdom, eighteen are conducted upon the cellular system, not including two cellular wards in the city of Brussells and in the central prison of Ghent. Of the six congregate prisons, four are undergoing alterations to adapt them to the system of separate imprisonment.

·IV. |For answer to the fourth question, which calls for the results obtained by these two systems, the reply of the government refers to a report made to the minister of justice by the administrator of prisons on the 31st of December, 1869, for the examination of which report there has been no time. The writer of the official reply having made this reference, goes on to say :] The Belgian legislature has given its preference to the cellular system, because it renders repression more efficacious, and because the reformation of the convict is thereby better assured.

V. The funds needed for the support of the prisons are derived from the same source as the funds required for the other departments of the public service.

The cost of each day's support is counted in gross, without taking account of the product of the prison labor, which is turned over to the treasury.

VI. The appointment of the directors and assistant directors is by royal decree. The other functionaries and employés of the prison are named by the minister of justice.

There is no limit to the tenure of office; it belongs to the government to judge whether the functionary ought to be retained or dismissed.

VII. The chief of a penitentiary establishment ought to be thoroughly acquainted with all the machinery of the service, whether relating to the moral, disciplinary, economic, of industrial administration. He should be able to conduct the government and discipline of the prison without extraneous aid, and to understand that the care which he is obliged to give to the material part of his establishment ought not to be to the prejudice of the zeal due from him to the moral part; and he should possess, in a high degree, the attribute of probity.

The director of a cellular prison, and especially of a penal cellular prison, has, so to speak, the charge of souls. He must be, at the same time, good, just, firm, intelligent, conciliatory; he must comprehend the whole extent of his duties; he must know men, and particularly criminals; he must be able to command respect and to secure submission to his authority from all without opposition. Above all, he must be animated by sentiments profoundly religious, for Christian devotion alone can sustain him in the path of his duty and give him the force and the perseverance necessary to overcome the obstacles which cannot fail to obstruct his progress.

The keepers are moral agents; they must, like all the other members of the staff, offer guarantees of morality, intelligence, zeal, and humanity. Their special service requires that they be in the vigor of their age, (they should not be admitted before the age of twenty-seven years;) that they have good health and a robust temperament; that they possess an energetic character; that they have a good primary education, and, if possible, the knowledge of one of the trades followed in the prison, so that they may be able to teach it to the prisoners.

Finally, they should have a complete and accurate knowledge of the regulations, whose practical application is confided to them.

VIII. Special training-schools are indispensable only for keepers, who generally enter on their functions without being prepared for the mission which they have to fulfill.

A school for keepers has existed for some years in the penitentiary of

Louvain. The directors are recruited from the *personnel* of the administration, where, in passing through the different grades, they have necessarily acquired the requisite knowledge. Special examinations are a condition-precedent of their appointment.

IX. The pension granted to directors and employés who have become incapacitated for a further discharge of their duties is regulated upon the footing of the average salary of their last five years of service, a salary determined by the whole number of their years of service.

In regard to the pension allowed them on retirement, they are placed on the same footing as all the other functionaries belonging to the public administration.

X. The difference between prisoners sentenced to simple imprisonment, to reclusion, and to hard labor, is, the first are confined in houses of correction ; the second, in houses of reclusion ; the third, in convict prisons.

The duration of correctional imprisonment is from eight days to five years; that of reclusion, from five to ten years; that of hard labor, when the sentence is not for life, from ten to fifteen years, or from fifteen to twenty years. Of the product of their labor, there is allowed to correctionals, five-tenths ; to reclusionaries, four-tenths ; and to prisoners sentenced to hard labor, three-tenths.

The privilege of receiving visits, and of writing letters, is accorded to correctionals every fifteen days; to reclusionaries, once a month; and to those sentenced to hard labor, every two months.

XI. As regards the classification of prisoners : In the congregate penal prisons, the prisoners are divided into three classes.

The first class comprises prisoners whose antecedents are the most unfavorable, and whose conduct is bad. This class bears the name of punishment division, (*division de punition.*)

The second comprises prisoners whose antecedents, without being decidedly unfavorable and their conduct absolutely bad, have, nevertheless, need to be subjected to a probation, longer or shorter, before being definitively classed. This class has the name of probation division, (*division d'épreuve.*)

The third is composed of prisoners who, by their antecedents or their good conduct in the penitentiary, have claim to a special distinction. This class bears the name of recompense division, (*division de récompense.*)

These three classes, although subjected to the same *régime* and the same exercises, are nevertheless the objects of special distinctions. In order to be able to recognize the prisoners who belong to each, a distinctive mark in the clothing is adopted for each division.

The prisoners of the punishment division are subjected to the most painful labors, are deprived of the *cantine*, and suffer various privations; especially that of visits from and correspondence with the outside, except in urgent cases, which are left to the judgment of the director.

The passage from one division into another is determined by the administrative commission, on the proposal of the director. To this end the records of conduct and of punishment are consulted.

The examination for classification takes place during the first third of each year, unless oftener made necessary by exceptional circumstances resulting from overcrowding in one or other of the sections.

The numbers of the prisoners assigned to each division are inscribed on a roster suspended on the wall.

The first classification is made by the director according to the known antecedents of the convict on his entrance, the circumstances revealed on the occasion of his conviction, and the notes which are forwarded by the courts.

This classification is, so to speak, the only possible one in the great congregate penitentiaries; but to obtain solid results, in a disciplinary and moral point of view, it would be necessary to appropriate special wards to different classes.

XII. The regulations relating to the penitentiaries authorize the administrative boards and those of the inspection of prisons to address to the minister of justice propositions of clemency, or of reductions of punishment, in favor of prisoners who distinguish themselves by their good conduct, or who, as the result of special circumstances, seem worthy to be recommended to the royal clemency.

XIII. As regards the participation by prisoners in their earnings: Prisoners receive a part of the earnings resulting from their labor. This part is three-tenths for those sentenced to hard labor, four-tenths for those sentenced to reclusion, and five-tenths for those sentenced correctionally. This proportion cannot be increased.

XIV. Other awards decreed to good conduct, to diligence, to zeal and progress in labor and school, to meritorious actions of whatever kind, are the following: 1. Admission to places of trust, to domestic service, and to certain exceptional labors. 2. An increase of the privilege of visits and of correspondence. 3. Permission to make use of tobacco, in the form of snuff, or by smoking it, save that the use in this latter form is limited to the time of promenade in the exercise yards. 4. The grant of certain diversions and alleviations, such as the gift of books, of engravings, of tools, of useful objects, &c. 5. Propositions of clemency and of reduction of punishment. No. 3 applies only to cellular penal prisons; the use of tobacco is absolutely forbidden in the penitentiary of Ghent.

The most frequent violation of prison rules are, in the cellular prisons, communications or attempted communications, verbal or by writing. In the congregate prisons they are infractions of the rule of silence and traffic.

XVI. The following are the disciplinary punishments in use: 1. Privation of work, of reading, of gratuities, of the *cantine*, of visits, of correspondence, and of other indulgences granted in pursuance of the regulations. 2. A diet of bread and water. 3. Confinement in a special cell, or in a dark cell, with or without the bread and water diet. 4. The withdrawal of rewards which might otherwise have been granted.

XVII. All disciplinary punishments are recorded in a special register, together with the causes for which they were inflicted. The offenses committed and the punishments administered are also placed in the moral account opened with each prisoner.

XVIII and XIX. Chaplains are provided in all the prisons and for all religions. They preside at all the different services and exercises of worship, and over all religious instruction; they visit the prisoners in their cells and give them counsels and consolations; they urge them to a conscientious performance of their religious duties; they direct their pious readings; they hear their confessions, preach to them, give special instruction to those who are ignorant of the essential truths of religion, and fulfill toward them all the duties of their ministry.

XX. The government has always attached the greatest importance to religious instruction as a means of reformation, and has given to it the most complete organization possible, and every facility is given to the prisoners for the performance of their religious duties.

XXI. The administration has declared in the regulations relating to penitentiaries that it would encourage and facilitate the formation of associations of persons of both sexes, with a view to offer counsels and consolations to the prisoners, to watch over their interests and those of their families, and to facilitate their re-entrance into society. But no such association has yet been organized, nor has even any private person ever offered himself for the performance of such services.

XXII. Sunday-schools have never been established in Belgium. The administration has no need of such schools, because schools are held daily during the week.

XXIII. In regard to correspondence: Except by special authorization of the director in urgent cases, or when the privilege is granted as a reward for good conduct, prisoners can write or receive only one letter each every fortnight, when they are sentenced to correctional imprisonment; every month, when they are sentenced to reclusion; and every two months, when they are sentenced to hard labor.

XXIV. To the question, whether the correspondence of prisoners with their friends exerts a good or evil influence upon them, we reply: The effect is evidently good. It maintains or renews the ties of family, and exercises a favorable influence upon the prisoners. It also aids the officers in the study of their character.

XXV, XXVI, and XXVII. The prisoners are permitted to receive the visits of their relatives: father, mother, husband, wife, children, brothers, sisters, uncles, aunts, and guardians, on the production of a certificate granted by the local authority of the places where they reside, authenticating their identity.

No other visits are permitted except upon a written order of the superior administration, of the governor of the province, or of the president or one of the members of the commission specially delegated to this effect.

In the penal prisons more particularly, these visits take place in the conversation-rooms, in presence of a keeper. This employé observes the persons of the prisoner and the visitor, without interfering with the privacy of the interview.

The moral effect of these visits is generally good. There are rare cases, it is true, where such visits have produced an effect morally unfavorable.

XXVIII. More than one-half of the prisoners, that is to say, about 51 per cent., are able to read on their admission to the prisons.

XXIX. Every prison, with a population of fifty inmates or more, is provided with a school, properly so called, or with a teaching lecturer.

XXX. At the penitentiary of Louvain attendance upon the school is obligatory for all the prisoners, except on a dispensation for cause, granted by the director of the establishment.

At the penitentiary of Ghent, appropriated to a class of reclusionaries and of prisoners sentenced to hard labor, attendance at school is obligatory for all prisoners under thirty years of age; it is permitted to prisoners who have passed that age; but these latter, once admitted, can withdraw themselves from the school only with the assent of the administrative commission.

In other prisons provided with a school, attendance thereupon is obligatory, 1. For prisoners sentenced to six months and over, and those who have not attained their fortieth year; 2. For juvenile delinquents, whatever may have been the cause of their imprisonment. Attendance on the school is permitted to the other prisoners.

XXXI. The instruction given in the penitentiary schools includes: 1. Religion, which is taught by the chaplains, or under their immediate direction; 2. Morals; 3. Reading; 4. Writing; 5. Arithmetic; 6. Elementary notions of grammar, history, and geography, particularly the history and geography of Belgium; 7. The elements of geometry and linear drawing in their relations with trades; as well as other branches of a practical utility.

Great progress is made by the prisoners in these studies.

XXXII. Libraries are found in all the prisons of Belgium. They contain three classes of works, which meet three several wants—that of reforming the prisoners, that of instructing them, and that of diverting their minds by reading, at once entertaining, moral, and instructive.

XXXIII. The prisoners are very fond of reading, and spend much time in that employment. Their choice of books depends on their degree of instruction and education. The preference is generally given by them to works containing recitals and adventures of voyages, pictorial magazines, and some of the romances of Conscience, of Snieders, and of Dickens, the first two being Flemish authors. The influence of these readings is excellent, and the formation of prison libraries cannot be made with too much care and discrimination.

The prison library ought to embrace three classes of works: those of a pious and religious character, those of an instructive character, and those of an entertaining character, but having at the same time a moral and educational tendency.

XXXIV. The sanitary state of the Belgian prisons is good. The drains for waste water and night-soil are cleansed every week by a strong current rushing through them, so that no emanation dangerous to health can ever issue therefrom.

XXXV. As regards the water supply, each prisoner in the cellular prisons has daily at his disposal from 12 to 15 liters of potable water. The water supplied to the prisoners is of good quality.

XXXVI. The ventilation and heating of the cells being intimately connected, it will be proper to speak of both under the same head.

The apparatus for heating is placed in the cellar. The fire is made in the center of a double cylinder filled with water, which forms the boilers for its propulsion. From the upper part of each of these boilers two perpendicular pipes ascend into the principal ventilating conduits, and conduct the hot water directly into a special reservoir placed in the chimney (cheminée d'appel) appropriated to each apparatus. This reservoir is fed by six pipes, which traverse horizontally each range of cells, returning afterward, by the same passage, to the principal apparatus. Two pipes, filled with hot water, thus pass into all the cells. They are placed in a horizontal conduit running along the floor, close to the exterior wall. These conduits, covered with a plate of perforated iron, form for each cell a little reservoir of heat.

Thus the caloric is utilized just where its action is required, since it is precisely in the cells that it disengages itself, supplying each with an equal quantity. Its center of radiation is in the cell itself. Here is found the first divergence from the English system of heating, and the caloric cannot, as in that system, concentrate itself against the parvises of a great conduit situated in the basement.

Let us examine now the mode of introducing fresh air. This introduction is twofold. In the first place, there is inserted in the window a ventilator of 30 centimeters (about 12 inches) in height and 44 centimeters (equal to 17½ inches) in breadth, through which the fresh air is introduced directly into the cell, without having come in contact with the heat-pipes. Secondly, at one of the extremities of the iron plate which covers the conduits from the hot-air furnace is left an opening, which allows the heat to circulate in the cells. The opposite side of the plate corresponds to an opening made in the thickness of the exterior wall, by which the pure air from outside penetrates into the reservoir, and so into the cells. A valve is fitted to this last opening, by which the prisoner can regulate the introduction of air, and by the same means can increase or diminish the heat of the cell. Let it be carefully noted that the reservoir of which we have just spoken, as well as the introduction of fresh air, is on a level with the floor.

The vitiated air is drawn off by a conduit placed in the thickness of the wall on the opposite side from that on which air and heat enter. This conduit, at its upper extremity, leads into a great pipe, which runs horizontally under the roof, discharging its contents into a vertical chimney, at the bottom of which is situated the reservoir which receives the hot water of the furnace, whose smoke-pipe also traverses the chimney.

This system of ventilation works naturally and without mechanism of any kind.

XXXVII. The cleanliness of the prisons is insured by the following measures:

An active ventilation incessantly purifies the different parts of the penitentiary establishment, throughout which there is always diffused a fresh and agreeable atmosphere.

A cleanliness the most minute is continually maintained. The daily cleaning of the premises, the varnishing of the pavement of the cells by means of a special process, and the waxing of the floors and the pavements of the galleries, have made it possible to give up washing with water, which is attended with great inconvenience.

The walls of the cells, galleries, &c., are washed of a stone-color at the beginning of every year, and partially whenever it becomes necessary to remove spots or stains. No deposit of dirt or dung is allowed within the inclosure of the establishment, and all necessary measures are taken to have the rain-water speedily carried off from the premises. In summer, fumigations are made every morning. They are less necessary in winter, and are, consequently, less frequent during that season of the year.

XXXVIII. To insure personal cleanliness on the part of the prisoners the hair is required to be kept short; whiskers, moustach, &c., are forbidden. The men are shaved twice each week. The prisoners are required to wash their feet once a week. Every two months in winter, and once a month in summer, they are required to take a full bath. The body-linen is changed every week.

XXXIX. As regards the arrangement of the water-closets, two good systems are in use—movable vessels and fixed seats, with a pressure of water. This last deserves the preference, particularly in penal prisons.

XL. The cells are lighted with gas; two stop-cocks are fitted to the lighting apparatus—one in the cell, under the control of the prisoner; the other on the outside, under the control of the keeper.

The consumption of gas is 39 liters per burner each hour.

XLI. The system of heating has already been described.

XLII and XLIII. The use of the hammock has been given up, having been replaced in the cellular prisons by an iron table-bedstead. This bedstead is folded up during the day, contains the bedding, and serves as a table.

The bedding consists of a mattress, a bolster, two cases for the mattress, two bolster-cases, two woolen blankets, and two pairs of sheets. The mattress and the bolster are made of ten kilogrammes of sea-weed.

XLIV. [This question is answered by referring to the special regulations of the central prison of Louvain, which the commissioner has not had time to examine.]

XLV. With regard to the treatment of sick prisoners. The infirmary occupies a part of the building at some distance from the cells, and the sick are distributed into spacious cells, well aired and comfortably warmed. These cells have a capacity of 40 cubic meters, and are provided with the necessary furniture and with clothing suited to the condition of the sick. The dietary is regulated according to a special tariff. The hygienic service leaves nothing to be desired. A cleanliness the most minute, a ventilation active and continual, frequent fumigations, the change of linen and of bedding—in a word, all desirable attentions are accorded to the sick.

Independently of the assiduous attentions of which the sick are made the object, they are regularly visited, at least once an hour, and can, at any time, call upon the nurses by means of a signal, whose movement reaches to each bed. Prisoners seriously sick have watchers, and all the necessary measures are taken that they receive the attentions required by their situation.

Experience proves that prisoners are better treated in an infirmary cell than in a common infirmary.

When the service permits it, the doors of the cells are left open. In this arrangement there is a moral and physical advantage. The rule of separation, which is the foundation of the penitentiary system, is not violated; and the prisoners have not under their eyes, during their sickness, the spectacle of other suffering.

XLVI. The most common disease in cellular as in associated imprisonment is phthisis; deficiency of blood is equally frequent. Caries of the ribs and the sternum, diseases rare in free life, are frequent in that one of our penitentiaries which is not cellular.

XLVII. Regarding the percentage of the sick. We give the figures taken from the statistics of 1870:

Average population penitentiary of Ghent 754
Number of days spent in the infirmary 14,503
Average population penitentiary of Louvain 515
Number of days spent in the infirmary 1,157

All the prisons together, during the same year, furnished the following results:

Days of imprisonment.................................... 1,916,949
Days of sickness 52,554
Giving a percentage of.................................... 2.74

XLVIII. Death-rate. We give the figures taken from the statistics of 1870:

Average population penitentiary of Ghent 750
Number of deaths 37
Average population penitentiary of Louvain 515
Number of deaths 6

It is worthy of remark that prisoners sentenced to hard labor for life undergo their punishment in the penitentiary of Ghent.

The average aggregate population of all the prisons was: Prisoners, 5,251; deaths, 93; being a percentage of 1.77.

XLIX. Penal, as distinguished from industrial labor, does not exist in the prisons of Belgium.

The industrial occupations, expressed by the designations of the persons engaged in them, are: Scriveners, lithographers of autographs, office boys, dyers, winders, warpers, weavers' boys, weavers. foil-makers.

cutters and tailors, menders, folders, hosiers, packers, shoemakers, book-binders, joiners, turners, clog-makers, blacksmiths, tinmen, founders, masons and stone-cutters, masons' laborers, painters and glaziers, white-washers, pit-sawyers, slate-quarriers.

L. We have no penal labor, properly so called. The law exacts work of persons sentenced to correctional imprisonment, to reclusion, and to hard labor. The employments introduced into the prisons are chosen, in preference, from among those which seem likely to afford to the prisoners after their liberation the means of procuring a livelihood.

It is our opinion that labor cannot be imposed as a punishment, for the first necessity of man in society, and, above all, of man in the lower classes, is labor, and the first sentiment to be developed in him is the love of work. To prevent crime in the honest population, or a relapse into crime of those who had been discharged from prison, in this consists the first guarantee of individual reformation and of social security. What would become of prisoners if they were restored to society with an aversion to labor? Is the hour of their liberation the time to say to them "Do you love work," when they have been taught to hate it? The liberated prisoner ought not to carry with him on his discharge from prison the idea that work is a punishment in this world, and that he has suffered it long enough during his imprisonment to hasten at the hour of his deliverance to free himself from his chains. Labor should be exhibited to him in the prison (as it is and ought to be in society) as the source of the physical and moral elevation of man. He ought, in all things, so to identify the life of man with the necessity and the at-traction of labor that even in captivity it should be still, if not the image of happiness, at least a solace attached to its exercise and an idea of punishment from its privation. In a word, if labor ought to enter as a penal element into penitentiary imprisonment, it is not in the use but the privation of it.

Labor in penitentiary imprisonment ought to be obligatory; but it is an obligation which ought not to be imposed on the prisoner under the empire of constraint, but as an obligation to which his reason, his interest, his position, everything, ought to urge him.

LI and LII. For our opinion concerning the moral and sanitary effect upon the prisoner of penal labor, see the preceding answer.

LIII. The industrial labor of the prisoners is in part directed by the administration itself, and in part awarded to special contractors. These latter are placed under the immediate surveillance of the directors of the prisons into which they are admitted.

LIV. The contract system, such as it exists in our prisons, is that to which our preference would be given, as well because of the certain and great benefits procured by it to the treasury, as because of the facility which it offers of diversifying the labors of the prisoners and of affording them employments suited to their particular aptitudes.

Nevertheless, the system of working the prisoners by the administration itself offers also, in our organization, certain advantages, especially when it is a question of labor of easy execution, or of the creation of products for the use of the administration itself.

LV. Different systems of contracting the labor of the prisoners do not exist in this country. That which is in actual use consists in awarding the labor to a contractor who offers at the same time remunerative prices and adequate guarantees of solvency and morality.

LVI. From 60 to 70 per cent. of the inmates of our prisons had not, at the time of their commitment, any regular business or assured means of support.

LVII. The apprenticeship of the prisoners, in the different trades

taught, is confided to the keepers of sections, under the special supervision and direction of the foremen. It follows that the keeper is not
only charged with the supervision of the twenty-five prisoners of his
section, and with the enforcement of the rules, but that he employs the
greater part of the day in instructing the prisoner in some one of the
branches of industry introduced into the establishment.

The mean duration of the apprenticeship is: twelve months for the
shoemakers; six months for the weavers; and three months for the
tailors. This time may be shortened by the aptitude or intelligence of
the apprentices. As a general rule, the apprenticeship is terminated
before the expiration of the date fixed upon, especially when, by dint of
repetition, the prisoner has been made to comprehend the necessity of
mastering a business, in order that, at the time of his liberation, he may
be able to work for his food, his clothing, his bed—in a word, to assure
the satisfaction of his essential wants.

Certainly it is important to effect the reformation of the prisoners,
but it is important also to place them, on their liberation, in a condition in which they may gain an honest living by work, since it is an
undoubted truth that ignorance of a business is the principal cause
which urges the greater part of men to crimes against property.

The theory of reformation includes, therefore, the industrial education which gives to the prisoner the means of being, some day, sufficient to himself, and the religious and moral education which instructs
him in his duties toward God and toward men.

LVIII. We regard it, as will already have appeared from the preceding answer, as a point of the greatest importance, that the prisoner,
during his imprisonment, should master the art of self-help. To this
end moral and religious conferences are held with him, and it is sought,
by means of the knowledge of various kinds imparted to him, to put
him into a condition of independence after his liberation.

LIX. The question relating to the effect of repeated short imprisonments, seeming to belong to a peculiarity in the legislation of the United
States, the committee has judged it expedient to abstain from formu-
lating a reply to it.

LX. As to the number of recidivists: Among the 795 prisoners committed, in 1872, to the central prisons, other than the establishment
specially devoted to juvenile delinquents, figure 626 recidivists; that is
to say, more than 78 per cent. This result evidently cannot be placed
to the charge of the cellular system, since nearly half of the penitentiary establishments are still conducted upon the congregate system.

The report addressed to the government in 1869, which is hereto an-
nexed, shows that the cellular system has considerably diminished the
number of recidivists.

LXI. Recidivists are more severely punished than persons committed
for a first offense, in proof of which are here cited articles 54 to 57 of the
Penal Code : .

ARTICLE 54. Whoever, having been sentenced to a criminal punishment, shall have
committed a crime which subjects him to the punishment of reclusion, may be sentenced to hard labor from ten to fifteen years.

If the crime involves a sentence to hard labor from ten to fifteen years, the convict
may be sentenced to hard labor from fifteen to twenty years.

He must be sentenced to seventeen years at least of this punishment, if the crime
imports a sentence to hard labor from fifteen to twenty years.

ARTICLE 55. Whoever, after a sentence to a criminal punishment, shall have committed a crime punishable by an imprisonment of from five to ten years, may be sentenced to an imprisonment of from ten to fifteen years.

If the crime is punishable by an imprisonment of ten to fifteen years, the convict
may be sentenced to an increased imprisonment.

He must be sentenced to seventeen years at least of imprisonment, if the crime is
one that necessitates an increased imprison-----

ARTICLE 56. Whoever, after a sentence to a criminal punishment, shall have committed a misdemeanor, may be sentenced to a punishment double the maximum permitted by the law forbidding such misdemeanor.

The same punishment may be awarded in case of a prior sentence to an imprisonment of a year at least, if the convict shall have committed the new misdemeanor before the expiration of five years after having undergone his prescribed punishment.

In these two cases the convict may be placed, by the judgment or the arrest, under the special supervision of the police during five years at least, and ten years at most.

ARTICLE 57. The rules established in case of a relapse shall be applied conformably to the preceding articles, in case of a prior sentence, pronounced by a military tribunal, for an act defined as a crime or misdemeanor by the ordinary penal laws, and to a punishment authorized by those laws.

If, for said act, a punishment authorized by the military laws has been pronounced, the courts and tribunals, in judging of the relapse, shall have regard only to the minimum of the punishment, which the act, punishable by the first judgment, might have warranted, according to the ordinary penal laws.

LXII. Debtors' prisons still exist in Belgium, but they are empty cases of incarceration for debt have become very rare since the publication of the law of the 27th of July, 1871.

The treatment to which imprisoned debtors are subjected is not the same as that applied to criminals. They occupy a special series of cells, have the exclusive enjoyment of an exercise yard, and may communicate with each other, receive four visits a week from their relatives and from persons with whom they have business relations, and may correspond freely with the outside world.

LXIII. The principal causes of crime are, in the army, want of occupation, and the system of substitution.

In civil life, they are the oblivion of religious and moral principles, ignorance of duty, want of a business, the creation of factitious wants, drunkenness, libertinism, thoughtlessness, distaste of work, and idleness.

LXIV. The two sexes are represented in the Belgian prisons in the following proportions: men, 88 per cent.; woman, 12 per cent.

LXV. As regards the object of penal treatment: The administration seeks, above all, to reform those whose punishment is exacted by society; but it punishes without subjecting them to any physical suffering. The execution of the punishment has in view the double aim of expiation and reformation.

LXVI. Regarding the moral condition of prisoners on their liberation: It is in proof that in the cellular prisons the moral state of the prisoners is, in general, better at the time of their discharge than at that of their entrance. Those who manifest evil inclinations are few in number; nearly all have sensibly modified the sentiments with which they were animated at the time of their commitment.

LXVII and LXVIII. No prisoners' aid or patronage societies are found in Belgium; but the government has not lost sight of this important point. Efforts were made in 1848 to organize such associations; but, unhappily, the measures taken were not crowned with full success. While waiting, the administration seeks the best means for assuring to liberated prisoners an effectual protection, so as to prevent their falling back into crime. A special credit figures even in the budget of the department of justice, permitting the administrative commissions of reformatory institutions to extend aid to their liberated inmates.

LXIX. To the question whether we are satisfied with our existing penitentiary system, our reply is affirmative in so far as it is not applicable to establishments on the congregate plan; but the transformation of these into cellular prisons is actively progressing.

N. B.—The following table, appended to the report, contains in condensed form much interesting information regarding the model prison of Belgium:

Penitentiary of Louvain.

	*1860.	1861.	1862.	1863.	1864.	1865.	1866.	1867.	1868.	1869.	1870.	Total or average.
Convicts admitted to the penitentiary	326	964	321	316	221	344	420	242	337	253	310	3,027
Number of days of maintenance	24,195	156,108	188,675	201,130	195,379	185,455	189,062	177,213	185,154	209,442	188,290	1,875,438
Average population	241	428	517	551	534	508	519	485	505	571	515	513
Average daily cost of maintenance, in francs	2.46	1.06	0.97	0.8982	0.8804	0.9259	0.9569	1.1719	1.1097	0.9951	1.0169	0.9987
Number of convicts admitted to the infirmary	7	36	42	33	52	36	41	37	40	41	28	386
Number of days of sickness	94	1,297	2,043	2,005	1,883	1,306	1,327	1,497	1,664	2,067	1,159	16,178
Number of punishments inflicted	20	175	149	167	76	95	129	86	88	102	85	1,152
Number of days of punishment	109	1,370	1,116	1,300	685	930	1,276	925	924	1,355	1,038	10,928
Average number of sick per day	1	4	5	5.49	5.15	3.57	3.63	3.91	4.55	5.66	3.17	4.41
Deaths	1	11	8	11	7	3	6	4	6	5	5	66
Suicides			2	4	1	1		3	3	1	1	15
Cases of mental derangement			5	3	2	2	1					14
Attempts at escape												
Escapes												
Crimes or misdemeanors committed by the convicts		1										1
Acts of rebellion or assault against the person												
Accidents, fires, and unusual occurrences				1								1
Amount of gratuities earned by prisoners, in francs	1,032.77	16,341.71	20,981.13	20,867.60	21,390.48	19,090.24	21,197.74	18,116.02	20,859.59	23,937.53	21,647.99	203,730.03
Average per prisoner, in francs	4.27	38.18	39.23	37.87	40.06	37.58	40.84	37.35	41.31	41.92	42.03	39.64

* The prison was opened on October 1, 1860. The first column (1860) is given only from memory, and should not be included in the totals. The totals comprehend only the years 1861–'70.

III.—THE NETHERLANDS.

[Translation.]

I. All the prisons in the Netherlands are under the superior direction and control of the minister of justice, and the general inspection of the prisons has hitherto been .made by an inspector, who has his deputy in the bureau of the department of justice. For the inspection of the buildings, an engineer-architect is attached to the same department. Further, according to the provisions of our code of criminal procedure, (article 421,) the courts and tribunals are required to cause the prisons to be inspected, from time to time, by members assigned to that duty, and the same obligation rests upon the attorneys general, and upon the officers of justice, (*procureurs du roi.*) These latter are bound to make this inspection at least twice a year. The reports of all these inspections are addressed to the minister.

The administration of the several prisons is confided to administrative commissions, named in each locality where a prison exists. The members of these commissions are named by the king, from among the notables of the locality, who receive no salary. Whatever appertains to the local administration, to the internal service, to the discipline, and to the execution of the general and special regulations, is confided to these commissions, or is done through their agency. They are in official relation with the minister, either directly or by the deputy of the royal commissioner (governor) of the province, their immediate superior and their honorary president.

II. There are four classes of prisons: The central prisons, for persons sentenced to more than eighteen months of imprisonment; the detention prisons, in the chief cities of the several provinces, for persons sentenced to eighteen months or less; houses of arrest, in the chief towns of the several *arrondissements*, for persons sentenced to three months or less; and police or cantonal prisons, in the chief places of the cantons, for persons sentenced to one month and under.

In some cantons these prisons are united together. Among the prisons there are several on the cellular plan. In the three last-named classes of prisons are also prisoners under arrest, and awaiting their trial.

III. The law has left it to the discretion of the judge to award either associated imprisonment or, when the circumstances of the offense or the character of the convict appear to him to require it, or he himself judges it useful, imprisonment on the cellular plan. This power, at first, in 1851, restricted to the case of a sentence to one year's imprisonment or less, was extended in 1864 to sentences of two years, and afterward, in 1871, to sentences of four years. In no case, however, can the sentence to cellular imprisonment exceed the moiety of the duration of imprisonment in association, which may have been pronounced by the judge. The maximum of cellular imprisonment is therefore actually two years. To persons sentenced for a violation of police regulations cellular detention is not applicable.

IV. To obtain decisive results, results of which a judgment may be formed with some degree of certainty on the relative merit of the two systems, it would be necessary that the application of the systems be made in a uniform and not an arbitrary manner, which would permit a fair comparison of the results obtained. Now this application is still made (see the description given under No. III) in a manner very irregular and little harmonious. Consequently there yet exists a great difference of opinion on the question of preference, and above all, on the results obtained, and which might be obtained, by a judicious application of the two systems. Still it may be said that the cellular system (in itself, and apart from the manner of applying it, and the limits which should be imposed upon it) scarcely encounters any adversaries; and for imprisonments of short duration the opinion which desires a universal application of this system is gaining ground. As regards imprisonments of long duration, public opinion is still too unsettled and too undecided to even permit a judgment of the direction which it will finally take.

V. The funds necessary for the maintenance of the prisons and the prisoners are placed, annually, on the budget of the kingdom. The product of the prisoners' labor contributes to them only in a proportion very inconsiderable, because only a part of it is retained for the state. This part is 60 per cent. for those sentenced to reclusion and military prisoners, 50 per cent. for other inmates of the central prisons, and 30 per cent. for those confined in other prisons.

VI. As to the appointment of officers: The directors of the central prisons are named by the king; the other employés by the minister of justice. They hold their offices until they are displaced, dismissed, or retire from the service.

VII. We hold it to be necessary that the directors and employés of the prisons be men of tried morality, intelligent, and gifted with tact and with the knowledge necessary to inspire the respect of the prisoners, even without the use of a severe discipline. This respect depends principally upon the spirit of justice, equity, and humanity which they exhibit in their relations with the prisoners. In the directors, especially, there is needed a high degree of mental culture and an enlightened understanding of their duties, we might say, indeed, of their mission. A knowledge of the more important foreign languages is necessary, that they may be able to read and study the best writings on prison discipline, and to communicate with the foreign prisoners. Unhappily, we cannot affirm that the majority of the directors and employés of our prisons possess these talents and qualities, a fact which is due chiefly to the circumstance that the salaries are too low, and that the service of the prison officers is, in general, too onerous, and held in too little esteem. As a consequence, young men of good family and education refuse to enter upon this career.

VIII. There are no schools specially designed for the education of prison officers, and we do not regret it.. The best school is a well-organized and well-governed prison, where are offered to the young employés the means of acquiring knowledge and developing their talents, by the reading and the study of the best writings on the subject of prisons.

IX. The pensions accorded to the directors and employés, who have become incapacitated for the performance of their official duties, depend on their state of service and on the number of their years of service, according to the general rules established by law in regard to the pensions of all civil officers.

X. This question calls for a statement of the difference between sentences to simple imprisonment, to reclusion, and to hard labor.

Our penal laws recognize only reclusion and imprisonment, (without reckoning imprisonment for a breach of public regulations,) besides the punishment, for military offenses, of the wheel-barrow and simple detention. Apart from the difference in the retention on the product of labor, (*Vide* No. V,) the treatment offers little variation, and the labor is the same. We endeavor to find for all some kind of useful and remunerative labor, and to teach a trade to all, at least, who are sentenced to an imprisonment of considerable duration.

XI. As regards separating the prisoners into categories : In the central prisons, there is a classification which permits the separation of the more hardened and the more dangerous, as well as of the recidivists, from the other prisoners. The results of this separation may be regarded as favorable. •

XII. Agreeably to a royal decree of 1856, the administrative commissions of the central prisons submit every year a proposition for pardons or remissions, to be granted to prisoners who have distinguished themselves by their good conduct. These propositions, however, include only persons who have been sentenced to more than three years, and who have undergone at least one-half of their punishment, and the remission does not exceed six months. Besides this, all prisoners have the ordinary recourse of applying to the king for pardon or remission ; and since, in general, a decision is made only after a report from the commission on the conduct of the prisoners, this conduct has, generally, a strong influence upon the decision.

XIII. The part of the product of labor not retained by the State (see No. V) is given to the prisoner. Such part is not increased by reason of his good conduct.

XIV. No other rewards are given to prisoners besides this participation in their earnings. The distribution of premiums has been abolished for some time, and the industry of the prisoners finds its recompense in the increase of its profits, which naturally results from its zeal and its capacity. Still, the re-establishment of premiums is under consideration.

XV. The kinds and frequency of the violations of prison rules differs sensibly in different prisons, and often depend on the more or less intelligent administration of the chiefs and the employés.

Insubordination and quarrels may be regarded as the most frequent infractions. Isolation by night, (which is not yet generally introduced,) has, in this respect, produced good fruits.

XVI and XVII. The disciplinary punishments in use are: restriction to bread and water, withdrawal of the privilége of writing and receiving letters, privation of books, the dungeon, fetters; and, in the central prisons, isolation in a cell.

All these punishments· are recorded in a register, which is consulted in the cases mentioned in No. XII.

XVIII and XIX. There are no special chaplains attached exclusively to any prison ; but in all the central prisons, in all the houses of detention, and in the greater part of the houses of arrest, the office of chaplain and the religious services are confided to one of the ministers of each religion, who is named by the minister of justice.

The duties of the chaplain consist in performing religious service on Sundays and feast-days, in making pastoral visits, and in imparting religious instruction.

XX. Religious instruction, given with intelligence, is considered by us of great importance as an agency in the reformation of prisoners. In some prisons there has also been introduced the system of proverbs. This consists in hanging on the walls of the halls and cells pithy moral sentences, and in changing them from time to time. In the opinion of experienced persons, this plan deserves to be recommended for general use.

XXI. Persons of both sexes, outside of the administration, are admitted into the prisons to labor among the prisoners, with a view to their moral regeneration. In some cities there are private associations to visit the prisoners, organized by the general society for the moral amelioration of prisoners.

XXII. Sunday-schools have not been established in the prisons of Netherlands.

XXIII and XXIV. The administration of each prison regulates the correspondence of the prisoners as it judges most expedient. There is no general rule upon the subject.

All the letters received for or written by the prisoners are subjected to the inspection of the directors, and are withheld when their contents are improper. There is, therefore, no ground to apprehend injurious effects, and, in general, the correspondence of the prisoners is attended with a beneficial influence.

XXV, XXVI, and XXVII. The prisoners are permitted to receive the visits of their friends as often, generally, as once a month.

A grating separates the prisoner from his visitor, and an employé is always present to supervise the interview, which, as a general thing, may not exceed a quarter of an hour. They cannot converse privately.

As in the case of the correspondence, it may be said that the general effect of these visits is good.

XXVIII. The percentage of prisoners able to read and write on their commitment varies from 62 to 65. The number of prisoners able to read, but unable to write, is not indicated in the official statistics.

XXIX, XXX, and XXXI. Schools exist in all penal establishments, except in the police and cantonal prisons. In the cellular prisons the instruction is given in the cells. All prisoners up to the age of forty years, who do not know how to read and write, are obliged to receive that instruction.

The branches generally taught in these schools are: reading, writing, and arithmetic. Yet the system of instruction leaves, still, much to be desired. In some of the central prisons important reforms have been already introduced; in others, they will speedily follow. In the two central prisons for juvenile prisoners, the system of instruction leaves nothing to be added.

XXXII and XXXIII. There are libraries in all the prisons, which include books on morals and religion, also histories, travels, &c. The books are specially classified according to the different religions. These libraries are designed exclusively for the prisoners, and not yet for the employés.

Most of the prisoners are very fond of reading, and they generally prefer books of history and, above all, of travels. Their reading has a happy effect upon them.

XXXIV. In some prisons the system of sewage is still imperfect, but effort is made to introduce reforms.

XXXV. The quantity of water, designed for the use of the prisoners, is nowhere limited. Generally the quality is good, but in some localities it is difficult and expensive to procure it.

XXXVI. The prisons are, mostly, well ventilated, particularly the central prisons. Where improvements are still needed, means are employed to accomplish them.

XXXVII. Regarding the means employed to insure the cleanliness of the prisons: The interior domestic service is performed by the prisoners. Earnest endeavors are everywhere made to insure cleanliness, which is, for the most part, satisfactory, and is energetically supervised.

XXXVIII. The personal cleanliness of the prisoners is assured by a vigilant attention to their dress and their persons, and by requiring them to bathe at stated periods.

XXXIX. The arrangement with regard to water-closets differs in different prisons. In a number of them, the system of inodorous portable vessels has been introduced, with a reservoir outside of the building. Preference is generally given to this system.

XL. The prisons are commonly lighted by gas or petroleum. Lights are kept burning in the dormitories during the night.

XLI. The system of heating varies in different prisons. In some the heating is effected by hot water or steam, in others by stoves.

XLII and XLIII. The prisoner's bed is made of straw; for the sick, of sea-grass or sea-weed. Hammocks were formerly in very general use, but by degrees they have been replaced by open bedsteads.

The bed, complete, consists of a mattress and bolster, two sheets, and one coverlet of a coarse material, and one or two blankets, according to temperature of the season.

XLIV. There is no general rule regarding the distribution of time. The hours of labor (including those of school) are ten in summer and nine in winter; and of sleep, eight and a half in summer and nine in winter. The remainder of the time is at the disposal of the prisoner, for meals, rest, study, and reading; that is to say, five and a half hours in summer and six in winter.

XLV. A distinct part of the prison building serves as an infirmary. In the cellular prisons, cells of double dimensions are appropriated to the sick. The medical service is confided to a military surgeon wherever there is a garrison; to a civil physician in localities where there is no garrison. The entire service is under the inspector general of the medical service of the army, and is performed in a highly satisfactory manner.

XLVI. The most common diseases in the prisons, as outside, are diseases of the chest, especially phthisis.

XLVII. The average of the sick and of deaths it is not easy to give. It differs a good deal in different prisons, depending on local circumstances and the class or species of prison. The difference in the duration of punishments, which is by no means inconsiderable, exercises a great influence on the proportionate number of the sick and of deaths. A comparison of the number of days of sickness and the number of deaths with the days of detention gives, during the period of 1861 to 1868, an aggregate annual average for 100 days of detention:

In the central prisons, 8.14 days of sickness, (varying from 6.35 to 12.57.)

In the houses of detention, 6.07 days of sickness, (varying from 4.47 to 7.74.)

In the houses of arrest, 6.39 days of sickness, (varying from 4.39 to 8.24.)

During the same period the deaths were at a rate of an annual average:

In the central prisons, one death to 8,225 days of detention, (varying from 4,973 to 21,177.)

In the houses of detention, one death to 17,896 days of detention, (varying from 10,737 to 35,204.)

In the houses of arrest, one death to 10,080 days of detention, (varying from 11,899 to 380,052.)

In the central prisons for juvenile prisoners, where the labor is performed in the open air, the sanitary state is highly satisfactory.

XLIX. The distinction between penal and industrial labor does not exist in this country. Penal labor is unknown. All the labor in the prisons of our country is industrial, with the exception of prisoners employed in the domestic or administrative service of the prisons. Agricultural labors are as yet pursued only in the two central prisons for juvenile delinquents.

L, LI, and LII. Penal labor, as has just been stated, does not exist in the Netherlands.

LIII. Industrial labor is everywhere directed by the administration. It is performed in part on account of the government; in part on account of contractors or individuals; and in some prisons, the contractors are allowed to participate in the control of the supervision of the labor.

LIV. It is our belief that the system followed in our prisons deserves the preference. Generally, we give the preference to labor performed on account of contractors or individuals, who offer a greater variety of handicrafts. But the labor done for account and service of the state has not the inconvenience of being sometimes interrupted for want of demand. We therefore judge that it is better to retain both systems.

LV. Different systems of contracting the labor do not exist here. The contractors furnish the raw material and pay the wages. Frequently they furnish, also, the necessary tools.

LVI. The percentage of prisoners not having a calling at the time of their commitment differs materially in the different prisons. One in four is, perhaps, the general average.

LVII, LVIII. It is sought, as far as possible, to teach prisoners a trade; but in short imprisonments the thing is impossible.

We regard it as of the highest importance to impart to prisoners during their incarceration the power of self-help, and this result is diligently sought by teaching to the prisoners, to the utmost extent possible, some useful calling.

LIX. We do not think that repeated sentences to short imprisonments produce any good effect upon the prisoner; but an equitable application of the penal law forbids the remedying of this evil by a long imprisonment for minor offenses. Yet considerable progress would be made in the right direction by applying the cellular system to all imprisonments of a short duration.

LX. In the absence of criminal registers, (*casiors judiciaires,*) a system devised by Bonneville de Marsangy, the statistics of recidivists are defective. The proportion given by our imperfect statistics for the general mass of prisons is 25 per cent.; and in the central prisons, 36 per cent.

LXI. According to our penal laws, a relapse may give occasion to an increase of the punishment in the ratio of one-third, when the first sentence was for more than a year's imprisonment; and in all cases it is a circumstance which may determine the judge to award the maximum of punishment allowed by the law.

LXII. Persons imprisoned for debt are placed in the houses of detention and of arrest, sometimes in the cantonal prisons. They are entered on a special register, and are not confounded with other prisoners. In the greater part of the prisons the best apartments are assigned to them, and a little better furniture. They do not wear the prison dress, unless, indeed, they have no other; and their food is of a better quality.

LXIII. The causes of crime vary a good deal according to the nature of the crime itself. The want of education, drunkenness, and the desire to make a figure beyond one's means and position, may generally be considered as the principal causes of crimes and misdemeanors. In the case of young prisoners, there may be mentioned, in addition, the influence, often pernicious, of a second marriage of their parents, which not unfrequently, by embittering the position of the children of the first marriage, deprives them of the salutary influence of family life.

LXIV. The general proportion in which the sexes are represented in the Netherland's prisons is about twenty women to one hundred men; but this proportion varies, especially in different provinces.

LXV. The aim is to make the punishment, as far as possible, contribute to the reformation of the prisoners. But the application of this principle, in most of the prisons, leaves much to be desired.

LXVI. Although it is very difficult to pronounce, with any degree of certainty, as regards the influence of imprisonment on the great mass of prisoners, it cannot be said, in general, that they leave the prison worse than when they entered it, and numerous cases can be pointed out, in which the instruction received in the prisons, the habit of labor formed, and the knowledge of a calling acquired there, have exerted a very happy influence upon the liberated prisoner.

LXVII. In answer to the question whether efforts are made to aid liberated prisoners in finding work, and thus to prevent a relapse, we answer that, officially, such efforts are not made. But many directors of prisons take great pains to find work for the liberated, and generally they have cause to congratulate themselves on the result of their efforts. The greater part of the directors, however, are too indifferent to concern themselves about the matter.

Zeal in this direction is an indication of a good director.

LXVIII. The Netherlands society for the moral amelioration of prisoners has for its object not only to visit the prisoners, but also to interest themselves in their welfare, after their discharge from prison. This society counts forty branches, scattered throughout the whole kingdom, and corresponding members in thirty-seven places where there are no branches. To some of the branch societies are attached committees of ladies. As regards the prisoners, a variety of methods are employed to encourage and help them. They procure places for them at service; they place them in the merchant marine; they supply them with tools; they obtain for them some little industry or business; they provide them with the means of emigrating, &c., &c. The results differ, as a matter of course; but it may be said, without exaggeration, that the society accomplishes much, and often sees its efforts crowned with success. Still, it can extend its activity only to a part of the liberated prisoners, and it is to be desired that its benevolent operations should be conducted upon a larger scale. Some time ago certain philanthropists sought to secure the organization of a special patronage society for juvenile delinquents, but without success.

LXIX. To the question, "Are you satisfied with your prison system as at present organized and administered?" we cannot return an affirmative answer. The greatest defect in our prison system is, in our opinion, that there is no system, or, rather, that the two systems of associated and cellular imprisonment are applied without any uniform rule, and without placing them in a harmonious relation to each other. Hence there is a pretty general agreement among us that a reform is necessary, and that it should have mainly two objects in view: a revision of our penal laws, which would introduce a more uniform and more harmonious system of imprisonment; and a serious effort to give greater dignity to the position of the directors and employés, and to open these offices to men of a higher education. Whatever differences of opinion may exist as regards the system to be followed, (and they are great, since all the systems which divide *savans* find their partisans among us,) on these two points there is a very general agreement.

IV.—SWITZERLAND.

[Translation.]

I and II. The Swiss Confederation, composed of twenty-two cantons and embracing twenty-five states, does not, by its own power, exercise any control over the administration of penal justice and of prisons, or over the penitentiary *régime*. Military and political penal justice, so far as it is called upon to punish offenses against the constitution and the federal laws, alone comes within its jurisdiction. Each canton is sovereign. It has its own special penal system and places of imprisonment. Its prisons are thus placed under the control of the cantonal executive authority, or of the council of state.

The supervision of the prisons belongs more especially to one of the departments of the executive power. In certain cantons the prisons are placed, wholly or partially, under the supervision of the department of police; in others under that of the department of justice or of the interior, according to the stand-point from which the importance of this public service is viewed. In the cantons in which recently constructed penitentiaries are found, the whole or a part of the supervision is confided to the director of justice, or to a special department, which gives its attention not only to prisons, but also to hospitals, insane asylums, &c., &c. This department associates with itself a commission of supervision composed of three to seven members, selected from among persons experienced in questions of penitentiary reform, of industry, and of commerce.

In the cantons where this machinery exists, an official regulation defines the functions of the commission of supervision.

The detention prisons in the districts and the places of detention for civil penalties are supervised by the agents of the council of state—prefects, counselors of prefecture, &c.

All the cantons of Switzerland, with the exception of Jug, Glaris, and Appenzell, have reclusion prisons, of which the number of inmates rises to thirty-four, without counting a considerable number of houses of arrest, and of district or correctional prisons for persons sentenced to short police punishments.

Of these twenty-four prisons, eleven are reserved exclusively for criminals, thirteen contain criminal and correctional prisoners, and some receive, in addition, prisoners awaiting trial.

Four establishments receive as boarders the convicts of cantons which, without penitentiaries of their own, have only imperfect and insufficient places of reclusion. Ten work-houses and houses of correction are exclusively devoted to the treatment of correctionals.

There are, besides, in Switzerland several agricultural establishments founded by the state, by communal corporations, or by societies of public utility, and designed for the education and moral reform of juvenile delinquents, or to that of vagrants and disorderly persons.

According to Professor d'Orelli, the prisons of Switzerland may be divided into four groups:

1. Those of the cantons of Uri, Schwytz, Obovalden, Nidwalden, and Valais, which are administered in an altogether patriarchal manner by Sisters of Charity.

2. Those of the cantons of Fribourg, Bâle-campagne, and Lucerne, which, in every point of view, leave much to be desired. Bâle-campagne, under the pressure of necessity, contemplates replacing its too contracted prison by a new structure.

3. The cantons of Saint Gall and of Vaud possess, especially the first,

good penitentiaries on the Auburn system. The Thurgovian establishment of Tobel, and that of Geneva, may be also considered as satisfactory. The same is true of Zurich, in which are found, at the same time, the systems of cellular and associated reclusion. Here, above all, on account of constructions in progress of erection, things will be better still. Solure, Grisons, Berne, and Schaffhause are making laudable efforts to reform their prisons, which will soon belong to this fourth class.

4. Finally, and as rising to a higher point of perfection, we cite the penitentiaries of Lenzbourg, (Argovie,) Bâle-ville, Neuchâtel, and Tessin, into which has been introduced, in different degrees, the progressive Irish penitentiary system.

III. The cellular system complete is applied only in the penitentiaries of Argovie, (Lenzbourg,) Zurich, Bâle-ville, and Neuchâtel. In the Auburnian penitentiaries, and the old convict or hard-labor prisons, (*maisons de force*,) cellular seclusion is an exception.

M. d'Orelli, in his work on the Swiss prisons, indicates the following numbers, which we group according to the systems introduced into the different establishments:

First group, patriarchal system, cellular reclusion, 1.02 per cent.
Second group, old convict prisons, cellular reclusion, 3.9 per cent.
Third group, system of Auburn, cellular reclusion, .3 per cent.
Fourth group, progressive system, cellular reclusion, 37.5 per cent.

The penitentiary of Neuchâtel alone shows a greater number of days of cellular reclusion than of labor in association. In this establishment, erected in 1870, separation by day and night is admitted in principle, without, however, excluding labor in common workshops.

As will have been seen, the system of congregate imprisonment predominates. Still effort is made to introduce individual separation, at least by night, in establishments in which common dormitories yet exist.

IV. There is a general agreement that the system of congregate imprisonment by day is favorable to industrial labor, and not unfavorable to the discipline, but incompatible with the moral education of the prisoners. Association in common dormitories by night is considered especially pernicious, and all that has been said by Obermaier and others on the harmlessness, and even the salutary influence, of this practice, is looked upon as illusory.

Imprisonment in common by day and night, condemned in Switzerland, would already have entirely disappeared if, in a number of cantons, financial questions had not caused the postponement of this reform.

Rigid cellular imprisonment is preferable to the Auburn system, without classification of the prisoners.

Mr. Kühne, director of the penitentiary of Saint Gall, (Auburn plan,) admits individualization as a principle, and the mixed system, if system it can be called, compounded of different elements of the progressive Irish prison system.

Penitentiary education imperatively requires cellular separation, at least in the initial stage; and it is on this sole condition that the prisoners can effectively enter into communion with themselves, a process which would be impeded by the contact and influence of some, at least, of the fellow-prisoners.

After the cellular stage, it is considered expedient to allow those prisoners to work together who furnish ground of hope that a moral reformation has been accomplished in them. It is under these conditions that we find associated labor in the recently constructed penitentiaries.

of Lenzbourg, (Argovie,) Bâle, Zurich, and Neuchâtel. But in comparison with the three first named, which have large workshops, Neuchâtel has but small ones, in which only three or four prisoners can
work, under the supervision of a foreman.

The public opinion of our country shows itself more and more favorable to the progressive Irish penitentiary system, with revocable liberation.

The exclusive cellular system should be reserved for houses of
preliminary detention. In some of the cantons reforms are needed in
this class of prisons.

V. In regard to the method of providing the funds necessary for the
support of the prisons, the treasury of the state (cantonal) covers the
deficit which exists between the entire expenditure and the special
receipts of the prisons. (Industrial labor, moneys paid by cantons
which place their convicts in the penitentiaries of other confederated
states, &c.)

The average annual cost of each prisoner is 250 francs in the smaller
establishments, and 350 to 400 in the large penitentiaries. The average
net gain in the majority of the cantons is from 89 to 90 centimes for
each day of labor.

In the penitentiary of Zurich the net gain of the prisoners, after
deducting the cost of tools and other accessories, has reached an average for the last five years of 1 franc 7 centimes.

Francs.

The expenditures for clothing, food, lodgings, &c., were........ 0. 773
Expense of the administration 0. 41

Sum total per prisoner for each day 1. 18

The canton of Argovie gives, as a subsidy, 55 centimes per man and
per day. The average daily earnings of the prisoners in the Lenzbourg
penitentiary amount to from 88 to 94 centimes to each prisoner.

The canton Neuchâtel gave for the first year (1870) an annual subsidy of 1 franc 90 centimes per day for each prisoner. The cellular
system, and the small number prisoners, (70 on the average,) involve
considerable of a general character. The net gain per prisoner in this
penitentiary rose, in 1871, to 1 franc 25 centimes for each day of labor,
a larger gain than had ever been reached in any of the Swiss prisons.

In the penitentiary of Saint Jacques (Saint Gall) the earnings of the
prisoners suffice for their maintenance, for their schooling and religious
instruction, for medical attendance, and for the administration of the
industrial service. The State, in this canton, includes in its subsidy,
besides the loss of the interest on the capital invested in the establishment, the expense of repairs to the buildings, the salaries of the officers
and employés, the maintenance of these latter, and, in short, the sum
which is annually granted to the prisoners as *peculium*.

VI. The officers and employés of the prisons are named by the council of state. In the cantons where penitentiaries of recent construction
exist, the officers (directors, stewards, instructors, chaplains, and physicians) are proposed by the department of justice or of police, which
takes the advice of the commission of supervision. The employés
(the foremen and overseers) are appointed by the commission of supervision, on the nomination of the director of the penitentiary.

In some cantons the officers are subjected to a re-election every three
years, (Zurich,) or every four years, (Argovie,) the employés every year,

(Zurich,) and in other penitentiaries the tenure of office is without limitation.

It may be affirmed that, as a general thing, the officers of the Swiss penitentiaries are not exposed to the influence of political changes, and that those whose position may have been endangered by the victory of a party have been effectually shielded by a public opinion which appreciated their merits and their devotion.

In some cantons the position of the directors is made difficult by the demands of doctrinaires, who do not give themselves the trouble to examine and weigh the facts which enter into the question.

V.II. In cantons where efforts have been made to introduce a rational prison system, it has yet been well understood that, under a bad administration, the prisons, instead of being hospitals for moral diseases, would become seminaries of criminals. For this reason, the greatest importance is attached to the choice of officers charged with the treatment of the prisoners.

As regards the moral and intellectual qualities which ought to meet in prison officers, there are found on this subject, in the literature of penology, details sufficiently numerous.

Whether in Switzerland the administrators possess the necessary talents and qualifications is a question which the writer of the present report cannot and does not wish to touch upon. The governments would be better able to answer the question, although the greater part of them do not take the trouble to examine thoroughly the organization and management of the penitentiary establishments. The director of a penitentiary does feel inclined to pass judgment upon the merits of his colleagues, and of the other officers, and still less upon their special aptitudes. At the same time, we judge that this question is one of great importance, and that it ought to have a prominent place in the deliberations of the congress. The speakers, in such an assemblage, occupy a position altogether different.

The penitentiaries of recent construction are presided over—

At St. Gall, by a distinguished man who, after having completed his university course, devoted himself to the profession of a teacher. After the decease of Mr. Moser, the first director of Saint Jacques, Mr. Kühne, known as a teacher of great intelligence, was unanimously chosen to fill his place.

At Zurich, by a former pastor who, before passing through his theological course, had been an artisan. For a number of years he discharged the duties of teacher in a secondary school. He has been a member of the legislative council of his canton, and of commissions of education.

The directors of the penitentiaries of Lenzbourg and Bâle belonged also to the ecclesiastical profession, and recommended themselves by their zeal in the study of social questions. Mr. Mühler, director of the penitentiary of Lenzbourg, has long been president of the commission of education in the city of that name.

The penitentiary of Neuchâtel is directed by a man who was previously engaged in the practice of medicine, and in that profession, from choice, much devoted to the science of public and private hygiene. He has retained the position of president of the commission of education in the city of Neuchâtel.

The penitentiary of Tessin will be directed by a man who has studied the profession of law.

The other officers and employés, foremen, and overseers, should on their part contribute, by their knowledge, their tact, and their example, to the success of the common labors.

Each penitentiary establishment (Zürich, Bâle, Lenzbourg, and Neuchâtel) has a band of intelligent employés, who contribute effectively to the mission which penitentiary education proposes to itself.

On all sides, notwithstanding, complaint is made of the difficulty which is experienced in finding for the corps of subordinate employés men possessing the requisite qualities and aptitudes.

VIII. Schools designed for the special education of prison officers do not exist in Switzerland.

It is generally felt that special schools would render an excellent service, especially if a just and sound idea should be given in them of the nature and aim of penitentiary treatment. Without wishing to exalt one system over another, that is, to dogmatize, a school of this kind would have the immense advantage of preparing the officers who, at present, acquire their experience at the expense of the institution. But this school would not be in a condition to form good officers and good employés with persons in charge who should not have the requisite qualifications, even though possessing the desired degree of intelligence. The education of our penitentiary employés is usually acquired after their entrance upon their official duties, which, for a long time afterward, will not be regarded as a profession.

Directors, when appointed, usually visit the model penitentiaries of other countries and study their organization. The employés receive, in their turn, from the directors, theoretical and practical instructions touching their official duties.

Perhaps an education for the penitentiary service might be obtained by establishing in some university a chair of penitentiary reform, and by making a course of instruction in that branch of knowledge obligatory for all those who intended to devote themselves to the moral reformation of criminals.

A normal school for the employés might be organized in establishments selected for that purpose, in which candidates might pursue a theoretical course, and might also be practically initiated into all the branches of the service.

In a well-organized and ably managed penitentiary we see novices who possess the necessary aptitudes becoming in a short time entirely competent to the discharge of their functions.

In Switzerland, pensions are granted only in exceptional cases to public functionaries. The directors and employés of our prisons, when they become incapacitated for their duties, form no exception.

There is sometimes granted to a functionary dismissed, because of age or sickness, three months' salary, and in case of death his family receives, in some cantons, the same gratuity.

The salary of the director of a modern penitentiary ranges from 3,000 to 3,500 francs, besides a residence; that of stewards, from 2,000 to 2,500 francs, with or without residence; of the chaplains, from 400 to 600 francs; of the teacher, from 1,000 to 1,800 francs; of the physicians, from 400 to 600 francs; of the chief keeper, from 900 to 1,200 francs; of the foreman, from 700 to 1,000 francs; and of the overseers, from 400 to 750 francs per annum.

X. The difference existing between sentences to simple imprisonment, to reclusion, and to hard labor, is greater or less in the different Swiss cantons. These, as has already been said, have all penal codes of their own, which differ materially from one another. For this reason it is not easy to give, in few words, an exact idea of the difference between the classes of imprisonment named above.

Simple imprisonment, whether police or correctional, in some cantons varies from a duration of twenty-four hours at least to five years at most. This punishment, when it is of short duration, is in some cantons undergone in the district prisons. The prisoner is permitted, at his own charge, to provide nourishment and occupation for himself, after having paid the damages caused by him, and the expense of his prosecution, without which he receives the ordinary treatment and is subjected to the customary labors of the prison.

In other cantons, prisoners of this class undergo their punishments in the same prisons as criminals, from whom they are more or less separated; still all are under the same regulations. In other cantons still, there exist special penitentiaries for persons sentenced correctionally. This punishment is not considered infamous; it may even, in some cantons, be replaced by a fine fixed at 5 francs per day.

Reclusion occupies a middle place between simple imprisonment and a sentence to hard labor; and the reclusionary undergoes his punishment in the work-house, where there is one, or in the penitentiary. A fine cannot be substituted for reclusion.

At Zurich reclusion has a duration of from six to ten years, and the convict is compelled to labor, and is subjected to the ordinary regulations of the prison. But he does not wear the prison dress, and does not lose his civic rights.

In some cantons, in Argovie, for example, the law leaves it to the judge to fix, in many cases, the duration of the privation of civic rights. Elsewhere, the dress alone differs; and the distinction between simple reclusion and hard labor is found in this, that the latter punishment is considered afflictive and infamous, whereas the former is simply afflictive.

Reclusion, with hard labor, varies in its duration from one year to fifteen, twenty, twenty-five, or thirty years, according to the cantons, or even to an imprisonment for life.

The death penalty is abolished in the cantons of Neuchâtel, Zurich, Thurgovia, Geneva, and Tessin. In the majority of the other cantons this punishment is abolished de facto if it is not by law.

In some cantons reclusion, with hard labor, is aggravated by wearing chains, by an infamous dress, and by physical privations. But these additional punishments are gradually disappearing.

XI. A methodical classification of prisoners, according to their degree of morality, exists only in the establishments of Zurich, Bâle, Lenzbourg, and Neuchâtel, and will also be introduced into that of Tessin.

In the other penitentiaries endeavors are also made to classify the prisoners according to their degree of morality; but frequently the architectural arrangement of the establishments does not afford opportunity to apply this classification methodically and with chance of success.

At Lenzbourg, where the progressive system has been for a number of years in use, there is found a first class, which is subjected to the cellular régime, and a second and third class, into which the prisoners, on leaving the first stage, are admitted to associated labor in the workshops during the day. The prisoners who belong to the higher class obtain an enlargement of privilege, are earliest proposed for admission to the benefit of conditional liberation.

Into the penitentiary of Neuchâtel has been introduced the following system of classification: A lower cellular class, in which are placed all the convicts on their entrance into the establishment; a middle class, comprising the prisoners who have been conspicuous for their good conduct and industry, and their zealous application to learning in the first stage. The greater part remain in separation, but if their character, their state of health, their kind of occupation, and the material conditions permit it, and if they themselves are not opposed to it, (a decree of the great council leaves them liberty of choice on this subject,) they are admitted into one of the small shops of the establishment. Finally, there is a higher class, (cellular, but with labor in common during the day,) which precedes liberation.

Each of these classes corresponds to a relative degree of liberty, of which the prisoner may make use to satisfy, in a larger measure, his moral, intellectual, and physical wants. The principle of conditional liberation, which will sooner or later be admitted into the system, will afford the means of conducting the prisoner gradually toward freedom, and of re-introducing him into society without a too abrupt transition.

At Zurich, where conditional liberation already exists, the same system of classification is applied, but, as at Neuchâtel, only for a time too limited to enable us to announce serious results.

In the penitentiary of Zurich the number of prisoners admitted to associated labor is proportionally larger than at Neuchâtel, where the cellular system is more highly esteemed.

At Saint Gall the prisoners are divided into four classes. The classification is revised and readjusted every three months.

As appears from the above statement, the progressive Irish system, where it is applied, is confined in its execution to one and the same establishment. We have no intermediate prisons. The financial resources of a single canton would not permit the realization of such a system, at least, unless several cantons should agree to unite in the common execution of a rational plan of penitentiary reform. On the other hand, public opinion, still more or less imbued with the old theory of vengeance and intimidation, would not be favorable to such a change.

XII. In all the cantons prisoners may, by their good conduct, obtain an abbreviation of their punishment by applying for pardon to the legislative authority, (great council,) which reserves to itself this right. Such reduction is rarely made conformably to fixed rules. In many of the cantons complaint is made that chance and caprice play too conspicuous a part, and that commissions of pardon do not always take account of grave and important facts. In some cantons clemency is exercised readily enough, while in others this is done only in exceptional cases.

In certain cantons a decree of the legislative authority confides to the council of state, or to the department of justice, or police, the right of remitting the latter portion of their punishment, (one-twelfth for example,) to convicts whose conduct has been good. There is here, as in the whole penal system, a great want of congruity, yet there is observed in the confederated states, where penitentiary reform has made some progress, a tendency to bring down the use of the right of pardon to its minimum, and to substitute in its place the principle of conditional liberation; in short, to confide this function to the direction of the department of prisons, which, having the supervision of the penitentiary administration, is alone capable of judging whether or not the re-entrance of a prisoner into society offers any danger, and whether a probationary liberation may be safely granted him.

XIII. In most of the cantons the prisoners have a share in the benefits of their labor. As a general thing this part has rather the character of a gratuity than that of lawful wages.

In the penitentiary of Argovie the prisoners receive their share in the following proportions:

Prisoners whose earnings do not reach 30 centimes a day receive nothing; those whose earnings amount to 70 centimes a day receive 5 per cent.; 1 franc 10 centimes, 10 per cent.; 1 franc 60 centimes, 15 per cent.; exceeding 1 franc 60 centimes, 20 per cent.; and that whether their conduct is more or less satisfactory.

Neuchâtel has adopted, provisionally, the same scale. At Zurich the participation in the benefits of the labor is fixed, according to the three penitentiary classes, as follows:

In the first class (cellular) it is from 5 to 8 per cent., conditioned upon the fact that the earnings of the prisoner are not less than 6 per cent. of the daily average earnings, obtained in the branch of industry in which he works. In the second class the portion of the prisoner is from 8 to 12 per cent. In the third class, which precedes liberation, it is from 12 to 16 per cent. on the same condition.

Elsewhere a percentage of the daily earnings has been introduced.

At Saint Gall the prisoners of the lower class receive no gratuity; those of the second class receive a sixth of their earnings; those of the third class, the fifth part; and those of the higher class, the fourth part.

The director of this penitentiary, Mr. Kühne, proposes, in a paper on the *peculium* of prisoners, to fix the rate according to the classes. For example: The day's wages being fixed at a franc, the prisoners of the lower class would receive 10 per cent., or 10 centimes; those of the second class, 20 per cent., or 20 centimes; and those of the superior class, 30 per cent., or 30 centimes.

The question of *peculium* is still in Switzerland a subject of discussions, and has not been resolved. It is the order of the day for the approaching meeting of the Swiss society for penitentiary reform.

Whatever may be the scale adopted in the different establishments, this gratuity is granted to all the prisoners who, conformably to the regulations, have rendered themselves worthy of it. It is adjusted every month, or at the end of every three months, and placed to their credit in their memorandum of savings.

XIV. The other rewards employed to stimulate the good conduct and zeal of the prisoners vary in kind and amount, according to the cantons and the degree, more or less advanced, of penitentiary reform.

In well-administered establishments we see granted to good conduct, to application, to zeal, and progress in labor and school, the following rewards:

In the second penitentiary class: liberty to choose books from the library and to attend the lessons given in class; the use of tobacco, limited, however, to the hours of promenade in the exercise yard; liberty to have served to them a supplementary or extraordinary ration of food, which is granted only exceptionally in the more recently erected penitentiaries, the dietary in these being sufficiently nutritive and varied.

In the third or higher class there are added to the above-mentioned rewards the privilege of promenade and free conversation with their fellow-prisoners of the same class, liberty to wear their beard, to work in their free hours for themselves and their family, to adorn their cells and to have plants in them; the use of a patch of land for a garden; and admission to places of trust, such as foreman, to superintend their fellow-prisoners in learning trades, or to execute certain exceptional labors in the administrative, industrial, and domestic services.

XV. In the cantons where the patriarchal system prevails, and where the old convict prisons still exist, the most frequent offenses against discipline are disobedience and insubordination; next come escapes or attempts to escape; then lies; and finally immorality in acts and words. In the penitentiaries in which the Auburn system has been introduced we find that the infractions' most frequent are disorder, want of cleanliness, and violation of the law of silence. In the penitentiaries of recent construction the want of propriety and dignity, lying, idleness, and disobedience.

XVI. The disciplinary punishments in use may be divided into three classes. In the prisons whose organization is imperfect, and where the reformation of the prisoners is not the aim of the imprisonment, we find existing the dungeon and corporal punishments. In penitentiaries on the Auburn system, more or less completely organized, corporal punishments are gradually disappearing and are being replaced by a diet of bread and water and by confinement in the dark or ordinary cell. In the modern establishments, we see coming into vogue a new series of punishments, of a moral order, among which figure, by the side of the dungeon and the diet of bread and water, admonition, privation of work, of reading, of visits, of correspondence, and, in general, of all or a part of the diversions, alleviations, and other indulgences above mentioned. Corporal chastisements are passing away, and in their place are substituted the strait-jacket and the cold douche-bath.

Those who, through mischief or negligence, destroy or injure the effects, objects, instruments, and raw material placed at their disposal, are obliged to pay the value of the damage done.

XVII. In most of the prisons are found registers in which the punishments inflicted are fully recorded. These registers, in the modern penitentiaries especially, give complete information as to the occasion, the kind, and the nature of the punishments inflicted.

XVIII. Ministers of the Reformed and of the Catholic religion act as chaplains in all the prisons. In well-organized penitentiaries, where the number of prisoners belonging to each creed is sufficiently large, two ecclesiastics are charged with the duties of their respective chaplaincies. The rabbi of the nearest locality is invited to visit such coreligionists as are occasionally found in the prisons.

XIX. In the establishments which are imperfectly organized, the chaplains, for the most part, confine themselves to the celebration of public worship. In proportion as they approach the category of penitentiaries that aim at the reformation of the prisoners, we see these officers paying regular visits to them, consoling and counseling them, superintending the religious instruction of the juvenile delinquents, and fulfilling toward them all the duties of their ministry. In some of the penitentiaries it is the chaplain who has charge of the distribution of books from the prison library.

XX. Religious instruction, as a means of reforming prisoners, is looked upon in Switzerland as of the highest importance and as exercising the happiest influence, particularly if the person charged with it possesses the special aptitudes suited to the high mission which he is called to fulfill, and throws aside, as far as he may, mere dogmatic questions. He should preach repentance with power and skill, set forth the divine mercy, and aid the prisoners in that self-communion which is the first step toward moral regeneration. Prisoners in whose heart the religious sentiment is not extinguished at the time of their entrance are easily impressed by the exhortations of the chaplains; on the other hand, such as do not possess it offer to the instructions of religion a soil arid and ungrateful. Among prisoners we often encounter self-deception and a tendency to hypocrisy; nevertheless, it often happens that individuals who repudiate or are ignorant of the Bible end by finding in its pages the consolations of which they are in pursuit.

XXI. Persons of both sexes, not connected with the administration, are admitted into the prisons to labor for the moral improvement of the prisoners. In the cantons which have new penitentiaries, such persons are authorized to visit the prisoners in virtue of decrees of the legislative authority. This is especially the case with members of aid societies, who have free access to the prisoners whom they seek to succor. The number of these benevolent visits is relatively few even in cantons where penitentiary reform counts many adherents. Such visits, however, ought not to be allowed without many precautions.

In some of the more modern establishments it is only the officers themselves who take part in the moral education of the prisoners.

In the female penitentiaries lady patronesses are more frequently met with, especially in the cities which were visited in 1839 by Elizabeth Fry, and where, at the instance of that good and charitable woman, ladies' aid societies were organized to console, to place, to watch over, and to sustain criminal women. At Zurich, where a society of this kind exists, the lady patronesses give to the female prisoners in the penitentiaries regular lessons, and take charge of their religious instruction.

XXII. Sunday-schools, properly so called, do not exist. Public worship is, on that day, celebrated in the prisons, or at least the chaplain makes a visit to the prisoners.

At Zurich the pastor holds a catechetical exercise in the afternoon, and afterward an instructor gives a lesson in sacred music.

XXIII. In most of the penitentiaries the week-days are so filled up with labor, school, exercise, and study, and Sunday morning by worship, that it is thought expedient to leave to the prisoners the free employment of Sunday afternoon. It is in these hours that they are able to write letters to their relatives and acquaintances. The frequency with which they are permitted to write letters differs in different cantons.

XXIV. In the establishments where the progressive Irish system has been introduced, prisoners of the middle class can write letters every two months, those of the higher class every month. But an extension of this favor is often granted, especially in cases where the correspondence is of such a character as to draw closer the ties of family, to exert a good influence, and contribute to the moral cure of the prisoner. This powerful means of moral reformation is more or less neglected in establishments where the organization is imperfect.

As the letters pass under the inspection of the director, his eye sometimes detects sentiments which have their taint of hypocrisy; but in spite of that, the correspondence of the prisoners manifests a strong family affection, and awakens tender household memories.

XXV. The visits of relations and intimate acquaintances are permitted the same as correspondence, and are most carefully regulated in the prisons where penitentiary education receives the greatest attention.

The internal regulations of different penitentiaries grant the indulgence of visits more or less frequently, but the average is about once a month. As in the case of correspondence, an extension of this is often accorded when the visits are found to have a salutary effect.

XXVI. The visits are received in the presence of the director, or, in his absence, in that of the chief keeper. The design is to supervise the interview. The director or his deputy place the visitors and the prisoners as much as possible at their ease, so that these latter may look upon them as friends in whose presence they may converse freely.

XXVII. As a general thing, the extension of the privilege of correspondence is more readily granted than that of visits, since the latter do not always have the good effect which might naturally be expected from them. Still, it sometimes happens that they have an excellent influence, especially on prisoners who believe themselves forgotten, ignored, and abandoned by the members of their family, and who see them approach in spirit of forgiveness.

Besides, the visits enable the director to understand better the character of the prisoner and the circumstances of his family, and sometimes enable him to lay his plans with greater certainty and efficacy in the interest of these latter.

XXVIII. The number of prisoners able to read at the time of their commitment may be estimated at 17 per cent. of the annual average number of the criminal population. In a number of cantons the convicts are not examined upon this point on their entrance into the establishment, so that the exact proportion cannot be stated.

Mr. d'Orelli gives the following figures :

Lucerne, out of 850 prisoners, 119 illiterate.
Schwytz, out of 27 prisoners, 9 illiterate.
Glaris, out of 31 prisoners, 1 illiterate.
Appenzell, J. R., out of 5 prisoners, 4 illiterate.
Bâle-ville, out of 298 prisoners, 3 illiterate.
Saint Gall, { criminals, out of 142 prisoners, 25 illiterate.
{ correctionals, out of 213 prisoners, 1 illiterate.
Argovie, out of 316 prisoners, 135 illiterate.
Tessin, out of 40 prisoners, 16 illiterate.
Geneva, out of 42 prisoners, 23 illiterate.

This table is incomplete, and the numbers indicated by it cannot be taken as a basis for estimating the degree of scholastic education of the prisoners.

We place more reliance on the following figures, furnished by the reports of the penitentiaries of Lensbourg, Saint Gall, and Neuchâtel :

Places.	Total number of prisoners.	Illiterate.	Per cent.	Inferior education.	Per cent.	Passable education.	Per cent.	Good education.	Per cent.
Lenzbourg	533	63	11.8	187	35.1	245	46.0	38	7.1
Saint Gall	1,286	668	51.9	194	15.08	347	26.9	77	5.9
Neuchâtel	146	18	12.3	101	60.9	27	18.4		
Average			25.3		36.9		30.4		4.3

These figures do not show the general state of public instruction in these three cantons, for a considerable part of the prisoners, especially in the canton of Neuchâtel, are foreigners.

But it is to be observed that although primary instruction is obligatory in Switzerland, (with the exception of Uri and Geneva,) and in fourteen cantons is also gratuitous,* it nevertheless happens that a certain

---

* Switzerland expends each year, as well for its primary as for its secondary and higher schools, the sum of twelve and a half millions of francs. The expenditures for education form one-seventh of the total budget of the Confederation and the cantons.

number of children escape the supervision and control of the school authorities, and reach the age of sixteen years without having regularly attended the lessons of the schools.

Many, after leaving school, neglect reading and intellectual recreations to such a degree as to almost entirely forget what they had previously learned. Thus one is astonished to see among the prisoners, who figure in the preceding table, in the "inferior" class, individuals who read with difficulty and in such a manner that reading cannot be resorted to as a recreation, and who can only write their own names.

The knowledge of arithmetic is also very limited in this class of "inferior," and the knowledge of geography and history is almost nothing, even among those who are placed in the table under the heading of "passable."

XXIX. Prison-schools are organized in the penitentiaries of Saint Jacques, (Saint Gall,) Lenzbourg, (Argovie,) Neuchâtel, &c. In many other establishments lessons are given by the chaplain. It even happens that these duties are confided to a prisoner if he is a teacher by profession, or if he possesses the necessary knowledge and aptitude. In the penitentiary of Zurich the school, which has been closed for some time, will be immediately re-opened. Instruction is a good deal neglected in the prisons of some of the cantons where the system is patriarchal, and in others where associated imprisonment by day and by night is still in use.

XXX. In penitentiary establishments in which schools are opened, all the prisoners, except those who are excused by age—above forty-five to fifty years—and those subjected to the cellular *régime*, attend lessons in classes. The prisoners receive, on an average, from four to five hours' schooling per week. Those who are in the cellular stage are visited by the instructor in their cells, and there commence their course of instruction.

XXXI. In the well-organized penitentiaries, the degree of education of the prisoners is verified at their entrance into the establishment. The result of this examination shows the necessity of maintaining three classes, whose programme corresponds to that of the three degrees of primary instruction. In the lower class the elementary branches are taught, and in the middle class progress is gradually made toward those branches which are taught in the higher class.

In the programme of the best-organized penitentiaries we see introduced even mathematics, physics, and technology, so far as these sciences are applied to arts and trades; even the modern languages are taught, French in the German penitentiaries, and German in the penitentiaries where French is the vernacular, (Neuchâtel.) Sometimes prisoners are permitted to take lessons in English, and often in linear drawing.

The progress made differs much in the case of different prisoners. Many are remarkable for their zeal and power of acquisition, while others advance but slowly. The organ of thought, little accustomed to being used, has lost its force. The power of memory is often wanting, and the result in these cases is a stupefaction, which leads to indifference. Still, the average progress made is highly satisfactory, especially in the case of juvenile delinquents, for whom, after all, this supplementary and tardy instruction can alone have any very great importance after their liberation.

XXXII. Circulating libraries are found in all the prisons. In those of the cantons where prison discipline is little advanced the number of books is limited, and works exclusively religious predominate. In the penitentiaries which are better organized the libraries are composed of moral and religious books, of works of general history and the history of Switzerland, of biographies, of travels, ethnography, natural history, of works on mechanics, agriculture, belles-lettres, &c., &c. Romances of a moral character (above all those of the Swiss authors, Bïtzins, Gottfried Keller, Urbain Olivier, Fritz Berthoud, Louis Favre) are not excluded.

The library of the penitentiary of Zurich, for example, possesses 800 works, consisting of 1,500 volumes; that of the penitentiary of Neuchâtel, though of recent creation, counts 500 volumes; that of the penitentiary of Saint Jacques has also a rich and varied collection of moral and instructive works. This establishment, like that of Zurich, Argovie, &c., has, in addition, a collection of special works, designed for the employés of the penitentiary.

XXXIII. The prisoners read, relatively, a great deal, in the penitentiaries where they pass Sunday in their cells, and where they have at their disposal a variety of works. They generally prefer moral tales, such as those of the authors just named, and those of D'Erckmann Charian and of Henri Tschokke; next come narratives of voyages, biographies, Swiss and general history, and works of popular science, (discoveries, inventions, technology, &c.)

Reading is found to have a very beneficial effect upon the prisoners. It enlarges the circle of their general knowledge, and, by fuller explanations of what they had learned in the way of routine, it develops also their practical knowledge.

It is by keeping their minds continually occupied by labor, or by moral and intellectual recreations, that that self-respect is oftenest awakened in prisoners which constitutes the best guarantee against self-abuse. These elevating and noble agencies calm an ardent imagination, and often put to flight ideas inspired by base passions and by vicious and criminal sentiments.

XXXIV. The greater part of the modern prisons, and of the old ones which have undergone recent changes in their construction, have a system of sewers which, in a hygienic point of view, are open to no serious objection. The system of pits prevails still, and it is only in the recent penitentiaries (at Lenzbourg and Neuchâtel, for example) that we find a system of drainage that leaves little to be desired. At Zurich, by the side of pits and *latrines*, arranged on the plan of Duspetian, (*Architecture des Prisons*,) is seen the system of movable vessels and of pipes for carrying off liquid substances.

XXXV. The water supplied for the use of the prisons is, for the most part, sufficient in quantity. The old prisons have each at least one fountain in the court. The penitentiaries of recent construction are abundantly supplied with water, which is distributed into all parts and to all the stories of the building.

At Zurich, for example, the penitentiary, which occupies the buildings of an old convent, has a spring of water which is reputed the best in the city. This establishment is also furnished with pipes by the company which supplies the city with water.

The penitentiary of Lenzbourg has, like that of Zurich, a spring which enables it to distribute water *ad libitum*. That of Neuchâtel receives its water from the city company, and has at its disposal, for an average of seventy prisoners, ten to twenty thousand liters for each twenty-four hours. The quality of the water is for the most part good.

XXXVI. A system of ventilation other than the doors and windows is found only in the modern penitentiaries, such as those of Lenzbourg and Neuchâtel. In them the ventilation is combined with a system of heating. Each cell is furnished with a ventilation pipe, whose opening is in a recess at the side of the door of entrance at the bottom of the wall; a recess closed on the side of the corridor by a little iron door, and in which is placed a water-closet, having a hydraulic fastening. Each pipe is in communication with larger condensing conduits, which communicate directly with the great chimney of the steam-boilers; this draught-chimney, about six feet in diameter and ninety or a hundred feet in height, incloses an inner one of iron, eighteen inches in diameter, which produces a powerful draught. A special furnace is so placed as in summer to heat the inner iron chimney, with the object of keeping up the ascending current, and increasing, as may be needed, the ventilation. The vitiated air thus drawn out from the cells carries off, in passing the recesses mentioned above, the emanations that have been generated there.

XXXVII. The best ventilation would be of no avail, especially in prisons where the aggregation of prisoners is relatively large, and where the cells and dormitories are not spacious, if means were not taken to insure their cleanliness. In all the prisons one or more prisoners are detailed to sweep and clean the corridors, the stairs, the courts, the water-closets, the workshops, the doors, and the windows. The special supervision of this important service is confided to the chief keeper.

In the cellular penitentiaries, each prisoner is charged with keeping his cell and its furniture in a condition of perfect cleanliness. The flagging of the cells of the penitentiaries of Lenzbourg, Bâle, and Neuchâtel is of asphaltum, which makes it easy to keep them clean. The yards of the cells are whitewashed every year or every two years. If their condition requires such a reparation before the regular time, it is done at the expense of the prisoners.

A clean cell and well-kept premises produce on prisoners accustomed to live in filthy apartments a hygienic and moral influence.

XXXVIII. Personal cleanliness is not neglected in the well-organized penitentiaries.

On his entrance into the establishment the convict receives a bath, and after having been examined by the physician, changes his clothing, often foul and filled with vermin, for the prison garb. The dress of the prisoners, in the modern penitentiaries, has nothing of a degrading character; the greater part of the cantons have continued, for prisoners, the striped costume.

The prisoner finds in his cell a wash-basin and towel; soap is furnished gratuitously, or at a very slight cost to the prisoner. A punishment is inflicted on those who neglect to wash the face and hands, to comb their hair, to brush their clothes, &c. The prisoners are shaved every eight days; their hair is cut once in six months. The wearing of the beard is permitted as a reward to those who distinguish themselves by their good conduct, and who, having reached the higher stage of penitentiary education, show themselves worthy to wear the token of manhood.

The body-linen, the pocket-handkerchiefs, the working-aprons, and the cotton stockings, are changed every week; cravats and woolen stockings every fifteen days; the sheets every month in summer, and once in six weeks in winter.

The prisoners take a bath regularly every month, (Neuchâtel,) and every two or three months in other modern penitentiaries.

The prisons which have no heaters to prepare the baths offer, as regards the cleanliness of the prisoners, conditions least favorable.

XXXIX. The privies are still very primitive in the old prisons, where association by day and by night still exists. They are adjacent to the hall, and are separated from it only by a door. In others are found large glazed earthen vessels, with covers more or less tight, which are regularly emptied into the adjoining *latrines*.

In the cells of the modern penitentiaries we find, in the recess indicated above, enameled iron vessels, whose cover closes hermetically. These vases are emptied regularly by a prisoner charged with this service. They are voided into the adjoining *latrines*, or into a movable pit, which is afterward emptied into another, that is immovable, at some distance from the buildings.

Workshops have privies situated in an angle, and isolated by one or two doors, which are sometimes glazed.

The water-closets in modern penitentiary establishments are placed on the north side, separated from the cells; they have basins provided with a deodorizing apparatus, and are abundantly supplied with water for purposes of cleansing. In the other prisons the privies fulfill only to a limited degree the conditions required by sanitary science.

XL. The method of lighting by gas has been introduced into the penitentiaries of Zurich, Bâle, Neuchâtel, and Saint Gall. Every cell is provided with one burner, which may be closed by a stop-cock placed outside the cell. Thus all danger of suffocation or attempts at suffocation is prevented.

At Lenzbourg petroleum is used for lighting the cells and the workshops. In winter, during the evening of Sunday, the prisoners are also permitted to have light.

In other establishments only the workshops are lighted with gas, Geneva and Lausanne.)

Finally, in the prisons of an inferior order we find the petroleum lamp or the simple candle, as a means of lighting the workshops and the common dormitories.

XLI. The heating, as the lighting, of the prisons differs very much, as they are of old or recent construction, and as the system of prison discipline is more or less advanced.

At Saint Gall, Lenzbourg, Bâle, Neuchâtel, and Zurich are found furnaces which warm, by steam, all the cells and other parts of the establishment. The detention prison of Neuchâtel is warmed by means of a hot-air furnace. Heating by steam is, as we have said, combined with the system of ventilation. The tube which is designed to warm the cell is a simple enlargement of the pipe. It is placed vertically in a recess, and is separated from the cell by an iron plate, perforated with holes, to allow the heat to pass through. On the side of the corridor there is an opening, opposite the tube, by which the amount of cold air to be admitted may be regulated.

In the greater part of the prisons we find ordinary stoves, made with varying degrees of excellence, and the heating is effected by means of wood or peat.

The penitentiary of Tessin, which is situated in a warm climate, has no system of artificial heating.

XLII and XLIII. Iron bedsteads are used in many of the penitentiaries. At Lenzbourg, Bâle, Neuchâtel, and Geneva they are fastened to the wall on one side, and are movable, so that they can be turned up and padlocked. Elsewhere, most commonly, the beadstead is of wood.

Everywhere the beds are composed of a paillasse, or of a sack filled with cow's hair or moss, of one or two linen sheets, of one or two woolen blankets, in summer, of two to four, in winter, and of a bolster or pillow filled with grass or straw.

XLN, *bis.* The dietary of the prisoners varies much in the different cantons, and according to the importance which is attached to penitentiary training. Where the moral reformation of the prisoners is not made the principal aim of the imprisonment, the dietary is but little varied, and is not sufficient to restore the losses caused to the bodily organs by hard labor. Meat seldom figures in the bill of fare, (in some prisons the prisoners have it only twice a year.) Prisoners long subjected to such a diet suffer more or less from a deficiency of blood. In proportion as penitentiaries become better organized and administered the dietary is improved, and substances containing nitrogen form a larger proportion of it.

The number of daily meals is three. Breakfast consists, in most of the prisons, of gruel or oatmeal porridge; and the quantity is, on an average, from a pint and a half to a quart.

In French Switzerland (at Neuchâtel, Lausanne, and Geneva) the prisoners receive from one-half to three-quarters of a liter of coffee, (*café au lait*). At Lenzbourg the breakfast consists on each alternate day of soup and coffee.

Dinner consists, once a week or oftener, of a soup (three-fourths to one liter) prepared with bread, pulse, or roots, or, according to the season, with meat. For the preparation of this meat soup, there is allowed 250 to 500 grammes of meat, without bones, per man and per week. In certain penitentiaries (Lenzbourg, Zurich, &c,) the quantity of meat authorized is spread over several dinners during the week. The meat is cut into little morsels and is distributed with and in the soup. In other penitentiaries it is given as a ration and by itself. At Lausanne there is added to the half pound of meat four ounces of raw bacon. At Geneva there are given on Sunday 250 grammes of boiled beef, and on Thursday the same quantity of hashed pork, prepared with potatoes. The distribution of this meat ration takes place, in certain establishments, on Tuesday and Thursday (Neuchâtel) of each week, so that these more substantial and nutritious meals may fall in the midst of the working days.

The evening meal consists of a soup prepared with rice, with barley or oats, with wheat flour, or with sea-moss, with or without the addition of potatoes or maccaroni.

The quantity of bread allowed to each prisoner varies from 750 to 800 grammes a day. Fresh water is the ordinary drink.

As a general thing prisoners in health are not supplied with wine. In some establishments there is accorded to those who have reached the higher penitentiary stage an authorization to furnish them at their own expense a ration of milk or of supplementary or extraordinary solid food.

Those who are engaged in toilsome labor receive a supplementary ration of milk, (Zurich, Neuchâtel,) and, in very exceptional cases, of wine, (Lenzbourg).

The choice and combination of aliments which should form the bill of fare of the three daily meals are but rarely regulated in such manner that the diet of the prisoners is varied as much as it might be, and that the food consumed in twenty-four hours contains the nutritive, nitrogenous substances in their just proportions.

A man insufficiently fed is little disposed to submit himself to the reformatory influence of the better penitentiary education.

XLIV. The hours of labor vary according to the kinds of occupation introduced iuto the different establishments. Where a large number of prisoners are engaged in agricultural labors or on public works there is less regularity than in penitentiaries where industrial labor predominates. Still it may be said that the number of hours of daily labor is, on an average, from ten to twelve.

In summer (from the 1st of April to 30th September) work begins at 5 o'clock in the morning, and in some establishments a half hour later. In winter (1st October to 31st March) at 5½ or 6 o'clock. On Sundays and feast days the signal for rising is given a half hour or an hour later than on working days.

Work is regularly suspended at 7 or half past 7 o'clock a. m., half an hour for breakfast; at noon, an hour for dinner; and in the evening, a half hour for supper. At a quarter past 10 a. m. there is very generally granted a recess of a quarter to half an hour. After the cessation of work, which occurs at half past 7 or 8 o'clock p. m., the prisoners have still a half to three-quarters of an hour at their disposal for intellectual occupations, but only in penitentiaries where they pass the night in separate cells.

An hour of exercise and an hour of school complete the day's programme. This last hour should be curtailed in those penitentiaries where there is no schooling, and where only an hour or two on Sunday are given to this object. The hour of exercise is accorded only to those who work in the cells or in the shops.

In the modern or reorganized penitentiaries, the average number of hours of labor is twelve; that of recreation (exercise, school-lessons in cell, reading, &c.) is four, to which must be added the hours of Sundays and feast-days. These last are more or less numerous according to the religious creed.

XLV. In regard to the treatment of sick prisoners: The above programme is applied only to prisoners in health. Those who are indisposed or sick are, on the order of the medical officer of the prison, excused from work.

Slight indispositions are treated in the cells or in the common dormitories; those more seriously sick receive medical attention in the infirmary, which is found in the penitentiaries of the two higher classes indicated at the commencement of this report.

The infirmary, presided over by the physician of the establishment, who has under his orders an officer detailed to duty therein, leaves little to be desired, especially in the modern penitentiaries. There is generally found there a small dispensary, and everything that is necessary for medical treatment.

Prisoners seriously ill cannot receive attention in the old prisons. The sick in this case are transferred to a hospital.

Prisoners who present symptoms of mental alienation are conveyed to an insane asylum.

XLVI, XLVII, XLVIII.—The diseases most common are inflammation of the bowels, bronchitis, inflammation of the pleura and lungs, rheumatic affections of the joints and muscles, pulmonary consumption, enlargement of the lymphatic glands, and diseases of the nervous system. Contagious diseases, typhoid fever, syphilis, the itch, &c., are always imported; and their number, especially venereal affections, chronic complaints, and the itch, are relatively numerous in some of the cantons.

At Lenzbourg the number of the sick varies between 2 per cent. (light cases) and 1½ per cent. (cases more serious) of the days of imprisonment. During the last six years this penitentiary has registered nineteen deaths, which is about 3 per annum on an average of 370 prisoners. Of the five who died during the year 1870, three owed their death to pulmonary phthisis.

In the penitentiary of Bâle we find, in 1867, 2.85 per cent. of days of sickness. Of 330 prisoners there were 126 cases of sickness, and two deaths, (apoplexy of the lungs and consumption of the liver.)

Zurich, with an annual average of 407 prisoners, has had, during the last six years, sixty-four cases of sickness, which is 15 per cent. of the whole number; or, in other words, 26 per cent. per annum of the average daily number of prisoners, which was 241. In this penitentiary the number of prisoners who died was 6.3 per annum, being 1.54 per cent. of the prisoners present during the year, or 2.61 per cent. of the average daily number.

The penitentiary of Geneva indicates 5 per cent. as the proportional number of its sick. That of Lausanne gives 3 per cent. as the average annual number of deaths. Of 307 prisoners who underwent their punishment in this establishment, there were 3,497 days of sickness, out of 63,217 of imprisonment; twelve persons alone counting about 2,000 days. The cases of chronic maladies cited are, phthisis, pleurisy, and scurvy. Four deaths occurred, two having been caused by pulmonary phthisis, and the other two by an affection of the heart and pulmonary œdema. There was one case of insanity.

The annual report of the penitentiary of Berne, for 1867, shows, out of an average daily number of 428 prisoners, 176 sick, who were treated in the infirmary, and 14 deaths, three of which were from pulmonary phthisis and two from pneumonia.

The number of deaths in the penitentiary of Saint Gall, from 1858 to 1863, during which years 1,286 prisoners were received into the establishment, amounted to 70.

At Lucerne, the average number of days of sickness was, in 1867, 25 to each prisoner for the year.

At Schaffhausen, there were 545 days of sickness out of 9,943 days of imprisonment.

The frequent catarrhal affections of the organs of digestion (dyspepsia, diarrhœa, colic, &c.) are, in a great measure, due to the too great uniformity of the living, and the want of sufficient exercise-in the open air, under the vivifying light of the sun. These injurious influences, added to sadness and remorse, give rise, secondarily, to that prison scrofula which is observed, in proportions more or less marked, in the different penitentiaries, and which often terminates in pulmonary phthisis.

During the three years, from 1868 to 1870, two suicides are noted at Lenzbourg, and fourteen cases of insanity, more or less grave, which were ascribed less to the imprisonment than to a hereditary or individual predisposition and the moral influence of remorse.

At Neuchâtel there were observed during the year 1870, out of 146 prisoners, two cases of insanity, one of which had already been treated in a hospital, and the other was occasioned by drink.

At Saint Gall, from 1858 to 1863, there were nine cases of insanity (six men and three women) out of a prison population of 1,286.

If there are observed in the prisons pulmonary phthisis and other diseases in proportions which demand serious examination, these establishments, and particularly those of recent construction, seem, on the other hand, to present a remarkable freedom from epidemic diseases. When the cholera prevailed at Zurich, not a single case developed itself among the prisoners. It was the same at Lenzbourg during an epidemic of measles which prevailed in the neighborhood, and by which adults were attacked. At the time of the entrance into Switzerland of the army of Bourbaki, there was established, close to the penitentiary of Neuchâtel, a lazaretto for persons affected with varioloid; and though the penitentiary establishment was required to furnish meals to the sick and to their nurses, and to apply disinfectants to the bedding, no case of small-pox occurred in the prison. It is true that a general re-vaccination had taken place.

Similar observations were made in the penitentiary at Bâle.

XLIX, L, LI, and LII. The distinction between penal and industrial labor is made, in the Swiss prisons, by law only in the cantons where there still exists the system of the old hard-labor prisons, in which a certain class of prisoners are subjected to public labor, viz, in sweeping the streets, making roads, diking rivers, agricultural labors, &c., &c.

This distinction is not made in the penitentiaries in which the reformation of the prisoner is proposed as the end. Doubtless many kinds of labor are disagreeable and little attractive, and the persons engaged in such labors would not voluntarily submit to them if they were free; these labors thus acquire a penal character. In some of the penitentiaries prisoners are sometimes subjected to labors of this kind on their entrance and during the continuance of the first part of their cellular stage, or those are thus employed who, from the intermediate stage, have been returned to their cells; or, again, the indolent, the intractable, &c., &c.

This penal labor is a sort of disciplinary punishment. The labors belonging to this class are: The sawing and cutting of fire-wood, the plaiting of straw, the culling coffee, the manufacture of envelopes and cornucopias, of wooden boxes, &c., &c.

Nowhere is there found in Switzerland a penal labor of the character of the tread-mill.

Hard, ignominious public labor, such as still exists in some cantons, is not unfavorable to physical health, but has a bad moral effect.

The penal labor introduced into our modern penitentiaries as a light disciplinary labor is applied only temporarily; it is not injurious to the health of prisoners, and, as it often produces *ennui*, they seek to regain the confidence they had lost, so as to be admitted to more interesting and more profitable labor.

We find in the greater part of the penitentiaries various branches of industry carried on, among which the more general and the more important are: Weaving, shoe-making, tailoring, carpentry, varnishing, upholstery, cooperage, working in wood, brush-making, locksmithing, blacksmithing, working in tin, book-binding, paper-ruling, lithographing, watch-making, turning, basket-making, laundry-work, embroidery, and knitting.

For persons sentenced to a short imprisonment: the stuffing of chairs, the making of slippers, the manufacture of mats, of sieves, of bee-hives, of envelopes, of paper monkeys, and of wire trellis-work. Then come domestic labors of various kinds, and office occupations.

LIII, LIV, and IV. Industrial labor in the prisons of Switzerland is managed by the administration itself. The attempts which have been made in some prisons to let the labor to contractors for a fixed daily sum have been very speedily abandoned. Orders are received in the penitentiaries. The raw material is furnished by the administration or by those who order the work; the tools belong to the establishment. The keepers, who act at the same time as foremen, superintend the work, and calculate the value of the workmanship and of the raw material employed. Account is taken in this calculation of the prices current. Everywhere they endeavor to deliver merchandise carefully manufactured; and thus, as a general thing, the industrial products of our prisons are in good repute.

Preference is given in the modern penitentiaries to the management of the administration over that of contractors in the interest of penitentiary training.

The administration, being supreme, can introduce a greater variety of industries, and suit to these latter the different aptitudes presented by the prisoners. The consequence of the distribution of the prisoners on a larger number of industries is, that each branch is restricted to a relatively small number of workmen, and hence free labor has no occasion to fear an injurious competition. We endeavor to create a demand for the products of prison labor, rather by the excellence and solidity of the manufacture than by the cheapness of the price. Were it otherwise, the penitentiaries which ought to be, at the same time, industrial schools, would be turned aside from their proper end. In Switzerland it is found that penitentiary training is incompatible with the system of letting the labor of the prisoners to contractors. It is the administration alone that can feel an interest in teaching a trade to every prisoner during his stay in prison, so that at the time of his liberation he may be independent, and able to gain an honest living.

LVI. The number of prisoners not having a regular business at the time of their commitment is relatively considerable. Nevertheless, the tendency is shown to be toward a diminution, if comparison is made between the results of statistics for the last twenty years in the penitentiary of Saint Gall. This belongs, evidently, to the progress of civilization.

By including in this category domestic servants, day-laborers, and people without any occupation, without homes, we obtain the following figures :

Domestic servants form 33 per cent. of the total number of prisoners; day-laborers, 9 per cent.; vagrants, 4 per cent.; making an aggregate average of 48 per cent. This average varies somewhat in various cantons, according as any particular industry is there more or less developed, and the population more or less floating. It must be remarked that among those who, when they enter the prison, are artisans or industrial workmen, many have but accomplished an insufficient apprenticeship; so that, of 50 per cent. who claimed to have learned a trade, there is scarcely a fourth part who can produce a respectable piece of workmanship.

LVII and LVIII. The preceding figures show clearly that the want of a trade is not without its influence in the law which controls the causes of crime. Hence it is sought in all the penitentiaries, particularly in those more recently built and organized upon a rational plan, to give a trade to the prisoners, and above all to juvenile delinquents, to those who have to undergo an imprisonment of one or several years. In all the penitentiaries, it has been remarked that numbers of the prisoners acquire, in a short time, the ability to do that which free workmen would be able to execute only after a long apprenticeship.

Apprenticeship to a trade, which requires a certain degree of intelligence, and is, at the same time, to the taste of the prisoner, is one of the principal agencies in reforming him. Without industrial labor of this kind, no satisfactory result can be expected from a penitentiary-system, and relapses will be inevitable. A trade learned in the establishment is worth more, as regards the support and succor of the prisoners, than a patronage society. It is well understood in the cantons somewhat advanced in penitentiary science that it is important, in order to prevent relapses, not only to make the prisoner an able workman, but also to teach him during his incarceration to help himself. In this view, there have been introduced in most of the prison regulations arrangements by which zeal and diligence in labor and the habit of saving are stimulated. The scale of the *peculium* rises, as has been said above, in many of the establishments with the augmentation of labor. In the better organized penitentiaries the further effort is made to attain this result by a careful apprenticeship to the trade chosen by the prisoner, by making him acquainted with the nature of raw materials, the places from which they are obtained, and their market value; also with the tools and machines employed; the price-current of the articles manufactured; and by teaching the manner of calculating the value of the workmanship. The prisoners are more or less associated with the administration through their industrial labors. If, by their good conduct and their aptitudes, they come at length to deserve the necessary degree of confidence, they are called to fulfill the functions of foremen.

There is thus afforded to every prisoner the opportunity of developing and manifesting his power of initiative.

Technical works and journals are placed in the hands of the workmen on different branches of industry. Writings of the character of Franklin's Poor Richard afford material assistance in this system of penitentiary education.

LIX. But all these salutary influences are lost in the case of prisoners sentenced to a short imprisonment. The directors of the Swiss penitentiaries are unanimous in regarding repeated short sentences for minor offenses as a pernicious judicial practice, which is followed without reflection. The sentiment of justice, as well as the moral reformation of the prisoner, requires that the repression be more serious and more adequately protracted in the case of individuals who take on the habit of crime, and who threaten to make it the basis of their character.

The effect of these short imprisonments becomes worse on each successive conviction. The recidivists fall deeper and deeper, and the prison cannot lift them up. During the short stay they make in the penitentiary establishment, it is impossible to teach them a trade, or even to make them apt at work.

The recidivists sentenced correctionally have more or less lost the moral sense and self-respect. The influence of the penitentiary education cannot affect the individual of this class who, on entering the establishment, counts the exact number of days which separates him from freedom.

These subjects undergo, more or less patiently, the restraint imposed upon them; they are indifferent, and little heed the present or the future which awaits them.

On the other hand, too protracted imprisonments (twenty to twenty-five years) plunge the prisoner at last into apathy and despair.

LX. The proportional number of recidivists can be given only approximately. The statistics in the different cantons are not made out in a uniform manner.

In some establishments, account is made of all prior sentences—police, correctional, and criminal; in others, they embrace only those which have been pronounced within the canton, or even notice only the punishments undergone in the same establishment. The greater part of the cantons expel from their territory liberated prisoners of foreign birth, and give themselves no further trouble about them; so that it may happen that the cantons whose penitentiaries contain numerous non-residents of the canton may have fewer recidivists to be registered. In spite of the defective state of the statistics, we may estimate an average of 30 to 45 per cent. as the proportion of recidivists in cantons where the penitentiary system has made least progress, and from 19 to 25 per cent. as that of the cantons whose penitentiaries are well organized.

The efficacy of a penitentiary system may be indicated, up to a certain point, by the number of its recidivists. But this rule has numerous exceptions in Switzerland. The diversity in the modes of punishment does not allow us to draw from the numbers indicated an indisputable conclusion. It would be necessary to take account of the preventive measures, which are more or less effectively applied in the different cantons.

In the canton of Argovie, (Lenzbourg,) where penitentiary education is conducted with care, there were counted, from 1865 to 1867, forty-five recidivists out of eighty-seven prisoners; and from 1868 to 1870 only forty-four to one hundred and fifty, among whom fourteen were not natives of the canton. Thus the recidivists form 25 per cent. of the criminals of Argovian origin, and 37 per cent. of those not born in that canton, making an average of 28 per cent. So that in the space of six years there was a cheering diminution in the number of recidivists, and it must be attributed, in great part, to the penitentiary system applied in that establishment, and also to the efforts made to aid and protect liberated prisoners. The correctional recidivists form, in that same canton, 50 per cent.

In the canton of Bâle-ville (one-third of the prisoners in cellular reclusion) the number of recidivists is from 18 to 19 per cent., and that figure is caused, in great part, by women abandoned to prostitution and vagrancy.

In the canton of Saint Gall, of 1,286 persons sentenced criminally and committed to the penitentiary of Saint Jacques, (Auburn,) during the first twenty-five years of its existence, (1839 to 1863,) the recidivists were 248, being an average of 19.5 per cent. This penitentiary has been, for many years, under the direction of a man as humane as he is enlightened.

In the canton of Lucerne, which possesses an old hard-labor prison, the number of recidivists rises, *per contra*, to 40.4 per cent.

The number of female recidivists is 50 per cent. in the canton of Argavie. The woman, more than the man, resists the seductions which lead to crime; but when she has once succumbed, her moral degradation is greater and more rapid than is the case with man, and her falls more frequent.

LXI. The existing codes denounce a severer punishment against prisoners convicted more than once. Some sentence them to the maximum of the punishment incurred; others add to this punishment its moiety, and even more, in excess of the maximum. Every sentence, for an offense exceeding six months, becomes an aggravating circumstance in the case of the person who, having suffered it, is prosecuted criminally.

In the cantons of Argovie and Zurich, it is only at the third relapse that the aggravation of the punishment commences for criminals, which punishment is then carried to ten years of reclusion in the first-named of these cantons. The recidivists of this class are besides subjected in the penitentiary to a cellular separation of longer duration, and even throughout the whole term of their punishment, if they show themselves depraved to a high degree.

This last system exists also in the cantons of Zurich, Bâle, and Neuchâtel.

LXII. Prisons for debt exist only in a few cantons, and it may even be said that, where such prisons are still found, the constraint of the body has fallen into disuse. In a number of cantons, the State authorizes the restraint of the body, in default of payment of the expenses of justice; but this imprisonment is of short duration, and often is not inflicted at all. This punishment is regarded as correctional, and has no character of infamy.

LXIII. In examining the table of crimes and misdemeanors, we observe that the number of those committed against property (petit larcenies, thefts, abuses of trust, &c.) constitute 65 per cent. of the total number; that the number of attempts against life (murders, homicides, infanticides) is 10 per cent.; acts of incendiarism, 5 per cent.; and the remainder comprises cases of counterfeiting, false accusations, &c., &c. These figures sufficiently indicate the direction followed by the will of the persons forming the criminal class. Mr. Mühler, director of the penitentiary of Lenzbourg, makes the following reflections on the causes of crime in the canton of Argovie:

The most frequent cause of crime is a malign education, which early gives to the will a fatal direction toward evil, or which, at least, stifles in the character the moral power to resist evil suggestions.

Among the correctionals the influence of an evil education is more marked than among the criminals. This is explained by the circumstance that the former are mainly recruited in the pauper class, which is deprived of everything that might give to the child a good education. Many of these correctionals have never enjoyed the family life; they are orphans or illegitimate children, who have been placed by the *commune* (we have in Switzerland obligatory communal assistance) or by philanthropic societies, with one, or, successively, with several keepers of boarding-houses. In both cases, these children are rarely in conditions favorable to their education. We find, on the other hand, among the criminals, a certain number belonging to the higher classes of society, whose education has been less neglected, who have themselves lived in favorable conditions, and who sometimes had gained an honorable position in society. Sensualism, which has been developed in them by an irrational system of education, is, in the greater number of cases, the predominant cause of their crimes.

Next, we encounter other persons who have learned a business and who have not yet arrived at that state of utter indolence which is so often remarked in the correctionals. In a higher degree than these last, the criminal prisoners have ties of family; either they are able to count on the support and succor of their relatives during their imprisonment and after their liberation, or they have a wife and children. The correctionals, on the contrary, are, for the most part, without family, without relatives, without friends, and possess neither sufficient energy nor sufficient perseverance to create for themselves a domestic hearth. The predominant characteristic of such a manner of living is levity and heedlessness, which, if other aggravating circumstances come in aid of them, (drunkenness, debauchery, &c.,) as often happens, degenerate into a depravity whose character is that of a stupid indifference, rather than the necessity of doing wrong.

Another source of crimes and misdemeanors, nearly as prolific as the preceding, is drunkenness, often accompanied by other excesses. The

·number of criminals, small and great, abandoned to drunkenness, or who at the moment of the criminal act were under the dominion of drink, is by no means inconsiderable, forming at least 50 per cent. of the total number of crimes committed by men, and this proportion is even higher among the correctionals. Governments and societies of public utility. have been occupied, and are constantly occupied, in seeking out the best means to combat this vice, but they are very far from having attained the object of their pursuit. The number of misdemeanors occasioned by wine is considerable in some of the cantons, and the liberty of the wine traffic, pushed to its utmost limits, causes, in a number of these cantons, (Neuchâtel, for example,) the commission of one crime as the effect of wine to every one hundred and four persons of the population. In others, an impost upon wine drives the pauper class to the consumption of brandy.

That which is worst in the vice of drunkenness is not the criminal act which it has directly or indirectly caused, but much more the moral waste which the drunkard gradually suffers, and which causes him to lose all perception of the most elementary laws of morality.

Happily, in Switzerland, there are generally few criminals by profession; that is to say, who are impelled toward evil as the result of a hereditary moral anomaly, or of a deplorable education. Nor is the number large of those who have become criminal by a deliberate purpose, through hatred of society and its laws, who find a fascination in crime, and who conceive that they have a right to the exercise of their vengeance. In the greater number of cases this criminal tendency is increased by drink and debauchery.

It may be admitted that all those criminal natures whose earliest movements are in the correctional domain reach at length that of crime. Anger, the absence of reflection, in a word, any sudden over-excitement, combined commonly with the influence of drink, is a frequent occasion of crime. In the majority of these cases it is observable that the moral character of the criminal had been previously, to a certain extent, vitiated.

Reverses of fortune, domestic troubles, the death of a good mother, may be an occasion of discouragement, followed by prolonged inactivity, drunkenness, and debauchery, vices which prepare the soil in which criminal thoughts speedily germinate. But such cases are less frequent among us than vulgar rapacity, sordid avarice, and the mania for litigation, which is also frequently a cause of crime of a kindred character.

Poverty and misery do not often, in Switzerland, become direct causes of crimes and misdemeanors. They act only indirectly, since, for the most part, they are the result of bad education, which is the easy road conducting to depravity of a greater or less intensity.

It often happens, again, that clothing, watches, money, are stolen, and that misery is indicated as the cause of these larcenies. But if these cases are carefully examined, it is found that want is rarely the impelling cause, and that more frequently the authors of these offenses were leading a dissolute life, and that their notions of morality were becoming weaker, if, indeed, they were not already totally effaced. Many of these petty thieves themselves excuse their crimes by alleging the destitution and misery in which they found themselves.

The following table, extracted from the triennial report (1868 to 1870) of Lénzbourg, and which may be applied to many of the Swiss cantons, gives an interesting view of the causes of crime. We transcribe it, however, under reserve, since it is impossible to classify with precision the immediate causes of crime.

Of one hundred and ninety criminals, among whom were one hundred and seventy men, we find ninety-two, equal to 42 per cent. of the men, who were addicted to drunkenness, or who committed their crimes in a state of intoxication. The proportion is 60 per cent. among the correctionals.

Of one hundred and ninety-two criminals thirty-nine, or 15.6 per cent., were criminals in the true sense of the word; forty-one, or 21.3 per cent,, were in a state of moral decay; eighty-five, or 44.3 per cent., became criminals through levity of character; thirteen, or 6.7 per cent., became so as the result of the wretched condition in which they lived; twenty-three, or 12 per cent., committed their crimes in a moment of sudden excitement. Of two hundred and forty-four correctionals nineteen, or 7.8 per cent., were criminals in the proper acceptation of the word; one hundred and five, or 43 per cent., were in a state of complete moral prostration; one hundred and six, or 43.4 per cent., had committed the fault through levity of character; twelve, or 5 per cent., in a moment of passion; and two as the result of unfortunate circumstances.

If the proportion of those addicted to crime, as a profession, is higher among the criminals than among the correctionals, that is compensated by the inverse proportion of correctionals who have lost all sentiment of duty and of honor.

The number of crimes would be reduced among us to its minimum if the education of orphans and of illegitimate and unfortunate children were the object of a solicitude more concentrated, more steady, and more methodical. Modes of relief are not wanting in Switzerland; we have communal assistance; we have numerous and well-inclosed alms-houses; and above all, we have voluntary aid, which is designed to supplement that of the communal corporations. These last are not sufficiently careful in choosing the familes to which they confide the education of orphans and deserted children. Honest families which, from charity and a true Christian devotion, receive under their care such unfortunates, are still too rare.

Old men who need assistance are sometimes placed by the communes at boarding in poor families, where they run the hazard of becoming mendicants, vagrants, and thieves.

Primary instruction is obligatory in all the cantons except two, and gratuitous in several; yet, in spite of this, it happens in these cantons that children escape from control and do not avail themselves of the benefits of instruction. It is the same with mendicity, which is interdicted by law, but which continues still in spite of the bureaus of relief and assistance, because many persons cannot refuse alms to paupers who knock at their gates, and make an appeal to their hearts.

Gambling-houses may be said no longer to have an existence among us. That which is opened in the canton of Valais is the object of general censure, and its license will probably not be renewed. The love of gaming exists notwithstanding, and the too numerous idlers who frequent the wine-shops seek habitually diversion and excitement in gambling. Public houses of prostitution are tolerated only in a few great centers of population. Secret prostitution is by no means wanting. Finally, there ought to be named as one of the sources of crime the defects of most of our systems of penal legislation and the absence of a suitable penitentiary system in several of the cantons. Efforts are made to dry up all these sources of crime, but this labor of moral hygiene does not proceed with sufficient concert of action. In the several cantons progress is made with different degrees of slowness. The result is that the success of those cantons which have introduced reforms into their penal and penitentiary systems are compromised by numerous cases of relapse, coming from neighboring cantons less advanced.

In order to hasten the realization of progress throughout all Switzerland many voices have been raised, on occasion of the revision of the federal constitution, to demand, if not the centralization, at least the unification of the penal code, the promulgation of federal laws to insure the greater diffusion of education, to regulate the assistance to be given to paupers, to abolish gambling-houses, &c., &c.

These reforms will be realized some day. But such a work requires time, which indeed is demanded by the general law of human progress.

LXIV. In the prisons of Switzerland, the two sexes are represented in the following proportions: The men form an average of 80 and the women of 20 per cent. This average varies slightly in different cantons. In some the women are but 15 per cent. of the total prison population.

LXV. The study of social questions, undertaken by numerous societies of public utility, and the reports presented in the meetings of the Swiss society for the reform of the penal system and of prison discipline, have enlightened public opinion to such a degree that the legislative assemblies of most of the cantons are favorable to the propositions made with a view to the introduction of penitentiary reform into all our prisons. On the other hand, public opinion declares itself in favor of expenditures designed to improve the condition of criminals only after the state has supplied the country with hospitals, insane asylums, orphan houses, schools, &c., &c., that is to say, with all needful establishments designed for the honest poor. In all the cantons where these institutions are found, the old theory of penal repression, based on vengeance, has given place to more humane ideas, the responsibility resting on society as regards the causes of crimes is better understood, and the system introduced into most of the prisons has for its aim the reformation of the prisoners. It is true that the penal codes of many of the cantons are based on punishment, intimidation, and expiation. But despite the text of the codes, which was often written prior to the reform of the prisons, it is sought in the penitentiaries, particularly in those which we have grouped in the two superior classes, to employ agencies which may combine at once repression and reformation. While in some cantons (those of the two inferior groups) the principle of repression is alone admitted, we see the canton of Zurich setting a good example by declaring, in its penal code, October, 1870, that the application of punishment ought positively to have for its object the reformation of the criminal.

This principle, which, some day, will be applied in its whole length and breadth, dates only from yesterday. Hence we need not be surprised that the country is found in that transitional period when the principle of intimidation still struggles against the moral reform of criminals. The spirit of vengeance is not entirely extinguished; it still shows itself whenever any atrocious crime has just been committed. But the moment of indignation is transient, which shows that an immense progress has already been realized, and that its development proceeds without cessation, in spite of occasional reactionary movements.

LXVI. The favorable results obtained in the moral reformation of prisoners, subjected to the penitentiary *régime* of the modern establishments, incite the others to a revision of their penal codes.

No doubt there are many criminals and correctionals in whose case the influence of the improved penitentiary system does not make itself felt. As among the insane, there are incurable moral maladies; persons in whom the moral sense has been completely perverted suffer themselves to be impressed in a penitentiary only by the evil which they find there, and show themselves insensible to the good which is sought to be accomplished. On the other hand, the greater number is far from being depraved, and the moral force of those who form this class increases in the prisons. At the moment of their liberation they feel themselves reconciled to society, and they have the firm intention of regaining, by their good conduct and by honest toil, the esteem of their fellow-citizens.

It is not easy for a prisoner to carry into effect his good resolutions. He has to confront many prejudices, to conquer many obstacles, and to resist many temptations, to which he would sometimes succumb if some charitable hand were not extended for his succor.

LXVII and LXVIII. It is with a design of preventing relapses among liberated prisoners, with or without a trade, that there are formed in most of the cantons patronage societies.

The canton of Saint Gall was one of the first to give its attention to this subject.

Thirty years ago the resolution was formed in that canton to establish a penitentiary house, organized on the principle of the reformation of prisoners; but its execution was essentially subordinated to the formation of a society which should have for its mission the supervision of liberated convicts.

In the autumn of 1838 the penitentiary of Saint Jacques was finished, and on the 24th of November of that same year there was passed on criminal punishments a new law, which declared in article 6:

After his liberation, it will be the duty of every prisoner who is a citizen of the canton, or has his domicile there, to place himself, for three months at least to three years at most, under the protection of a patronage society.

On the 15th of the same month the grand council of Saint Gall adopted, in regard to the administration of its penitentiary, the following resolution: •

ARTICLE VI. The commission of direction will take care that all the liberated prisoners find an honest support and be placed under patronage. In this view it will endeavor to found a special society, to which the minor council will be able to confide the care of the liberated prisoners, in conformity to a rule approved by him.

These arrangements greatly facilitated the organization of the patronage society of Saint Gall. Thus, on the 10th of June, 1839, the society was organized, and on the 21st of the same month its statutes were ratified by the minor council, which, in its letter missive, expressed the hope that it would accomplish by incessant devotion what the law could not exact.

The system on which this society was founded has undergone no modifications down to the present time, and it has even been confirmed anew by a decree of the 16th August, 1860.

It is to be remarked that the committee is authorized to hand over to the police of the canton every individual whom it is unable to keep under its supervision, or who has rendered himself unworthy of its protection—an authority which has hitherto proved almost useless.

In the canton of Zurich a patronage society was founded in 1865. It differs from that of Saint Gall, inasmuch as it is based on liberty of action, and is subject to no governmental constraint.

Its protection is granted, in preference, to juvenile delinquents, and it extends its aid not only to prisoners discharged from the penitentiary, but also to those who have undergone their punishment in a district prison.

At Saint Gall the patronage committee receives from the director, six weeks before the liberation of the prisoner, information relating to his age, his conduct, his trade, and the causes of his sentence, and decides at that time whether the prisoner is deserving of patronage, and what measures ought to be taken in regard to him ; whereas at Zurich the director and the chaplain of the penitentiary, being themselves members of the central committee, are officially called upon to give it, orally, the information required, and to submit to it the propositions which they judge suitable as regards the patronage of the discharged prisoner. When that is done, the president selects from among the members of the committee, for each prisoner, a reporter charged with drawing up a paper in relation to the cases, and, after discussion, the committee takes a definitive resolution.

In order that the patron may become acquainted with the prisoner and question him concerning his plans for the future, permission is granted to visit him before his liberation.

It is admitted, in principle, that the society is not to bestow its care upon those who, morally and materially, have no need of it, or refuse it, or give no hope of improvement from it. This fact, like many others, shows that there are reforms necessary in our penal legislation in regard to the duration of punishments.

The annual reports of the central committee of Zurich show that the work of patronage is there in full activity. The patronage society of Berne, organized in 1864, owes its existence to the Society of Public Utility. Its organization does not differ in any essential point from that of the societies of which we have just spoken, and, like that of Zurich, it is based on the principle of free action.

In the report of the labors of the first year the committee makes the following observations :

At first we had in view only the patronage of prisoners whose previous and present conduct offered sufficient guarantees. It was necessary that the first essays should not be an occasion of discouragement to the society. Our earliest efforts disappointed us. We had no success, and it was only when we had the courage to afford aid to recidivists and great malefactors that our success became complete. Although Mr. Dick, chaplain of the establishment, did not cease to speak to the prisoners of the many benefits of patronage, both in the pulpit and in his personal visits, we had only now and then an application for assistance. There is occasion to propose this question, which is worthy of a serious examination, to wit, Whether it would not be expedient that the patronage society have, by law, an official position ?

In the canton of Bâle-ville it is now some years since the Philanthropical Society and the Society of Public Utility have added to their vast and laudable field of activity the patronage of prisoners sentenced criminally and correctionally. They give their attention specially to juvenile prisoners, whose moral regeneration offers a better chance of success, and they take great pains to find places for them as apprentices. Hitherto the results obtained have been highly satisfactory.

In 1835 a patronage society was formed at Neuchâtel, and for some years was actively engaged in its appropriate work. Its labors were resumed in 1844 by a new committee, which had at first the material and moral support of the government, but subsequently had no other resources than those obtained through voluntary contributions. It obtained no moral results, became disheartened, and ceased to exist during the political events of 1848.

The principal cause of these disappointments was, as we think, the absence of a rational penitentiary system.   Hence at the opening of the present penitentiary, by a spontaneous movement, many persons residing in the six districts of the canton started the project of the formation of a patronage society for liberated prisoners.   This society was organized and its regulations adopted the 6th of April, 1871.

Like all the voluntary societies, it manifests, at the commencement of its career, much zeal and enthusiasm for the object to which its efforts are directed.

The cantons of Lucerne, Thurgovia, Appenzell, Vaud, and Glaris have also societies organized similar to those of which we have just spoken.

In the canton of Argovie much zeal is shown in the patronage of liberated prisoners, and as in this canton conditional liberty is authorized by law, it has been proposed to charge the consistories, that is, the elders of the churches, with the supervision and care of liberated prisoners.   But as in this canton the principle of the separation of church and state has just been decided upon, patronage will now be confided to the officers of the civil state.

Wherever they exist patronage societies aid discharged prisoners by their counsels, watch over their conduct, shield them from evil enticements, and purchase the clothing, tools, &c., which may be needed by them.   They endeavor to aid their beneficiaries by procuring work rather than by giving them assistance in money.

In spite of all these efforts, the results do not correspond to our desires, and, as may be seen from what has been said, there is not sufficient unity in the organization of patronage.   This is a great inconvenience, which the Swiss society for penitentiary reform is seeking to remove, by bringing into mutual relation all those persons who, in the different cantons, occupy themselves with the patronage of liberated prisoners.

LXIX. The restricted limits of the present report do not permit us to discuss the imperfections of our penal system, and of the discipline of our prisons.   What has already been said gives indications of the reforms to be desired   We therefore limit ourselves to a *résumé*, under the following heads, of the reforms which still remain to be accomplished:

1. The unification of the penal code, based on the principle of the moral reformation of prisoners.

2. The reform of our detention prisons for persons awaiting trial.

3. The increase of the number of reformatories for juvenile delinquents and vicious boys, and also the reform of work-houses and houses of correction for vagrants and idlers.

4. The erection of penitentiaries in cantons which have only the old-fashioned prisons, which are incapable of rational transformations.   Two or more cantons might come to an agreement to establish a penitentiary in common, or they might make arrangements with a canton which already has one, or found other establishments to be used as intermediate prisons, agreeably to the progressive Irish prison system.

5. The special education of prison officers and employés.

6. The reform of the disciplinary and educational *régime* of the penitentiaries, with a view to the moral regeneration of the prisoners.

7. The direction and supervision not only of the administration of all the prisons, but also of preventive institutions, (such as public assistance, orphan houses, agricultural colonies, refuges, patronage societies, &c.,) in the hands of special officers of the government.

8. The united action of the State and voluntary philanthropic societies, and societies of public utility.

9. Finally, the perfecting of all institutions whose aim is the preven-

tion of crime, whether in the domain of education, instruction, social conditions, &c., or of that of police and of justice.

In the name of the committee of the National Society for Penitentiary Reform,

The President-Reporter,

DR. GUILLAUME

NEUCHÂTEL, *December* 18, 1871.

V.—ITALY.

[Translation.]

I. Every prison in Italy—whether for the punishment of criminals or the safe-keeping of prisoners awaiting trial—is under the immediate control of the minister of the interior, who places at the head of its administration a director, who is subject to his own orders.

The general direction, besides a secretary attached to the office of the chief, comprises three divisions, which make part and parcel, with the other departments, of the ministry of the interior.

The first division is charged with the direction and oversight of the *personnel* (the officers) of the prisons.

The second has charge of the prison supplies; takes care that the expenditures of the local administrations do, not exceed the funds assigned to each establishment; sanctions the contracts for supplies, where they are given to private persons, as well as those for the labor of the prisoners made by the directors; and, in short, exercises in behalf of the state the vigilance necessary to insure, on the part of contractors and officers, the fulfillment of their obligations toward the government and the prisoners, and a faithful observance of the general laws of accounts.

The third division is in charge of the prison buildings, and is aided by a bureau of professional engineers, established in connection with the general direction. To this division belong also the distribution and transfer of prisoners to the different penal establishments, the size of the prisons and the different punishments to be undergone being taken into account. These dispositions are made with the special view of preventing the removal of dangerous prisoners to penitentiaries which offer facilities of escape, or to avoid overcrowding, which is always prejudicial to health and to discipline.

In connection with the general direction there is established a bureau of statistics. This gives information to the country, by the publication of an annual report, not only of the movement of the prison population, but also of the sanitary, legal, economical, and moral condition of the said population, and places the government and parliament in a position to appreciate the effects of the national penitentiary administration, of which it gives a thoroughly accurate account.

In addition to the above-named administrative functions, the director general is aided by a superior prison council.

This council is regarded as a consultative body, and its advice is taken in regard to the construction of new prison buildings and alterations in old ones, as well as in relation to administrative affairs, on which the director general thinks proper to ask their opinion. He consults them also with reference to promotion and measures of discipline relating to the officers and employés in the prisons.

This council is composed of the central inspectors—of whom two at

least must be present to insure the validity of its deliberations; of the head of the division to whose jurisdiction belong the matters from time to time brought before the council; and is presided over by the general director of the prisons. The functions of secretary, without the right of voting, are devolved upon an officer selected by the director general.

The directors of penal establishments, detention prisons, reformatory institutions, governmental or private, male and female, as well as the directors and administrative authorities of the judicial prisons of the whole kingdom, depend upon the director general, and receive orders from him.

II. The classification of the penal establishments in Italy is as follows:

For men: bagnios 21, in which are confined criminals sentenced to hard labor for life, or for a limited term; bridewells, 11, for prisoners sentenced to the punishment of reclusion; establishments of banishment 3; houses of correction 6, for persons sentenced to simple imprisonment; special establishments 10, (classed under the general title of houses of punishment,) for persons sentenced to a bridewell, agreeably to the Tuscan code, during the first stage of their punishment.

For women: there are 5 of these, in which all the different kinds of punishment are inflicted; also, 2 detention prisons for young girls, and 1 for young boys.

For youths: government detention prisons, 2.

III. There are 2 prisons in which a system of absolute separation prevails, containing a population of 362; 2 on a mixed system, (partly Pennsylvanian, partly Auburnian,) containing a population of 582; 5 in which the Auburn system complete is used, with 2,105 inmates; 48 in which the system of association by day and by night prevails; and 2 on a mixed system, partly Auburnian and partly associated, with a population of 600, making a total prison population for the whole kingdom of 21,706.

IV. In proportion as the Italian provinces came gradually to form a single nation, the authority of the general direction was extended over the prisons already existing in the said provinces.

From this single fact of the gradual coalescing of the prisons of different states under one government, every one can understand that it was impossible at once to introduce a perfect uniformity of discipline into so many and so various penitentiary establishments. The introduction of a uniform system of prison treatment was obstructed by the differences between the penal code of Sardinia, of 1859, which extended over almost the whole kingdom, and that of Tuscany, both of which were in force at the same time. It was obstructed, also, by the old style of penitentiary buildings in vogue before the practice had become general of employing punishment as an agency in the reformation of prisoners.

Notwithstanding these differences in the penal codes, the general direction holds itself in such a position that it will not be obliged to cause too profound a shock to the service when the new criminal code is promulgated; and, in the mean time, it follows, as far as possible, those rules of discipline which have elsewhere been put to the test, and which general experience has shown to be an effective means of penitentiary reform. It is, therefore, evident that, before rejecting or adopting, definitively, any one of the various systems employed in the several provinces of the kingdom, or which have been adopted by foreign nations, the general direction of the prisons in Italy has need to collect a greater number of facts, to arrange them, and to investigate their causes and bearings. In this view it occupies itself, from year to year, with the study of statistics. The results of this study will, ultimately, enable it to propose to the Government a penitentiary system, which may be applied to the whole kingdom. For these reasons the general direction does not think that the time has come, in so far as it is concerned, to answer categorically the second part of the present question; that is to say, it cannot declare from mature examination and conviction its own preferences for the system proper to be adopted.

If the author of the present series of questions will carefully consider the matter he will see that the very naming of a commission, charged with the duty of studying the questions connected with modern penitentiary discipline, and of proposing their solution to the government, shows of itself that the general direction does not regard the results hitherto obtained by its own efforts as all that might be secured by the discipline which it has adopted.

But the results of the two systems chiefly practiced by us are readily seen from the character of the numerous facts furnished by our statistics. At any rate, in questions of such importance, it is but just to weigh the opinion of the directors of our prisons, which is as follows: Three-fifths of them favor the Auburn system, some of these, however, with modifications suggested by themselves; the other two-fifths incline to the system of absolute separation, with or without mitigations.

V. The funds for the support of the prisons are drawn from the general budget of the state.

The financial results of the prisoners' labor are shown in the statistics; recourse must, therefore, be had to the figures to form an accurate judgment. No doubt there is a remarkable disproportion in the economical results obtained by different establishments; but this is due to the fact that some of the prisons, situated in unfavorable localities, cannot compete with others which are placed in the great centers of population, where commercial and industrial life has a high activity.

VI. The directors and officers of the prisons, whether central or local, are named by royal decree; the keepers and foremen by decree of the minister of the interior on the proposal of the director general.

The tenure of office for the higher functionaries is for life; nor can they be removed except for causes which would render them unfit for the service, or unworthy of a place among the officers of the State. The keepers are chosen for six years; and as to the foremen, their engagements with the penitentiary administration depend in each case on special arrangements.

VII. On the general gifts of mind and character which should distinguish a good prison officer, the general direction cannot express any special opinion. It confines itself to the remark that, as a general thing, it recognizes in its higher officers a degree of aptness and competency which leads it to continue them in their respective charges. It simply adds that, beyond the needful probity, it selects in preference those who had made some attainments in juridical knowledge, who possess a more than ordinary energy and activity in their work, who are endued at once with courage and coolness, and of late those whose personal appearance is calculated to inspire a certain degree of respect in the minds of the prisoners.

VIII. To the present time no special schools have been established for the preparation of good officers to be placed in our penitentiary establishments. The general direction has thought it sufficient, as regards the qualifications of those who apply for office in the prisons, to comply with the royal decree of 10th March, 1871, and with the subsequent ministerial decree of 20th of May of the same year, which regulate the examinations to be undergone by all applicants for the higher penitentiary positions.

As regards the *personnel* of the keepers, the general direction has already taken steps to establish, at a few central points of the state where there exist, in near proximity, detention prisons and female establishments of different classes, certain (so to speak) novitiates, or training schools, for keepers, by way of experiment. Here it is to be hoped the pupils will be able to gain a knowledge of every branch of that difficult service with which, from the start, they need to be somewhat acquainted, if they would not injure the discipline of the establishments to which they are attached as probationers, and do, perhaps, irreparable damage to their own future career.

IX. The pension to which the directors and officers of the prisons are entitled, after a service of at least twenty-five years, is determined on the same principle as that of every other officer in the civil service of the state. Thus, when retired after twenty-five years of service, they have as many fortieths of their salary, when it does not exceed two thousand Italian livres, and as many sixtieths when it is more than two thousand livres, as their years of service.

But without regard to the twenty-five years of service there are cases of pensions granted to all classes of officers, when any of them become incapacitated by a wound or disease caused by some extraordinary act performed in the discharge of his official duties.

X. The differences, not only in the length of the sentences, but also in the judicial consequences, and in the treatment of prisoners sentenced to the different punishments, whether penal or correctional, are determined by the penal code, (lib. 1, title "Of punishments.") Our penitentiary regulations are conformed in their spirit to the literal provisions of the code, which has fixed the degree of punishment.

XI. If by the classification of prisoners is meant their assignment to different penal establishments according to their several crimes and sentences, we must answer that a complete system of classification does exist in our prisons.

In the detention prisons the following categories are, as much as possible, separated from each other; the accused; the indicted; those sentenced for terms of six months and under; those sentenced for longer periods, who are awaiting their transfer; the arrested, who are at the disposal of the authorities of public safety; those detained in transit; persons imprisoned for debt; women; and minors.

In the prisons for correctionals and reclusionaries the classification for different treatment is as follows: the idle; the laboring, including apprentices; boys; masters.

In the bagnios there are recognized four divisions, with separate dormitories for each. They are: those sentenced for military crimes or assaults; those sentenced for theft; those sentenced for highway robbery; those convicted of atrocious crimes, such as assassination, homicide, &c. Each of these four divisions is subdivided into three categories, distinguished by marks on their dress, according to their terms of sentence, from ten years to life.

XII. The general regulations of the prisons ordain that, when the council of discipline, legally convoked by the local director, is of the opinion that there is ground for invoking the royal clemency in behalf of any prisoner, and formulates its judgment, it is the duty of the said director to send the application to the general direction, which, after duly recording it, transmits the papers to the keeper of the seals, whose duty it is to submit them to the royal decision.

Besides the conditions which naturally limit such applications to the case of prisoners of exemplary conduct, the regulations provide that the crime of which the candidate for the royal pardon was convicted should not have been one of those betokening a profound corruption and perversity of mind, and that he should have already undergone the one-half of his punishment. Moreover, the applications for pardon made by each director must not exceed the proportion of 5 per cent. of the whole prison population confined in the establishment to which he belongs.

XIII. Participation in the products of their labor is not the right of the prisoners, but is conceded to them as a gratuity. Such gratuities commence at one-tenth, and increase in inverse proportion to the gravity of the punishment assigned to the prisoner.

These tenths constitute a fund laid up against the time of the prisoner's liberation.

Apart from the gratuities just mentioned, the prisoners obtain, by way of reward, a certain amount of food in those prisons in which the labor is managed by the administration. Instead of this additional food, they have two-tenths of their disposable *peculium* in prisons where the labor is let on contract; and with these two-tenths they are at liberty to purchase for themselves additional food of their own choice, always, however, within the limits of a short list of simple eatables, at prices agreed upon between the contractor and the director, and posted in every workshop.

XIV. Other rewards granted to prisoners who are industrious and otherwise well conducted are: permission to receive visits and write letters; the use of their savings up to one-third (provided the two remaining thirds are not less than twenty-five livres) for the relief of their parents, their wife, and their children under age; liberty to purchase under-clothing, books, and tools; and finally, positions of responsibility and trust awarded them by the administration.

A reward, justly held in much higher esteem by convicts distinguished for good conduct, has been recently introduced; only, however, in the case of those who should have completed a certain part of their sentence, provided their offense was not one indicating a profound perversity, and who should have passed six months continuously without disciplinary punishment; said premium consisting in sending them to an agricultural penal colony, situated for the most part in some Italian island.

XV. The most common offenses against discipline in the bagnios are insubordination and quarrels between prisoners, (constituting a fourth part of all violations of the rules,) conspiracies, mutinies, and clandestine possession of contraband articles.

In the ordinary prisons the most common offenses are violations of the rule of silence and refusal to work.

XVI. The disciplinary punishments in use are admonitions, isolation in the cell of rigor from one to three days with ordinary bread, and with soup only once; isolation with a diet of bread and water; and isolation in a cell from one to six months, but with the legal rations. Let it be noticed that even the punishment cells are furnished with a camp-bed.

In the bagnios there are used as punishments—the hard bench; increasing the weight of the chains, (*il puntale;*) and the solitary cell.

The graver punishments cannot be inflicted by the director alone, but there must intervene a sentence by the council of discipline, composed of the president-director, the vice-director, and an officer of the prison. On the invitation of the president, the chaplain, the medical officer, and the superior of the sisters take part in the deliberations of the council, but without the right of voting; the lady superior being present only in the female prisons, or in male prisons in which sisters have charge of the kitchen and the wardrobe.

If the punishments awarded, even by the council of discipline, exceed three months, they cannot be applied until they receive the official sanction of the minister of the interior.

The punishments most frequently employed in the bagnois are the hard-bench and simple arrests; in the houses of correction, the cell of rigor, with bread, water, and soup once, and admonitiòns.

XVII. Every punishment incurred by a prisoner is entered at length in his individual register; and an abstract of it is afterward copied into the general register of the establishment to which the prisoner belongs. It is the records contained in this last register which furnish to the general direction the *data* for the annual penitentiary statistics.

XVIII. Every prison, even for persons awaiting trial, has a priest, who is its titular chaplain. As in Italy the great mass of the citizens are Catholic, there are no ministers of other creeds attached to our prisons. Whoever belongs to a different religious communion is permitted to confer with a minister of his own creed on application to the director, who cannot refuse to admit the individual named by the prisoner, unless he has reason to believe that the safety of the establishment would be thereby endangered.

XIX. Besides the spiritual service, (public worship and the administration of the sacraments,) the chaplain gives lectures to, or holds moral conferences with the prisoners; visits them when sick, administers the consolations of religion to the dying, delivers a sermon to them once a week in the chapel, visits in their cells newly arrived prisoners, and those about to be discharged, admonishes and comforts such as are confined in punishment cells, and often conducts the prison school, or aids the master in doing it.

XX. The Italian government attaches great importance to a service such as that rendered by the chaplains; to such an extent is this true, that, in order to secure it, the government has not hesitated sensibly to increase the budget of the prisons.

XXI. The general direction has kept up the system of volunteer visitation of the prisons in those provinces in which it found that system in existence; and at this moment it makes it the object of a special study whether it would be well to extend the system; if so, in what manner and whether with a connection more or less direct with the central government, or with the local agents either of the prisons or the administration.

In short, it is proposed to solve the problem whether or not the plan of volunteer visitation ought to be considered as a useful or necessary complement of a good prison system.

XXII. Every penal establishment in Italy has elementary schools to which the prisoners, by turns, are admitted three times a week. On the working days the school continues an hour and a half. On Sunday conferences are held with the prisoners, which sometimes last two hours or two hours and a half, in which a variety of topics, scientific, moral, and miscellaneous, are made the subject of discourse.

XXIII. Prisoners are ordinarily permitted to write and receive letters once a month. The regulations suggest the necessary cautions to prevent the correspondence from becoming a source of danger to the internal security of the establishment, and from being used as a *stimulus* to the illicit passions of the prisoners. Hence these regulations prescribe that every letter of a prisoner (unless directed to the minister, to the director general, or to the central inspectors of the prisons) should pass under the inspection of the director, without which the prisoner is not permitted either to send away or to receive a letter.

XXIV. The general opinion of the directors as to the effect of the correspondence of the prisoner with his family is that it is excellent. They are not so unanimous in their opinion as to the effect of the correspondence of the prisoner with persons who are not related to him. The general direction, for itself, is of the opinion that the fruits to be expected from the liberty of correspondence conceded to the prisoner are good or bad, according to the wisdom or tact of the director who grants it. This officer, if he attends assiduously to his duty, ought to know the degree of affection felt toward their families by the prisoners under his care, and how far communications from outside would contribute to render certain prisoners better or worse, and to inspire them with sentiments of submission and obedience, or the reverse.

XXV and XXVI. According to our penitentiary regulations the convict in our prisons, whether for detention or punishment, is not prevented from receiving the visits of a few friends. Various provisions introduced into the regulations of the several penitentiary establishments add the precautions to be observed in the concession of visits, their frequency, and, in fine, the cases of serious sickness in which the visitor is permitted to see the sick prisoner in the interior of the penitentiary.

As regards the exercise of vigilance, it is established that the visits take place always in the presence of a keeper or officer in the male prisons, or of a sister in those for women; besides which, it is positively forbidden to have any communication by signs or conventional expressions, which might tend to defeat the object of the continual presence of the officer.

XXVII. As regards the good or bad results of the visits of relatives or of strangers to the prisoner, the general direction does not think that it can give an opinion different from that already expressed concerning the favorable or unfavorable influence of epistolary correspondence; nor, on the other hand, can we doubt the wisdom of the rule which makes the liberty of receiving visits a premium on good conduct, since it thus serves as a *stimulus* to a constant respect on the part of the prisoner for the discipline of the prison.

XXVIII. The proportion of prisoners who at the time of their entrance are wholly illiterate is as follows: In the ordinary prisons the illiterate constitute 40 per cent. at least; in the bagnios it is 30 per cent.

XXIX, XXX, and XXXI. Schools exist in nearly all the penal establishments of whatever kind.

The prisoners admitted to the benefits of the school in the penal prisons form nearly 70 per cent. of the total population; in the bagnios the proportion is somewhat less. Of those admitted two-thirds are illiterate.

In establishments where the premises are too contracted to permit the organization of a school composed of a considerable number of individuals, the young are accepted in preference to those more advanced in age.

To the foregoing statistical *data* it may be added that, in a number of penitentiary establishments, besides the classes of elementary instruction, we have schools of design, of vocal and instrumental music, and of chemistry as applied to soils in our agricultural penal colonies.

Those prisoners alone are considered deserving of admission to the school who, besides, the aptness they show for profiting by it, have uniformly conducted themselves well. Attendance on school is not allowed to a prisoner in punishment, and he is always expelled from it when he is guilty of insubordination to the master.

The progress made in their studies by the prisoners forms an element in the annual statistical reports. The subjects taught are the same as those prescribed by the government in the programme of elementary instruction. The schools are under the general care of the school inspectors of the several districts.

Should some particular case seem to make it necessary, instruction may be carried to a greater extent than that specified above; but the director must, in each case, receive a special authorization from the minister.

In the prisons for juveniles attendance upon the school is obligatory, the prison school being divided into four elementary classes, precisely as the communal school is.

Musical instruction in these juvenile prisons receives much attention.

XXXII. Nearly all the prisons of Italy have small libraries, purchased by the minister of the interior, or given by the minister of public instruction, or contributed by philanthropic associations.

The greater part of the works composing these libraries are books written specially for prisoners and others selected from educational works, written in a pleasing style, and presenting clear and elementary notions of the national history, mechanics, moral tales, &c.

XXXIII. As soon as the prisoners acquire the ability to read they show a great inclination to it; but almost invariably they seek in books some diversion from their monotonous life or food for the imagination, rather than a fund of solid knowledge; consequently few of the books read by them are of a didactic character, but the greater part are novels or romances, of course always of an unimpeachable moral tendency.

XXXIV. In prisons recently constructed the systems of drainage are, without exception, those which architectural science has shown to be the best. In old prison buildings, provided they are such as ought to be preserved and will admit the introduction of improved penitentiary systems, new *latrines* and sewers are introduced of the most recent and best construction. In this respect, therefore, the prisons, either recently erected or which have undergone material alterations, are so constructed and arranged that the health of the prisoners is not endangered.

XXXV. In regard to the water supply of our prisons, the general direction has, from the local directors, positive and satisfying assurances both of its sufficiency and its quality.

On an average, there are required for cleaning from 8 to 10 liters *per capita*, not including what is needed for purposes of personal cleanliness and for drinking.

XXXVI. The ventilation of the old prisons is in a more or less satisfactory condition. In the new ones, and those which have undergone or are undergoing extensive repairs, we require an exact observance of all the rules of modern architectural science for the purification of the air, for its renovation, for regulating the heat, &c., to the end that the prisons be free from all exhalations injurious to the health of the prisoners permanently confined in premises which, in cases by no means rare, we could wish were larger.

XXXVII. Cleanliness is made an object of special attention in every prison, and whoever visits our penal establishments, where the arrangements of the buildings are satisfactory, will find their condition, in this respect, worthy of commendation, as a sufficient number of hands are detailed for this purpose, and the floors are swept daily, and even, in those parts which require it, two or three times a day.

XXXVIII. Without going into all the minute particulars, we can affirm that the convict, and even the prisoner awaiting trial, (when he does not wear his own clothing,) can, in our Italian prisons, keep himself neat and clean. He has a change of clothing in winter, and in summer he has two changes, of cotton or linen, with the necessary supply of shirts, socks, &c. Every one may satisfy himself of this by examining the list of articles furnished in the detention prisons as well as the penal establishments, which list is published by the general direction of prisons.

XXXIX. Re-affirming what was said above in answer to the thirty-fourth question, we simply add that the water-closets are fixed or movable as the conditions of the building permit; but we always seek to secure in them the quality most desirable, viz, that they be inodorous.

XL. The dormitories and cells are commonly lighted with oil; in some prisons they are lighted with petroleum; in others, more recently constructed, gas has been introduced.

XLI. In the prisons of the northern provinces of Italy heaters are used to soften the rigors of winter, and they are constructed according to the latest improvements of science.

XLII and XLIII. All the new bedsteads are of iron. The old ones are made of sail-cloth, and are suspended in the same manner as a hammock. The bed is composed of a tick filled with straw, corn-husks, or moss; a pillow or bolster, two hempen sheets, and one or two blankets, according to the rigor of the season. In the infirmaries each bed has, besides, a mattress and a linen or cotton counterpane.

XLIV. The regulations prescribe work every day, with the exception of half an hour in the morning for personal cleansing and another half hour in the evening before retiring.

The time of rising varies according to the seasons. In the winter it is at 7; in March and October at 6, and from 1st of April to 3d September at 5. Besides the two half hours above mentioned for rising and retiring, the prisoners enjoy a half hour's rest at each of the two daily meals, besides which they have an hour for walking in suitable yards; and if they attend school, they have an hour and a half for this purpose three times a week. On Sunday both exercise and school are continued for a longer time.

XLV. Every penitentiary has an infirmary, to which the sick prisoner is sent at the request of the medical officer of the establishment, who attends him during his sickness.

XLVI. The diseases most common are those of the digestive and respiratory organs and fevers. The diseases that cause proportionally the greater mortality are those which attack the organs of respiration. The mortality from fevers is less.

XLVII. The number of days passed by the prisoners in the infirmary is in the proportion of 4 to 5 per cent. of the number of days spent in prison by the entire prison population.

XLVIII. The mortality, viewed in relation to the average number of prisoners, is about 7 per cent. of the inmates on the first day of each year, while it is scarcely 5 per cent. of the total population for the whole year.

XLIX. In our penal establishments, unproductive or merely penal labor is unknown.

L. As penal labor, properly so called, does not exist with us, the general direction would be unable, reasoning from the national character, to express an opinion on the question whether, in Italy, this kind of labor would be deterrent.

LI and LII. For the reason above stated, the general direction is equally unable to express a judgment as to the possible moral and sanitary effects of strictly penal labor.

LIII. In our prisons, the usage varies as regards the mode of managing the prison labor; in some, it is managed by the administration, in others by contractors. For the last three or four years the general direction has sought, and with success, to find contractors for the labor of the prisoners; and already, in many penitentiaries, the labor has been let to contractors, as well as that of a sedentary kind, to wit, that which is done by the prisoners in workshops within the prisons, as that given to agriculture in the open air.

LIV. In respect of financial results, labor let to contractors is undoubtedly to be preferred; no political economist denies that government is, universally, the worst of producers.

As regards the discipline, though the general direction is convinced that the letting of the labor to contractors ought not to produce a bad effect upon the general discipline of a prison, because the director, freed from the numerous cares imposed upon him by the management of the industries, and by the sale of the merchandise, whether at retail or by wholesale, has more time left to devote to the moral improvement of the convicts, and to attend, without other preoccupations, to the internal order and security of the prison; yet about one-third of the directors, interrogated by the ministry of the interior, have shown themselves inclined to continue the system of managing the labor by the administration, or of restoring it, and the remaining two-thirds have approved, and do approve, the contract system recently introduced.

LV. The general direction, before adopting a universal rule, feels the necessity of continuing still further its observations and studies; too little time having, as yet, been given to the trial of the contract system, the experiences gained are neither solid nor regarded as sufficient to decide, absolutely, whether it is expedient to have a general contract for all the industries, or a special contract for each.

LVI and LVII. Very small indeed is the number of those committed to our prisons under the title of idlers, vagrants, or mendicants. Nor is the number great of those who leave our penal establishments without, at least, a rudimentary knowledge of some trade.

LVIII. The general regulations, by prescribing that, at the end of the first period of trial, every prisoner shall be introduced into a workshop to exercise some trade, that he shall not change it except in case of showing himself unfit for it, or the labor proves injurious to him, or he might, through the exercise of it, put in peril the quiet of the workshop or even the safety of the prison, together with the rewards accorded to the prisoner who goes on perfecting himself in his trade and producing a greater amount of good merchandise, are a clear proof how important it is regarded, among us, that the prisoner, on his discharge, be in possession of the power to earn for himself an honorable livelihood.

LIX. The criminal code does not inflict sentences of a short duration upon recidivists. Indeed, it regards as a recidivist even a person guilty of a minor offense, whenever he commits a new transgression. In that case, the relapse always brings upon the delinquent a relatively longer punishment.

LX. In 1871, of convicts sentenced to a punishment of more than a year's duration, the number of. recidivists was, for the men, 30 per cent.; for the women, 17 per cent.

LXI. Recidivists always receive severer punishments than one who has committed the same offense for the first time and has not, previously, undergone any criminal or correctional sentence.

LXII. In the detention prisons of some size, there are commonly sections destined to the imprisonment of civil debtors. In none of them is there wanting at least an apartment for whomever is imprisoned on the demand of his creditor.

In Italy, however, the number of those imprisoned for debt is exceedingly small. The maintenance of the debtors is a charge upon the creditors, and therefore his treatment differs from that of other prisoners maintained at the charge of the state.

LXIII. The cause of crimes of blood was, in 1871, the sentiment of revenge; of crimes against property, cupidity.

LXIV. Women form only 3 per cent. of the entire prison population in Italy.

LXV. When once a convict has been assigned to the prison in which he is to undergo his punishment, the discipline to which he is subjected looks not only to his safe-keeping, but also to his reformation.

LXVI. The general direction of prisons can only repeat, in reply to the present question, what it has already said in answer to the fourth question, to which, therefore, it begs to make reference.

LXVII and LXVIII. Certain religious associations possess funds that may be used in aid of liberated prisoners; an occasional patronage society exists in some of the cities of Italy. Such societies are what remains of institutions more or less ancient, but prior to 1859, which were religiously preserved and even protected by the Italian government; but there are none of any great importance, except at Milan, Turin, and Florence. The government has sought to extend institutions of this kind; but down to the present time, such institutions are too few in number and too limited in means to enable us to predict whether they will take root in our social soil, or, if so, whether their rules should be preserved or modified in order that the best fruit for which they were founded may be obtained from them.

LXIX. We refer for all answer to the present question to the statements made and the conclusions drawn in replying to the fourth question.

VI.—GREAT BRITAIN.

1. THE CONVICT PRISONS OF ENGLAND.

1. What is the number of government convict prisons in England, distinguishing between those designed for the different sexes ?

Eleven; eight exclusively for males, one mixed, and two exclusively for females.

2. What is the aggregate capacity of the convict prisons, (*a*,) the males, (*b*,) for the females?

Males, 8,764; females, 1,239; exclusive of infirmary cells, punishment cells, &c.

3. How many of these prisons are wholly upon the separate system?

Two, and parts of two others, but separate sleeping cells are general, except for invalids of certain classes, and some of the women.

4. In how many is there provision, after the first period of imprisonment, for other stages of discipline, including associated labor?

All but two of the above are prisons in which convicts are employed in associated labor.

5. How, in each class of prisons, is separation carried out, as regards work, exercise, (other than work,) attendance in chapel, and sleep?

By the construction of the prisons in some respects, and internal regulations in regard to others.

6. How many convict prisoners are placed (under contract with the local authorities) in prisons not belonging to the government?

None.

7. What is the aggregate number of cells?

Nine thousand and fifty-seven cells, exclusive of infirmary cells and punishment cells. This number is being added to considerably.

8. What are their ordinary dimensions?

In the model prison, at Pentonville, they are 13 feet by 7 feet by 9 feet, but in others they vary.

9. What furniture do they generally contain?

Blankets and bedding; washing utensils, &c.; eating utensils; table and stool; slate and books.

10. What are the rules, framed according to law, in regard to the certification of the cells, and their visitation by officers; and in respect to the visits to the prisons by the inspectors of prisons?

Their fitness for their purpose is certified by the surveyor general of prisons. They are visited by the directors of convict prisons, but not by the inspectors of prisons.

11. How far are these rules carried into effect?

Completely.

12. What has been the average number of prisoners in the convict prisons in the last five years?

Sixty-seven hundred and thirty-three males, and 1,100 females.

13. What are the chief internal regulations of these prisons?

See books of rules.

14. How are the officers appointed, and what is their tenure of office?

By the secretary of state for the home department, on the recommendation of the directors. Tenure of office so long as they are efficient and are wanted.

15. What qualifications are required, and in what manner are they tested?

Examination by civil-service commissioners; former character and experience, and actual probation.

16. What provision is made for superannuated and disabled officers?

By act of Parliament regulating civil-service pensions.

17. Are rewards employed to stimulate the prisoners to good conduct and industry? If so, of what kinds, and to what extent?

Yes. The mark system.

18. Is there a system of progressive classification? If so, how is it worked, and with what results?

Yes; (see rules for classification.) The results are considered satisfactory.

19. What punishments are used for breaches of prison rules or other misconduct?

Loss of marks, degradation of class, close confinement, reduction of diet, and corporal punishment.

20. Is corporal punishment ever employed?

Yes.

21. Is a full record of punishments kept?

Yes.

22. What kinds of offenses are most common?

It is difficult to say. They vary in different prisons.

23. In what convict prison last year was the number of punishments least, and what was it?

Millbank, (males,) Fulham, (females.)

24. To what circumstances is this comparative exemption from punishment attributable?

No accurate statement can be made on this point.

25. Are prisoners always allowed to make complaints of grievances, real or fancied? If so, to whom; and what attention is paid to their complaints? And what security is there that the complaints shall be properly examined?

Yes; to the foremen, and, if necessary, to the directors, or by petition to the secretary of state. They are always investigated.

26. How far are moral forces used in the discipline of the convict prisons; and what is found to be the comparative efficacy of moral and coercive agencies?

Moral forces are employed in preference to others, but the effect depends upon the individual prisoners.

27. Do the inmates of the convict prisons wear a party-colored dress?

Yes, in certain cases.

28. Is your own opinion for or against such a prison dress; and, in either case, upon what grounds?

For it, in those cases.

29. Is the mask worn in convict prisons? What is your judgment of its utility or the reverse?

No; I do not think it is of any use.

30. To what extent are chaplains employed, and of what denominations are they?

Church of England and Roman Catholic are employed in all convict prisons.

31. What religious services are held on Sunday, and during the week?

Two services on Sundays and daily morning prayers.

32. Are religious tracts and papers distributed to the convicts?

Books of this kind are supplied by government, and furnished to prisoners at the discretion of the chaplain.

33. Are volunteer working visitors, of either or both sexes, admitted into the prisons? If so, under what restrictions, and with what results?

Not generally.

34. In what spirit do the prisoners receive efforts for their moral and religious improvement?

See the chaplain's reports.

35. What are the regulations relating to the correspondence of prisoners?

Periodical letters to respectable acquaintances are allowed; the frequency varies according to the class.

36. What, in relation to visits from friends?

The same as the above.

37. Are the letters and visits of friends found to be beneficial to the prisoners or otherwise?

They are found to be beneficial.

S. Ex. 39——8

38. What proportion of prisoners are found, on their admission, either wholly illiterate or so imperfect in their knowledge of reading as to derive neither instruction nor entertainment from it?

See the directors' annual reports.

39. What provision is made for the schooling of prisoners?

A staff of schoolmasters is provided, and schooling takes place after working hours.

40. What branches are taught, and what progress is made therein?

Elementary education, and the progress is considered satisfactory.

41. Is there a library in each convict prison, including secular as well as religious books?

Yes.

42. What, about, is the average number of volumes?

About three or four volumes to each prisoner.

43. Do many of the prisoners show a fondness for reading?

Yes.

44. What time have they for reading?

Generally after work.

45. What, in a general way, are the sanitary arrangements and condition of the prisons?

Good. No epidemic or other diseases prevail in these prisons. They are generally in a high state of cleanliness, and the medical officers are required to examine and report frequently on these points.

46. What are the prevailing diseases?

See medical officers' annual reports.

47. What has been the average annual death-rate for the last five years?

Per 1,000—males, 13.7 ; females, 14.5.

48. In what prison last year was the rate of mortality smallest, and what was that rate?

The prisons must all be considered as one; no trustworthy inference can be drawn from considering them separately.

49. To what circumstances is this small rate attributable?

No answer.

50. Is there a distinction made in the convict prisons between penal and industrial labor? If so, what kinds of each are in use?

Convicts are all employed on industrial labor, unless oakum-picking, in which a few are employed, is considered penal labor.

51. Is the deterrent effect of penal labor found to be considerable? What is found to be its effect upon the health of the prisoners? What its moral influence?

No answer.

52. Is penal labor utilized in the convict prisons? If so, what is its average daily value in money *per capita?*

Crank, tread-wheel, &c., are not used for convicts.

53. Upon what principle is the industrial labor of the convict prisons organized? On a contract system or some other?

Not on the contract system. All work is performed directly under officers.

54. What have been the average annual net earnings per head of the prisoners in the last five years, exclusive of any portion allowed to the prisoner himself?

Annual earning per head, (last two years,) £22 18s. 1¾d. on the average number of prisoners.

55. In what prison, last year, were the net earnings the highest per head; and what was the amount?

Chatham and Portsmouth; annual earning from £38 16s. to £38 18s. on average number of prisoners.

56. What is the average number of prisoners there?

Chatham, 1,586; Portsmouth, 1,219.

57. What are the chief kinds of work there?

Engineering works, brick-making, &c.

58. To what circumstances are the comparatively high earnings attributable?

Suitability of the work.

59. Is a prisoner allowed any portion of his earnings? If so, how is that portion determined?

No.

60. Is overwork encouraged by the prisoner being allowed all the earnings so obtained?

No.

61. Do the prisoners work by the hour, or are tasks and piecework employed as far as practicable?

Generally by the hour.. Tasks encouraged when practicable.

62. How many hours each day, as measured either in time or by piecework, do the prisoners generally labor?

About eleven hours in summer and nine in winter.

63. What, during the last five years, has been the average annual cost of each prisoner, including food, clothing, and a proportionate share of salaries, and of the estimated rent, (say at the rate of 5 per cent. on the cost of the building,) and of every other expense whatever, but deducting the money received for prisoners' work, (if sold to the public,) or its value, if employed on public works belonging to the government, and unconnected with the prison?

For the last two years the net annual cost per prisoner each year has been £12 10s. 10d., cost of buildings not considered.

64. How much of this cost is put down for rent?

None.

65. What proportion of the prisoners had not learned a trade or calling prior to their committal?

There is no complete information. See returns in directors' annual report.

66. Is it made an object to impart to them the art of self-help; that is, the power to earn an honest living on their discharge; if so, in what manner, and with what results?

Yes; by employing them at suitable trades, &c.

67. What has been the average length of sentences for the last five years?

About seven years.

68. What has been the proportion of life sentences for the last five years?

See criminal returns.

69. Do prisoners for life receive the same treatment as other prisoners?

Yes; in every respect.

70. What portion of the prisoners committed in each of the last five years had been in a convict prison before?

No regular returns. Return in directors' report for 1869, page 5, gives the necessary information at a certain period, (April, 1869.)

71. What portion had been previously committed to any prison?

No answer.

72. From what *data* have the recommittals been ascertained?

From actual records of men still in prison.

73. What proportion of the prisoners were minors when committed ?
See return of ages in annual report of directors.

74. Is deterrence or reformation made the primary object ?
Both.

75. Are the prisoners able, by industry and good conduct, to shorten
their periods of confinement; if so, to what extent ?
Yes; one-fourth of the time on public works.

76. What do you think of the policy of substituting unlimited for
limited periods of imprisonment, to which criminals are sentenced, so
as to make the time of liberation depend on the prisoner's moral condition, and the reasonable expectation of his not relapsing into crime?
Prefer limited periods.

77. Under present circumstances, are prisoners often set free before
their liberation can be considered safe to society, or really beneficial to
themselves; whether because their moral cure cannot be deemed complete, or because they have not the means of getting an honest livelihood, either for want of a sufficient knowledge of some handicraft, or
from physical or mental weakness ?
Probably they are.

78. On the other hand, are prisoners often detained beyond the time
when it is fully believed that they can safely be liberated ?
It is impossible to say.

79. Is the "intermediate system" for gradually preparing prisoners
for liberation in use; if so, to what extent and with what results?
The whole system is designed gradually to prepare prisoners for liberation.

80. Do the mass of prisoners, as a matter of fact, leave the prisons
better or worse, morally, than they entered them ?
Better, it is believed.   See the chaplains' reports.

81. Are female prisoners, needing such instructions, taught to cook
and to sew; and, generally, are efforts made to enable a man or woman,
on liberation, to avoid a wasteful expenditure, and to turn their wages
to the best account ?
Taught to work; cooking not specially taught in domestic economy.

82. Is any attempt made to give the prisoners good tastes, such as
that for music, so as to diminish the danger of their falling, when liberated, into habits of drunkenness, or other debasing pleasures ?
So far as church services go.

83. Is any effort made to induce the prisoners, from their share of
their earnings, to help to support their families, or to make restitution
to those whom they have robbed or otherwise injured ?
They devote their labor to the benefit of society, whom they have
injured, and whom they put to heavy expense.

84. If not, is there any other way in which they can practically give
that evidence of moral improvement which is afforded by a willingness
to forego selfish advantages for the benefit of others ?
No.   They have only bare necessaries, and, therefore, cannot forego
any advantages.

85. Are efforts made to keep up the domestic ties of prisoners, such
as allowing them to see members of their family, from time to time,
except when, under the circumstances, these ties must be hurtful ?
Yes.

86. What agencies are employed to provide discharged prisoners
with work, in order to prevent their relapse; and with what results ?
Discharged prisoners' aid societies.

87. Are any other efforts made through prisoners' aid societies, refuges, or otherwise, to encourage discharged prisoners, desirous of doing well, and to prevent their relapse?
Yes.

88. What means are taken to trace prisoners after their discharge, in order to ascertain what is their subsequent career?
Registration of criminals.

89. General and miscellaneous remarks.

A view of the English convict system, which embraces the prisons in England only, is in a great degree imperfect, because transportation has been such an integral part of the system, and though no convicts have been sent to Australia for some years, the system has had the effect of withdrawing many of the prisoners who were most likely to reform and have reformed, and left those who were more likely to be again convicted.

ERON CARU CAPLER,
Chairman of Directors, and Surveyor General of Prisons.

2. BOROUGH AND COUNTY JAILS IN ENGLAND.

1. What is the whole number of borough jails in England?
Thirty-five.

2. What of county jails?
Eighty-seven.

3. What, if any, is the exact distinction between these two classes of prisons; and what the specific functions of each?
None, except that the county prisons are governed by the county magistrates, and the borough prisons by the borough magistrates.

4. What is the aggregate number of prisoners which the two classes of jails are together calculated to receive?
Twenty-seven thousand one hundred and sixty-nine.

5. What, about, is the average period of confinement?
Somewhat under one month.

6. About what portion of the prisoners are confined for periods not exceeding one month?
About three-fourths.

7. About what portion for periods of from one month to six months?
About one-fourth.

8. About what portion for periods exceeding six months?
Less than one per thousand.

9. Is there a separation of the prisoners—complete or partial—in any of the prisons, by day as well as by night?
As a rule, all prisoners are separated by night, where there is sufficient cell accommodation. Prisoners in many prisons work to a certain extent in association, but under such supervision as the governors consider sufficient to prevent communication.

10. What, in general, are the dimensions of the cells; distinguishing cells used during the night only from those used both by day and night?
The cells in the several prisons vary from about 400 to 1,000 cubic feet. As a rule the smaller cells are used for sleeping-cells only, or are certified for very limited periods.

11. What is their ordinary furniture?
Bedstead or removable hammock, table, and stool, washing apparatus, and chamber-pot, the last utensil being omitted in cases where the cells contain a water-closet.

12. What are the rules, framed according to law, in regard to the

certifications of the cells used both by day and night, and their visitation by officers; and in respect to the visits to the jails by the inspectors of prisons?

Vide clause 18, prisons act, 1865, as to certificates of cells. The visitation of officers is regulated by the rules of the several prisons, and inspectors are required to visit each prison at least once a year.

13. How far are these rules carried into effect?

Complied with in all respects.

14. Do the prisoners work in the cells or in association?

Both in cells and association, according to the capabilities of the prison and the character of the work required.

15. Is the mask worn in any of the prisons?

In very few.

16. Has it been discontinued in any where it was formerly worn; if so, with what effect?

Not since the present inspectors assumed office.

17. What is your own judgment as to its utility or the reverse?

We think but slightly of its utility.

18. What has been the aggregate average number of prisoners confined in the borough and county prisons, jointly, for the last five years?

We have no records by which to furnish the necessary reply to this query as to a five years' aggregate average.

19. Are the internal rules and regulations of all these prisons the same; if not all the same, do they differ materially?

The rules of all prisons are founded on the prisons act, 1865, by the respective county and borough visiting justices, and they do not differ materially.

20. Can you supply copies of some of the best?

Copies of rules of three prisons are herewith forwarded.

21. How are the officers appointed; and what is their tenure of office?

Officers are appointed by the visiting justices, and are retained at their pleasure.

22. What provision, if any, is made for superannuated and disabled officers?

Vide clause 15, part 1, prisons act, 1865.

23. Are rewards employed to stimulate the prisoners to good conduct and industry; if so, of what kinds, and to what extent?

Gratuities may be given under clause 42, same act.

24. Is there a system of progressive classification; if so, how is it worked, and with what results?

This system obtains in some few prisons, and is considered to work well.

25. What punishments are in use for breaches of prison rules and other misconduct?

Vide clauses 50 to 60, schedule 1, prisons act, 1865.

26. Is corporal punishment ever employed for criminal offenses?

Yes.

27. Is a full record of punishments kept in every prison?

Yes.

28. What kinds of offenses are most common?

Idleness and insolence.

29. In what large prison last year, and in what small one, were the numbers of punishments least; and what were they?

Durham County prison, and Lincoln County prison. In the former the punishments for prison offenses, as follows:

	Males.	Females.
Whipping..	2	..
Solitary, or dark cells.............................	29	18
Stoppage of diet	27	2
	58	20

In the latter, solitary, or dark cells, 2 males.

30. To what circumstances are these comparative exemptions from punishment attributable?

So many different causes may contribute to this result in different prisons, that it would be invidious to give a categorical reply.

31. Are prisoners always allowed to make complaints; if so, to whom, and what security is there that the complaints shall be properly examined?

Yes; to inspectors of prisons, visiting justices and governor; on the supposition that these gentlemen do their duty, all complaints receive attention.

32. How far are moral forces used in the discipline of the prisons, and with what effect? What is found to be the comparative efficacy of moral and coercive agencies?

We believe that the chaplains are, as a rule, very assiduous in their endeavors to improve the minds and character of the prisoners, and that the governors adopt the same course, and in our opinion with good effect. The comparative efficacy of moral and coercive agencies depends so much on the individual temperament of prisoners that no conclusive reply can be given.

33. Do the prisoners wear a party-colored dress? What is your judgment as to the necessity or utility of such a garb?

Vide clause 23, schedule 1, prisons act, 1865. This dress is not necessarily party-colored, though in many instances it is so. In our opinion, a distinctive dress is all that is required.

34. To what extent are the prisons provided with chaplains?

Clause 10, part 1, prisons act, 1865, is complied with.

35. What religious services are held on a Sunday, and during the week?

[This question was passed by the inspectors without answer, no doubt from inadvertence.]

36. Is there a Sunday-school in any of the prisons?

We are not aware.

37. Are religious tracts and papers distributed to the prisoners?

Yes; at the discretion of the chaplain.

38. Are volunteer working visitors, of either or both sexes, admitted within the prisons; if so, under what restrictions, and with what results?

Not that we are aware.

39. In what spirit are the efforts made for the moral and religious improvement of the prisoners received by them?

As a rule, the efforts of the chaplain are received in a becoming manner.

40. What are the regulations relating to the correspondence of prisoners?

Prisoners, as a rule, are permitted to write and receive a letter (subject to the inspection of the governor) after the conclusion of the first

three months, and once during each subsequent three months of detention. In special cases the governor has power to relax this rule.

41. What, in relation to the visits of friends?

The same rules as above generally apply to the visits of friends.

42. Are the letters and visits of friends found to be beneficial or
otherwise?

In our opinion they are generally beneficial.

43. What proportion of the prisoners are found, on admission, either
unable to read, or to read so imperfectly as to derive neither instruction
nor entertainment?

Out of the total committals for the year ending September, 1870, viz,
157,223, 53,265 prisoners could neither read nor write, and 98,482 could
read, or read and write imperfectly.

44. What are the provisions relating to the schooling of prisoners?
What branches are taught, and what progress is made therein.

Vide clause 53, schedule 1, prisons act, 1865, the provisions of which
are carried out.

45. Is there a library in each prison, including secular as well as
religious books?

Yes.

45 *bis.* Do the prisoners show a fondness for reading?

Generally.

46. What time do they have for reading?

The usual time is during the dinner-hour, and after the conclusion of
their daily labor till bed-time.

47. What, in a general way, are the sanitary arrangements and condition of the prisons?

Satisfactory.

48. What are the prevailing diseases?

If one class prevail, it is probably chest affections, a great proportion
of the more severe of which cases might be traced to predisposition
previous to admission.

49. What has been the average death-rate for the last five years?

Same answer as last.

50. In what large prison and in what small prison was the rate of
mortality smallest, and what, in each instance, was that rate?·

We have no *data.*

51. To what circumstances are these small rates attributable?

Same answer as last.

52. Is a distinction made in any or all of the prisons between penal
and industrial labor? If so, what kinds of each are in use?

Yes. Clause 19, part 1, prisons act, 1865, which is carried out in all
prisons, determines the character of penal labor. Industrial labor consists of various kinds of weaving, mat-making both by hand and loom,
oakum-picking, teasing hair and cocoa-fiber, and the various trades,
viz.: tailoring, shoemaking, carpentering, gardening, blacksmith work,
&c.

53. Is the deterrent effect of penal labor found to be considerable, as
shown by the fewness of recommittals? What is found to be its effect
upon the health of the prisoners? What its moral influence?

We believe that it is so; but to what extent it tends to the "fewness
of recommittals" we are unable to state, as all prisoners sentenced to
hard labor are, as a rule, (in compliance with clause 34, schedule 1,
prisons act, 1865,) placed at hard labor for the first three months at
least after conviction, and for the whole of their sentence if not
exceeding three months. As a general rule, the health of the prisoners

does not suffer by this form of labor. In individual instances where it does, the surgeon of the jail has full power to alter the character of the prisoner's punishment. As to its moral influence, we believe, as stated above, that it has a deterrent effect.

54. Is penal labor utilized in the prisons? If so, what is its average daily value in money, *per capita?*

Penal labor (or hard labor of the first class) is in many prisons turned to account, but is not as remunerative as-hard labor, (second class or industrial labor.) We have no means of giving the daily average value per head.

55. Upon what principle is the industrial labor of the prisons organized.

Task-work is required in some instances, in others so many hours' labor *per diem.*

56. What have been the average annual net earnings, per head, of the prisoners in the last five years, exclusive of any portion allowed to the prisoner himself?

We have no *data.*

57. In what large prison last year, and in what small prison, were the net earnings the highest per head, and what were the amounts?

Wakefield County prison, £6 13s. 9¾d.; Grantham Borough prison, £5 2s. 9d.

58. What is the average number of prisoners in each of these prisons?

In Wakefield, 1,290 was the daily average for the year 1870; and in Grantham, 9.

59. What are the chief kinds of work in each?

In Wakefield, rope and oakum beating, hand-weaving with heavy looms, stone-breaking, tread-wheel, the power of which is applied to industrial purposes; mat-making, to which steam-power is applied to a great extent; industrial trades, &c. In Grantham, stone-breaking, wood-cutting, and mat-making, &c.

60. To what circumstances, in each case, are the comparatively high earnings attributable?

In Wakefield to the employment of steam-machinery principally; and in Grantham to a ready and profitable market for the sale of prison produce.

61. Is a prisoner allowed any portion of his earnings? If so, how is that portion determined?

As a rule prisoners are not allowed a portion of their earnings, but well-conducted prisoners who have served any length of time generally receive a small gratuity on discharge.

62. Is overwork encouraged by the prisoner being allowed all the earnings so obtained?

Such is not the rule.

63. Do the prisoners work by the hour, or are tasks and piecework employed as far as practicable?

Both plans are in use.

64. How many hours each day, as measured either in time or by piecework, do the prisoners generally labor?

Not more than ten hours, nor less than six, in accordance with clause 34, prisons act.

65. What, during the same time, has been the average annual cost of each prisoner, including food, clothing, and a proportionate share of salaries, and of every other expense, except rent; but deducting the money received for prisoners' work (if sold to the public) or its value, if done for government?

The average annual cost of each prisoner varies very considerably in the several prisons, ranging from £10 7s. 3d. in the county prison, Montgomery, to £128 14s. 4d. in the county prison at Oakham.

66. What proportion of the prisoners had not learned a trade or calling prior to their committal?

Out of 157,223 prisoners committed during the year 1870, 20,219 had no occupation.

67. It is made an object to impart to them the art of self-help; that is, the power to earn an honest living on their discharge? If so, in what manner, and with what results?

Prisoners sentenced for any lengthened period have generally facilities for learning some trade or occupation.

68. What has been the general length of sentences for the last five years?

We have no means of stating.

69. Are repeated short sentences for minor offenses found to be of much use; if not, what remedy would you suggest?

We are of opinion that repeated short sentences for minor offenses are not of much use, and that the length of sentence should, as a rule, be increased on every successive conviction.

70. What do you think of the policy of substituting unlimited for limited periods of imprisonment, to which criminals are sentenced, so as to make the time of liberation depend on the prisoner's moral condition and on the reasonable expectation of his not relapsing into crime?

We believe that the difficulties attending such a policy would be insuperable.

71. Under present circumstances are prisoners often set free before their liberation can be considered safe to society or really beneficial to themselves; whether because their moral cure cannot be deemed complete, or because they have not the means of getting an honest livelihood, either from want of a sufficient knowledge of some handicraft or from physical or mental weakness?

Prisoners must be released according to the existing law at the termination of their respective sentences.

72. On the other hand, are prisoners often detained beyond the time when it is fully believed that they could safely be liberated?   ·

Same answer as last.

73. Are any of the prisoners confined for debt; if so, is the number large?

Yes; but only under the provisions of the act for the abolition of imprisonment for debt. (32 and 33 Vict., chap. 62.) The numbers so committed are small.

74. What is the longest term for which they are held?

The length of sentences is regulated by the above act.

75. Are they treated like other prisoners or differently?

Generally differently.

76. What has been the average proportion of recommittals for the last five years, and upon what *data* have they been ascertained?

We have no means of stating.

77. Are sentences increased on reconviction?

Not necessarily so.

78. About what proportion of the inmates owe their committal, it is believed, directly or indirectly, to drink?

We have no *data*.

79. What proportion were minors when committed?

Same answer as last.

80. What proportion were orphans by the loss of one or both parents?
Same as last.

81. What is the average proportion of the sexes?
In the year 1870 were admitted 116,240 males and 40,983 females.

82. Is deterrence or reformation generally made the primary object?
In the shorter sentences, deterrence; in the longer sentences, both systems are combined.

83. Is the "intermediate system" for gradually preparing prisoners for liberation in use; if so, to what extent and with what results?
The "intermediate system," as in use in certain Irish government prisons, is not adopted in either county or borough prisons in this country.

84. Do the mass of the prisoners, as a matter of fact, leave the prisons better or worse morally than they entered them?
We believe that, as a rule, prison discipline is beneficial.

85. Are female prisoners, needing such instruction, taught to cook and to sew; and generally are efforts made to enable a man or woman, on liberation, to avoid a wasteful expenditure, and to turn their wages to the best account?
When the length of sentence admits, female prisoners are generally taught cooking, washing, and sewing.

86. Is any attempt made to give the prisoners good tastes, such as that for music, so as to diminish the danger of their falling, when liberated, into habits of drunkenness or other debasing pleasures?
Not aware of any prison in which music is taught except for devotional purposes.

87. Is any effort made to induce the prisoners, from their share of their earnings, to help to support their families or to make restitution to those whom they have robbed or otherwise injured?
Not that we are aware.

88. If not, is there any other way in which they can practically give that evidence of moral improvement which is afforded by a willingness to forego selfish advantages for the benefit of others?
By willing industry and cheerful obedience to the rules of the prison and the orders of their officers.

89. Are efforts made to keep up the domestic ties of prisoners, such as allowing them to see members of their family, from time to time, except when, under the circumstances, these ties must be hurtful?
Yes.

90. What agencies are employed to provide discharged prisoners with work, in order to prevent their relapse, and with what results?
Prisoners' aid societies, reformatories, training ships for boys, &c., of all of which we believe the visiting justices to avail themselves as far as practicable.

91. Are any other efforts made, by means of the visits of officers or through prisoners' aid societies, refuges, or otherwise, to encourage discharged prisoners desirous of doing well, and to prevent their relapse?
Yes.

92. What means are taken to trace prisoners after their discharge in order to ascertain what is their subsequent career?
To enable the police to carry out such duties, descriptive returns and photographs are forwarded to Scotland Yard.

HENRY BRISCOE,
T. FOLLIOTT POWELL,
Inspectors of Prisons.

3. REFORMATORIES OF GREAT BRITAIN.

1. What is the number of reformatories in Great Britain?
December 31, 1871, 65.
2. What quantity of land is generally attached to each reformatory?
No fixed amount; quantity varies from 1 to 400 acres.
3. What is the aggregate amount of land belonging to or rented by them?
About 4,000 acres.
4. How are the funds provided for their support?
Allowance from treasury, 6s. per week per head, contributions from county or borough rates, industrial profits, and voluntary subscriptions.
5. Is the principle of the responsibility of parents for the full or partial support of their children, while inmates of the institution, recognized and enforced? If so, what is the average annual sum per inmate received from this source?
Parents are chargeable, under the reform-school act, up to 5s. per week for each child. The majority are too poor to contribute. Payments, when practicable, average 1s. 6d. per week. Rate of assessment, 1d. in 1s. of wages.
6. What is the total average sum?
About £4,000 per annum.
7. What is found to be the effect of the practical application of this principle?
It is a check on the parents' neglect of their children, and counteracts the attraction which the advantages of the reformatory might possibly present.
8. What are the ordinary kinds of work in the reformatories?
Farm-work and gardening, tailoring, shoemaking, turning, carpentry, wood-chopping, and, in some, weaving or printing. For girls, laundry, house, and needle work.
9. What, about, has been the net average annual value per inmate, of the work; distinguishing that of work employed on articles sold to the public from that of work done for the reformatory?
Such a distinction is impracticable; the same workshops, boys, and teachers being employed for both sorts of work.
The average industrial profits will be about £2 per head per annum, (not quite 1s. per week.)
10. In what large reformatory, last year, and in what small one, were the net earnings the highest per head; and what were the amounts?
Of large reformatories. 1870: Highest, Red Hill, £1,529 profit; lowest, North Lancashire, £237. Number of inmates: Red Hill, 300; North Lancashire, 100.
The amount of industrial profit has nothing to do with the size of the school. Many small schools make a larger return than some of the large ones, from having better opportunities for the employment of their inmates in the neighborhood of the school.
Profits depend on the locality of the school, the demand for labor, the quality of the soil, the capital sunk in drainage and improvements, the market for the articles manufactured, &c.
11. What is the average number of inmates in each of these two reformatories?
12. To what circumstances, in each case, are the comparatively high earnings attributable?
See answers to previous question.

13. What has been the average annual cost of each inmate, including food, clothing, and a proportionate share of salaries, of the estimated rent, and of every other expense whatever; deducting the money received for work, but not the payment by the parents?

Boys—England, 1870 : £18 17s. 9d.; Scotland, £17 1s. 3d. Girls—England £17 17s. 10d.; Scotland, £13 13s. 6d.

14. What has been the total average annual cost, so reckoned, of all the inmates?

1870. £108,035 6s.

15. Is the family or congregate system in use?

Most of the schools are on the associated system. Red Hill, Northeastern, Calder Farm are on the family or distribution plan.

16. For what kind of offenses are the children usually committed?

Mostly for theft; in some cases for arson and homicide.

17. What is the process of committal?

Mostly summary conviction before two magistrates; also sentence by courts of assize or quarter sessions.

18. What are the usual periods of sentence?

The act prescribes a minimum of two years and a maximum of five years. The average period about three and a half or four years.

19. Must the full term be served out, or may the children be discharged, as reformed, prior to the expiration of their sentence?

The inmates of a reform school can be placed out on probation, under a license, after eighteen months' detention.

20. If they can be so discharged, with whom is this power lodged?

They can be discharged at any time by the secretary of state for the home department.

21. Are the children, who have been discharged as reformed, considered still, to some extent, under the care of the institution, so that they can be returned to it if not doing well, or is their discharge unconditional?

While on license they can be recalled to the school at any time, if they misconduct themselves, or the situation they have been placed in proves to be unsuitable. When once discharged they are free from any further control.

22. Within what ages are children admissible?

Maximum age, 16; minimum, 10, except for children who have been before convicted, or who are tried before courts of assize or quarter session.

23. Are both sexes received into the same institution?

No; boys' reformatories and girls' reformatories are entirely distinct.

24. In what ways are the children disposed of on their discharge?

Emigration, (mostly to Canada;) enlistment in the army; merchant service at sea. The majority to trades or farm, or domestic service.

25. How is the time divided in regard to labor, schooling, sleep, and recreation?

School and work about ten hours daily; sleep, meals, washing, prayers, and recreation about fourteen.

26. Is the discipline most like that of a prison or of a family school?

Everything prison-like is entirely avoided. There are no wardens, and, in most cases, no walls.

27. Do the inmates sleep in common dormitories or in separate apartments? If in common dormitories, what supervision is had over them?

In common dormitories, usually holding from ten to twenty-five, (some are larger.) One of the assistant teachers sleeps in an adjoining room, or in a cubicle parted from the dormitory. The master usually has supervision of one or two of the rooms from his own room by a window.

28. What proportion of the children are found wholly illiterate on committal?

Probably about one-third, but we have no exact return.

29. What branches of learning are taught; and how far are the children carried therein?

Reading, writing, ciphering, In some cases drawing and geography; school-ships, a little navigation.

30. Has each reformatory a library, including secular as well as religious books? If so, do the children make much use of the books? What time do they have for reading?

Most reformatories have a lending library of both sorts of books. They are generally much used on Sundays and on winter evenings.

31. Has each institution a chaplain? If so, what are his duties, and how much of his time is devoted to them?

Of the Protestant schools, three, Red Hill, Castle Howard, and Woodbury Hill, are superintended by a clergyman. A few others have a chaplain attached, who visits, instructs, &c., once or more in the week. All Catholic schools have a chaplain to visit, receive confessions, &c.

32. If there be no chaplain, how is his place supplied? ·

The superintendent, or schoolmaster, or both, give religious instruction.

33. What rewards are employed as a *stimulus* to good conduct?

Privileges of food or liberty; distinctions of dress, money, or other prizes.

34. Is the principle of progressive classification in use? If so, how is it worked, and with what effect?

The boys (or girls) rise from class to class by proficiency and merit.

35. What disciplinary punishments are employed?

For small offenses, fines and loss of privileges, or partial deprivations of food; for serious ones, confinement in a cell or corporal punishment.

36. In what large reformatory, last year, and in what small one, were the numbers of punishments least; and what were they?

[No answer.]

37. To what circumstances are these comparative exemptions from punishment, in each instance, attributable?

[No answer.]

38. Are the antecedents of the inmates made matter of record?

Yes.

39. How far is their history, while connected with the institution, recorded?

A monthly or quarterly report is usually drawn up and entered in the "register," or each fault is noted in this on the date of its occurrence.

40. To what extent, and in what ways, are a knowledge of, interest in, and care over them, kept up after their discharge; and with what results?

The managers of each school are required to report for three successive years, after each inmate's discharge, on his (or her) character and circumstances. A yearly return is obtained also from each prison of any offender in jail during the year who is recognized as having been in a reformatory. By this the managers' reports are checked.

41. What proportion of the children are orphans by the loss of one or both parents?

Of the 1,612 admitted in 1870, 591 were orphans.

42. What proportions are otherwise outside of the normal family re-

lation, by reason of having vagrant, vicious, or criminal parents, or from any other circumstances?
[No answer.]

43. What in general is the sanitary state of each reformatory as regards food, drainage, ventilation, water supply, hospital accommodation, means and enforcement of personal cleanliness, &c., &c.?
Good.

44. What are the prevalent diseases, and what the average death-rate?
Disease is scarcely known. There are a few cases of consumption, and some of scrofula. The average death-rate is under 5 per thousand, (or one-half per cent.)

45. In what large reformatory, and in what small one, were the rates of mortality smallest; and what were they?
[No answer.]

46. To what circumstances are these small rates attributable?
[No answer.]

47. What are the regulations regarding the correspondence of the inmates and the visits of friends; and what influence are these found to exert upon them?
Letters are allowed once in two or three months. Visits usually once a month, or two months. The influence is good, natural affections being kept up.

48. What is the average period of continuance in the reformatories?
About three or three and a half years.

49. Is there any special arrangement for training officers for reformatories?
There is no training institution. But the treasury allows for the training of a man £40, and of a woman £27, for twelve months, if received into a good reformatory. Very few are trained.

50. What proportion of the inmates are believed, on their liberation, to be reformed; and upon what *data* is this belief grounded?
About 75 per cent., average. In some schools from 85 to 95 per cent. In some under 55 per cent. The *data* are furnished by the returns and reports. See question 40.

51. General and miscellaneous remarks.
The reform-schools act, the rules and regulations, and the printed report of the inspectors for 1870, will supply the above particulars and much extra information in matters of detail.

Rev. SYDNEY TURNER,
Her Majesty's Inspector of Reform-Schools, 15 Parliament Street.

4. INDUSTRIAL SCHOOLS IN GREAT BRITAIN.

1. What is the number of industrial schools in Great Britain?
December 31, 1871, ninety-two.

2. What quantity of land is generally attached to each reformatory?
Most industrial schools are in towns, and have no land attached. Some few are in the country, and have a garden or a few acres of farm land.

3. What is the aggregate amount of land belonging to them?
Probably about 100 acres.

4. How are the funds provided for their support?
Treasury allowances, English schools, 5s. per week; Scotch schools, 4s. 6d. per week. Voluntary subscriptions. Payments from county or school rates; industrial earnings.

5. Is the principle of the responsibility of parents for the full or partial support of their children, while inmates of the institution, recognized and enforced? If so, what is the average annual sum per inmate received from this source?

The law makes the same provision as in the case of reformatories. In Scotland the parish is liable to contribute if the child has been chargeable within three months.

6. What is the total average sum?

Including payments by parishes in Scotland, about £5,000 per annum.

7. What is found to be the effect of the practical application of this principle?

8. What are the ordinary kinds of work in the reformatories?

See answer to questions on reformatories.

9. What, about, has been the net average annual value per inmate of the work; distinguishing that of work employed on articles sold to the public from that of work done for the reformatory?

About £1 per annum per head, or less than 6d. per week.

10. In what large reformatory, last year, and in what small one were the net earnings the highest per head; and what were the amounts?

The children are mostly too young for their work to be profitable.

11. What is the average number of inmates in each of these two reformatories?

[No answer.]

12. To what circumstances, in each case, are the comparatively high earnings attributable?

13. What has been the average annual cost of each inmate, including food, clothing, and a proportionate share of salaries, of the estimated rent, and of every other expense whatever, deducting the money received for work, but not the payment by the parents?

Industrial schools are of two sorts. One class are for boarders only; the other for boarders and day scholars who are only partially fed. In these last the cost per head cannot be accurately distributed. In boarding schools, the cost is, for England: boys, about £17 per annum; for girls, £16; for Scotland, boys and girls, about £12.

14. What has been the total average annual cost, so reckoned, of all the inmates?

In 1870, £188,788 14s. 10d.

15. Is the family or congregate system in use?

The congregate.

16. For what kind of offenses are the children usually committed?

Vagrancy, begging, companions of thieves, &c., up to fourteen years of age; petty theft, up to twelve years. (See industrial school act, § 14.)

17. What is the process of committal?

By two magistrates in England; one magistrate in Scotland. (See act.)

18. What are the usual periods of sentence?

From three to seven years, or up to sixteen years of age.

19. Must the full term be served out, or may the children be discharged, as reformed, prior to the expiration of their sentence?

20. If they can be so discharged, with whom is this power lodged?

The rules are the same as for reformatories. See answer for these.

21. Are the children who have been discharged as reformed considered still, to some extent, under the care of the institution, so that they can be returned to it if not doing well; or is their discharge unconditional?

Same as for reformatories.

22. Within what ages are children admissible?

The act prescribes no minimum age; but practically very few are sent under six years of age. The Treasury makes no allowance for any younger than six; maximum age, fourteen.

23. Are both sexes received into the same institution? If so, are they kept entirely separate, or is association permitted within certain limits?

Some schools receive children of both sexes, but most are for either boys or girls; when both sexes are received they usually meet and associate at meals, prayers, and school hours.

24. In what ways are the children disposed of on their discharge?

25. How is the time divided in regard to labor, schooling, sleep, and recreation?

26. Is the discipline most like that of a prison or of a family school?

27. Do the inmates sleep in common dormitories or in separate apartments? If in common dormitories, what supervision is had over them?

In all these points the answers are the same as for reformatories.

28. What proportion of the children are found wholly illiterate on committal?

Probably more than half; we have no exact returns.

29. What branches of learning are taught; and how far are the children carried therein?

Reading, writing, ciphering.

30. Has each industrial school a library, including secular as well as religious books? If so, do the children make much use of the books? What time do they have for reading?

Yes; Sundays and winter evenings.

31. Has each institution a chaplain? If so, what are his duties, and how much of his time is devoted to them?

The Middlesex industrial school has a chaplain who officiates in the chapel of the institution, and superintends the school-teaching and correspondence.

32. If there be no chaplain, how is his place supplied?

The superintendent conducts the weekly prayers, and gives religious instructions. On Sunday the children attend some church or chapel.

33. What rewards are employed as a *stimulus* to good conduct?

34. Is the principle of progressive classification in use? If so, how is it worked, and with what effect?

35. What disciplinary punishments are employed?

The same as for reformatory schools.

36. In what large industrial school, last year, and in what small one, were the numbers of punishments least; and what were they?

[No answer.]

37. To what circumstances are these comparative exemptions from punishment, in each instance, attributable?

[No answer.]

38. Are the antecedents of the inmates made matter of record?

39. How far is their history, while connected with the institution, recorded?

40. To what extent, and in what ways, are a knowledge of, interest in, and care over them, kept up after their discharge; and with what results?

Same as for reformatory schools.

41. What proportion of the children are orphans by the loss of one or both parents?

42. What proportions are otherwise outside of the normal family rela-

tion, by reason of having vagrant, vicious, or criminal parents, or from any other circumstances ?

The whole number admitted in 1870 was 2,599 ; of these were orphans, 398 ; illegitimate, 164 ; lost one parent, 843 ; deserted by parents, 340 ; one or both parents criminal, 165.

43. What, in general, is the sanitary state of each industrial school as regards food, drainage, ventilation, water supply, hospital accommodation, means and enforcement of personal cleanliness, &c., &c. ?

Good.

44. What are the prevalent diseases, and what the average death-rate ?

A large proportion of the children, especially of those sent to Scotch schools, are scrofulous and consumptive ; but the death-rate for 1870 was only 1.75 (1¾) per cent.

45. In what large industrial school, and in what small one, were the rates of mortality smallest ; and what were they ?

[No answer.]

46. To what circumstances are these small rates attributable ?

[No answer.]

47. What are the regulations regarding the correspondence of the inmates and the visits of friends ; and what influence are these found to exert upon them ?

Same as for reformatory schools.

48. What is the average period of continuance in the industrial schools ?

Five or six years.

49. Is there any special arrangement for training officers for industrial schools ?

No.

50. What proportion of the inmates are believed on their liberation to be reformed ; and upon what *data* is this belief grounded ?

Of 1,729, discharged in 1867, 1868, 1869, we had the following results : December 31, 1870, died since discharged, 44 ; doing well, 1,175 ; doubtful, 138 ; unknown, 270 ; convicted of crime, 102. The *data* are the same as for reformatories.

51. General and miscellaneous remarks.

The industrial school act, the inspectors' annual report, and the rules and regulations for industrial schools, will afford further details.

SYDNEY TURNER,
Her Majesty's Inspector of Industrial Schools, 15 Parliament street.

VII.—IRELAND.

THE CONVICT PRISONS OF IRELAND.

1. What is the number of government convict prisons in Ireland, distinguishing between those designed for the different sexes ?

The whole number is four—three male and one female.

2. What is the aggregate capacity of the convict prisons, (*a*,) the males, (*b*,) for the females ?

Male: Mountjoy, 496 ; Spike Island, 712 ; Lusk, 100—1,308. Female: Mountjoy, 547.

3. How many of these prisons are wholly upon the separate system ?

4. In how many is there provision, after the first period of imprisonment, for other stages of discipline, including associated labor ?

The Mountjoy male and female prisons are on the separate system, but after the first stages of imprisonment, the prisoners are worked in association by day.

5. How, in each class of prisons, is separation carried out, as regards work, exercise, (other than work,) attendance in chapel, and sleep?

See copies of the daily routine of the respective prisons forwarded herewith.

6. How many convict prisoners are placed (under contract with the local authorities) in prisons not belonging to the government?

None.

7. What is the aggregate number of cells?

Mountjoy, male, 496; Spike Island: ward cells, 688; light punishment cells, 22; dark cells, 6—716. Lusk: no cellular accommodation. Total, 1,212. Mountjoy, female, 505.

8. What are their ordinary dimensions?

Mountjoy, male, 13 feet long, 7 feet wide, 9 feet high. Spike Island: 372 cells are each 6 feet long, 3 feet 7 inches wide, 7 feet high; 316 cells are each 7 feet long, 4 feet wide, 7 feet high; 11 cells are each 11 feet long, 7 feet wide, 8 feet 6 inches high; 11 cells are 11 feet long, 7 feet wide, 10 feet 9 inches high; and 6 cells are 8 feet long, 6 feet wide, 8 feet 10 inches high. Mountjoy, female, 7 feet long, 4 feet wide, 7 feet 6 inches high; and 12 feet long, 7 feet wide, 9 feet 6 inches high.

9. What furniture do they generally contain?

Mountjoy, male: table, stool, hammock, &c., washing-basin, quart-tin, and plate. Spike Island: hammock, mattress, pillow and bedding, form table, water-can, washing-basin, urinal, drinking-cup, salt-cup, spoon, candlestick, comb, towel, coir cell brush. Mountjoy female: table, stool, bed, bedding, and towel, dusting, shoe, and hair brushes, combs, (2,) quart tin, tin dish, basin, spoon, and chambers, (2.)

10. What are the rules, framed according to law, in regard to the certification of the cells, and their visitation by officers; and in respect to the visits to the prisons by the inspectors of prisons?

See copies of rules approved of by the Irish government, forwarded herewith.

11. How far are these rules carried into effect?

They are fully carried out.

12. What has been the average number of prisoners in the convict prisons in the last five years?

See appendix to annual report for 1870, herewith. .

13. What are the chief internal regulations of these prisons?

See daily routine, and copies of rules for prisoners herewith.

14. How are the officers appointed, and what is their tenure of office?

They are appointed by the Irish government, at whose pleasure they hold office.

15. What qualifications are required, and in what manner are they tested?

Test examination by civil-service commissioners. See candidates' form herewith.

16. What provision is made for superannuated and disabled officers?

Pensions and compensations are awarded by the lords commissioners of Her Majesty's treasury, under the scales laid down by the superannuation acts.

17. Are rewards employed to stimulate the prisoners to good conduct and industry? If so, of what kinds and to what extent?

Yes; classification, gratuities, and a remission of portion of imprisonment by release, or license, &c. Fully explained in rules and forms herewith.

18. Is there a system of progressive classification? If so, how is it worked, and with what results?

Yes. See rules which explain the working of classification. Results are satisfactory.

19. What punishments are used for breaches of prison rules or other misconduct?

Privation of diet and reduction in classification. See rules.

20. Is corporal punishment ever employed?

Very rarely.

21. Is a full record of punishments kept?

Yes.

22. What kind of offenses are most common?

Insolence, unnecessary talk, and inattention to orders.

23. In what convict prison last year was the number of punishments least, and what was it?

In Lusk.

24. To what circumstances is this comparative exemption from punishment attributable?

Entirely owing to the exceptional circumstances of the establishment and to the class of prisoners sent there.

25. Are prisoners always allowed to make complaints of grievances, real or fancied? If so, to whom; and what attention is paid to their complaints; and what security is there that the complaints shall be properly examined?

Yes; to directors, or governors, or superintendents of the prisons. Statement taken down in writing, and decision made accordingly. See rules.

26. How far are moral forces used in the discipline of the convict prisons, and what is found to be the comparative efficacy of moral and coercive agencies?

See rules. We are unable to state whether good prison conduct is the result of the moral or coercive agency of the system.

27. Do the inmates of the convict prisons wear a party-colored dress?

The male prisoners wear frieze, with a distinctive stripe. · The female prisoners are, as at all large institutions, dressed alike.

28. Is your own opinion for or against such a prison dress; and, in either case, upon what grounds?

Yes; as a precaution against escape, and to secure uniformity.

29. Is the mask worn in the Irish convict prisons? What is your judgment of its utility or the reverse?

No.

30. To what extent are chaplains employed, and of what denominations are they?

Chaplains of the Episcopal, Presbyterian, and Roman Catholic denominations; regularly appointed officers of the prison, who devote their time to the religious instruction of the prisoners. See rules.

31. What religious services are held on Sunday and during the week?

See daily routine.

32. Are religious tracts and papers distributed to the convicts?

No; but approved religious books are supplied to the prisoners.

33. Are volunteer working visitors of either or both sexes admitted into the prisons? If so, under what restrictions and with what results?

Not at the male prisons. Ladies of a religious community visit the

Roman Catholic convicts, and ladies of their own persuasion the Episcopalians and Presbyterians, to prepare them for the refuges.

34. In what spirit do the prisoners receive efforts for their moral and religious improvement?

Generally satisfactory.

35. What are the regulations relating to the correspondence of prisoners?

See rules.

36. What in relation to visits from friends?

See rules.

37. Are the letters and visits of friends found to be beneficial to the prisoners or otherwise?

Usually beneficial.

38. What proportion of prisoners are found, on their admission, either wholly illiterate or so imperfect in their knowledge of reading as to derive neither instruction nor entertainment from it?

Males, 21.74 per cent.; females, 63.22 per cent.

39. What provision is made for the schooling of prisoners?

Schoolmasters and schoolmistresses are attached to each prison.

40. What branches are taught, and what progress is made therein?

See schoolmasters' and schoolmistresses' reports, in directors' annual reports.

41. Is there a library in each convict prison, including secular as well as religious books?

Yes.

42. What, about, is the average number of volumes?

Mountjoy, male, 592. Mountjoy, female, 290. Spike Island—secular books, 380; religious books, 4,180; total, 4,560. Lusk—library books, 50.*

43. Do many of the prisoners show a fondness for reading?

Yes.

44. What time have they for reading?

About an hour each evening, and on Sundays and holidays.

45. What, in a general way, are the sanitary arrangements and condition of the prisons?

The sanitary arrangements of the prisons are excellent, and the condition of the prisons satisfactory.

46. What are the prevailing diseases?

Colds, mild febrile and pulmonary affections. See reports from medical officers in directors' annual reports.

47. What has been the average annual death-rate for the last five years?

See appendix, directors' annual report for 1870.

48. In what prison last year was the rate of mortality smallest, and what was that rate?

Mountjoy, male, no death in the year 1870.

49. To what circumstances is this small rate attributable?

The satisfactory sanitary state of the prison, as well as the limited periods of detention therein.

50. Is there a distinction made in the convict prisons between penal and industrial labor? If so, what kinds of each are in use?

The only penal labor in use is oakum-picking in Mountjoy Male Convict Prison for the first three months of a prisoner's confinement in sep-

* The religious books are chiefly Bibles, prayer-books, and catechisms of the Episcopal and Roman Catholic Churches.

aration. The industrial labor in use consists chiefly in making mats, matting, mattresses, and shoes in Mountjoy Male Convict Prison. Tailoring, shirt-making, and washing in Mountjoy Female Convict Prison. Agricultural work at Lusk Prison, and out-door employment on public works, as stone-cutting, masonry, quarrying, and laboring at Spike Island Prison.

51. Is the deterrent effect of penal labor found to be considerable? What is found to be its effect upon the health of the prisoners? What its moral influence?

Its effect upon the health of the prisoners is not injurious. We are unable to give a decided opinion upon the other parts of this query.

52. Is penal labor utilized in the convict prisons? If so, what is its average daily value in money *per capita*?

Each prisoner, for the first three months of his confinement in Mountjoy Male Convict Prison, is required to pick daily four pounds of oakum, value about $2\frac{1}{4}d$.

53. Upon what principle is the industrial labor of the convict prisons organized; on a contract system or some other?

See tables of the estimated value of prisoners' labor in the published annual reports.

54. What have been the average annual net earnings, per head, of the prisoners in the last five years, exclusive of any portion allowed to the prisoner himself?

We are unable to give any further information on this subject than what is contained in the published annual reports for the last five years, herewith. See also reply to query 59.

55. In what prison, last year, were the net earnings the highest per head; and what was the amount?

See reply to query 54.

56. What is the average number of prisoners there?

Same answer as above.

57. What are the chief kinds of work there?

Same answer as above.

58. To what circumstances are the comparatively high earnings attributable?

Same answer as above.

59. Is a prisoner allowed any portion of his earnings? If so, how is that portion determined?

The only allowance given to a convict is a gratuity, which is dependent on his classification. A prisoner has no claim to any portion of his earnings.

60. Is overwork encouraged by the prisoner being allowed all the earnings so obtained?

No; see reply to query 59.

61. Do the prisoners work by the hour, or are tasks and piecework employed as far as practicable?

Chiefly by the hour; piecework is in use as far as practicable in the female prison.

62. How many hours each day, as measured either in time or by piecework, do the prisoners generally labor?

See daily routine.

63. What, during the last five years, has been the average annual cost of each prisoner, including food, clothing, and a proportionate share of salaries, and of the estimated rent, (say at the rate of 5 per cent. on the cost of the building,) and of every other expense whatever, but deduct-

ing the money received for prisoners' work (if sold to the public) or its value, if employed on public works belonging to the Government, and unconnected with the prison?

A complete answer to the question cannot be furnished from this department, portions of the expenditure, as for fuel, light, buildings, repairs, rents, and taxes, being defrayed by another department.

64. How much of this cost is put down for rent?

See reply to query 63.

65. What proportion of the prisoners had not learned a trade or calling prior to their committal?

About 35 per cent.

66. Is it made an object to impart to them the art of self-help, that is, the power to earn an honest living on their discharge? If so, in what manner and with what results?

This can only be done to a certain extent; the results are satisfactory.

67. What has been the average length of sentences for the last five years?

Males, seven and one-third years and life; females, six years and eighty-five days.

68. What has been the proportion of life sentences for the last five years?

Males 3¼ per cent.; females 1.35 per cent.

69. Do prisoners for life receive the same treatment as other prisoners?

Yes; excepting that they are not sent to intermediate prisons or refuges.

70. What portion of the prisoners committed in each of the last five years had been in a convict prison before?

Year.	Males.	Females.
1867	$3\frac{9}{11}$	$2\frac{2}{51}$
1868	$\frac{9}{31}$	$\frac{5}{75}$
1869	$\frac{5}{16}$	$1\frac{1}{63}$
1870	$\frac{5}{29}$	$\frac{4}{41}$
1871	$1\frac{4}{16}$	$\frac{2}{13}$

71. What portion had been previously committed to any prison?

Year.	Males.	Females.
1867	$\frac{54}{62}$	$\frac{77}{81}$
1868	$\frac{23}{61}$	$\frac{74}{75}$
1869	$\frac{60}{80}$	$\frac{41}{63}$
1870	$\frac{34}{81}$	$\frac{34}{44}$
1871	$\frac{13}{16}$	$\frac{66}{73}$

72. From what *data* have the re-committals been ascertained?

Personal identification, records received with prisoners from county and city jails, and by photography.

73. What proportion of the prisoners were minors when committed?

Year.	Males.	Females.
1867	8.43	1.81
1868	12.97	.75
1869	13.66	2.53
1870	9.31	4.68
1871	15.62	1.73

74. Is deterrence or reformation made the primary object?
Both deterrence and reformation are combind in the Irish system.
75. Are the prisoners able, by industry and good conduct, to shorten their periods of confinement? If so, to what extent?
Yes. See scale herewith.
76. What do you think of the policy of substituting unlimited for limited periods of imprisonment, to which criminals are sentenced, so as to make the time of liberation depend on the prisoner's moral condition, and the reasonable expectation of his not relapsing into crime?
Mr. Murray is of opinion that, subject to the modifications suggested to the transportation committee of the House of Commons, first report 1856, by Mr. M. D. Hill, unlimited imprisonment would be a wise and most valuable addition to the criminal code of the nation. See, also, Mr. Hill's charge for October, 1855, and the sequel to it in his "Suggestions for the repression of crime." Captain Barlow does not approve of such a policy.
77. Under present circumstances, are prisoners often set free before their liberation can be considered safe to society, or really beneficial to themselves; whether because their moral cure cannot be deemed complete, or because they have not the means of getting an honest livelihood, either from want of a sufficient knowledge of some handicraft, or from physical or mental weakness?
Mr. Murray replies to all the points arising in this query in the affirmative, and hence one of his grounds of belief, as stated in his reply to 76, are the advantages of unlimited imprisonment.
78. On the other hand, are prisoners often detained beyond the time when it is fully believed that they could safely be liberated?
Some such cases occur. Mr. Murray states that in his opinion such cases do beyond all doubt occur.
79. Is the "intermediate system," for gradually preparing prisoners for liberation, in use? If so, to what extent, and with what results?
Yes; with satisfactory results. Details will be found in annual reports.
80. Do the mass of prisoners, as a matter of fact, leave the prisons better or worse, morally, than they entered them?
If not re-convicted, it is to be assumed that improvement has taken place.
81. Are female prisoners, needing such instructions, taught to cook and sew; and, generally, are efforts made to enable a man or woman, on liberation, to avoid a wasteful expenditure, and to turn their wages to the best account?
Yes; to sew, and, to a certain extent, to cook. Our answer to the second part of the question, is: As far as possible.
82. Is any attempt made to give the prisoners good tastes, such as

that for music, so as to diminish the danger of their falling, when liberated, into habits of drunkenness, or other debasing pleasures?

We should consider any such arrangement as teaching music unsuitable in a prison.

83. Is any effort made to induce the prisoners, from their share of their earnings, to help to support their families, or to make restitution to those whom they have robbed, or otherwise injured?

The only case in which convicts can assist their families is where they had, on conviction, private property; this, under certain regulations, they can send to their friends.

84. If not, is there any other way in which they can practically give that evidence of moral improvement which is afforded by a willingness to forego selfish advantages for the benefit of others?

No.

85. Are efforts made to keep up the domestic ties of prisoners, such as allowing them to see members of their family, from time to time, except when, under the circumstances, these ties must be hurtful?

Yes; such efforts are made; prisoners are allowed to be visited by friends when their conduct merits it. See rules.

86. What agencies are employed to provide discharged prisoners with work, in order to prevent their relapse; and with what results?

An agent in the case of male prisoners is appointed, with satisfactory results. See reply to query 87.

87. Are any other efforts made, through prisoners' aid societies, refuges, or otherwise, to encourage discharged prisoners, desirous of doing well, and to prevent their relapse?

Yes; by the "Golden Bridge Refuge" and the "Shelter," for females.

88. What means are taken to trace prisoners after their discharge, in order to ascertain what is their subsequent career?

Not beyond expiration of sentence. While on license the convicts are under police supervision provided by fifth section of prevention of crimes act, 1871. (Copy herewith.)

89. General and miscellaneous remarks.

Such full details are given of the working of the system, in the annual reports, that we consider remarks unnecessary.

PATRICK JOSEPH MURRAY,
J. BARLOW,
Directors.

MARCH 6, 1872.

MOUNT JOY MALE PRISON.

Daily routine of prisoners in separation and association.

In summer—hours.	Disposal of time—prisoners in separation.	In winter—hours.
5.30 a. m.	First bell, prisoners rise, wash, make their beds, and sweep their cells.	6.30 a. m.
6 to 7 a. m.	Exercise	7 to 8 a. m.
7 to 9 a. m.	Work in cells	8 to 9 a. m.
9 to 9.30 a. m.	Breakfast hour	9 to 9.30 a. m.
9.30 to 2 p. m.	Work in cells, except one hour's schooling, daily, for first and second school classes, and one hour's schooling three days in the week for third school class.	9.30 to 2 p. m.
2 to 3 p. m.	Dinner hour and school-teaching in cells	2 to 3 p. m.
3 to 7 p. m.	Work in cells	3 to 7 p. m.
7 to 7.15 p. m.	Supper, and double-lock prisoners retire to bed at 8¼ o'clock, and gas extinguished in cells at 8¼ o'clock, p. m.	7 to 7.15 p. m.

Ten and a half hours' work daily in summer and nine and a half hours in the winter months.

Roman Catholic prisoners, in separation, attend chapel from 7 to 8 o'clock a. m., on Tuesdays, Thursdays, and Fridays. Protestant prisoners, in separation, attend church from 10 to 11 o'clock a. m., on Mondays, Fridays, and Saturdays. Sundays and holidays Roman Catholic prisoners attend mass from 7 to 8 a. m. Religious instructions from 12 to 1 p. m. The Protestant prisoners at Divine service from 10 to 11 a. m.; Presbyterian prisoners from 8 to 9 a. m. The remainder of the day is devoted to reading in cells, except two hours for exercise.

In summer—hours.	Disposal of time—prisoners in association.	In winter—hours.
5. 30 a. m.............	First bell, prisoners rise, wash, make their beds, and sweep their cells.	6. 30 a. m.
6 to 8 a. m...........	Work......	7 to 8 a. m.
8 to 9 a. m...........	Exercise......	8 to 9 a. m.
9 to 10 a. m..........	Breakfast hour......	9 to 10 a. m.
10 to 2 p. m..........	Work......	10 to 2 p. m.
2 to 3 p. m...........	Dinner hour......	2 to 3 p. m.
3 to 6 p. m...........	Work, except one hour's exercise daily to the advanced class...	3 to 6 p. m.
6 to 7 p. m...........	School......	6 to 7 p. m.
7 to 7. 15 p. m.......	Supper, and double-lock prisoners retire to bed at 8½ o'clock, and gas extinguished in cells at 8½ o'clock p. m.	7 to 7, 15 p. m.

Nine hours' work daily in summer and eight hours' in the winter months.

Prisoners, in association, attend chapel from 7 to 8 o'clock a. m., on Tuesdays and Fridays; with these exceptions, the routine is the same as on the other days. On Sundays and holidays the Roman Catholic prisoners attend mass from 7 to 8 a. m., and for religious instructions between 12 and 1 o'clock p. m., and the Protestant prisoners attend Divine service from 10 to 11 a. m., and the Presbyterian prisoners from 8 to 9 a. m. The remainder of the day is devoted to reading in their cells and exercise.

The Protestant prisoners attend at religious instructions on Mondays from 10 to 11 a. m., and on Fridays at Divine service from 10 to 11 o'clock a. m., and on Saturdays, for issue and exchange of books, from 10 to 11 a. m.

P. N. HACKETT,
Governor.

FEBRUARY 9, 1872.

MOUNT JOY FEMALE CONVICT PRISON, JANUARY 23, 1872.

Daily routine for summer months.

Prison unlocked at 6 o'clock a. m.
Prisoners' breakfast served at 6.30 a. m.
Matrons' breakfast hour, 1st, 6.45 to 7.45 a. m.
Matrons' breakfast hour, 2d, 7.45 to 8.45 a. m.
Prisoners' dinner served at 11.30 a. m.
Matrons' dinner hour, 1st, 11.45 a. m. to 12.45 p. m.
Matrons' dinner hour, 2d, 1 to 2 p. m.
Prisoners' supper served at 5.15 p. m.
Prison locked at 6 p. m.

PRAYERS.

Roman Catholic prisoners, probation class, 8.40 to 9 a. m.

Morning.

Protestant and Presbyterian prisoners, 6 to 6.20 a. m.
A, First, second, third, and probation classes, (morning.)
Roman Catholic prisoners, second and third classes, 4 to 4.20 p. m.

Evening.

Roman Catholic, first and A classes, 4.45 to 5.5 p. m.
Protestant and Presbyterian prisoners, 4.45 to 5.5 p. m.
First and A classes, evening.

SCHOOL HOURS.

From 8 to 11 a. m., and from 2 to 4.30 p. m., daily, (Saturdays excepted.)
Second and third class prisoners attend daily from 2 to 3 o'clock p. m.
Probation class, from 3 to 4.15 p. m., daily.
First and A class prisoners on alternate days, from 9 to 11 a. m.; of these classes, the prisoners in third and fourth books, and those employed in cleaning the prison, join the others from 10 to 11 a. m.
Refuge class not employed in laundry, (those employed in laundry do not attend at all,) from 8 to 9 o'clock a. m., daily.
Hours of labor, 9½ daily.
Prayers, exercise, school, and labor go on simultaneously.

DELIA I. SIDWILL,
Superintendent.

MOUNT JOY FEMALE CONVICT PRISON, JANUARY 23, 1872.

Daily routine for winter months.

Prison unlocked at 7 o'clock a. m.
Prisoners' breakfast served at 7.15 a. m.
Matrons' breakfast hour, 1st, 7.30 to 8.30 a m.
Matrons' breakfast hour, 2d, 8.30 to 9.30 a. m.
Prisoners' dinner served at 12 m.
Matrons' dinner hour, 1st, 12.15 to 1.15 p. m.
Matrons' dinner hour, 2d, 1.30 to 2.30 p. m.
Prisoners' supper served at 5.15 p. m.
Prison locked at 6 p. m.

PRAYERS.

Roman Catholic prisoners, probation class, 9.40 to 10 a. m.

Morning.

Protestant and Presbyterian prisoners, 7 to 7.20 a. m.
A, first, second, third, and probation classes, morning.
Roman Catholic prisoners, second and third classes, 4.30 to 4.50 p. m.

Evening.

Roman Catholic, first and A classes, 4.45 to 5.5 p. m.
Protestant and Presbyterian prisoners, 4.45 to 5.5 p. m.
First and A classes, evening.

SCHOOL HOURS.

From 8.45 to 11.30 a. m., and from 2 to 4.30 p. m., daily, (Saturday excepted.)
Second and third class prisoners attend daily from 2 to 3 p. m.
Probation class prisoners attend from 3 to 4 p. m.
First and A class prisoners on alternate days from 9.30 to 11.30 a. m. Of these classes, the prisoners in third and fourth books, and those employed in cleaning the prison, join the others from 10.30 to 11.30 a. m.
Refuge class not employed in laundry, (those employed in laundry do not attend at all,) from 8.45 to 9.30 a. m., daily.
Hours of labor, 9 daily.
Prayers, exercise, school, and labor go on simultaneously.

DELIA I. SIDWILL,
Superintendent.

MOUNT JOY FEMALE CONVICT PRISON.

Sunday routine for winter months.

Prison unlocked at 7 a. m.
Roman Catholic service (1st) from 7.15 to 8 o'clock a. m.
Roman Catholic service (2d) from 8.15 to 9 o'clock a. m.
(Half the number of prisoners attend the first service and the other half the second service.)
Protestant service from 7.15 to 8.15 a. m. (For all Protestant prisoners.)
Presbyterian service from 10 to 11 o'clock a. m. (For all Presbyterian prisoners.)
Benediction for the Roman Catholic prisoners who attended the first service from 11 to 12 a. m.
Prayers for all creeds from 12 noon to 12.30 p. m.
Matrons' breakfast hour (1st) from 8 to 9 o'clock a. m.
Matrons' breakfast hour (2d) from 9.15 to 10.15 a. m.
Prisoners' breakfast served at 9 o'clock a. m.
Matrons' dinner hour (1st) from 11.45 a. m. to 12.45 p. m.
Matrons' dinner hour (2d) from 1 to 2 o'clock p. m.
Prisoners' dinner served at 12.40 o'clock p. m.
Probation, third, second, laundry, and invalid classes, exercised before the dinner hour, and the first and advanced classes from 2.15 to 3.15 p. m.
Prisoners' supper served at 4 o'clock p. m.
Prison locked at 5 o'clock p. m.

DELIA I. SIDWILL,
Superintendent.

FEBRUARY 12, 1872.

MOUNT JOY FEMALE CONVICT PRISON.

Sunday routine for summer months.

Prison unlocked at 6.30 o'clock a. m.
Roman Catholic service (1st) from 6.45 to 7.30 o'clock a. m.

Roman Catholic service (2d) from 7.45 to 8.30 o'clock a. m.
Protestant service from 6.45 to 7.45 o'clock a. m.
Presbyterian service from 10 to 11 o'clock a. m.
Matrons' breakfast hour (1st) from 7.30 to 8.30 o'clock a. m.
Matrons' breakfast hour (2d) from 8.45 to 9.45 o'clock a. m.
Prisoners' breakfast served at 8.30 o'clock a. m.

All the other arrangements same as given in winter months, Sunday routine.

DELIA I. SIDWILL,
Superintendent.

FEBRUARY 12, 1872.

SPIKE ISLAND CONVICT PRISON.

Detailed statement of the daily routine.

SUMMER.

First bell, 5 o'clock a. m.—Prisoners arise and make up beds; officers same and collect in the prison from outside.

Second bell, 5¾ a. m.—Parade of officers; unlock prison, draw rations, and serve breakfast.

Third bell, 6¼ a. m.—Breakfast, officers and prisoners, the intern guard (second relief) continuing on duty.

Fourth bell, 6¾ a. m.—Parade of day-officers; prison unlocked, and officers and prisoners attend their respective places of worship. Prayers read for the Protestants and Presbyterians by officers of these persuasions, the Roman Catholic chaplain or his assistant officiating in chapel; time occupied in prayers from fifteen to twenty minutes.

Fifth bell, 7¼ a. m.—Parade after prayers. Prisoners marched to their respective places of employment, where they remain until dinner-bell, at quarter to 12 noon.

Sixth bell, quarter to 12 noon.—Prisoners recalled from work for dinner. Prison locked up at 12 o'clock noon, the two night-reliefs (with the exception of those on leave) posted on extern and intern duty during the dinner-hour.

Seventh bell, 1 p. m.—Warders parade and unlock prison. Prisoners marched to labor under their respective officers and remain on the works until 6 p. m., when the recall-bell rings and supper is served out. Schooling is carried on in the prison up to 8 o'clock p. m.

WINTER.

The winter routine is the same as the summer, except that the unlocking in the morning and the locking up at night varies with the light, according as the days shorten and lengthen, and that during the winter months the warders breakfast before going on duty.

The Protestant and Presbyterian chaplains attend two days a week each, viz: Tuesday and Saturday, and on Saturday afternoons portions of the prisoners of each religious persuasion are withdrawn from the works and receive instructions from their respective chaplains for two hours.

The entire body of the convicts leave off work two hours earlier on Saturdays than on other week-days for the purpose of bathing and feet-washing, cleaning shoes, exchanging clothing, &c.

Sunday routine.

First bell, 6¾ a. m.—Prisoners arise and make up beds.

Second bell, 7 a. m.—Parade of officers; unlock prison, draw rations and serve breakfast.

Third bell, 7½ a. m.—Prisoners parade and attend mass till about 8½ a. m.; they are then marched to their respective wards and locked up.

Fourth bell, 8½ a. m.—Prison officers paraded and dismissed to breakfast, the intern duty being taken up by the first relief of the previous night.

Fifth bell, 9½ a. m.—Officers parade after breakfast and unlock prison, the sick are taken to hospital, the Presbyterian prisoners attend service, and the others are exercised by classes round the prison square.

Sixth bell, 10.55 a. m.—Roman Catholic service, which is over about 12 o'clock or soon after, exercise till 12¾ o'clock. Protestant service from 11¾ to 12⅛.

Seventh bell, 1 p. m.—Dinner served. Dinner hour from 1¼ to 2¼ for both officers and prisoners; 2¼ o'clock parade of prisoners, and their persons and clothing inspected by the chief and principal warders. Prisoners at exercise or reading in their wards till lock-up, which is at 6 o'clock in summer and varies with the light in winter.

PETER HAY,
Governor.

JANUARY 19, 1872.

LUSK CONVICT PRISON.

Daily routine of duty for prisoners.

5 a. m. Ring bell; fold bedding and dress.
5.30 a. m. Ring bell; officers parade, unlock huts, and roll-call.
5.45 a. m. Ring bell; prayers.
6 a. m. Ring bell; breakfast.
6.30 a. m. Ring bell; parade prisoners in classes to work.
12 p. m. Ring bell; dinner.
1 p. m. Ring bell; resume work.
5 p. m. Ring bell; return from work, and supper.
5.30 a. m. Ring bell; to school and lecture.
7.30 p. m. Ring bell; make beds.
7.45 p. m. Ring bell; to prayers.
8 p. m. Ring bell; count prisoners; lock up.
9 p. m. Ring bell; to bed.

R. GUNNING,
Superintendent.

LUSK CONVICT PRISON.

Daily routine of prisoners' employment on Sundays and holidays.

6.00 a. m. Ring bell; fold bedding and dress.
6.30 a. m. Ring bell; officers parade; unlock huts.
6.45 a. m. Ring bell; breakfast.
8.00 a. m. Ring bell; prisoners let out to exercise.
8.30 a. m. Ring bell; count all; Roman Catholics to prayers, at village chapel.
11.00 a. m. Ring bell; Roman Catholics from prayers; parade all.

11.45 a. m. Ring bell; parade all; Protestants to prayers at village church.
  12.30 p. m. Ring bell; prisoners to read in hut.
   1.30 p. m. Ring bell; prisoners let out to exercise.
   2.00 p. m. Ring bell; Protestants return from prayers; dinner.
   2.30 p. m. Ring bell; lecture.
   3.00 p. m. Ring bell; prisoners let out to exercise.
   4.00 p. m. Ring bell; general parade.
   4.45 p. m. Ring bell; make beds.
   5.00 p. m. Ring bell; supper.
   6.00 p. m. Ring bell; to read in hut.
   7.45 p. m. Ring bell; to prayers.
   8.00 p. m. Ring bell; count prisoners; lock up.

LUSK CONVICT PRISON.

Employment of time in school.

Day.	Subjects.
Monday	Reading, spelling, writing, arithmetic
Tuesday	Reading, writing, English grammar.
Wednesday	Geography from maps, exercises on ship.
Thursday	Reading, spelling, writing, from dictation.
Friday	Competitive examination.
Saturday	Simple accounts.
Sunday	Moral lessons.

Hours of instruction from 5¼ till 7¼ p. m.

C. DALY,
School Instructor.

VIII.—RUSSIA.

[No answers were furnished by the Russian government to the questions submitted; but Count W. Sollohub, the originator, six years ago, of an exceedingly interesting experiment in prison discipline at Moscow, communicated a paper, detailing the progress and results of that experiment down to June 1, 1872. He had previously, several years since, communicated, for publication in one of the annual reports of the New York Prison Association, a more general paper, giving a full description of the prison system of the Russian empire. The essay now furnished is a sequel to the former; and as that gave an account of the establishment and early workings of the house of correction at Moscow, this gives the results of six years of intelligent and earnest work in it; results which must be regarded as equally remarkable and gratifying. Its perusal cannot fail to interest and instruct all who watch the signs of progress in this important department of social philosophy.]

1. COUNT SOLLOHUB'S REPORT.

[Translation.]

The paper sent to the Prison Association of New York was written at the time when the house of correction at Moscow had just inaugurated a new prison system. That system took for its basis a theory of prison labor till then unknown. It maintained, so far as the execution of the sentence was concerned, the most inflexible rigor. But it did not lose sight of the day when the prisoner should recover his liberty. In view of that day it prepared for the liberated convict the possibility of acquiring habits of order, useful knowledge, and a capital in money, indispensable as a shield against new temptations. The system thus offered a twofold combination—that of preventing relapses and that of augmenting the resources of the administration by giving to the prisoners an interest in the profits of the establishment. It was necessary to await, from time, the results of this experiment. We are already able to cite some statistics which have a mute eloquence.

The prison entered upon its untried path in 1865, though still embarrassed by the progress of the constructions, and amid the hesitations which always accompany a new experiment. A report, published June 1, 1871, furnishes the following results: There were admitted into the two houses of correction—male and female—from 1865 to 1871:

	Men.	Women.
Sentenced for a term of more than a year	1,316	200
Sentenced for a term of less than a year	486	207
Imprisoned by desire of their parents	17	2
Total	1,819	409
		1,819
Grand total		2,128

It is necessary here to call attention to the fact that, as the fixing of the minimum of one year for correctional imprisonment is made the object of general legislative measures, the house of correction of Moscow could not be an exception. It is, therefore, only from a population of 1,316 men and 200 women that a judgment can be formed of the effect of the new system. The results of the industrial workshops, shown by the statistics, are as follows:

Prisoners recognized in the prison as master-workmen and who have become entitled to wages:

Boot-makers	164 since 1865.
Hosiers	136 since 1865.
Weavers of linen	84 since 1868.
Weavers of woolen stuffs	103 since 1869.
Weavers of ribbons	93 since 1868.
Weavers of galloons	110 since 1867.
Weavers of belts	50 since 1868.
Weavers of scarfs	17
Shoemakers	69 since 1865, closed in 1868.
Book-binders	29 since 1865, closed in 1868.
Preparers of chips	35 since 1866, closed in 1867.
Glovers	1 since 1866, closed in 1866.
Cotton-spinners	2 since 1866, closed in 1868.
Makers of binders' boards	8 since 1865, closed in 1871.
Tailors	58 since 1866.
Makers of cigarettes	56 since 1868, closed in 1871.
Total	1,015

Thus the prison has given back to society 1,015 artisans, the majority of whom had previously no knowledge of a trade.

The following table affords proof that the prisoner, moved by the hope of regaining for himself a position above want, becomes an excellent workman, and so is able to break off from those vicious habits which were sure to plunge him again into misery.

The report shows that the industrial labors thus executed have produced—

Boots	15,425	pairs.	Shoes	41,733	pairs.
Hosiery	22,888	pieces.	Binders' boards	9,065	pieces.
Thread	64,015	archines.	Cuttings of chips	1,653	pounds.
Woolen cloth	57,363	archines.	Gloves	1,710	pieces.
Ribbons	1,156,192	archines.	Calicoes	9,600	pieces.
Galloons	1,324,803	archines.	Manufacture of wearing		
Girdles	36,653	pieces.	apparel	4,132	pieces.
Scarfs	27,016	pieces.			

In addition to the above, the women have knit 20,162 pairs of stockings and made 310 nets.

Each workman being pushed on by his own interest and the fear of fines, which have not in the aggregate exceeded 216 rubles 51 copecks in six years, there is no occasion to stimulate his zeal or to have recourse to measures of severity.

The earnings of the master-workmen amounted, during that time, to the sum of 10,062 rubles 79 copecks for the day of liberation, and 4,020 rubles 55 copecks spent in the purchase of tea, which the master-workmen distributed to their apprentices. The earnings received by the prisoners have, therefore, amounted to 14,082 rubles 34 copecks. The treasury of the administration has received for its share of the profits only 6,705 rubles 98 copecks, the result of the skilled labor, but it has gained abundantly from the unskilled labor. The washing done for the hospitals and alms-houses in the neighborhood has brought in 7,812 rubles 97 copecks. For the prison itself it has saved an expenditure, which would otherwise have been necessary, of 3,932 rubles 95 copecks, to say nothing of mending to the value of 650 rubles 75 copecks. The products of the kitchen-gardens represent a sum amounting to 6,867 rubles 73 copeks.

In addition to the above, there were made 3,949,459 wrappers for newspapers, realizing to the administration 1,036 rubles 50 copecks.

In a word, if the value of the unskilled and gratuitous labor of the prisoners had been estimated, they would have represented 135,705 days of labor, amounting in value to at least 9,840 rubles 61 copecks.

The sum total of the general revenue of the prison, it will thus be seen, has amounted to 50,498 rubles 70 copecks. If there be added the savings on the expenses allowed on the maintenance, &c., which have amounted in six years to 10,267 rubles 35 copecks, spent in the purchase of linen, clothing, &c., the general balance-sheet will represent a total gain of 60,766 rubles 17 copecks, of which sum about one-fourth will have gone to the prison workmen and three-fourths to the administration. This proportion seems normal, and it would be difficult to obtain a proportion more advantageous, at least without impeding the reformation of the prisoners and lowering the quality of the work.

The treasury of the house of correction of Moscow contained on the 1st June, 1871, the sum of 20,603 rubles 75 copecks in vouchers and coin. The administration had not received a stiver in the way of capital for the organization of labor. The state had only altered the old buildings and added some new ones, which involved an expenditure of about 90,000 rubles. Thus it will be seen that about one-fourth of this sum had been re-imbursed in June, 1871.

The honor of such a result belongs not alone to the idea of the new system, but still more to its execution. We cannot pass in silence the services rendered in this regard by Lieutenant Colonel Mertz, immediate director of the prison. It is to his energy, his spirit of order and economy, his extraordinary integrity, and his entire devotion, that the establishment under his direction owes its reputation, and has been able to attract the attention of the students of penitentiary science.

Do not the statistics cited above go far toward the solution of the most difficult problem in the establishment of penitentiaries, viz, the financial problem?

Who has not heard a thousand times that society, not being able to command pecuniary means for citizens who behave well, has not the moral right to draw upon them, to any great extent, for citizens who behave ill? Does it not follow that no civilized country possesses a complete and rational system of means for attaining the various ends of penitentiary discipline? Has not every country some prisons which it willingly shows, and others which it would like to conceal?

A correctional prison, such as that which we propose, is no longer an expense to the state; it is an investment. Nothing is easier than to effect a loan, with redemption guaranteed by the state. Such loan would be largely paid from the labor of the prisoners, when once they saw in that labor not simply a sterile vexation, but the only means of escaping the misery which threatens them in the future. Thus have we demonstrated by figures not only that payment might be effected without weighing heavily upon the state, but there would even be an excess of income, which would gradually form a capital for each prison, and would enable it, in time, to become self-supporting. This same calculation would serve as a guide in the case of penal prisons, which, not implying the return of the prisoners into society, would have no need to organize, professional or mechanical labors, but might be devoted to great enterprises, such as improving lands, working mines, &c., &c. Joint-stock companies might, in this case, furnish capital *ad hoc*, under a stipulation that the product of the prison labor should be set apart to the re-imbursement of the loan. This would become an unfailing resource, when once the prisoners should have a share of the profits laid up against the day of their colonization, either in the mother-country or on some foreign shore. Perhaps the prisoners ought not, at first, to have the right of sharing in the profits, and the prisons might, in this view, be organized somewhat after the plan of the Irish system. But this would be a matter to be determined by experience. The general financial plan for the support of the prisons would have, in all cases, the following solutions:

The preliminary detentions to be at the expense of the municipal government.

The houses of amendment (cellular with a maximum of three months) at the expense of the state.

The houses of correction (from one to five years) to stipulate for a loan re-imbursable by the labor of the prisoners.

The penal prisons would undertake, on the same principle, enterprises to be managed either by private companies or by the administration of the state.

We had expressed the opinion, in our paper on the prison question in Russia, that imprisonment in the house of amendment should be from one day to a year. This classification was suggested by the existing laws in relation to the jurisdiction of justices of the peace. A prison established on this principle at St. Petersburg has yielded the most brilliant results as regards revenue from the workshops. It appears from this experiment that even the houses of amendment need not be a burden upon the State, and may be established by loan. But the imprisonment was too short to produce much effect upon the habits of the prisoners. Moreover, they had not time to gain from their earnings a capital with which to commence a new life. Numerous relapses were the result. Grave disorders ensued. The director barely escaped assassination. An event sadly memorable, the death of the Prince of Aremburgh, was the consequence of a mutiny of the prisoners, of some days' continuance. The conclusion we draw from these facts is, that the state ought to give up the idea of material profits, and establish houses of amendment, rigidly cellular, with a maximum imprisonment of three. months. Such, in a few words, is the result of the experiments undertaken at Moscow and St. Petersburg—experiments which have not, as yet, been elsewhere conducted, in Russia, upon a larger scale.

No doubt a great many objections, as has heretofore been the case in other countries, will be raised against a system which seems to be too favorable to wretches in revolt against the laws of society. It will be said, "Why give premiums to criminals, while you give nothing to honest people who are struggling against misery?" These objections will be offered by persons who have never made a special study of penitentiary science, and have never had a near view of prison life. This will be the opinion of the great majority, who will find it quite natural that men, made in the image of God, should be buried alive, or confined in corrupting dens, should there prepare new crimes and new disorders. Such persons will not admit that a criminal who applies himself to labor, in order that he may lead a new life in the future, thereby performs a meritorious action—the action of an honest man—an action which he certainly would not accomplish with the zeal, the sole condition of success, if it had been imposed on him simply as a barren task. With too little reflection, the majority cries out for punishment, always punishment, nothing but punishment. But they forget that punishment alone makes the burden greater, and does not arrest relapses. The majority, therefore, defends the principle of excessive and useless expenditures, since the social security gains nothing by them. The interesting little sheets published in London by the Howard Association, cite the almost incredible fact that the same woman had been arrested at Bristol for the two hundred and fiftieth time. Does the majority desire the repetition and perpetuation of facts like this? Is it so flush of money that it can afford to throw it out at the window, all for the barbarous pleasure of taking vengeance once, and of reserving the right to revenge itself again? Crime, like misery, is a disease. It should be cured, not propagated. Relapses are but falls, which prove that the disease has not been cured, and that the punishment had no reason for its existence, since it only produced a new crime.

We do not address ourselves to the majority, but we call the attention of specialists to the results of the treatment of crime by discipline, instruction, and participation in the earnings.

The house of correction at Moscow has received, as we have seen above, in the course of six years, 1,719 men and 409 women. During the whole of this period it has re-admitted, as recidivists, only eight men and one woman. Of the whole number there was only one person who had been married, and he had not reached the point at which a share in the earnings is allowed in the establishment. It has been remarked that the most zealous of the workmen were those who had families. They labored with intense earnestness to be able to buy a dray-horse, to build a small house, to set up some little business. Later in the history of the institution, we saw a large number who exhibited tokens of intelligence in public positions. They were employed as salesmen of the products of the industries which had been taught them in prison. Many of these liberated prisoners have found excellent places as foremen in factories, the ordinary working class in Russia not being distinguished for sobriety or for precision of workmanship.

We cannot forebear citing the following fact: One of our discharged prisoners had made a fortune. He had established the hosiery business in his native city, which, as well as the whole surrounding district, had never seen among them a hosier. Orders rained upon him from all sides. This person passed from misery to affluence. His wife dressed herself in silks; his children attended school. He rented a house for which he payed 500 rubles, or more than a thousand francs, per year. In short, it was riches, consideration, complete regeneration that he had attained. One fine morning he was seen to arrive at Moscow completely robed in velvet. He came to throw himself at the feet of those whom he looked upon as his benefactors. He recounted his successes, but he added, " I am so happy that I fear I shall become intoxicated."

Does not this story demonstrate that the true aim of all education is to form the will? There are many natures, especially in certain nations, in which the will lacks energy. This defect of organization can be supplied only by creating an artificial will by the force of habit. On the other hand, everything which is obligatory instantly awakens the desire of revolt and disobedience. The great difficulty in reformatory prison discipline is to attain the end without weakening or discrediting the means. Nothing, certainly, could be more efficacious than the religious sentiment; but we have always feared to enforce the application of it. We have made obligatory only the presence of the prisoners at public service on the Sabbath at morning and evening prayers, and at grace at the hour of meals. But we have placed in each separate division of the common dormitories an image of Christ for the men, and an image of the Holy Virgin for the women.

Nothing is more touching or more solemn than the moment when absolute silence pervades the prison in the evening. The bolts are drawn on the cells, the prisoners have retired, but through the gratings all, or nearly all, are seen kneeling before the symbol of their worship. They make their prayer, their own prayer, which they do not confound with the ceremonial of the discipline. They are not required to do it. It is a necessity of their conscience, of their habits; and it is precisely because there is no constraint upon them that the habit, contracted in infancy, has become a second nature—perhaps a salutary one. We feel a commiseration for wretches endued with such instincts, and are impelled to ask whether society is not more culpable toward them than they are toward society. We ask ourselves also whether personal conference with the prisoners is more beneficial than hurtful, and we think we are not deceived in affirming that it will be efficacious only when confided to ecclesiastics possessing not only large human sympathies, but also a keen penetration and a great knowledge of the human heart. It cannot be sufficiently kept in view that every prisoner is, naturally, always on his guard, always defiant, always in a state of antagonism to whatever proceeds from the constituted authorities. It is the natural reaction of lost liberty against the power that has taken it away. Give to the prisoner who has a medium or long sentence the means of earning money. That he will comprehend, for money needs no explanation. This is already one form of liberty; but every other measure will awaken illwill, unless it allows of a comparative freedom. We have made obligatory the presence of the prisoners at the service of Sunday, but we have thought it proper, under the circumstances in which we were placed, to leave it optional with them to attend or not to attend the school, of which religious instruction is made the basis. We have only determined in principle that the time spent in school should be counted as time employed in gratuitous labors, which the prisoners avoid as much as possible.

Our experience has convinced us that it is altogether inexpedient to limit the instruction given in prisons to the elementary branches. When once you have made it your aim to wrestle with low instincts, to induce better habits, and to strengthen the power of the will, you cannot too much enlarge the horizon of intelligence. Many prisoners, even in Russia, bring into the prisons a knowledge more or less extended. Is it just to carry their civilization no further? It is a matter of course that there should be no schools in detention prisons, nor in houses of amendment, which, in our opinion, ought to be cellular, and the imprisonment should not exceed a duration of three months; but in correctional, and even penal prisons, it would be highly desirable that progressive pedagogical instruction should, without ceasing, go hand in hand with the skilled and unskilled labors of the establishment. Here the aid of philanthropical societies might be of the greatest utility. We have been able, in this view, to make only timid essays, but we have had the good fortune to find a devoted schoolmaster in the person of Mr. Savenko. We think that the chaplain, who inspires by his noble character a certain reverence, a kind of awe, a principle of salutary authority, ought to be charged only with the religious instruction of the catechism, of sacred history, and the like; but that secular instruction should be confided to one or more professors, who should be toward the prisoners rather friends than judges. It is this which Mr. Savenko has thoroughly comprehended. He has the air of a person who does not know in whose presence he finds himself. He treats his pupils with the most perfect politeness, and his pupils, knowing that they are not obliged to attend his instructions, flock to them with alacrity and eagerness. He has divided them into three categories: the elementary course, the higher course, and the conferences of Sunday. In the elementary course there are 124 pupils; in the higher course, 54. The conferences of Sunday, which relate to history, geography, and, above all, the skilled industries carried on in the establishment, draw nearly all the prisoners sentenced for a considerable time. They question the professor, to the end that they may be sure that they understand his lessons. Never is the least rudeness permitted in their intercourse with him. Mr. Savenko is an intelligent worker, an enthusiast in his vocation. He writes instructive treatises for the prisoners. His books of elementary instruction are remarkable, and enable the pupils to make rapid progress. His Sunday conferences are simple and popular. This man is unostentatibusly useful, and we are happy to bear public testimony to his worth.

An attempt has been made to teach choral singing by note, according to the system of Galen-Paris-Chevé. Never, perhaps, has this system produced more surprising results. Persons, unable either to read or write, have become able to read music at first sight. Instruction, however, was confined to the forms and names of the first seven notes, which were learned in a single lesson. Unhappily, the course was suspended for want of professors. We cannot too earnestly recommend instruction in music for the inmates of correctional and penal prisons. Beyond the fact that singing is a part of worship, there is in it a reformatory and tranquillizing principle, which paralyzes the instincts of debauchery, hatred, and rebellion. It is an error to suppose that a residence in a spacious, well-aired, well-kept establishment, affording, besides, high wages, with freedom from all care as regards life's necessities, and offering gratuitous progressive instruction, not even omitting music, becomes a paradise which would awaken the desire to commit a crime simply to enjoy the benefits of incarceration. We have encountered in six years eighteen attempts to escape. We are compelled unceasingly to keep up the most active vigilance against incendiaries who would burn the establishment. There have been registered, within these same six years, one hundred and twenty-two cases of disciplinary punishment. Of this number, seventy-nine cases, nearly two-thirds, belong to the years 1869 and 1870; that is to say, the period in which the inflexibility of the discipline was definitively established. The prohibition against receiving alms from without, which still defray in Russia the expense of drunkenness; against peculations in the prisons; against going out with an attendant, either to visit the confessional or for any labors whatever; against receiving visits except in a grated conversation-room; the enforcement of separation and silence by night; pitiless labor during ten hours of the day, (each minute regulated by the tick of the clock;) a scrupulous cleanliness maintained, by the dread of fines, military discipline, a monastic diet, punishment always present, always executed, always inflexible, down to the day of liberation—all this must provoke the most vivid dissatisfaction. Many of the prisoners spoke with delight of those fetid dens in which they swarmed together in numerous apartments. There they were suffocated with foul air; they had no labor, no gain to expect, no useful instructions, no care for the future; but they had liberty of low debauchery. They related histories to one another, they formed copartnerships for thieving while drinking brandy and playing at cards or dice. They even enacted comedies, as shown in a programme which we have actually had in our hands. All that debauchery can offer that is most foul, all that crime can present that is most hideous, is taught in these vulgar haunts. There is found what those moralists who cry out against solicitude in regard to penitentiary reforms desire to perpetuate, without giving much thought to the matter. They do not at all comprehend that it is only by measures strictly penitentiary that real punishment is accomplished, that the liberty of doing evil is paralyzed, and that the society which does not accept the Christian duty of turning a feeble man from the path of crime only pushes him further on it, and is as guilty as himself. We expected an open revolt; but nothing of the kind occurred. Those who were most exasperated dared not assail the life of their chiefs, as is often the case in prisons given up to idleness. We attribute this fact to the good sense of the mass, and especially to the money gained by their labor. The discipline alone, without the alleviation afforded by the expectation of a better lot, would, undoubtedly, have led to the gravest disorders. It was remarked by us that the most turbulent prisoners were found among the shoemakers, among the tailors, and, in general, among the artisans who work near each other, while the weavers, who are separated from their comrades by noise and distance, have a far more tractable character.

Man clings, above all, to life. The privation of life is, therefore, the greatest punishment that can be imposed upon him. But the punishment ceases at the moment of its execution. Next to life, man's most precious treasure is liberty. Privation of liberty is a punishment all the more terrible in that it does not cease as soon as inflicted, that it is always intense, always present, and that it would be intolerable if hope, that benefactor of man, did not come to his support. It is not necessary to suppose that the putting of criminals inside the walls of a great edifice constitutes the absolute essence of the privation of liberty. Nothing could be less exact. The privation of liberty does not consist in the mere place of abode, but rather in the constraint put upon a man during all the hours of the day and night. It is only then that the punishment weighs like an iron ball. We have seen, in many prisons, the semblance of the privation of liberty, but not the real privation. Where the prisoners sleep in common dormitories, where labor is not systematically organized, where the discipline cannot, therefore, be rigidly maintained, where the building is not adapted to the special aim of punishment—there are there always intervals of relative liberty, which paralyze the action of justice. It has happened to us many times to exhibit the correctional prison of Moscow to visitors. At sight of the long range of dormitories, of their walls stuccoed and washed in colors, of the cells painted with oil, of the floors covered with rope matting, of the church, of the refectory, of the storerooms, of the flower-gardens, of the court, of the workshops, presenting a scene of animation like a great manufactory, they cried out, "This is not a prison; it is the land of promise; a crime would be committed to get here." A man came—a man of mark. He looked about him and said, "This is very severe; this must be extremely painful to them." He had comprehended the case. In truth, nothing is more painful than to be always in a state of constraint, like the machinery which moves a clock. "Rise, dress yourself; clean your cell, make your bed; the keepers are waiting; the companies are forming; forward, march. It is the time of making the toilet; if you are not clean you will be punished; forward, march. You will eat bread if you do not become a master-workman, and if you have not the means of drinking tea with your comrades. The clock strikes again. Forward, march. To the workshops, each in his place; to the kitchen-garden, every one in his place; the monitor, the overseers, the elders, the sentinels, are at their posts. No conversations, no songs, no rest. Work, without reward, or strive to earn money for your future. That is your affair. You will work none the less. Don't depart from the regulations. If you do, a fine or the dungeon."

And in the prison, as is generally the case in a reformatory discipline, the punishment must be severe, for punishments which are not so, and especially in prison, irritate. Severity alone inspires awe. Work is finished. "Forward, march, to the refectory. You will have meat only on Sundays and festival days. Halt a moment. Forward, march, to work;" and so on to the moment in which the last company enters its dormitory, where silence reigns, and where one would hear the motion of a fly's wing. This constant pressure of the discipline throughout the duration of the imprisonment would end in making the prisoner mad, if it were not balanced by an anticipation of the time when the punishment, once undergone, will no longer have any reason to exist. All constraint is essentially hateful, and it is for this reason that our judgment is in favor of admitting a certain degree of liberty in whatever may be advantageous to the future of the prisoners. We believe it necessary to give freedom of choice between gratuitous and waged labor; freedom in the selection of trades; permission to go or not to go to school, or to the Sunday conferences; liberty to read or not to read. One does really well only what one does of his own will.

We think it proper to add some words regarding the sanitary results of the experiment made at Moscow. There were recorded in six years 27 deaths out of 2,128 prisoners, about 4 per cent. This number is considerable, but it is explained by the fact that the greater part of the persons brought to the prisons are already enfeebled by debauchery.

Some of the diseases that have been cured have had perhaps their cause in a too restricted dietary, insufficient for men in the flower of their age. We are not permitted to go beyond the existing laws on this subject, but it appears to us that a more substantial diet would be desirable.

Such, in brief, are the statistics which we have thought proper to add to our memoir upon the prison question in Russia, as published in the report of the New York Prison Association. We were far from expecting that that memoir would cause any sensation, or that it would procure for us the distinguished honor of a correspondence with eminent specialists and the flattering privilege of being enrolled as a member of philanthropical societies of high repute.

Among the ideas which our conscience has constrained us to put forth—that which has enlisted universal sympathy—is the proposition to call an international congress to establish definitively the laws of an improved penitentiary discipline. This proposition, however, was but the natural sequence of pre-existing facts. The secretary of the Prison Association of New York had already addressed himself to different governments, with the view of collecting information concerning the modes of prison administration of all countries. This collection of materials should evidently be only a preface. The materials necessitated a critical examination, the critical examination a conclusion, and the conclusion demanded publicity. The task undertaken by the association of New York involved, necessarily, the international congress. We cannot sufficiently testify our gratitude to the respectable secretary of the association, Mr. Wines, for the energy with which he has pushed the preliminaries of the greatest movement for reform of which the prison question has ever been the occasion. Within a period of less than three years, propositions to this effect were sent to all the civilized points of the globe, and received unanimous adhesions. A preliminary congress, held in October, 1870, at Cincinnati, declared itself on thirty-seven questions, founded the national association of the United States, and laid down definitive rules for the international congress fixed at London for the month of July, 1872. Mr. Wines, clothed with an official character, came to Europe to confer with the different governments and with specialists of highest renown.

Penitentiary science, then, thanks to the indefatigable activity of Mr. Wines, is about to enter upon a new phase. The congress, accepted everywhere, becomes an event of the highest importance. This importance, nevertheless, depends on the direction which shall be given to the conferences, and on the conclusions which shall be reached.

Mr. Wines is devoting himself to this question as well as to all the others connected with the congress. In the midst of his immense correspondence and of his numerous voyages, he has found time to prepare a series of questions addressed to the different governments, relating to the prisons and prison administrations of their several countries.

This series of questions continues the work commenced, and seeks to complete the documents and statistical *data* on what concerns the prisons of all countries. The idea of Mr. Wines, without doubt, is that it will belong to the congress to declare itself as to what ought to be determined upon as definitive axioms in relation to penitentiary science. It is this manifesto of science which we invoke with all our heart.

Every country has its exigencies, its traditions, its habits, its routine. Every country has its vestiges of barbarism, living ruins of an ancient order of things; but these ruins have not yet been transformed into symmetrical edifices. The troubles of war and the labors of peace have left them still extant, perhaps from want of time, perhaps from lack of means; perhaps, also, a little through indifference. There is no country which can boast of being able to serve as a model in its penal legislation. There is no country which does not feel the pressing need of important modifications in this regard. But we do not suppose that all these sincere confessions, these tardy acknowledgments of national shortcomings, can take the place of, or be an equivalent for, a congress. There is no government, however civilized it may be, which can feel complacency in appearing before such a tribunal to enumerate its faults. Matters of this kind can only be talked of, so to speak, in the family at home. We must acknowledge that when we received the invitation to prepare for America a memoir on the state of the prisons in Russia we were singularly embarrassed. We well knew that, on the one side, it was disloyal to disguise the truth, but that, on the other, it was cruel to lay bare before foreigners the bleeding wounds of one's own country. We therefore determined to speak the truth only in some words; to glide over it, as it were; but to extend our remarks upon the essays that had been confided to us in view of the future. There resulted from this a misunderstanding, for the essay was taken for the exhibition of a complete system already existing; and special sheets, published in England, in America, in Italy, praise the organization of the Russian prisons; a representation which was, unhappily, premature.

There is, it seems to us, another rock still to be avoided by the congress—that of falling into questions of detail. Every country having its exigencies and its peculiarities, it will be very difficult to separate great humanitarian considerations from those of a local character.

The direction of the debates, the choice of the principles to be definitively established in the name of science, render necessary, as we think, some preliminary understanding, some preparatory labors. We look upon the congress as a tribunal which will have to pronounce judgment, after having heard the pleadings of the advocates, but will not have the time to study the questions and to make *résumés* of general statistics. It should direct its attention not so much to what has been or what is, as to what ought to be. Our opinion is, that the different governments should send to the congress not official representatives, which might embarrass them, but unofficial ones, who might take part in the debates, without making the conclusions of the congress rigorously binding upon the countries of which they might be the delegates. Such is also the opinion of the English government. An official international congress could be, it seems to us, only political. The congress of London ought to be an affair quite different from this, if it would be generally recognized as useful. It should be, no doubt, supported, patronized, and its expenses shared by all the powers; but it ought to guard its special character, so as to avoid all embarrassment in the debates, and everything that looks like binding the administrations which are represented in it. It is only after the close of the congress that each government will be able, on the report of its delegation, to determine what it will accept and what reforms it will undertake.

The form of the questions framed by Mr. Wines seems to us particularly happy as a basis of preliminary labors in view of the congress. We also take leave to submit a series of questions, which we offer to the examination of the students of penitentiary science.

Our opinion is that collective reformation is more important than individual reformation; that detention prisons ought to be connected with the centers of preliminary proceedings, and with the judicial tribunals, and should be governed by special regulations; that prisons for punishment can be of only three classes, and must be determined by the duration of the imprisonment; that the same prison ought not to be used for different objects; and that the same object cannot properly be sought in different prisons.

What we would desire above everything is, to establish the system of classification, for upon an exact classification depend the different modes of architecture, of discipline, and of public utility. If the congress does no more than fix the fundamental boundaries of the classes of prisons and the functions which each class is to perform, it will, by so doing, have rendered an immense service to humanity.

———

2. QUESTIONS PROPOSED BY COUNT SOLLOHUB IN VIEW OF THE APPROACHING INTERNATIONAL PENITENTIARY CONGRESS.

1. Do you consider it the aim of the congress to secure, among civilized nations, a unanimous judgment on the most desirable legislative and administrative plan for the general management of prisons?

2. To avoid the loss of precious time, do you not think it desirable that the congress engage neither in abstract discussions nor in studies relating to what is peculiar to each several country, but that it seek to come to an understanding on fundamental principles, on practical axioms, which every civilized state should henceforth have in view in the managements of its prisons?

3. Do you not think that these axioms should be divided into—

(a) General principles applicable to all countries;

(b) Local considerations necessitating exceptional measures?

4. In determining principles, do you not consider it necessary to avoid confounding questions of detail with general questions, so as to avoid confusion in the discussions?

5. Do you not think that general questions are summarily comprehended in the principles of classification and organization, and questions of detail in the principles of discipline and practice suited to the different aims which they should have in view?   •

6. Do you think it proper that the congress decline all discussion of the death penalty, as having no connection with its special aim?

7. Do you judge it proper that the congress decline all discussion on political rights, social order, bail, fines, &c., it being impossible to treat these matters thoroughly in a first meeting?

8. Ought not the congress to recognize from the start, as a binding principle, the fundamental proposition of Rossi's Treatise on the Penal Code: *"Imprisonment is punishment, par excellence, among all civilized people?"*

9. Should not the congress add to this the following declaration: *"Preliminary imprisonment is a necessary evil, imposed from considerations of social security?"*

10. Should not the general principles, applicable to all countries, lead to the following declarations:

(a) All imprisonment ought to have a special aim, and that strictly determined;

(b) The same prison cannot serve different ends;

(c) Prisons of different kinds cannot serve the same end?

11. This being admitted, do you think that all the prisons of a civilized country must belong to one of the four well-marked follow-

ing forms: (*a*) detention, (*b*) amendment, (*c*) correction, (*d*) punishment?

12. Do you think that detention prisons (*maisons préventives*) should be made the object of special solicitude, and that prisoners awaiting trial (*détenus préventifs*) ought not to be subjected to the humiliations and servitudes which should be applied only to persons found guilty by the courts?

13. Are you of opinion that the theory of detention of prisons ought to be made the object of special deliberations and categorical decisions on the part of the congress? Will you not give special thought to this subject, which, as being the most difficult point in penitentiary science, requires the convergence of all the lights that can be directed toward it?

14. Do you think it absolutely necessary to fix a definite minimum period for the custody of arrested persons prior to their transfer to the detention prison?

15. What would this period be in principle, apart from local considerations?

16. Do you think it indispensable that the examinations be continued subsequently to those of a preliminary character, within the precincts of the detention prison itself, and that, in this view, there be established in all these prisons offices of committing magistrates and of deputy attorneys general?

17. Do you think it necessary to establish strict regulations touching the proceedings of committing magistrates, with a view to shortening as much as possible the period of preliminary imprisonment?

18. Are you of opinion that detention prisons should be adjacent to the court-rooms, (*palais de justice*,) so as to spare the prisoners needless humiliation and loss of time, and save to the administration the expense of carriage-hire and police escort?

19. Would you be able to suggest any means to accelerate the progress of justice?

20. What in your opinion are the best styles of architecture and modes of discipline for detention prisons?

21. Do you not think that a uniform rule for all prisoners awaiting trial would lead to needless vexations, and that we might properly recognize three classes of this sort of prisoners:

(*a*) Those who should be in complete isolation;

(*b*) Those who should be subjected to certain restraints;

(*c*) Those who might properly enjoy comparative liberty?

22. Do you not regard as equitable the following principles:

Every prisoner awaiting trial has the right—

(*a*) To an apartment for himself individually;

(*b*) To the preservation of his clothing and his ordinary modes of life as far as possible;

(*c*) To purchase for himself better food than the customary fare of the prison;

(*d*) To smoke, read, and occupy himself in manual labors without being subject to a detention of his earnings;

(*e*) To receive visits authorized by the committing magistrate;

(*f*) To exercise in the open air, except in cases of absolute isolation, where cellular yards should be provided;

(*g*) To be free from every privation, every humiliation, every inconvenience, other than those required by the order of the prison and the necessities of the preliminary proceedings?

23. Do you not think that, nevertheless, it would be useful to neutral-

ize the evil influences which the prisoners might have on one another?
What would you propose to be the best means to this end?

24. Will you please trace the normal plan for a prison construction,
uniting the several localities requisite for trial, preliminary proceedings,
and detention?

25. Do you think it necessary to establish separate detention prisons
for the two sexes, or may such prisons consist of two separate sections
in the same establishment?.

26. What would be the maximum number of prisoners that might
properly be confined in a detention prison?

27. What are the special exigencies of the country or city in which you
happen to reside for the improvement of detention prisons?

28. What would be the proper discipline to be introduced for the
maintenance of order in the establishment without being irritating to
the prisoners?

29. Are you of opinion that it is not logical to admit into the codes
only two degrees of guilt, when there are three?

30. Do you not think it necessary to treat this subject in the congress in a manner very exact? Does not it appear to you that confusion
in prison discipline has proceeded from confusion in the penal laws,
which admit two forms of guilt, *misdemeanor* and *crime*, whereas there
are three forms of guilt, corresponding to the three forms of comparison—minimum, medium, and higher—which may be designated as misdemeanor, crime, and felony, (*délit, crime et forfait.*) Would not this
classification draw after it the corollary that against each form of guilt
there should be established a special system, which should not be confounded with the others? The system for misdemeanors would take for
its aim amendment; for crimes, correction; for felonies, punishment.

31. Do you not think it of great importance to ordain that each
degree of penal imprisonment, answering to a particular aim, be rigidly
determined by the minimum and maximum of the duration of detention,
so that the classification of prisons shall be controlled by the continuance of the imprisonment?

32. Do you consider it necessary that all existing penal prisons be
modified in this sense, and that all those which are not conformed to
the above classification be regarded as abnormal?

33. Do you accept as logical the following propositions:

(*a*) The house of amendment has for its aim to inflict on the prisoner
a salutary terror, to arrest him at the moment in which he is entering
upon an evil course, and to withdraw him from the bad influences to
which he might be subjected as well outside of the prison as among his
prison comrades.

(*b*) The house of correction has for its aim to give to the prisoner a
new education, and to prepare him for a return to society under conditions which would render his return safe. In this view, the correctional
system should use its best efforts to the end that the prisoner on his
liberation may carry with him a capital of good habits, a capital of
newly acquired knowledge, and, above all, a capital of money, without
which the other two might remain inefficacious. This capital would be
acquired under the form of wages, agreeably to principles to be hereafter explained.

(*c*) The convict prison (*maison de force*) or galley (*bagne*) has for its
aim to positively cut off from society its members, recognized as unworthy to re-enter it, to the end that they may serve as an example,
and to protect the general safety. The galleys must not, in any case,
be confounded with deportation. Distant or near, they ought to con-

tain individually convicted criminals, and to release them only at the end of the sentence fixed by the laws for their imprisonment.

(*d*) The system for the convicts would be the same as for the correctionals, but the discipline more severe. The money gained as wages would not be given unconditionally to the liberated convicts as to the liberated correctionals, but would be applied to a system of colonization, based on capital, landed property, and family, the only principles which can assure the future of a colony. The place chosen for colonization would depend upon the topographical conditions of each country.

(*e*) The architecture and discipline of each class of penal prisons would be determined by special considerations?

34. The houses of amendment having for their object to inspire delinquents with a salutary terror, thereby leading them to avoid pernicious influences, ought they not to be rigidly cellular, although for short imprisonments?

35. Do you not think that it would be useful to discuss at the congress the following motion :

The congress declares that cellular imprisonment is to be recommended only in the following cases :

First. For short sentences in the houses of amendment.

Second. As a disciplinary punishment in the houses of correction and convict prisons.

Third. It would be desirable that all existing cellular prisons be reorganized in this sense.

36. Do you not think that the duration of detention in the cellular prisons of amendment ought not to exceed three months, a term sufficient for the end proposed, while a longer captivity might offer serious inconveniences?

37. Would you not think it necessary to propose to all governments adopting the cellular system for houses of amendment, to eliminate from their legislation all penal detentions from three months to a year, on the ground that that period would be too prolonged for repressive and too short for correctional action?

38. Guilt of the first degree being divisible into infractions and delinquencies, (*contraventions et délits*,) do you think it necessary to establish, besides houses of amendment, houses of arrest for persons guilty of the first of these offenses, or do you think it would be sufficient to establish, for this purpose, sections in the houses of amendment, or, in short, do you think that such a distinction would be useless, and that a slight degree of culpability should only draw after it a minimum term of detention in the house of amendment?

39. Admitting that the houses of correction should have for their object the regeneration of the prisoner, do you think it wise to enact that no one shall be detained in a house of correction less than one year or more than five years, and that the penal laws should be modified to conform to this principle?

40. Do you think that every penal detention should have in view, above all, the time of the prisoner's liberation, and that the entire discipline of prisons should be organized with a view to prevent relapses? If by short imprisonments it is important to give an energetic notice so as to hinder the propagation of evil, is it not important by means of sentences of a longer duration to prepare, in a manner more sustained and efficacious, the correctional prisoner for his re-entrance into society?

41. Does it not appear just that every penal imprisonment should be executed rigorously and without the least feebleness, but that the epoch at which the punishment shall end be made the object of a special soli-

citude? In admitting, to the fullest extent, the utility of moral instruction, it is impossible to deny that this alone is insufficient, where a man finds himself, without defense, exposed to misery, scorn, and temptation, when the gates of the prison are opened for his egress. Is not, then, what follows the prison more grave than the imprisonment itself, and is it not true that in nearly all cases of relapse, the cause is found rather in the prisons than in the recidivists? Is it not the object of correctional detention, while maintaining the rigor of the punishment, to impart to the liberated correctional the means of earning a livelihood, and to afford him the opportunity of laying by such a portion of his earnings as will be sufficient for the new struggles which he is about to encounter?

42. Is it not at the same time highly useful to point out without ceasing to the prisoner the end which he may gain, to arouse in him a regenerative aspiration, to enable him to gain a constant victory over himself, and thereby to accomplish his complete reformation?

43. Inasmuch as labor affords a constant occupation to the mind, and constitutes besides the sole source of income possible to prisoners, do you not think that the theory of prison labor ought to be made an object of special attention by the Congress?

44. Do you think it would be an error to confound under one general signification the three forms of labor which may serve either as punishment, or as a mechanical occupation, or as a means of regeneration?

45. Are you not of the opinion that this third form of labor should be liberally remunerated in order to form a *peculium* for the prisoner, since this must serve as a safeguard to him after his liberation?

46. Do you regard as equitable the following regulations respecting correctional prisoners:

(*a*) Every prisoner, received into a correctional prison, is under obligation to work without remuneration, ten hours a day, at rough manual labors, the product of which belongs to the administration.

(*b*) Every prisoner has the right, if he so elect, to redeem himself in part from labor unproductive as regards himself, and to be subjected to the rough occupations only four hours a day; if he express the desire to pass to mechanical occupations, the product of which shall be divided in the following manner—one-third for the laborer, two-thirds for the administration.

(*c*) If the prisoner manifests the desire to learn a trade, he is subjected only two hours a day to the rough work, but receives no wages so long as he remains an apprentice. On becoming a master-workman, he receives two-thirds of his earnings for himself, and the administration only one-third.

(*d*) The prisoner who is already master of a trade at the time of his incarceration receives but a moiety of his wages; the other moiety goes to the administration.

(*e*) No prisoner has the right to touch his money before the day of his liberation.

(*f*) Every prisoner has his little book, in which is inscribed, each week, the sum that he has earned by his labor.

(*g*) The money of the prisoners is placed in a particular case, inclosed within the strong box of the establishment, but the key of the case is in the hands of a cashier, whom the prisoners choose from among themselves, and who is always present when the money is deposited in the case, and when it is paid out to the prisoners.

(*h*) The trades taught to the prisoners should be simple and not requiring any great expenditure of funds, such as tailors, shoemakers, hosiers, book-binders, weavers, &c. The trade should be taught as a whole, and not in part.

(*i*) The wages should be distributed in such manner that the same degree of application would secure the same benefit.

(*j*) The infraction of a disciplinary regulation should involve a fine, to be deducted from the *peculium* of the workman.

(*k*) The prisoners should have the right to establish their own tribunal, whose acts must be ratified by the director of the establishment.

(*l*) The *cantine* should be rigorously prohibited.

(*m*) If the customary rations of the prison are not sufficient for the support of the prisoners, a fourth part of the wages might be devoted to the expense of a more substantial nutriment, but only on the request of the prisoners themselves, and under their inspection. The purchases for this purpose should, nevertheless, be confided to the overseer of the establishment. It is a matter of course that only master-workmen should be permitted to enjoy this privilege.

(*n*) The superintendence of the work should be in the hands either of the authorities of the prison or of manufacturers by profession; but no contractor should be in charge of several branches of business at once?

47. Might not the congress resolve that in countries which offer vast productive forces and few arms, the labor of prisoners cannot be too much encouraged as an auxiliary to private industry; but that where population exceeds the productive forces, it is impossible not to recognize the possibility of competition between prison labor and free labor?

48. What would be your opinion in this last case? How could the injustice be avoided that would be done to the free and honest laborer in favor of the criminal, whose crime would thus become a title to public assistance?

49. Do you not think that this question ought specially to engage the solicitude of the congress?

50. Since the principle of reformation should effect a reconciliation of the prisoner with himself, are you of opinion that the cellular system and the law of silence can only lead to a result diametrically contrary to that which is proposed? It would then be rational to prevent the irritation occasioned by both systems by replacing the cells with separation at night in common dormitories, and the law of silence with a discipline by day which would prevent dangerous conversations, cabals, or even orgies. The regulations for the night should require that all the dormitories be lighted, that attendants circulate through them, and that silence be enforced in them in order not to disturb the sleep of the prisoners—an arrangement which in no case could be regarded as a cause of irritation. The discipline of the day should require a triple *surveillance*, viz: on the part of the overseer of the shop, the regular monitor, and an old man chosen by the prisoners themselves from among his comrades.

51. The rations of the prisoners being fixed by law, do you not think that the prisoners ought to have delegates, whose duty it would be to be present at the reception of the provisions, and even to be responsible for their good quality?

52. Do you think it would be unwise to confine the education of prisoners to the mere elements of learning, and that it would be desirable to establish in correctional prisons two courses of instruction—one for beginners, the other for prisoners who already possess knowledge of a higher order? Do you not think it also indispensable that men specially qualified give to the prisoners, every Sunday, lectures on scientific subjects, having relation to history, geography, chemistry, physics,

the natural sciences, and, in general, to everything that can enlarge the intellectual horizon of persons who are rather ignorant than guilty ?

53. Do you not think that prison libraries ought to be the object of special solicitude on the part of the congress, and that it would be desirable that the congress offer a premium for the best work which might be written for the use of prisoners ?

54. Since the congress will contain representatives of different religions, do you not think that it should content itself with resolving that religious instruction ought to be made obligatory in every prison, without enlarging on the mode and nature of such instruction ?

55. Do you not think that to establish order in a prison, it is indispensable to pay special attention to its architectural arrangements ? Do you accept as desirable the following principles :.

(a) Every correctional prison should have a large kitchen-garden to serve as the base of a system of labor, being made at once a branch of revenue for the administration and a center of unremunerated manual labor ;

(b) No one, except the director and the chief keeper, should have lodgings within the prison itself;

(c) There should be a special court outside of the prison to contain the residences of the chaplain, the surgeon, the assistant surgeon, the schoolmaster, the midwife, (for female prisons, which should be central, like those of the men, but established at a distance, although under the same administration,) the monitors, and the keepers. This court of service should contain also the magazines of provisions, the stables, the garden-tools, &c. The overseers of the prison should go there only to discharge the duties of their service, and, beyond the time of their service laid down by the regulations, should not have the right to remain there;

(d) The hours of rising and retiring, of labor and rest, should be announced by the bells of the establishment;

(e) The building of the correctional prison should be divided into three courts, in the following manner :

First court. Wicket, guard-house, chancery, kitchens, laundry, store-rooms for the effects of prisoners. The main building, facing the court of entrance on one side and the second court on the other, should contain the residences of the director and the chief-keeper, and the apartment where prisoners are allowed to see their friends.

Second court. Chapel, refectory, store-room for clothing furnished by the administration, school and library, dungeons, dormitories.

Third court. Workshops for trades.

N. B.—The hospital and baths should be placed in the kitchen-garden, to avoid the danger of contagion and fire, but within the general inclosure of the establishment, which should be marked by a deep fosse, and, if necessary, by a wall. The prison for females should be established near by; its bases should be the same as that for the men; but the wash-house should there replace agricultural labors.

56. What would be your objections to this plan ?

57. Do you not think that the utmost cleanliness ought to be maintained in an establishment of this kind, and that cleanliness has also its reformatory side ?

58. Do you not think that military discipline in an establishment of this kind would be too rigorous ?

59. Do you not think it desirable to offer an international premium to the architect who shall furnish the best plan for a house of correction ?

60. Do you not think it highly desirable that the congress offer an in-

ternational premium to the engineer who shall propose the best system for the ventilation and the water-closet (*lieu d'aisance*) of prisons? Cheapness should be one of the absolute conditions of this premium.

61. In general, are you not of opinion that cheapness in the construction of prisons ought to be a constant aim of penitentiary science, and that establishments requiring large expenditures of funds deform the action of justice by applying it only to privileged prisons, to the detriment of the great principle of equality, which ought to make men equal even in the presence of punishment and the benefits which may come in its train?

62. Do you not think that houses of correction, as they ought to be central, should contain not more than six hundred inmates?

63. Is it not your judgment that the congress ought to occupy itself specially with the question of legislation for young criminals? Do you not think that short and medium terms of imprisonment ought to be avoided, but that society, on assuming the charge of a minor who may have committed a crime, should be bound to charge itself with his entire education to the day of his majority?

64. Would not the system of the agricultural colony, in the vicinity of a model farm, be the best means to this end, as an agency both of instruction and of profit? What are your views upon this subject as regards the country of which you are a citizen?

65. Do you think that deportation, pure and simple, without regard to the time passed in the convict prison, and without the principles of a rational colonization, can be of any utility whatever? If such is your judgment, are you not of opinion that the congress might make the following declaration: The deportation which should only cause criminals to be transported from one place to another would but shift the danger of impunity, and therefore would have no reason for its existence.

66. Do you not think that we should be careful not to confound exile for political causes with deportation inflicted for crimes, since exile is but a banishment with liberty of locomotion, while deportation should be admitted only with the clause requiring the convicts to undergo the punishment which they may have deserved, affording them, however, at a later period, the opportunity of colonizing by means of the money which they should have been able to lay up during their imprisonment?

67. Do you not think that the Irish system might be applied, wholly or in part, to the management of convict prisons in other countries?

68. Do you think that the galley-slaves might be admitted to a participation in their earnings from the moment of their entrance into the bagnio, or should they remain a certain time without the right to any remuneration whatever in order to increase the severity of their punishment?

69. Do you not think that the disciplinary severity of the bagnios ought to admit—

(*a*) That separation by night should be effected in little cells of brick or stone;

(*b*) That the prisoners be compelled to wear chains during a certain time, and that they be permitted to lay them aside only after the time prescribed, and not even then unless they should have deserved such indulgence by their conduct and their application;

(*c*) That for a violation of discipline they be subjected to corporal punishment, which could not be tolerated in any other class of prisons?

70. Do you not think that the bagnios should be placed near the localities in which the criminal acts have been committed, in order to avoid the useless expense of transportation, and to serve as a continual

example in sight of the people; and that the establishment of bagnios in distant colonies is admissible only when the topographical conditions of a country show a too great agglomeration of inhabitants in view of a marked insufficiency of the productive forces of that country?

71. The want of money being always the great objection which is urged against the establishment of a complete system of rational prisons, do you not think that the financial problem relating to this important branch of the administration of each country would find its solution in the following proposition:

(a) The houses of detention, connected with the centers of preliminary proceedings and of judicial sentences, should be established and maintained at the expense of the municipalities, as having relation to the civic rights of the citizens whom justice has not yet declared guilty, and for that reason having a right to the protection of their fellow-citizens;

(b) The houses of amendment (cellular, from one day to three months) should be established and maintained at the expense of the state;

(c) The houses of correction (separation by night, labor stimulated, from one year to five) should be established by the aid of a loan reimbursable from the product of the labor of the prisoners. The maintenance of the correctionals would devolve upon the state until the formation of capital funds, which the prisons of this category would have to provide;

(d) The convict prisons or bagnios, with sentences from five years to life, remissible conditionally, should be established by joint stock companies, as great enterprises are set on foot, or by the state in a similar manner. The formation of an obligatory capital, realizable only by the participation of the prisoners in the profits of the enterprise in view of their colonization, should take for their base the principles proposed for the correctional prisons?

72. Are you not of the opinion that the ideas above set forth might be made the object of the special attention of the congress? Do you think that questions of colonization, being outside of what relates specially to prisons, could not be properly debated by the congress?

73. On the other hand, do you think that the question of prison administration ought to be the object of an unanimous judgment?

74. Do you think that every prison, in order to maintain all the rigors of discipline, ought to be conducted on a war footing, like a regiment in service or a vessel in commission?

75. Do you think that the prisons of a country ought to depend on the ministry of the interior or on the ministry of justice, or that the detention prisons alone ought to depend on the ministry of justice, and the others on the ministry of the interior?

76. Do you not think that the topographical features of the different countries should have an influence on the mode of administration of their prisons; that a country of little extent may centralize the inspection of its prisons, while countries covering vast territorial regions must parcel out the inspections, yet uniting them in a general administrative focus?

77. Do you not think that since the immediate directors of certain prisons are called upon to exercise rights of great importance, and to accept obligations no less grave, it would be essential to raise the dignity of directors of the central prisons? The houses of preliminary detention and amendment might be confided to officers of a scrupulous probity, but the houses of correction and the bagnios ought evidently to be intrusted only to men of a high civilization, whom it would be

unnecessary to subject to the complications of a too minute administrative machinery. Should they not be subjected simply to an inspector general, who, on his part, would be obliged to have recourse to the central administration placed in charge of the prisons?

78. Do you not think that the directors of the great prisons should be chosen from among the officers of the prisons of a lower order, and that the inspectors, whether of *arrondissement* or general, according to the necessity of different countries, should be chosen from among the directors of the great prisons? Might not this order of things create a new specialty of administration, the absence of which is now widely felt?

79. Do you not think that the assistance of philanthropic prison societies might be of an indisputable utility, but that it would be desirable that the congress sanction the following proposition, enunciated in one of the works of Mr. Charles Lucas: "The action of philanthropic societies begins where that of the administration ends?"

80. Should not philanthropic societies take for the object of their efforts—

(*a*) The establishment and embellishment of prison chapels;

(*b*) Aid to their schools and libraries;

(*c*) The moral instruction of the prisoners by ecclesiastics chosen for this end;

(*d*) The establishment of asylums for the children of prisoners;

(*e*) The guardianship of liberated prisoners;

(*f*) The observations and propositions for ameliorations which they should have the right of proposing to the authorities?

IX.—THE GERMAN EMPIRE.

[In the latter part of February, or early in March, a letter was received from Herr Steinmann, counselor in the ministry of the interior, who is specially concerned with penal affairs, and to whom the preparation of the report for Germany was assigned by the minister, in which he said that the report had been completed, and would be forwarded in a few days. Its arrival has been vainly expected to the present time, (May 15,) when this report is placed in the hands of the printer. It is feared that the failure is due to some mischance in the mails. Whatever may have been the cause, (whether this or some other,) the non-reception of the document is deeply regretted, and must be felt by all as a serious loss to science.]

B.—ALEXANDER MACONOCHIE AND HIS PRINCIPLES OF PRISON DISCIPLINE.

No one familiar with the literature of penology can have failed to recognize in Alexander Maconochie one of the profoundest thinkers and most vigorous writers on that subject the world has ever seen. His writings are marked by a fullness of knowledge, a clearness of thought and expression, and a force of reasoning, united to a love of truth and a spirit of candor, which render them as charming as they are instructive. Yet he produced no good book, nor did he develop, in any single publication, his whole system of prison organization and prison management. He was pre-eminently a pamphleteer; and his works, which are numerous, consist rather of tractates, dashed off on special occasions and for particular purposes, than complete and exhaustive treatises, evolved through a process of long and patient thought, continued through months and years of solitary study. For this reason he continually repeats himself; and it is not even uncommon with him to give the same title to different publications. I have, therefore, thought that it would be a useful service to those who are devoted to studies of this nature, to the greater part of whom, probably, the writings of this author are not accessible, and have judged that it would be especially timely, in view of the approaching international penitentiary congress of London, to bring together, under a series of propositions, embodying the essential principles of prison discipline held and advocated by him, the substance of what he has published on this subject. In doing this, I shall sometimes condense what he has writen, and, at others, make use of his own language unchanged, but without the formality of quotation marks, since, as I make no pretense to originality in this paper, and aim to be simply a faithful mouth-piece to Captain Maconochie, such characters would only serve to disfigure the page.

Without further preface, I proceed to the work in hand, putting in, however, this *caveat;* that while I heartily concur in most of the positions taken by this able and excellent author, as well as successful prison-governor, there are a few of them to which I cannot give an unqualified assent.

I. *In lieu of the customary sentences on conviction for crime, imposed for a fixed time, there should be substituted a specific task, to be computed in marks of approval, given for diligence and good conduct, or if sentences as recorded in court are still imposed for a definite period, they should be commutable, at a fixed valuation, into labor and good conduct.*

The essential principle of the mark system is the substitution of task for time sentences. It proposes that, instead of criminals being sentenced to so many months or years of imprisonment, they be required to earn so many hundred or thousand marks of approval or commendation in the same condition, subject to whatever rules may be otherwise imposed. This change would not benefit the prisoner, as regards the duration of his imprisonment, because to earn a considerable number of marks, or considerable amount of time must be employed, and it would be easy so to adjust the quantity of marks to be earned, that the task sentence, with reasonable diligence and good conduct, should be nearly the measure of the time sentence. But there would be this important difference: that in the one case the reasonable diligence and good conduct are indispensable to the completion of the sentence, and in the other they are not; and there would be this further difference, that the time sentence, being the only thing required, is commonly sought to be whiled away, as far as possible, in idleness, self-indulgence, prurient thought, word, or act, pretended sickness, and the like, and is thus necessarily deteriorating; while, in the other case, the task sentence, by making diligence and good conduct the first object, and thus giving a strong interest in activity, exertion, ingenuity, and perseverance, would be, from necessity, a period of great improvement; and in this sole contrast between the two systems, will be seen, at a glance, the immense superiority of the one over the other.

In administering punishment, we should in every case seek primarily to reform the individual criminal, without directly aiming to make an example of him. For this purpose we ought, while endeavoring to gain and direct him, carefully to avoid doing anything calculated to enfeeble him either in body or mind. On the contrary, we should seek, in all possible ways, to invigorate and strengthen him. If this end be judiciously sought; if we endeavor to improve the prisoner, morally and physically, by properly stimulated self-exertion and self-restraint, (the only way in which it can be successfully done,) we shall find that the sight of this process, and the known fact that all convicted persons must pass through it before being again released, will prove more deterrent than anything we now inflict for the special purpose of deterring. In other words, by making reform our first object, and seeking it through properly stimulated industry and self-command, with the necessary moral and religious instruction, we shall find that we both *reform* and *deter;* whereas at present we rather corrupt and incite. Or, in other words still, by making punishment primarily a school of hardy reform, reform through sustained hardy exertion, we shall gain our ends in it; but by making it primarily a school of suffering, with reform a subordinate object, we practically lose them.

As a rule, reform can be attained only through a severe training. It is in a system of (so to speak) well-devised adversity, by a victory over opposing forces, that all the manly virtues are generated, all the manly energies called out. Before a task, to be accomplished as the indispensable condition of release, time becomes valuable. It is sought to be improved, not cheated. A purpose is given to life. Idleness is shunned, industry courted. Prurient and other distracting thoughts are rejected. Evasion brings with it its own punishment, by prolonging detention. Moreover, the impulse to exertion is thus made moral instead of physical; it is internal, not external. This accustoms the prisoner to act for himself, instead of requiring him to be led by others. Above everything, such a training would prepare him to meet subsequent temptation. And the habit of self-command necessarily generated in prison by such a system, would remain after his discharge, almost of itself a compensation for the sacrifices by which it was acquired.

Sentences measured by time convert time into the great enemy of prisoners; and thus, instead of being systematically taught to value it, as the laboring free are compelled to do outside, they are systematically taught to hold it of no account, and to cheat and idle it away by every means in their power. It is impossible to overrate the moral injury thus alone inflicted, which might and would all be avoided by substituting sentences measured by tasks instead. Indolence, evasion of labor, and habitual pruriency of thought, act, and language, are among the direct results of time sentences; whereas the result of task sentences would be industry, active effort, a healthy influx of new thoughts and motives, and a toning up, strengthening, and general improvement of the character.

Long fixed sentences are always morally injurious by leading criminals to accommodate themselves to existing circumstances of whatever kind, while they undervalue and neglect distant prospects. This evil would be lessened by an accompanying task, measured, as proposed, by marks; for then, from the very start, they would, by their exertions, their idleness, or their contumacy, be sensibly advancing or receding, day by day, toward or from the anticipated discharge, and would thus have constantly before them a motive to activity and self-denial. Nevertheless, a very distant minimum will ever be found to damp their zeal, and be otherwise disadvantageous. On the other hand, the task, while fairly proportioned to the accompanying time sentence, should be made rather hard, never easily to be performed in the whole minimum time assigned with it, and impossible to be done in less. In any case, advance toward it, with good conduct, will always be certain; with industry and economy, it may even be rapid, and the character must improve with every step. This constant approach to liberty, through the prisoner's accumulation of marks over and above both expenditure and forfeiture, is the key-stone of the arch. Apart from executive pardon, nothing should release a criminal once under bondage, except the literal fulfillment of his task; nor, when this is done and his minimum time served out, should anything short of a new charge retain him. The excessive applications for pardon now made, too often on false grounds, yet also too often listened to, give excessive trouble to the executive, while the hopes and systematic misrepresentations which they suggest among prisoners also do them much mischief. At present, when punishment is known to be almost universally deteriorating, it is hard to resist these applications; but when it shall come to be known as universally improving, this reason for leniently considering individual petitions will be at an end.

II. *The prisoner's destiny, during his incarceration, should be placed, measurably, in his own hands ; he must be put into circumstances where he will be able, through his own efforts, to continually better his condition.*

One of the gravest errors in the existing system of prison discipline is that it requires only submission and endurance on the part of those subjected to it. No means are offered to prisoners to improve their condition under it, and their minds consequently become, in a short time, stagnant. They accommodate themselves to the position in which they are placed with little feeling of pain, as they would accommodate themselves to a worse, if they were placed in it; for it is of the nature of man, after a time, thus to submit with resignation to an invincible necessity. If it were possible for prisoners, by exertion, to better their position, they would feel its privations far more. They would contrast, in thought, their actual condition with that to which they might, by a succession of efforts, raise themselves. They would become daily more and more dissatisfied with the first, and would more and more crave the last. They would be willing to make any sacrifice to attain and, when attained, to preserve it. Their fate being thus placed in their own hands, their manly purposes and energies would be strengthened; whereas now, these, kept in quiescence, become every day more and more enfeebled. They would, almost of necessity, be improved by such a form of adversity, by such voluntary self-effort and self-denial; whereas, under prison discipline as at present conducted, they are, as a general rule, deteriorated. And, when discharged, they would go out prepared to contend successfully with the difficulties of free life, instead of, as now, weaklings, incapable of consistent effort, except under the eye of a task-master, and thus compelled, for the most part, by absolute want, to yield to the first strong temptation to renewed criminality.

The first and essential step to be taken in improving prison management, and making imprisonment at once formidable outside and improving within, is, therefore, to reduce the accommodations and comforts allowed in prisons as a matter of right to the lowest standard consistent with proper seclusion, decency, and support of life; but to enable good conduct and exertion to acquire better and better, as they are, progressively, more and more signally and steadily displayed. In this stage all should remain till they had undergone a fixed probation, performed so much work, and otherwise complied with every prison requisition, and the task, though graduated according to strength, should in every case be made a hard one, the object being to stimulate exertion.

by a strong motive. The first removal should then be a second stage, in which a little more comfort should be given, but still with a reserve suited to maintain the impulse thus once started; and thence to a third, a fourth, and so on, always upon the same plan. But from each higher stage misconduct should remove to a lower, or even the lowest, position, according to its degree. As exertion and self-command had raised, so must these continue in order to sustain. An upward tendency would thus be given to the prisoner's mind, a looking to his own actual and active exertions, and not to mere submission or evasion, in order to improve or make his condition tolerable; on which tendency might, by degrees, be founded almost any amount of better feeling and purpose—with, at the same time, a demand for exertion and a degree of hardship involved, with which, as leading to a beneficent end to the prisoner himself, public opinion would readily sympathize, which it would not do with an equal amount of suffering without such end, and to which, notwithstanding, the unreclaimed and unregenerated mind outside, little appreciating the ultimate benefit, would look with unmixed aversion.

The type of a prison, thus organized and managed, would be characteristically industrial, because industry, in every way, would be its special requisition, and the spirit of its administration would be, not arbitrary nor merely authoritative, but kindly, persuasive, and benevolent, though stern. Its first effect would be to improve the officers; its second, their charges; for it would be impossible to watch each man's conduct from day to day and week to week, constantly noting it, and suiting the exhortation to the deficiencies and the approbation to the improvement, without coming at length to take a kindly interest in the progress made; and equally impossible for the object of so much care and solicitude not in the end to respond to and endeavor to repay them.

It is thus that the stern school of punishment would be made really reformatory. Every man would have his fate in his own hands. His imprisonment would be very tolerable, and its duration comparatively short, if he were steadily diligent and well conducted; but if he were otherwise, it would be most painful, and might be even interminable. The most refractory could not but be thus at length subdued. Where a man keeps the key of his own prison he is soon persuaded to fit it to the lock; and even if the inner purpose continued unchanged, he could be much more cautious after a probation of this active character than after a period of mere endurance, and be much more able to contend with subsequent difficulties, and, consequently, be exempt from much subsequent temptation.

III. *Severe suffering, consequent on conviction of crime, by way of example and warning, has not hitherto been very effective in preventing its recurrence; the example of necessary reform, or at least of sustained submission and self-command through a period of probation determined by the results of voluntary exertion, as the essential condition of release, would be found practically more deterrent than severity.*

The idea thus presented to the criminal would be more definite, more intelligible, and more humbling to the false pride which usually attends the early practice of crime, and which derives gratification at once from its successful perpetration and from the bravado of thereby defying menaced vindictive punishment. With reform as the object of penal administration, the better feelings of even the most abandoned criminals would, from the beginning, sympathize; whereas, when merely suffering and degradation are imposed, it is precisely these better feelings that are most revolted and injured by them.

The direct object of public punishment should, therefore, it is conceived, be the reform, if possible, but, at all events, the adequate subjugation and training to self-command of the persons subjected to it; so that, before they can regain their full privileges in society, after once forfeiting them, they must give satisfactory proof that they again deserve and are not likely to abuse them. This principle neither prescribes punishment as such, which will, it is believed, always be necessary to induce submission and penitence; nor does it lose sight of the object of setting a deterring example. But it raises the character of both these elements in penal treatment, placing the first in the light of a benevolent means instead of a vindictive end, and securing the second, by the exhibition of law constantly and necessarily victorious over individual obstinacy, instead of being, as now, commonly defeated by it. It cannot be doubted that very much of the hardness of old offenders arises at present from the gratified pride of having braved the worst that the law can inflict, and maintained an unconquerable will amid all its severities; but for this pride there would be no place, if endurance alone could serve no useful end, and only submission and voluntary effort would restore to freedom.

The example of punishment may deter the fearful, the hesitating, those who have, as yet, scarcely entered on the paths of guilt; but it falls powerless on the bolder, the more advanced, and more dangerous criminals. These, like the baited bull-dog, are rather irritated and spurred on by such examples, which they interpret as so many challenges to persevere. They rush on with their eyes shut to the danger, and derive at once an animal gratification within themselves, and encouragement from their companions, who look on and applaud their daring.

In the evidence taken before various parliamentary committees, no testimony is more uniform than that of the small deterring value of mere severity in repressing crime. Indeed, so little to this end has the example of mere suffering proved, that it has passed into a proverb that "crime thrives on severe penalties." On the other hand, nothing would probably tend to check criminality more than the sight of a prison system which would uniformly subjugate all brought under its influence, and reclaim most of them, because such general defeat would be peculiarly distasteful to the criminal mind outside.

It should never be forgotten, but rather strongly insisted on, that the principles of example and reformation may and should be made to concur. In many prisons hard labor is introduced in the shape of the tread-wheel. This punishment is certainly an object of fear, and so far falls within a sound principle; but then, instead of reforming the prisoner, it has a directly opposite tendency. Indeed, no labor can be imagined more irritating than this. It is utterly valueless, since, with very few exceptions, no corn is attempted to be ground by it; and even where this is the case, the prisoner knows perfectly well that he is only employed in the place of the elements. Instead, then, of acquiring a habit of labor which may be useful to him when his term is expired, his abhorrence of all work, and his revengeful feelings toward those who impose it, are only aggravated and confirmed. Another grave objection to tread-wheel labor is, that it is destructive of free agency. In it neither willingness nor unwillingness can have any scope, since it is weighted to a pace, and reduces the zealous and the reluctant to the same dead level. This is always most demoralizing. Whatever the occupation, and whether productive or not, some scope for free agency should always exist in it.

It is certainly more for the interest of society as tending much more effectually and directly to check the spread of crime, to endeavor earnestly and judiciously to reform criminals while in prison, and discharge those desirous of doing well in time to come, than vindictively, retributively, or, as it is called, exemplarily, to punish them there. It is not necessary, at the same time, while acting on this principle, to give up the object, highly useful in its place, of deterring from crime by setting an example of suffering in our prisons. On the contrary, it is held that a comprehensive and manly reform, not evaporating in professions, but exhibited in subsequent actions, can only be attained by subjecting each prisoner to a course of severe suffering, from which his own exertions can alone extricate him; but in every case this suffering should be studiously subordinated to the object of individual reformation; it must never be inflicted capriciously, or for the mere sake of example.

If the ordinary purpose and process of prison discipline were changed, and reformation made the specific end, and suffering only a necessary means, there would still be quite enough of the latter, since it is by fire, properly applied, that gold is purified, and not merely scorched and defaced. But when suffering is made the end, and reform a mere accident by the way, not only is it often disregarded altogether, but the position has even been assumed that it ought not to be pursued at all, because it is incompatible with the suffering necessary for example. Too much importance is at present attached to the agency of mere force in the production of moral effects in prison management. We thus habitually mistake even the nature of that on which we expend our efforts. We improve the mechanical appliances of our prisons, their means of coercion and supervision, and all the clock-work of their arrangements, and we think and talk of this as an improvement in their discipline; whereas, in truth, the more of all this there is, the more is true discipline, the discipline of the mind and will, impeded. The process that moves, directs, and strengthens these high intellectual. and moral powers is infinitely different from any that makes or guides an automaton.

IV. *Punishment for the past should be distinctly separated from training for the future.*

Both these processes, when their object is reform, are equally benevolent, because equally essential to the end in view. There can as little be true reform without true penitence, as there can be the growth of the man without the birth of the child. But the necessity of both is not equally evident to criminals. Many such who would object to any restriction imposed as mere punishment, and evade it if possible, would nevertheless desire the reform, and ardently devote themselves to giving such a demonstration of it as would entitle them to their release, thinking nothing a hardship which tended to such an issue. It is only the separation of the two objects and processes that can overcome this difficulty; but that does it effectually, and the means employed are in strict conformity to the analogies of nature, which to follow, in such a case, is to obey the finger of the Creator. A fever must be reduced before its ravages are sought to be repaired; a wound must be probed and cleansed before it can be properly healed up. To do one thing at a time, and each well, is the rule in all nice operations; and the recovery of a fellow-being from habits of crime to virtue, by many considered even a hopeless undertaking, is at least worthy of an equally methodical and careful procedure, and is not likely to be promoted by a more unscientific or slovenly one.

This proposed separation may be placed in another light. Subjection to direct punishment is essentially an unnatural position. It interferes, necessarily, with that free agency, a sense of which belongs to the instinct of man, (an interference from which, in great measure, no doubt, springs the deteriorating and disappointing effect of punishment, when long continued;) whereas, on the contrary, a state of probation, of difficulty, of hardship even, supported by the influence of hope, and with its objects to be attained by means of voluntary exertion and self-denial, is a highly natural and improving state, the very state in which we are all placed when sent into this world, and to which, accordingly, our faculties are especially accommodated. Can the two processes, then, be combined to advantage; or, rather, can they be combined at all? We may try to combine them; we may even claim to have done so; but nature is too strong for us. Either the restrictions involved in the idea of punishment destroy the free agency which is the essence of probation, or the concessions made to the latter destroy the former; and so between these two horns of a dilemma the arrangements of our existing penal institutions are constantly fluctuating.

A subordinate proposition regarding the nature of punishment may be here brought in to advantage. It should be severe but short, and melt into probation, as that again into entire freedom, as gradually as possible, thus resembling the acute pain caused by some great calamity which at first is overwhelming, but by degrees gives way to renewed hope and elasticity. The analogy of nature is ever to be studied on this subject, for only as we conform to that analogy can any system of moral influence be reared. Two stages of separate imprisonment—the first intensely penal, the second softened and relieved by some indulgences—with moral and religious instruction anxiously and affectionately inculcated in both; social labor by day, but under separate confinement at night, with increasing privileges and liberty as earned by voluntary effort and self-control, and a final stage of natural training, under an imprisonment rather moral than coercive, are the gradations recommended by our author as, in his view, the best for a reformatory prison discipline. But if the principles of the system are seized, we need not be solicitous, in any of the stages, about the perfection of the apparatus by which they are worked out. The error of modern penal science is the importance attached by it to mere physical arrangements, as admirably constructed prisons, &c. In operating on the human mind, the less store that is set on such appliances the better, provided always that the structure and philosophy of the mind itself be rightly apprehended, and that this knowledge be judiciously applied. It is the will that is to be gained, not the body only; and just in proportion to the importance attached to fettering the latter, it is to be feared is the carelessness about winning the former. Bad workmen never have good instruments; good ones rise above petty inconveniences. Men are most easily compelled by a strong external apparatus; they are best led without it. Men never turn from crime *per force;* this is a work of persuasion, rather than of coercion; and generally of persuasion applied under an organized system, which powerfully, though naturally, acts upon the will by its inherent forces.

The entire course of punishment and probation together, under this system, should not, and need not, be made nearly so long or so severe as that usually allotted at present to punishment alone. The end proposed—individual reform—should be distinctly and prominently kept in view throughout; and nothing is likely to operate worse, for such a purpose, than a necessarily long punishment. Such a punishment is, in some respects, worse than a corporal infliction; for men accommodate themselves to a system which is unavoidably destined to embrace them for a long time; and they study rather to endure than to rise above it.

Ordinarily, a man convicted of crime should not be sentenced to a course of purification, through which industry, good conduct, and economy of marks would not carry him within from two to four years; and for minor offenses, the indispensable time should be considerably less. Continued misconduct may, indeed, prolong these periods to five, seven, or even ten years; but without the moral torpor and injury produced at present by the four, six, and eight years of necessary incarceration before any indulgence can be obtained. The strongest spirits are unable to bear up against "hope deferred" through such a period; and they either sink into a sullen despair, or seek to forget, in present dissipation, the long duration of their captivity.

V. *Fixed rations, beyond bread and water, should be abolished in prisons; and the prisoner should be required to earn his food, as well as all other privileges and comforts, by good marks; that is, by diligence and good conduct.*

The great point with the prisoner, under Captain Maconochie's system of prison discipline, is to earn good marks, attainable only by diligence at work and lesson-learning, and by general good conduct. These marks have a manifold value. There is one sentiment common to all prisoners, and that is, a passionate desire to regain their freedom, or even a sensible approach toward it. Now, the essential value of the marks earned consists in this, that the accumulation of them contributes to this end. But they have other elements of worth, for they are used, and are indispensable to this purpose, in the purchase of whatever conveniences, comforts, and opportunities the prisoner is provided with during his confinement, such as food, clothing, bedding, room-rent, books, stationery, postage-stamps, schooling, and the like. Marks, therefore, are a species of wages in this system, and are greedily coveted as such; but they are, and must be, expended as well as earned; and it is only the accumulation of them that tends to the attainment of liberty. It is evident that the balance may be on the wrong side here, as it often is in free life; and the motive, therefore, is as strong to economize marks within the prison as it is to economize in the expenditure of money outside. Marks, then, as a form of wages in prison, at once raise the men above the demoralizing condition of slavery, in which they are otherwise plunged. The forfeiture of these marks for misconduct supplies the place of lashes for prison offenses. Their convertibility, at the prisoner's own will, into immediate gratifications, thereby, however, prolonging detention, tends strongly to promote and prove steadiness and self-denial, that is, will-power; and, in a word, the whole scheme, it is claimed, is pregnant with untold moral good.

So much, preliminarily, in general explanation of the mark system. I come now to the special subject of this section, as set forth in the proposition at its head.

Fixed rations, especially when ever so little too good, have an injurious effect on the minds of prisoners and on the community outside. To the latter, when in distress, they become a temptation; and they accustom the former to having their wants met without forethought or exertion of their own. If each prisoner was required to pay in marks, that is, in labor, for what he consumes, besides the whole tale that he must render for his liberation, both the above-mentioned effects would cease, and with them much collateral evil. A prison would no longer be looked to as a refuge in hard times, and questions of dietary would not arise. The improvement would be vast, both moral and physical, if all were required to diet themselves at their own cost, paid in the currency to them most precious, as being the only coin with which they can buy back their freedom. They would in this way be made to feel, most beneficially to themselves, the burden of their own support; would learn economy, and would become inured to and content with coarse, because cheap, fare.

In existing prison systems, fixed rations are issued to all alike, without regard to any effort made to earn them. The necessity of exertion, previous to enjoyment, so beneficially as well as forcibly pressed on the laboring poor in society, is here entirely lost sight of, and a bounty is almost directly offered to indolence and crime. The supply of rations without cost to the prisoner is justified on the plea that, as he is, by the very fact of imprisonment, debarred from his customary means of earning a subsistence, he must be otherwise supported. This is true, and readily granted. But must he, therefore, be *gratuitously* supported? He cannot earn a subsistence by ordinary means, but may he not be supplied with extraordinary ones instead, viz: a judicious mixture of moral and physical task-work, in the accomplishment of which he may have presented to him precisely the same motives to exertion, diligence, economy, prudence, self-denial, and the other minor virtues of social life, and be kept habitually active in bondage as when virtuously exerting himself in free society? Nor is this all. A criminal who has forfeited his liberty through misconduct may surely be justly required, besides maintaining himself, to purchase back his liberation by a proportionate period of good conduct. This postulate being granted, the whole mark system is admitted, since the marks are proposed as mere counters, like money in free life, by which exertion and obedience may be appraised and their exchange facilitated.

But apart from the motives to good conduct lost to prisoners by making their support gratuitous, it is disadvantageous, morally, to relieve laboring men for a time from solicitude and daily effort specifically for their subsistence; it operates injuriously on the habits of soldiers and sailors, as well as of prisoners. If made to pay (in marks earned by effort) for their maintenance, these last should also have a discretion (and not too much restricted either) both as to its quantity and quality, with a strong interest given them at the same time in economy. They would thus be trained not only to habits of steady industry, and that from an inward impulse, always the most healthy, but also to those of self-guidance and self-control. Nothing could be more easily arranged than this in the management of prisoners; nor, were the motive only strong enough to restrain them, could anything be, to self-indulgent minds, as usually possessed by prisoners, either more immediately painful or prospectively improving. The limits of a strict prudence might in the beginning be frequently exceeded; but, after a time, as the consequent prolonged detention became irksome, and especially as its end approached, the tendency will be rather to excessive economy than to excessive expenditure.

VI. *The primary aim of public punishment should be the reformation of the criminal—the making of upright, industrious freemen, rather than orderly and obedient prisoners; and this is always practicable, when sought by proper methods and agencies.*

The words of our Saviour, and much more the whole spirit of his instructions, may be adduced on this head: "Seek ye first the kingdom of God and his righteousness, and all these things will be added unto you." Seek first the reform of the individual culprit. This is a Christian, an indispensable duty. Beginning thus at the right end, laying the foundations right, the other objects of punishment will fall into their places, and be readily attained. But by reversing this process, and omitting this element from our calculations, we only proceed from difficulty to difficulty; and we almost systematically exclude religion from our penal science by excluding from its purview that object—individual reform—on which religion peculiarly fixes her regard.

The great error in existing systems of prison discipline is, that they aim too exclusively at making orderly, obedient, and submissive prisoners, and not nearly enough at training active, efficient, industrious freemen. The only apparatus at present employed in prisons to effect the latter object is religious instruction—the highest and holiest of all agencies in itself, and which, when duly combined with others, purifies and elevates them also. But alone even religious instruction is not sufficient for what is here required. It only teaches virtue theoretically; whereas a field of practice must be associated with it to give its lessons their highest value and their greatest effect. The lessons of virtue and piety, without this, often evaporate in mere words. And many of the most useful social qualities—energy, activity, ingenuity, industry, prudence, economy, and the like—have little distinct connection with religious instruction. They are often strikingly present where there is little of this, and as strikingly absent where there is much. A mixed training is thus required, temporal as well as spiritual, worldly as well as religious; the first, to give the power to do well, the second, the will to direct that power aright.

It is to the want of a due combination of these elements in our ordinary prison discipline more than to any necessary circumstances in the condition of discharged prisoners that their frequent reconvictions and the difficulty in disposing of them seem mainly due. Were men systematically taught in prison to be active, industrious, prudent, economical, and capable of guiding themselves, instead of depending on the guidance of others, their difficulties on returning to society, and their conduct and reception in it, would soon be very different from what they now are.

It is the duty, and still more the interest, of society, in dealing with its criminals, to try earnestly, while they are in custody, to reform them, to develop especially manly virtues in them, to qualify them to contend successfully after their discharge with the difficulties besetting their social condition, and so to direct their thoughts upward, instead of allowing them to blindly struggle on, as too many now do, without thought, or care, or hope, or, consequently, desire to rise in life, under the belief that they are born to steal or starve, and preferring the former to the latter alternative. How must the general moral tone of the lower classes be sunk through contact with individuals entertaining such thoughts! On the contrary, how would this tone rise if the liberations from the prisons were, instead, to carry into society a healthy current—men with their powers developed, their purposes improved, their characters strengthened, and their aspirations and efforts all directed upward! "It is impossible, it is a mere Utopia," is a thought which, on such a suggestion, doubtless rises to the lips of many in the community. But have we ever tried? Have we ever used the means suited to bring about such a consummation? We have not; we have bounded our endeavors by the object of making good, obedient, and in many cases professing, but in few performing, prisoners. We have lowered their moral tone to make them submissive; and having thus sown tares, we have assuredly not reaped wheat; but are we thence to infer that wheat, by a different husbandry, may not be raised at all? The mark or task system seems alone competent to compass the end in view, its essential principle being to influence by hope more than by fear, thus lifting the prisoner up, instead of crushing him to the earth—the whole being so organized that the rewards, and chiefly that of restoration to freedom, shall be certain, affording thus motives for steady, consistent exertion, and not merely to occasional or fitful effort. Prison life would thus be made to closely resemble ordinary life, and for that reason the arrangements of the former could best prepare for a return to the latter. Its machinery, too, once set in motion, would nearly work itself, and be little liable to abuse; its provision of labor, wages, purchases, and for-feitures, all explaining themselves, and nothing being wanted in it but that punctuality of account which is maintained in every well-regulated factory. A criminal once convicted and imprisoned should never, under this system, get away till he has earned his marks. No application should be listened to on this head. However, this is but a detail of the system, and not a vital part of it. It is to the fundamental principle that value is to be really attached; and to this, the highest. The system of public punishment cannot be radically improved, without letting this principle in; and attempts to amend it will, in practice, be successful only in proportion as they approach it. For, consider what that principle is, and how it proposes to operate. The basis of the mark system, that on which the entire superstructure is raised, is this simple idea, that if we would reform criminals, and really fit them to re-turn to free life, we should subject them, while yet in bondage, as far as possible, to the same checks and impulses as make men prudent, honest, industrious, and otherwise well-doing in society; avoiding at the same time, as far as may be, treating them as slaves, assured that with what-ever slavish virtues we may endow them, as obedience, submission, and the like, there will always be generated in them a superabundant admix-ture of slavish vices too—cunning, falsehood, self-indulgence, subjection to external influence, and so forth. The great point, then, in a reforma-tory prison discipline, is so to arrange and regulate our prisons as to stimulate and call into exercise, in and by them, the motives, impulses, and habits which make good men and women outside of them, and ear-nestly to discourage and, as far as possible, discard those which generate weakness or lead to vice.

It is peculiarly important that reformatory principles and processes should be introduced and energetically acted on in county and munici-pal prisons, those minor or, as we may say, elementary penal establish-ments, through which criminals usually pass when entering on their career of crime—their infancy in it, so to speak—and in which, accord-ingly, it is important that the most strenuous efforts should be systemati-cally made to turn them aside from it. For the repression of crime, very much, aside from the rescue of individuals, will depend on the na-ture of the influence exercised by discharged prisoners on the society again receiving them. If really turned from crime, and desirous of avoiding it in time to come, they become each, as it were, an apostle of virtue in the community. Not to lose caste among their fellows on account of their altered conduct, they seek to justify this by such argu-ments as occur to them, many of them the same as were addressed to themselves while in prison, and which had most influence over them there. The good seed planted in them becomes thus widely cast on the waters, and even where individuals fail in their own persons of exempli-fying its fruits, it is not altogether lost; it becomes diffused over the whole class usually supplying criminals, and beneficially influences their thoughts and 'manners. While, on the contrary, the influence of pris-oners discharged, unreclaimed, impenitent, and hardened, as they now commonly are, is equally extensive, and more than proportionally pernicious; it is a match set to gunpowder. This aim is most important, it is even fundamental, to the system; and it throws extraordinary interest on the reform of prisoners; but its practical utility will of course depend on the degree in which we may hope to succeed in effecting it. From long experience Captain Maconochie is confident that, by the use of right measures, success may be very great in this endeavor; only, however, by altogether reversing the arrangements now commonly enforced in prisons. These, having been organized without reference to reform, and looking only to coercion and example, are almost as if specially intended to be opposed to improvement in moral character—a comprehensive charge, but whose justice is incontrovertible.

This view of the susceptibility of criminals to reformatory influences deserves the most serious attention of all who are interested in the question of prison discipline, and are duly impressed with its vast and vital importance, morally, socially, politically, and religiously. Considering the interests involved, and how deeply they concern the whole community, it is deplorable to see existing prison management guided, in the main, by almost diametrically opposite views, and to consider how flagrant the error on which these views are founded. They begin by confounding the opposite aims of punishment, example, and reformation, making it almost impossible, as a rule, to attain either. All that ought to be made contingent on good conduct alone, as food and immediate comforts, is made certain and gratuitous, whatever the demeanor evinced by the prisoners; and that good conduct, which ought to be sternly and even peremptorily required, is left so uncertain, and is indeed so generally dispensed with, that criminals, in crowds, are daily discharged through mere flux of time, who are proclaimed altogether incorrigible. On the ground of actual experiment, it is denied that there are any such whatever. There are many prisoners weak, and some deplorably wicked; but so long as Divine Providence is pleased to retain men in this world of probation at all, our right may well be disputed to regard or pronounce any to be irreclaimable. Our duty is first to try some new method, to try indeed any and all hopeful methods, to reclaim them. But under present notions we reject all rational means of promoting their recovery; and, these failing, we quietly pronounce them irreclaimable, just as an engineer might do who, charged to reduce a strong fort, should fling away his trenching tools and then pronounce it impregnable. In such a case, with whom really lies the blame, the prison officers or the prison inmates? And which are the irreclaimable while such a system is persisted in? It was the opinion of this able writer, and equally able, as well as successful, prison manager, that prisoners could be saved to a man by the application of right principles and methods in prison administration. He feared neither bad habits nor any other difficulties. He believed that, while life and sanity are spared, recovery is always possible, if properly sought. There is infinite elasticity in the human mind if its faculties are placed in healthful action, and neither diseased by maltreatment nor locked up in the torpor of a living grave.

It is impossible to overrate the value of reformation as the primary aim of prison management, and difficult to appreciate even its real importance. The reform of prisoners has a wide bearing. Its systematic pursuit, apart from the repression of crime by positive punishment, would have a strong tendency to raise the moral tone of the masses. Discharged criminals constitute our most direct channel of communication and influence with the morally lowest classes of the community. If our prisoners, on liberation, return among these either weak or wicked, their discourse and example must tend powerfully to countenance and aggravate their already downward tendencies; whereas, if they return to them well-purposed and firm in their virtuous intents, they will, beyond a doubt, as speaking the language of experience and deliberate repentance, contribute to check such tendencies, and to promote the growth of better sentiments and aspirations.

VII.—*Prison discipline, to be truly reformatory, must work with nature, not against it.*

This principle has already come into view in several of the previous extracts, but its importance entitles it to a more distinct consideration. In his account of Norfolk, which he found "a turbulent, brutal hell, but left a peaceful, well-ordered community," after a detail of the remarkable results accomplished in that most remarkable experiment, Captain Maconochie adds:

My task was not really so difficult as it appeared. I was working *with* nature, not *against* her, as all other prison systems do. I was endeavoring to cherish, and yet direct and regulate, those cravings for amelioration of position, which almost all possess in some degree, and which are often strongest in those otherwise most abased. Under the guidance of right principle they rose easily to order and exertion. I did not neglect the object of punishment in my various arrangements, but I sought it within the limits assigned alike by the letter and the spirit of the law, not by excesses of authority beyond them. The law imposes imprisonment and hard labor, and these, in the fullest sense of the words, my men endured. Every one of them performed his government task, besides the labor bestowed, as he could catch the opportunity, on his own garden or other personal interests; but he was saved, as far as I could save him, from unnecessary humiliation, and encouraged to look to his own steady efforts for ultimate liberation and improved position. And this—not the efforts of an individual, zealous as they certainly were—was the real secret of the altered aspect of Norfolk Island, in my time, from what either preceded or followed it.

The principle thus set forth, in its application and issues, is directly to existing systems of convict management. Seeking their ends, whatever those ends may be, by a species of domestic slavery, this feature alone (even without others of like deformity) sets them aside as *media* of individual reform. Such a plant never grew in such a soil. This principle is opposed to the silent system, which not only groups men for punishment alone, and, through its minute and artificial regulations, demoralizes, by familiarizing them with resistance and evasion; but it acts thus precisely with a view to crush those social feelings which, on the contrary, it is the object of a natural treatment to encourage and train. Such rough-riding over human nature is irreconcilable with every principle legitimately founded on its study. Gardening with a pack of hounds, and thus studiously defacing what we seek to beautify, seems the nearest approach to such folly.

Prisons should be great workshops or industrial establishments, where the inmates are systematically trained to be skillful, steady, sober, and *voluntarily* industrious; where all the arrangements for labor are at the same time so like real life, so identical with, as fully to prepare for it. The voluntary character of the labor cannot be too strongly insisted on. Compulsory labor is, as a rule, rude, reckless, unskillful, and therefore unprofitable; it is free and still more emulative exertion that is ingenious, skillful, and productive. The economical improvement under such a system would be felt almost as soon as the moral; it is a mistake to suppose that these can ever be successfully dissociated, but it would require great care and discretion, in the first instance, to organize such establishments. The art employed must be of that high character which conceals itself; which is artful by being artless, and which is content to sow good seed and wait, without forcing, the corresponding return. In such a situation it will always be easy to produce immediate results;

the real difficulty will be to be early persuaded that they are likely to prove worthless nearly in proportion as they rise to the surface with a slight compression. It is doubtful if this wisdom will, in any hands, be attained until taught by experience. The unerring test of renewed convictions after discharge will at length teach it. When the lesson is sufficiently impressed to move forward too fast, to give free agency a large scope, to suffer temptation to assume all its customary forms, to regulate but encourage much, then complete success may be hoped for, in what should ever be the great aim of public punishment, the reformation of the fallen.

It is argued that, however the combination of prisoners with free persons might be advantageous to the former, that of prisoners with prisoners cannot be so to each other. But this is a gratuitous and even demonstrably erroneous assumption. It is much easier to influence numbers together than the individuals separately of whom they are composed, and when moved they will thus go much further; they mutually assist each other and beget a common enthusiasm. There is, besides, strange as it may appear, a specific tendency in numbers toward right feeling. The clap-traps of a theater are generally high moral sentiments. The better feelings of a mob are rarely appealed to in vain. In the army and navy the most heroic self-abnegation, even unto death, is often called out at a word. In none of these instances, probably, could the same responses be obtained from even a single individual, which he renders spontaneously when he forms one of a body. On Norfork Island, Captain M. avers he could have done nothing with each prisoner separately; the best of them would have remained only dogged under his exhortations. In Birmingham he would neither have gained the boys as he did, nor would they have been able to influence each other outside as they did, if they had been shut up in separate cells. And Colonel Montesinos's experience at Valencia was all of the same nature.

The use of marks as wages, under this system, would enable its managers to make life within prison a close copy of that without, for a return to which it would, accordingly, be the best possible preparation. At present nothing could be more dissimilar than the two; and the lessons inculcated in the prison are not only inapplicable in free society, but even, in most cases, directly opposed to what it is most desirable that men should possess when they go out. The patience, docility, and ready subservience to external impression, which make an excellent prisoner, equally contribute to make a ready dupe in another sphere. Moreover, prisoners, as at present managed, are clothed, fed, lodged, and even allowed indulgencies, all by regulation, without the least reference to their conduct, and without care or sacrifice on their part to obtain them. The victims of this management are thus kept together without immediate solicitude, and are but as so many automata in a master-mechanic's hand. Surely this is no suitable preparation for returning to a work-a-day world, with its anxieties, its responsibilities, its troubles, its infinite varieties of choice among daily recurring perplexities; and if some of the difficulty in adequately preparing to encounter these is necessarily inherent in imprisonment itself, at least it would be much lessened by the introduction of marks and their use as money within the allotted pale.

The rigorously coercive systems, by whatever names known or under whatever forms existing, viewed as reformatory agencies, are based on an essentially wrong principle. They pull down, but do not build up; they subdue, but do not reclaim. By their minute and artificial regulations they destroy individual character and the power of self-direction, and so hoop prisoners about in prison that they are ready to fall to pieces afterward at the first touch of difficulty or temptation. Such systems cannot be called good; no system can in which, as in free society and the ordinary conditions of life, men cannot, under a strong, certain, and universal motive, be themselves the chief agents in the work required, that of subduing their evil and nourishing their good tendencies. The mark system will certainly secure such co-operation. Its machinery, though acting chiefly on the will, is more stringent than that of the most coercive system. It must be yielded to, and even willingly. But its force lies in appeals to the judgment, feelings, and interests of prisoners, all for their own advantage; and the most stubborn will thus give way to it. By granting its prisoners some latitude of action, guided by motives, it cultivates the powers of self-direction, prudence, foresight, self-denial, self-command—in a word, all the qualities which enable men to maintain a purpose once formed.

From the foregoing detail it will be seen that the closest possible resemblance is given, in arranging the form of society, to the type of free life. It is as a preparation for return to this that the whole scheme is organized.

VIII. *The principle of mutual responsibility, that is, of grouping prisoners together in small companies, made to resemble as closely as possible ordinary family life, will be found to be highly conducive to their reformation; the social principles and relations of humanity are the great springs of improvement, and of vigorous and efficient exertion, in free society; duly regulated, they will prove equally so in the treatment of persons imprisoned for crime.*

There are four essential principles of the mark system of imprisonment. The first is, that instead of sentences for a fixed time being passed on criminals, they be required, by diligence and good conduct, to earn, in a penal condition, a certain number of marks of approval. The second is, that the marks so earned be used to stimulate and restrain them, precisely as money is used to stimulate and restrain free people in ordinary life. The third is, that a reasonable number of marks be credited to them daily for work performed, for attention to lessons, and for general good conduct; that a fair charge be made for provisions and other supplies furnished; that moderate fines be imposed for misconduct; and that the clear balance, the actual surplus accumulation, over and above all deductions thus made, alone count toward liberation. There is a fourth principle, regarded by the author of the system as scarcely less important, viz: that when men are associated under this system, they be required to distribute themselves into small parties (say) of six or eight, *with common interests;* so that each man shall be made to labor and refrain for others as well as for himself, and exertion and good conduct shall be thus rendered popular, and idleness and misconduct unpopular, in the community, because each exhibition of them affects, favorably or unfavorably, the fortunes of several together.

In the earlier stages of treatment, devoted peculiarly to punishment, the prisoners should not be combined in social parties; and the first stage of all should be, as mentioned under another head, separate imprisonment, for men will repent best alone. But the object is an important one at an early period to call forth social virtues by creating social ties. This is, indeed, the key-stone of the whole system, the essential principle, without which its other parts would be of comparatively little value. A prison system must study to make good members of *society,* or its efforts will be vain, because they will be directed too low, and because they will leave untouched the selfishness which gives to vice its worst character of malignity, and deprives even good conduct of all pretension to virtue. In modeling the social parties, however, too much strictness should not be exercised. The type of families in ordinary life should be followed, but not exceeded. Thus *interests* should be common among the members, but not necessarily either occupations or dwellings. On the contrary, by admitting separation in these particulars, friends will be enabled to combine and support each other, though of different mechanical tastes and powers; their friendships will be cemented, which is precisely the object desired; quarrels will be prevented in the several parties; the educated and uneducated will be enabled to combine without pain or a feeling of degradation, and consequently without deterioration on either side; and the influence of each individual on his companions, and of his companions on him, will be more moral and less material by their occasional separation.

Prisoners, thus distributed into small parties with common interests, both labor and refrain from generous and social, and not merely from selfish and personal impulses. Great importance is attached to this feature in the mark system, and its value was abundantly proved on Norfolk Island. As before stated, it makes good conduct popular and bad conduct unpopular, since each affects others as well as the actor himself. It thus deprives offense of a great stimulant which it now has, arising from the sympathy, sport, or other excitement which the sight of it creates in the lookers-on. It transfers this *stimulus* rather to good conduct. It opens the hearts of those who sacrifice a personal gratification to the good of their companions, and thus tends to raise them in the scale of being. It gives every man a certain number of custodians—his most intimate friends and companions—all interested in supporting his good tendencies and suppressing his bad, investing him with a right to the same supervision over them. And by giving a social and almost family influence over them, as opposed to a merely gregarious one, it directs a flood of wholesome influences on all. Without some social organization, it is almost impossible to make a general impression on numbers together. Each impulse communicated perishes as it enters, for there is nothing in the man's own position to sustain it; and the least improving state of society in which men can be placed is thus one of gregarious assemblage, without common ties, or interest, or concert, or combination, among themselves. Instead of bringing prisoners together, and yet endeavoring to keep them separate and uninfluenced by each other, (which is impossible,) the true and natural policy is to combine them in circumstances which will make their mutual influence necessarily beneficial. And few who have not, as our author says he has, tried and proved this plan, will easily conceive the power it gives a superior employing it. The change produced on the convicts at Norfolk Island under this system was, he avers, most remarkable. He gives the following interesting detail of the process by which it was effected:

The men previously locked up every night in a barrack, in which there were lodged fifty and sixty together in large dormitories, without lights or any immediate superintendence to prevent abuse, were gradually thinned out and hutted in the bush near their field labors. The best men were taken first, and under the check of the officers they were allowed to choose others as companions when able to accommodate them, on condition that they became severally responsible themselves for their good conduct. A strong field police was at the same time formed of prisoners, but with a considerable value attached to their situations, and who, under the immediate direction of the chief constable and police-runner of the island, both free, behaved generally remarkably well. Gradually many men were thus got out. The best conducted were always taken, and, their privileges being much coveted, others behaved well to obtain the same. They had all small gardens allotted them, on which they were encouraged to grow vegetables, and to rear pigs and poultry, both for their own use and for said among the officers, as they were able. They thus all speedily acquired a little property; and with its possession they also acquired an interest in its rights. Theft became unpopular among them, and at last almost unknown. There was every temptation to it, and every facility for its commission; yet it was abstained from. The writer had himself a large garden in the midst of them, almost uninclosed, and with a deep well in it of peculiarly fine water, which all were allowed to draw from at will. His borders were full of the finest fruits, pine-apples, bananas, grapes, melons, figs, guavas, and the like; yet nothing was ever taken, and the other officers' gardens were equally respected. At the same time, the tale of government work required was not abated, and the men were even seen sometimes to work at their little allotments by moonlight in order to do them justice. The scene was a remarkable proof of the power of mere arrangements to call out the favorable points in human nature, even in the most unfavorable circumstances; and though some of the facts seem scarcely credible, they are still well attested, and the effect of the discipline was not merely transitory. Two years after he left the penal colonies, the writer obtained returns of the conduct subsequently of these men, both in New South Wales and Van Diemen's Land, which were remarkably favorable. And in a private letter written from Van Diemen's Land, about four years afterward, (May 20, 1848,) are these words: "The conduct of your Norfolk Island men generally has been most exemplary; they have shown that a reformation far greater than has hitherto been effected in any body of men by any system, either before or after yours, has taken place in them. With scarcely an exception, the whole are doing well, and some are in a respectable way of business advancing fast to prosperity. They are a credit to the name they bear of Captain Maconochie's men."

Captain Maconochie, in his writings, insists much upon this point, that man is a social being, and that his duties are social; whence he deduces the principle that only *in society* can prisoners be duly prepared *for it*. Only thus can a field be provided for the exercise and cultivation of the active social virtues, and for the habitual voluntary restraint of active social vices. To prepare for society in society seems just as requisite as to send men to sea to prepare them to command ships, or, in any case, to accommodate the preliminary education of individuals to their ultimate destination. Penitence, good resolution, moral and religious principle are an excellent foundation—they are, indeed, the only sure foundation; and if only once really instinct with life, they will ascend and pervade whatever superstructure is raised on them. But where their dictates have been originally weak or systematically disregarded, it seems as idle to expect that their mere theoretical inculcation late in life, however enforced by suffering, will be sufficient to make them the dominant guides of future conduct, as it would be to hope in this way to teach a trade, or any other practical application of abstract rules. Moral lessons, to be taught profitably, require a field of progressive experimental application the same as engineering does. In the one case, as in the other, if the important element of friction is omitted in the pupils' studies and in their training, if they are only inculcated from books, and their respective truths are not enforced by experience, the end sought will not, ordinarily, be attained. *Non vi, sed sæpe cadendo*—not by violent or artificial machinery, but by frequent failures—moral habits, like mechanical skill, are developed and strengthened.

The superiority of such a system, that is, of a social training over any ascetic or merely individual treatment, may be placed in various lights:

1. It would be more natural. Man is born with social instincts and tendencies; his impulses, habits, and virtues are social; and hence in society only can they be suitably exercised. Moreover, only in society is hope usually vigorous and exertion sustained. Solitary beings are uncertain in temper; and solitariness of feeling, that is, selfishness, is the known and admitted source of every description of vice. Hence proceed, in great measure, the vicious tendencies which at present prevail in prisons. But with a social existence a different result might

be looked for. With common interests, their hearts, which are now shut, would open. They would become alive to others' feelings, instead of brooding over their own. They would recognize their relation to society at large, and the obligations involved in it. Reformers are too anxious to re-create. Instead of following nature they seek to change it. They impute their failure to *its* perversity, when it is *their own* that is in fault. They do not seek to imitate natural agencies, but to improve on them. Instead of training and guiding, they try to re-model. Can we wonder that they are, for the most part, so little successful?

2. Being more natural, this mode of discipline would be also more easily organized and maintained. The opposite of this is, indeed, often asserted. The difficulty of finding suitable agents to work the system has been much insisted on. But this idea is a misconception, founded on a superficial examination of the question. The difficulty in other systems of prison discipline arises from the importance attached in them to minute regulation and to mere physical restraints, without any adequate effort being made to gain the prisoners themselves, to control their wills, and so to change the character, and not merely to restrain the manifestations of their impulses. But the mark system reverses this process. The difference of effort that would be required to overcome the obstacles in its way, as compared with that required in others, would thus be like that between the strength required to confine steam in a highly expansive state and when it is chemically altered by condensation. Natural agencies assert an immediate mastery, whereas artificial restraints operate with difficulty, and too often with a melancholy destruction of material, which, in this case, is men, and not mere material objects. Aspiring after marks of commendation, which they may in turn exchange for immediate gratifications or ultimate release, prisoners, under a social system of training, would be exactly as freemen laboring for wages, and be just as easily managed; or rather they would be more so, for both their dependence and stake would be greater. And as every description of good conduct would have a marketable value, as well as labor performed, the corresponding habits of order, submission, self-command, and the like, would be more generally formed, and their effects more uniformly exhibited.

3. It is easier to create an *esprit de corps* in a body of men than to regulate the impulses of any single individual. Man is a social being; nor can he wholly resist any given social tendency, however opposed to it may be his personal inclinations. The cowardly soldier yet maintains his place in the ranks; the unprincipled man yet pays the homage of hypocrisy to virtue. The facility of working a social system of prison management would be in nothing more striking than in the fetters which it would thus throw around even the most hardened; fetters which would be only the more effectual because they would be unseen, and because they would proceed from the prisoner's own class, unconsciously to himself, and therefore unresisted.

4. The next interesting point of view, accordingly, in which the system here advocated may be placed, is this uniformity of its action. All would be impressed by it, more or less, and the greater number very much. Good prisoners are now the exception. Under the system proposed they might be expected to become the rule; and the circumstances being made favorable to virtue, as they now are to vice, the exhibitions would as punctually correspond in the one case as in the other. The efficiency of an army is in proportion to the discipline, intelligence, and consequent uniform action of all its members, and not.

to the superiority of a few. Thus virtue is maintained in a community, not by a few high examples of it, but by an elevated general standard.

5. The superior efficiency of a social school of reform, even for obtaining a high measure of individual virtue, constitutes another strong recommendation. It may aim far higher than any system of individual treatment, and may much more confidently hope to compass even the highest. Men are excitable in society. Where one goes another will follow, and he will seek not merely to follow, but to outstrip. It is thus that armies rush impetuously where the bravest would hesitate to advance alone, and boys at school exhibit, under an impulse of emulation, a patience and self-denial foreign to their age, and which none of them, probably, would singly command. Is there any reason why this excitability may not be enlisted in the service of moral reform, as well as of military or moral excellence? It is presumable that, if moral reform were distinctly pursued as the first object of penal management in associations properly combined to promote it, and with those encouragements which, in dealing with ignorant men, are often as necessary to define virtue to their comprehension as to stimulate them to its practice, it would, in the great majority of cases, be attained. Once actuated by any common impulse, uneducated minds are always more entire in their subjection to it than those whose views are more extended through culture; and where they act in the mass, their movement becomes accelerated at every step.

6. A prison discipline, organized as proposed, would be much more accommodated to varieties of temper and character than any that depended on mere physical or coercive apparatus. Every man's lot under it would be in his own hands; his companions would be of his own choice, and on his and their conduct and industry would depend both his daily comfort and the length of his detention. No system, accordingly, could be at once so benevolent and so just. Its object being personal reformation, it would seek such reform by the most agreeable of all means—the mutual action of chosen companions on each other. Rising above the justice which aims to accommodate punishment to mere past offense, at best an erring and often a false criterion, it would put every one on a trial of *character* merely, and deal with him on this only, which is what society has chief interest in. For much more important is it to a community to ascertain, before a prisoner is released, whether he is likely again to commit offense than whether his suffering has been made adequate, in a vindictive sense, to that which is past. And much more would even abstract justice be satisfied by making penal treatment bear a relation to habitual disposition than by accommodating it to that which may have been only an accidental extreme evidence of it. To this quality in the system the greatest value is to be attached. It not only renders punishment benevolent as well as just, but it rests its claims to these qualities on higher grounds than are usually taken in recommending them. The benevolence is not that of inflicting the least possible unnecessary hardship, but of conferring the greatest possible necessary benefit; and the justice, humbly copying that ascribed to omniscience, looks beyond one occasional action, and seeks rather to grapple with the impulses which may excuse, or in many cases constitute, its demerit. Its language to the criminal would not be, "I will keep you till you have paid a certain forfeit for a past offense," but, "Having exacted a certain moderate penalty for that, I now retain you till I have qualified you to meet the requisitions of society, on your return to it, that you may not again fall, as you have done." The balance would not be, as now, the uncertain and, to all practical purposes, useless one be-

tween crime and suffering, but the highly practical and useful one between the demands of society and the attainment of the power and will
to meet them.

7. The proposed system of prison discipline would be almost self-work-
ing, which would be another strong point in its favor. Scarcely any
discretion is lodged in any part of it; and its close resemblance to real
life would insure the action of the same principles in maintaining it.
The only difference is in the circulating medium by which it is proposed
to balance its accounts. By making this to consist of marks of commendation, exchangeable in the right hands for anything, but in the
wrong utterly without value, a great many good effects would be produced. All occasion of dishonesty would be removed; attention would
be fixed solely on proper methods of obtaining indulgences; these methods would rise proportionally in estimation; the connection between
them and their beneficial consequences would be obvious to the meanest
capacity, and they would thus be imprinted on the habits, as well as
made clear to the understanding, of all concerned. But in no other respect is innovation on the habits of ordinary life sought to be made; and,
under its arrangements, injustice even in this would be scarcely practicable, and if it were ever so easy, it would be almost without motive.

8. Such a system would be self-checking—another great advantage.
Its object, personal reformation, being a tangible one, obvious to the
senses, the attainment or non-attainment of this end would exhibit
wisdom and ability, or the want of these qualities, in its administration,
and that without delay or uncertainty. Slow progress in reform, whether
through idleness or extravagance, would be the result of one set of
errors; renewed convictions after discharge, of another. At present
there is no similar check on any faults of administration, however grave.
This is, doubtless, one of the main causes of the prevailing difference of
opinion as to the comparative efficacy of existing systems. It is impossible to estimate the value of vindictive examples, perhaps because
they have none; and the sad result of general deterioration, with its
concomitant of repeated convictions, is overlooked as unimportant. It
would be quite otherwise if a fixed object were in view, which could not
be mistaken. The very pursuit of such an end, the attainment or non-
attainment of which must be at once obvious to every observer, would
close the avenues to carelessness on the one side, and malversation on
the other, even if the fear of detection from missing it were less co-
gent than, in such circumstances, it would of necessity be.

9. There is another consideration, which strongly recommends a
social prison discipline. It is this: Power in a society, by being under
the direction of virtue, naturally increases, and has a necessary tendency to prevail over opposite power, not under such direction, just as
power, by being under the direction of reason, has a tendency to prevail
over brute force. Union, and more especially virtuous union, is power.
Men can do jointly what they cannot do singly. The union of minds
and hands works wonders. Men become efficient in proportion as
they concentrate their powers. Joint effort conquers nature, hews
through mountains, rears pyramids, dikes the ocean. Man left to himself, living without a fellow, if he could so live, would be one of the
weakest of creatures. Associated with his kind, he gains dominion
over the strongest animals, over the earth and the sea; and, by his
growing knowledge, due almost wholly to association, he may be said
to obtain a kind of property in the universe.

Nor is this all. Men not only accumulate power by union, but they
thereby gain warmth and earnestness, which raises and intensifies

power. The heart is kindled by association. An electric communication is established between those who are brought into contact and are bound to each other by common labors and interests. Man droops in solitude; no sound excites him like the voice of his fellow-man. The mere sight of a human countenance, brightened with generous emotion, gives new strength to do or suffer. Union not only brings into play forces which before existed, and which were ineffectual through separation, but, by the interest and feeling which it arouses, it becomes a creative principle, calls forth new forces, and gives the mind a consciousness of powers which would otherwise have remained unknown.

A current objection to the system of discipline here proposed and advocated is the alleged necessary demoralization attending the association of prisoners together. It is readily admitted that if only their worst feelings are called out, as is commonly the case under existing systems, their association cannot but aggravate the evil. But if, instead, we will bring their better impulses into play—and it is quite easy to do this under proper combinations, without sacrificing any portion of reasonable punishment—prisoners will be found just like other men. They are born social beings, are so fashioned by the hand of the Creator, and it is in society, not in seclusion from it, in the society of their equals, not in exclusive contact with superiors, that their best qualities will infallibly be called out. To say that men can be best fitted to return to society in solitude, or in the company only of their superiors, without any other social relations whatever than that of prisoner to jailer, seems as great a solecism as it would be to say that admirals may be best taught their special duties by being kept on shore, or artists by being debarred the use of their implements. Both instruction and practice must go to fit a man to meet the difficulties and temptations of social life; and if either is omitted, the discharged prisoner must inevitably go lame and halt. Like handcuffs and strait-jackets, separation has a good special application, and, as a medicine, is excellent for certain phases of moral disease; but it is no more fit for habitual diet than senna or ipecacuanha. It is alleged that it facilitates the return of prisoners outside by lessening the chances of recognition; and in aid of this property in it, masks have been introduced into many prisons further to conceal the person. But it is a delusion to suppose that such a device can ordinarily be successful; prisoners rarely fail to know and recognize each other. Besides, is it really desirable or wise to try to qualify men to go forth into the world with a lie in their mouth? Would it not be better to make prisons so improving, and the principles on which men are discharged from them necessarily bear such testimony to their amended character, that the prejudice against receiving them when discharged will gradually fade away, and cease to be an obstacle to their ultimate advancement?

IX. *It is the living soul which a true system of prison discipline will seek to win, not the inert and obedient body ; hence minute regulations should not be greatly valued, and the multiplication of conventional or artificial offenses is to be sedulously avoided.*

To make the mark system consistent with itself, and carry out the principles on which it is founded, the head of a penitentiary establishment under it must propose to himself a purely benevolent object, and repudiate everything which is merely vindictive, as well as what is called exemplary. He will not by so doing lose the little benefit that may be derived from any example without principle; but he will raise the character of the example that he sets by making it one of successful reform. Whenever he is in doubt he must refer to the ordinary operations of society as a guide; and, in particular, he must study by every means to create a representation of its social ties by diffusing common interests and responsibilities, extending and subdividing these as on experience he shall find best. He must set no store by minute regulation, and carefully avoid multiplying conventional offenses. He must also encourage men to love labor, by assisting it with all the usual aids and appliances to make it productive. There cannot be a greater mistake than to make penal labor necessarily rude and ineffective. His object must be thus to persuade, not coerce; to create the good will, and reward, without commanding, the good deed. It is the living soul, and not merely the inert and obedient body that he must seek to gain; and precisely as he attaches value to the latter he will probably be indifferent to the former; and, conversely, as he comprehends the worth of the former he will appreciate at only its just value the minutely scrupulous eye-service which is often rendered by the worst men. Of his general success on these principles he need entertain no doubt; and the more confident he is on this head the better, for such confidence will make him inventive of the methods proper to the attainment of his end.

In dealing with prisoners we habitually make a variety of mistakes, to which, nevertheless, professed disciplinarians are all zealously attached. We draw no proper distinction between moral and merely conventional offenses. By minute regulation we multiply the number of these latter, and at the same time exaggerate their importance. We thus wear out the spirits of our men, and exhaust their feelings of submission and obedience by incessant demands upon them for pure frivolities. We also sear their conscience by familiarizing them in this way with petty transgression. We trust altogether to force to compass our ends. We seek to bend men like osiers, or to cast them, as we would dough, in stone molds. We allow the higher principles of human nature to lie dormant in our prisoners; we afford no scope for their exercise; we make our sole appeal to immediate and absolute submission; we give no charge to men of their own destiny; we keep them as automata in our hands; we treat them as such mainly, if not wholly; and having thus done everything in our power to weaken them, we look to make up for our blunders afterward by placing them in "favorable circumstances." Is this a school of virtue? Is not the whole process an absurdity? *Nitimur in adversum*—a struggle against opposing forces—is the real road to improvement; and we give our prisoners neither opportunity for making this manly struggle, nor the chance of acquiring energy and independence of character through the battle. We make them look and act to order while in our hands, and we wonder and cry out at their perverseness, when they afterward fall, either through the weakness which we have ourselves induced, or from the want of strength which we have failed to impart.

The system devised by Maconochie avoids these errors, without falling into others of any great gravity. It may be improved in its details, as it has been by Sir Walter Crofton, but its fundamental principles cannot be advantageously dispensed with. It grants no weak or unmeaning indulgences, but it seeks to gain soul as well as body; to influence and to mold, not merely to coerce. It draws the line of duty under the guidance of religion and morality, not of conventional regulation. It seeks to punish criminals by placing them in a position of severe adversity, from which nothing but long-sustained effort and self-denial can extricate them; but it does not aggravate their position by unworthy scorn, hatred, or contempt; on the contrary, it respects our common nature, however fallen or diseased. It does not encourage a man approaching his freedom by an abatement of task or improvement of diet, the low rewards of existing low systems, which flatter the spirit of self-indulgence, that leads most criminals to their first fall; but it at once proves, stimulates, and cheers him on by an ever-increasing scope of free agency, with motives to guide it, yet not unmingled with difficulty to resist its temptations. Seeking thus to train men for discharge into any circumstances, it does not distrust its power to qualify them for even the most difficult; but it seeks this end by strengthening the will, not by fettering it, believing that thus only can men be trained, whether in free society or in prison, who will be able to meet successfully the trials and difficulties of active life; for to aim at virtue by fencing it from without, instead of by strengthening it from within, is as perfect an exemplification as can well be conceived of dropping the substance to pursue its shadow. We cannot have worse success by seeking to gain the minds of our prisoners than we have had by aiming merely to fetter their bodies; and, on the other hand, we may, by using a more rational method, solve a problem which all concur in pronouncing difficult, and which the dispassionate reasoner can scarcely avoid pronouncing incapable, on present principles, of being solved at all, viz, how we may so organize public punishment as to check crime and yet recover criminals.

X. *The prisoner's self-respect should be cultivated to the utmost; everything tending to destroy this sentiment should be avoided; all unnecessary humiliation of the prisoner is of evil tendency and effect.*

The principle should be of constant and of universal application in prisons, not to degrade further those who come to them already degraded by their crimes. Self-respect is one of the most powerful sentiments of the human mind, for the reason that it is the most personal; and he who will not condescend in some degree, according to circumstances, to flatter it, will never attain his object by any series of chastisements, the effect of harsh treatment being to irritate rather than to correct, and thus to turn from reform instead of attracting to it.

Stripes, the imposition of a degrading dress, and everything else tending to destroy men's self-respect, should be abolished, and instead, the punishment for prison offenses should be the withholding of some privilege to which the prisoner would otherwise be entitled, or the forfeiture of a proportion, suited to the offense, of the progress already made toward liberation, with or without a period of stricter imprisonment, as the case may be. There is no greater mistake in the whole compass of penal discipline—fertile as it is in such—than its studied imposition of degradation as a portion of the punishment. It destroys every better impulse. But, on the contrary, no imposition would be so improving, none so favorable to the cultivation of prudence, self-command, self-respect, and a proper deference and respect for others, as that of making every deviation from the required line of right bear on ultimate release. Such a punishment would be as the drop of water that wears away the hardest stone; and without the possibility, under suitable regulations, of being ever wantonly cruel, would yet speedily subdue even the most refractory.

Captain Maconochie assures us that, while he did not neglect the object of *punishment* in his various arrangements on Norfolk Island, he sought it within the limits assigned both by the letter and the spirit of the law, not by excesses of authority and of suffering beyond them. The law imposing imprisonment and hard labor he executed to the fullest extent. But, while every one of his men was required to perform the government task allotted him, without abatement, he was saved from all unnecessary humiliation, and was encouraged to look to his own steady efforts for improved position while in prison and for his ultimate liberation from it. And this, he avers, not the efforts of an individual, zealous as they certainly were, was the real secret of the altered aspect of Norfolk Island in his time from what either preceded or followed it. He sought, by all practicable means, to recover the men's self-respect, to reinstate their manhood, to gain their own wills toward their reform, to visit moral offenses severely, but to reduce the number of those that were purely conventional, to mitigate the penalties attached to these, and thus gradually to awaken better and more manly feelings among them. He believed that needless humiliation, which it is the fashion to impose on prisoners over and above what is required by law, does more moral injury than all other incidents put together of ordinary prison life. Its tendency is to crush the weak, irritate the strong, and indispose all to submission and reform. It is, in truth, neither intended by the law, nor consistent with the professions made by lawgivers when framing them. It is merely one infirmity of human nature, one exhibition of its worst qualities, aggravating others. It is trampling where we ought to raise, and is therefore at once unchristian and impolitic.

No one will ever beneficially influence prisoners, or indeed any others, who does not cherish and seek to strengthen in their breasts manly sentiment, which is the religion of uncultivated minds, and perfectly compatible with their most improved aspirations.

XI. *Moral forces should be relied upon both for discipline and reformation in prisons, with as little resort to physical force as may be; the military type of discipline, particularly, is not suited to the nature and design of public punishment.*

A broad distinction is to be made between *physical apparatus* and *moral appliances* in prison management. By physical apparatus is to be understood is intended merely to coerce, regardless whether it persuades or not; by moral appliances is to be understood whatever offers a choice, and thus strengthens the mind even when guiding it. An invincible necessity, however produced, may, in this sense, be called physical; it may be caused by *moral* means, as intimidation, without affecting its real character; and, on the other hand, a *moral* appliance has frequently a tangible *physical* form, without losing its proper character. The essential [distinction—and it is a very important one—is that between *force* and *persuasion*, the fitting of the body and the gaining of the will. Whatever conduces to the latter may thus have place in a system of moral influence, but that place will be more or less high, according to its more or less directly persuasive or coercive character.

The chief influence at present relied on, both for preventing crime and weaning from it, is fear. Fear is no doubt among the most active impulses of the human mind; we all, in a degree, daily experience it; and it ought therefore to have a place, and even a large place, in every agency directed to repress crime. Yet if we consider it dispassionately and philosophically, there is not an impulse of any kind whatever, whether love, hatred, desire, covetousness—be it what it may—that does not continually overcome it even in the most timid. Is it rational, is it feasible, to rest our chief confidence on so feeble an agency in the endeavor to repress crime, to which the promptings usually proceed from the strongest feelings of the human breast? It is unworthy the intelligence of our age to state such a proposition. There needs to be introduced into prison discipline a higher aim, enforcing management that seeks to gain the wills of prisoners, and not merely to confine and macerate their bodies. We must train them to become again virtuous freemen, not merely for a time reduce them to the position of well-ordered bondmen, taught the virtues of a state of slavery—obedience, submission, punctuality, order, and the like—but necessarily with these a large admixture of its vices also—concealed but cherished resentment, duplicity, evasion, a thicker cloak of hypocrisy, which, however, only conceals with a little more art the continued rottenness within.

We too commonly consider criminals as the representatives of crime, and pharasaically fancy that, in being harsh to them, we show our detestation of it. If we would consider them rather as its first and saddest victims, to be pitied as well as blamed—to be pitied all the more for being bankrupt in virtue as well as in means, and if we would earnestly seek to raise them from this position, not indeed by pernicious indulgence, but by a judicious course of adversity and instruction, developing their manly and stimulating their moral nature; if we would do all this, we would much more correctly appreciate the whole subject, much better understand our own duties in relation to it, much better exhibit a Christian spirit to our fellow-men, and much more successfully repress crime. Only let us try—try in good faith and with good will, not halting between two principles, but acting steadily and energetically on one. The result would not long be doubtful, and the greatest moral problem of our day would be at length satisfactorily solved.

All past systems of prison discipline have been, in the main, different modifications of *force*. Whether separation, or silence, or enforced labor, or artificial privation, or whatever else may have been the leading principle, still, authority has been their chief, if not the exclusive reliance; and, so far as reforming criminals is concerned, they have all signally failed. Let *organized persuasion* now have a trial—not coaxing, not coddling, but persuasion with such forces behind it, resulting from a judicious application of motives, as, while leaving the will free, will yet, by a sort of moral necessity, determine it to a right choice.

It was charged against Maconochie that the only secret of his management on Norfolk Island was indulgence, and that his prisoners behaved well because they had all their own way. They little know prisoners who say this. Mere weakness never yet guided or controlled such men. They behaved well with him because they were reasoned with, not bullied; because they were sought to be raised, not crushed; *because they had an interest in their own good conduct*; because the public sentiment of the establishment was at once a restraining and an impelling force; and because they knew that if, notwithstanding, they behaved ill, they would be otherwise vigorously repressed.

It was objected by a writer in the Edinburgh Review that prisoners are selfish, and he argued that the way to cure them is to urge their penal sufferings to the maximum, and so make them feel that "the wages of sin is death;" and he endeavors to illustrate the analogy of such treatment to the doings of the supreme intelligence in the effects of continued intemperance on the body of the drunkard. But what is the real analogy of this case? As long as a drunkard continues to besot himself, his bodily suffering and decay increase; but if he turn from his infatuation, after the pain of the first effort is over he gains health and ease day by day. Just so it is with criminals under a moral as distinguished from a coercive *régime*. They come in selfish—desirous only of ease, evasion, and self-indulgence, but, under the strong impulse afforded by the system, they gradually become social, generous, active, and well-purposed throughout. "They wash and are cleansed." Religiously they may not be converted. But even in this respect many come, through their temporal good, to see and embrace their spiritual; and it is beyond all controversy that a right agency will make improved social agents of even the worst; or if this be considered doubtful, it will be time enough to pronounce authoritatively to this effect when a right agency shall have been fairly tried.

The coercive system of managing men appears to be an essentially vicious one, insomuch that precisely where most perfect, it will be found ultimately most unsuccessful. Mind can be gained only by appealing to mind. Fettering the body is even directly opposed to this. It has its immediate and apparent advantages no doubt; but they are too dearly purchased. If we will actively employ our prisoners, and by suitable means cultivate in them the daily practice of manly and social virtue, they will protect themselves from degrading vices much better than we can protect them by walls and bolts. And the moral triumph thus achieved will be as improving and strengthening to them as the physical triumph, even when achieved, is humiliating and enfeebling.

An extravagant degree of importance has been and is attached to the mere construction of prisons, and attention is drawn off by this from what is much more important. A good system in a bad prison is far better than a bad system in a good prison; and as no one ever heard of a regiment fluctuating according to the construction of a barrack, so neither is there any sound reason for that of prisoners being more dependent on the construction of their prison. Discipline is a science of moral much more than of physical arrangement; and in this department alone is this consideration utterly disregarded. In all other directions influence has in great part superseded force; here only has force superseded influence almost altogether; and the natural result—want of success—has followed. We cannot have worse success by seeking to gain the minds of our prisoners than has hitherto resulted from seeking merely to fetter their bodies.

Little effort is made, generally, to call the better impulses of prisoners into habitual exercise, while much in their treatment tends to keep the worse in activity. Further punishment is denounced if they misbehave; but no fixed encouragements are held out for sustained good conduct. Their more abject feelings are thus kept habitually active, while their more manly ones are allowed to sleep. Consequently, the powers and impulses most likely, on their discharge, to keep them from again falling, are impaired by disuse, while those of concealment and evasion, the sources, probably, of their first error, are continually being sharpened. Their character being thus modified, and themselves subjected to increased temptation on discharge, while their powers of resistance are necessarily weakened, the expression, "once a prisoner, always a prisoner," has become proverbial, but in a great degree through the training to which criminals in prison are thus habitually subjected.

The ability on the part of the prisoner to better his condition while in prison—in other words, a regulated self-interest—is one of the mightiest and healthiest moral forces that can be introduced into prison management. Captain Maconochie, in one of his publications, refers to the remarkable experiment in prison discipline of Colonel Montesinos, in Valencia, Spain, and makes the following extract from one of his reports:

The establishment of one workshop, and the difficulties experienced in managing it, showed me both how to introduce more, and how to enlarge those already in operation; and I thus further acquired the intimate conviction that without the *stimulus* of some personal advantage accruing to themselves from their labor, it is difficult to obtain work even from the already skilled, and almost impossible to get the unskilled to learn. Repeated experiments convinced me of the practical lesson involved in this maxim of social economy, and that what neither severity of punishments nor constancy in inflicting them could exact, tho slightest personal interest would obtain. In different ways, therefore, during my command, I have applied this powerful stimulant; and the excellent results it has always yielded, and the powerful germs of reform which are constantly developed under its influence, have at length fully convinced me that the most inefficacious of all methods in a prison, the most pernicious and fatal to every chance of reform, are punishments carried to the length of harshness. Moreover, the love of labor cannot be imparted by violent means, but rather by encouragement and persuasion; and although it is quite possible to obtain a given amount of work from prisoners by the aid of the stick, yet the consequence is, necessarily, aversion to an employment which involves so many penalties, and of which such a bitter recollection must always be preserved. The moral object of penal establishments is thus also, in effect, defeated, which should be not so much to inflict pain as to correct—to receive men idle and ill-intentioned, and return them to society, if possible, honest and industrious citizens. It was not till after making many experiments of severity that I came firmly to this conclusion; but ultimately I made the principle the basis of all my operations on the minds of the prisoners, and the extraordinarily small number of recommittals to my prison, and the excellent health and perfect state of submission in which those confined in it have always been kept, seem to me to leave no doubt of its soundness.

The comment of our author on these statements is:

The most depraved human nature, the lowest, the most sunk, has yet elasticity sufficient to rise at the call of a regulated self-interest, and can thence be made gradually to ascend under the influence of higher motives.

One of the moral forces most confidently relied upon by Captain Maconochie in the management of prisoners is the law of kindness. The kindness proposed, however, is neither morbid nor mawkish, seeking merely to alleviate the immediate suffering of prisoners, which they have deserved, and ought to undergo. It is rather a manly, rational, Christian, prudent, forecasting kindness, seeking to raise them again. Such a spirit introduced into our prisons would speedily work wonders, both on the character of prisoners and on the general movement of crime. This spirit once there, the principle admitted, the aspiration after moral improvement recognized by the officers as a duty, it would prove inventive in their hands. It would *find* or *make* means to accomplish the reform of their prisoners, and when driven from one agency, it would have recourse to others; it *would* not be wholly defeated. Further, such a spirit once having found a lodgment in the breasts of prison officers, and constantly working itself out, would not long be confined within the prison walls, but would follow those who had felt its beneficent power while in bondage into society, after their discharge, and would thus tend prodigiously to repress crime.

What a change, what a revolution we might say, would the general possession and manifestation of such a spirit on the part of prison officers make in the tone and temper in which prisoners are now treated in prison! This is at present supercilious, in many cases even contemptuous or denunciatory, whereas it should be rather that in which patients are received into a hospital. The hatefulness of the crime that has been committed should be, indeed, freely expressed; on this head there should be no compromise; but apart from this the criminal should be sincerely regarded and studiously treated as an object of compassion, sadly fallen, indeed, but yet recoverable, and sent to prison to be recovered. A tone of hopefulness for his case should thus be maintained, and of confidence that, when put in the right way, he will be manly enough to abide in it. This idea of manliness, as attached to virtue, and of cowardice and abjectness, as shown in yielding to vice, should be especially insisted on. The greatest benefit has been seen to result from it in dealing with rough and fallen natures. It is an idea that comes home to many bosoms, otherwise hard to be permanently impressed, and to whom, on the other hand, any approach to whining is distasteful and an object of scoffing.

And it deserves to be noted here, in passing, that a liberal application of the law of kindness to prisoners is not incompatible with a calm, steady, resolute discipline. Tenderness may be fitly and successfully blended with justice in the treatment of them. It is not a just rigor against which the prisoner rebels, for that may be wise and kind; it is against capricious harshness, which is cruel and irritating, because it lacks the element of equity. Criminals are not much accustomed to kind treatment, and therefore they are the more readily touched by it. Show them that you have humanity, that you feel a genuine sympathy, and their gratitude is at once awakened. This principle appears to keep a lingering hold of our nature, even in the last and lowest degree of human wickedness. When all other generous principles are gone, this still survives, and shows itself even in the most hackneyed and hardened malefactors. There is, somehow and somewhere, a softer part about them, which will give way to the demonstrations of tenderness. This one ingredient of a better character, this one germ of a dormant virtue, is still found to survive the destruction of all the others, insomuch that, fallen as a brother may be from the moralities which at one time adorned him, the manifested good-will of his fellowmen still carries a charm and an influence along with it; and in this there lies a regenerative and redemptive operation, which no degradation and no depravity can extinguish.

Moral power over his prisoners was sought by Captain Maconochie, and attained, too, in a very high degree, by frequent, frank, kindly, judicious conversations with them. On this point the captain says:

I very early adopted, in the penal colonies, two practices, to which I owed much of the minute information that I gradually acquired about prisoners, and much of the influence that I gained over them. One was that of conversing with them all very freely, and encouraging them to speak to me in like manner, and to give me, without hesitation or reserve, their views and sentiments on whatever was our subject. By this means I was enabled to sound their impressions and the sources of them much more deeply than would otherwise have been possible. I derived infinite advantage, in the beginning especially, from this practice. My second habit was that, whenever a prisoner was brought before me judicially, especially for a moral, as distinguished from a mere disciplinary or conventional offense, I always strictly interrogated him about his early youth and training, his parents, the lessons they had taught him, the example they had set him, and so forth. My immediate object was to call up the associations connected with the days when he was yet comparatively innocent, and thus endeavor to revive in him the impulses which guided his conduct before he became corrupted and seared by the scenes he had subsequently gone through. I was often much struck by the manifestations of tenderness and regret that passed before me; yet distressed, too, by their too often fleeting character. Still, I had reason to think that they did some good, as recurring to the men's minds afterward, and insensibly influencing their conduct. They were sometimes quoted to me months afterward by prisoners as having had that effect on themselves; but at the moment I certainly was not always convinced of this beneficial effect. At times I had even cause to suspect artifice in the exhibition of them.

Again:

I carried constantly about me a little book, in which the names and characters of all were entered, by which I was enabled at all times to address them according to their occupations and general demeanor. If they preferred applications to me, as was common, I would immediately reply to them; and talking freely, almost familiarly, with all, I could both probe their characters and insinuate much useful instruction, especially among the leaders of them, for I knew that if they were gained, the others would follow; while, on the other hand, this process could not be reversed. I thus especially pressed a distinction, which I was anxious to draw, between what I termed (by comparison) manly offenses and unmanly, including especially among these latter grossness and petty thefts; and I found generally that I could by no other means so effectually discountenance such faults as by thus pouring contempt on them. I encouraged all to address me with freedom, and would not even listen to a man unless he stood erect and spoke to me like one. I even said to them frequently that I would rather have a man insolent to me than cringing; and I encouraged all, if they wanted anything, to come to me themselves with their requests, instead of seeking to make friends among those more immediately about me. To facilitate this, I walked and rode about the island generally quite alone, and rather invited than discouraged, conversation with any who came in contact with me.

For every really useful purpose, the discipline in our prisons is at present far too military in its whole conception. The objects of military and prison discipline are diametrically opposite; and yet the latter is very much modeled on the former. The object of military discipline is to train men to act together; that of prison discipline, when rightly viewed, is to prepare them advantageously to separate, and to act each for himself. The purpose of the first is to absorb individuality, to make each man, as it were, a portion of a well-adjusted machine in the hands of a skilled regulator. Its aim is to teach all to look to orders only, not principles, as the guides of their actions. It is precisely the unhappy result of this spirit in existing systems of prison discipline that produces its injurious effect, and shows the false principles on which they are founded. Were it the express purpose of society to destroy the moral strength of prisoners, and to utterly unfit them to regain a place among free and self-acting men, the means could not be more perfectly adapted to the end.*

The aim is to reform these criminals. To compass their reformation we must quit the military type, and seek a more suitable arrangement. A military barrack, despite the presumed original innocence of its inmates, and a high point of honor studiously cultivated in it—for which no substitute can be found in a prison—yet notoriously demoralizes, and can it be deemed possible that a similar organization can reclaim criminals? Instead of this, we must carefully copy the incidents of that frugal, honest, self-denying, and laborious poverty, to which we wish to restore our criminals, and for which, therefore, it should be our earnest endeavor to qualify them. No more hot meals without previous exertion to earn them; no more undervaluing of time, nor consequent *stimulus* to skulking or evasion; no more interest but in industry; no indulgences save those purchased by exertion and self-command; no progress toward liberty except through diligence in work, and the exhibition of every other description of good conduct, proved not by words but by acts, not by lip submission, but by active, strenuous effort in the fulfillment of all duty. It is thus, and thus only, that the stern school of punishment would be made really reformatory.

The military type must therefore be abolished in prison management, and a discipline by moral forces substituted in its place. The objects of military and prison discipline, being directly opposed to each other, cannot be pursued by the same road. The one is meant to train men to act together, the other to prepare them to act separately. The one relies upon force, which never yet created virtue; the other on motives, the approved agency for obtaining moral ends. The special object of the one is to suppress individual character, and reduce all to component parts of a compact machine; that of the other is to develop and strengthen individual character, and, by instilling right principles, to encourage and enable it to act on these independently.

---

* The Rev. Mr. Luckey, late chaplain of Sing Sing prison, used to relate the case of a man who, being discharged after a long imprisonment, was unable to walk otherwise than after the fashion of the lock-step; and, accordingly, he would invariably get behind the person with whom he was walking, and laying his hand on his shoulder, tread with the greatest precision in his steps. One day, walking in the streets of New York with a brother clergyman, accompanied by this man, who was following himself in the manner described, and feeling, as he expressed it, "a little wicked," he managed to slip from before the ex-convict and place him behind his companion, to the great consternation and fright of the latter, and his own abundant amusement.

Upon the whole, the questions which heretofore have chiefly occupied public attention—questions of separation, association, kinds and methods of labor, and the like—are but the husk; the kernel is found in the question, "What shall be the spirit, what the moral apparatus, with which punishment shall be inflicted under any system?" External circumstances have had far too much attention. On the principles of the mark system, or, more generally, of *systematized persuasion* in any form, better results are likely to be obtained in the most unfavorable circumstances than any modification of force will give in the most favorable. And no great advance seems probable or possible in the application of penal science till this truth is seen, acknowledged, embraced, and acted on.

XII. *Unsuitable indulgence in prison management is as pernicious as unsuitable severity. The true principle is, to place the prisoner in a position of stern adversity, from which he must work his way out by his own exertions—by diligent labor and a constant course of voluntary self-command and self-denial.*

The writer in the Edinburgh Review, cited under the last head, objects to Captain Maconochie's discipline as a system of indulgence and pampering; but certainly there is nothing in it to warrant such a representation. On the contrary, it proposes to place criminals in a state of utter poverty, destitution, and bondage, from which nothing but their own steady, unflinching, persevering effort can extricate them. They are to be at the bottom of a well, with a ladder provided by which they may ascend if they will, but without any bolstering or dragging up by other than their own exertions. If they even halt, the effect is to make them go downward again, for their maintenance from day to day is to be charged to them. Are there not here, then, sufficient elements of suffering to produce a deterring effect? And yet everything is strongly conducive to reform. Why, therefore, go further? Why introduce, in addition, chains, and dungeons, and factitious offenses, and all the other apparatus of slavery, so much clung to in ordinary prison discipline, yet so injurious to both officers and men? Why stigmatize that system as overindulgent which merely rejects these, while substituting, at the same time, conditions far harder than they to a degraded mind? A fallen spirit can put up with a little more humiliation, a little more contumely, a few more harsh restrictions, which there is always a contemplated pleasure in evading or resisting; but to set his shoulder to the wheel, to struggle steadily out of his position, to command his temper, his appetites, his self-indulgent propensities—and all voluntarily, all from an inward impulse stimulated by a moral necessity—this is a far harder imposition.

In the same spirit the reviewer quotes all his intellectual apparatus as though they were intended as mere *solatia*, mere devices to while away time. But he introduced them for the express purpose of awakening, stimulating, and keeping the mind active, as well as the body, storing it, at the same time, with better thoughts and images than the impure and disgusting ones otherwise most familiar to prisoners. And in this light they cannot, surely, be too highly valued. It is in the intervals of entire repose, of an absolute want of occupation, which, in ordinary prison management, are allowed to alternate with severe bodily toil, that such men corrupt each other. His music, readings, schools, novels, horticulture, and other like machinery, kept out (as they were designed to) many a devil, and let some angels in.

Reform by adversity, deter by improving criminals—such is the fundamental precept of Maconochie's system; and it cannot be justly charged against it that it is either weak or mawkish. On the contrary, it is obvious that a much firmer, more consistent, and even more formidable and deterring system may be founded on this principle than on arbitrary, vindictive punishment. It is substance, not forms, at which it aims. It leaves little to administration, and requires higher sacrifices than lip professions, or mere external, and often hypocritical, submission and obedience.

As a rule, reform can be attained only through a course of severe training. It is in well-devised adversity that all the manly virtues are generated. "Sweet are its uses," therefore, to prisoners; though they, like others, would gladly shun its school. It is a consideration here of no little force, that when suffering is inflicted with a benevolent aim the very weakest will enforce it. And all the ends of public punishment may be thus more surely gained. We reform and deter at the same time and by the same process. The judicious pursuit of the first object will give us also the second.

Beyond the restrictions necessary for the order and safe custody of prisoners, every part of their treatment should be directed exclusively to their improvement. Unless this position be distinctly and steadily acted upon, we shall be liable to be constantly drawn aside to the infliction of mere hardship and suffering, which will be quite unnecessary, for if improvement be but wisely sought, there will be enough of these, and even far more than are at present imposed. In truth, nothing could be devised more distasteful to the habitually idle, dissolute, and criminal, than an imposed necessity to be, for a length of time, orderly, steady, industrious, and otherwise self-restrained, under penalty of prolonging their detention. The necessity of thus even *electing* to be well-conducted, of choosing to *make effort*, and not merely consenting to *endure*, would be more felt by most prisoners than a much greater amount of physical hardship, incurred under other conditions; for this would make it evident that their wills were subdued, as well as their persons, and bravado, then or afterward, would be out of the question.

The true principle, then, is, that a man incurring punishment should, like one who has fallen into a pit, be required to *struggle* out of it, and not be allowed, as at present, simply to *endure* out of it. In the one case, his more active and better qualities are called into play, and thereby necessarily improved; in the other they are all put to sleep, or, to change the figure, they are consumed by rust, if, indeed, others most pernicious do not supply their place.

XIII. *The education of prisoners is a matter of primary importance as a means of reforming them.*

To develop the minds and powers of prisoners, schools should be established in all penal institutions; or, rather, such an establishment should be one vast school, in which everything is made subservient to instruction in some shape, moral, religious, intellectual, or industrial. Libraries, museums, and all other appliances calculated to excite and gratify a rational curiosity, should be liberally furnished. But, except in the early stages, when the first start is to be given, and when the treatment should be more like that of a hospital, in which whatever is most suitable is given without regard to expense, Captain Maconochie would not have the benefit of these aids extended to any gratuitously. He would liberally reward proficiency where it did occur, but he would, in every case, require a sacrifice of marks to obtain the means of acquiring it. These means would be thus valued, and the analogy of ordinary society would be still preserved, a rule of supreme importance in a reformatory prison discipline. The most active means should be taken, the most assiduous efforts made, to expel old thoughts from the minds of prisoners, and supply them with new materials for reflection. The captain devised a curious arrangement iu aid of this desigu. In a separate prison, which he caused to be built on Norfolk Island, an apartment was contrived, in which a reader's voice could be heard in twelve contiguous cells; and, during the greater part of each day, some description or other of reading aloud was maintained in it. By closiug a sliding panel iu his door, each prisoner could be absolutely alone, if he wished it, while, by opening it, he was again within hearing of some entertaining and instructive reading. The effect, in a great degree, even through this power of choice, was most beneficial. It is vain to talk of ignorant, inert, and corrupt minds profiting by their own unassisted reflections. They sleep over these, or do worse; and they cannot be *compelled* to do better, for what is forced on them soon becomes nauseous, and hence unprofitable. Really to serve them, their occupations and progress must be made immediately profitable, and their time thus be rendered important to themselves. They must be assailed from without, also, by continuous, rather than by vehement intermitting efforts; and, being for the most part either adults, or very precocious, they cannot be treated with permanent advantage as mere school children. Any progress they so make will be found ou trial deceptive, disappearing with the machinery used to produce it.

Captain Maconochie, in the management of Norfolk Island, was most anxious to encourage education among his men; however, as he refused them rations, so neither would he give them schooling gratuitously, but compelled them to yield marks to acquire it. He balanced this by visiting the schools regularly on the last Saturday of every month, and inspecting them with some degree of formality, examining the men, and distributing prizes, in marks, for attention and proficiency; so that, with diligence and assiduity, school was rather a source of gain than expenditure, though the idler found it only the latter. Altogether the plan worked admirably. He never saw adult schools make such rapid progress or be carried on with greater spirit. He further, on his Saturday visitations, gave prizes, in marks, to the educated prisoners employed to read aloud in the jail, hospitals, dormitories, and larger huts, from which practice of loud readings, very great advantages were derived. It enlarged the minds of even the most ignorant and stupid; and, by showing them the use and value of being able to read, it invited them to diligence in acquiring the power.

XIV. *Religious instruction and culture are all-important as a means of reforming criminals.*

Among other agencies for the recovery of the prisoners on Norfolk Island, religious instruction and exhortation occupied much of our author's thoughts, and not a little of his time and effort personally. Besides visiting almost daily the jails and hospitals, and supplying them with books and readers—the latter educated prisoners, mostly infirm and unable to do any work besides this, (and it was marvelous how much they improved both themselves and their companions by this exercise)— he established adult schools; furnished these also with books and other intellectual apparatus; employed even his own family tutor to teach and to preach in them; held monthly examinations, at which he distributed prizes to the meritorious; and, in addition to all these efforts, every Sunday afternoon for four years, after attending morning service with the prisoners on the settlement, he went regularly, attended by some of his family, to a distant station in the bush, where he read the evening service, with a sermon for the benefit of the shepherds and others whose

avocations made it difficult for them to attend punctually on the service
at the settlement. Further, he built two churches in the settlement
during his incumbency, one Protestant, the other Roman Catholic.
Previous to his coming, though the island had been fifteen years a penal
settlement, there had not been even one, and the services had been read
to the prisoners, often by one of themselves, in a most slovenly and
irregular manner, in barns and mess-rooms, as they could be hastily and
very imperfectly arranged for the purpose. His church edifices, though
plain, were, at least, convenient, and never used in any other way; and
the moral benefit that accrued from making the religious observances
thus decent, and, in aspect at least, reverential, was prodigious. He'
was assisted in all these efforts by a moderately strong clerical staff,
consisting of two principal chaplains, Protestant and Roman Catholic,
both able, zealous, and even eloquent men, and by two Catholic and
Protestant catechists. The men were all (he did not doubt) morally and
socially improved; the tone of feeling, action, and still more, of opinion,
among them was sensibly raised; vice of all kinds, as well as theft, was
discountenanced; scurrilous and reproachful epithets addressed to each
ether, which had been previously common, became comparatively rare
and even unpopular; evidence in all cases of transgression was much
more easily obtained; and there was no longer, as it were, a conspiracy
among the men on all occasions to defeat the ends of justice. But the
captain was constrained to acknowledge that he did not think that any
great part of this general and marked improvement proceeded from
religious motives, though it was clearly the result of religious teaching.
Few, he conceived, could be considered as religiously impressed even in
thought, and fewer still, in difficult circumstances, evinced self-denial
as the result of religious impression. Still, after citing a variety of
illustrative examples, Captain Maconochie adds:

> From these anecdotes, to which more might be added, it appeared to the writer that
> some important lessons might be deduced, bearing both on education and prison disci-
> pline. They illustrate the extreme importance, as regards recovery from crime, of ex-
> tending as widely as possible among our population early devotional teaching, directed
> to stimulating conscientiousness and instilling an early sense of personal responsibility.
> It did not appear to me of much importance with what specific code of theology this
> was combined, provided it was instilled early, and thus, almost of necessity, dwelt
> more on the points in which nearly all agree than on those in which some differ. In
> this case, however, the impression may have been overborne for a time under the influ-
> ence of youthful levity, strong temptation, or other adverse circumstances; it was
> easily renewed, especially if presented under the forms with which it was originally
> connected. On the other hand, if youth, the season when the sentiments are most ex-
> citable and retain impressions made on them with the greatest tenacity, has once been
> passed without any such feelings being kindled, it seemed almost impossible to awaken
> them afterward in mature years.

In this connection may be fitly introduced what Captain Maconochie
says in regard to the burial of deceased prisoners. Very soon after his
arrival at the island he set himself to improve the prisoners' funerals,
previously most disreputable. The attention of prisoners to their sick
companions, he avers, is usually very striking; and their emotion, on
occasion of a death, far exceeds what is usually seen in either army or
navy. The feeling exhibited is not, he thinks, the expression of fear,
but rather of sympathy with one who has passed from among them, and
from their trials to another audit. He often observed this thought in
the minds of otherwise rather hardened men, and in no case did he ever
witness a trace of that disgusting levity with which death is sometimes
adverted to in military and even in high civil society. Before he went
to Norfolk Island only a limited number, not above twelve, were allowed
to attend any funeral; and no head-stone was permitted to be erected at

a prisoner's grave. In the belief that a high moral benefit would be the result of an opposite course, he abrogated both these regulations. Two or three hundred men would thus often accompany an interment, all dressed in their best, and walking most respectably in files together; and a decorum, modesty, and even taste (occasionally) were exhibited in their headstones which were really wonderful. He speaks of one which greatly impressed him. It was a low, humble stone over an old man, with the words, "The weary are at rest" above, and the name and date beneath. It seemed to him very touching, and at the same time highly characteristic. It expressed that *tædium vitæ*—weariness of life—which elderly prisoners, who especially feel the discomforts of their position, and have outlived their relish for its palliations, almost always testify. The prison burying-ground was in a somewhat romantic spot, picturesquely placed between a high cliff on one side and a portion of sea-beach on the other, on the bar fronting which a heavy surf broke, even in the calmest weather. A considerable clump of trees, of stunted growth, because much beaten by the prevailing sea-breeze, and hanging low, in consequence, over the rear portion of the ground, contributed both to sequester and, with its associations, to give the place a funereal character. A broad gravel walk ran through the whole length of the cemetery. The little "heaving" mounds rose thickly on either side, with their simply epitaphed headstones; and, eventually, the place was seldom without one or more prisoners "walking among the tombs," scaning the inscriptions, and meditating on the stern or touching lessons and recollections thus brought to mind and impressed upon the soul.

Anxious to improve the funeral rites in every proper way, and so make them not only more decent but more impressive, Captain Maconochie desired to provide the prisoners a mort-cloth; but true to his principle of giving nothing for nothing, on which his inflexibility was as unchanging as "the laws of the Medes and Persians," he required three hundred marks to be yielded for one, which thus became the property of the individuals subscribing them, and was hired out afterward as wanted, and much valued, "and in time valuable."

XV. *Industrial labor in prisons is the only occupation that has an amendatory power; the tread-mill, crank, and shot-drill are deteriorating rather than reformatory in their effect.*

Captain Maconochie cites a passage from a report of M. Demetz, director of the agricultural colony of Mettray, to the effect that, while in England the crank and tread-wheel are employed both for ordinary and disciplinary punishments, the young criminals committed to his institution universally object to this, and express great indignation at being set, as they call it, "to grind the air," (*à moudre l'air;*) adding, "We find it of much importance that our occupations, whether ordinary or for punishment, produce a sensible result." Upon this Captain Maconochie observes, "The difference, in moral effect, between sawing wood or other *useful* employment, and 'grinding air,' appears to me to be nearly the whole difference between improving and deteriorating occupation. Even lunatics are soothed by what they consider useful employment, and are irritated by what produces no useful result. In a reformatory course it is of much importance to study every point of this kind. Unless a sphere of useful active exertion is provided, I have always found one of the two results—almost equally disadvantageous—to ensue, viz: either morbid irritation, tending at length to insanity or stupid acquiescence, deriving amusement from frivolous occupations."

We may introduce at this point, though perhaps not exactly falling here, what is said on the question of the competition between free labor and convict labor: "It has been urged," he says, (quoting from the committee on criminal law of the Society for Promoting the Amendment of the Law,) "against the introduction of useful employment in our jails, that an impolitic competition between convict labor and free labor will thereby be established. We consider this an utterly futile objection, and one the fallacy of which has been so often exposed, when raised against the introduction of machinery, that it requires no labored efutation from us; but we may observe, in passing, that it is infinitely less applicable to convict labor than to machinery, since the convict must be supported, while undergoing imprisonment, from some funds, and that it is far better for the interests of the community that he should be kept wholly or in part by his own industry than by taxes levied on the industry of others. If every rug, net, and mat used in England were made in our prisons no evil results would follow, but, on the contrary, unmixed good, since the public would be supplied with these articles at a cheaper rate than at present, and those who now gain their livelihood by rugs, nets, and mats would, by degrees, find employment in other trades equally remunerative. We have thought it necessary to allude to this objection, not because we deem it, intrinsically, of the slightest importance, but because we know that at present a foolish prejudice on the subject prevails."*

XVI. *Arbitrary classification, that is, classification by age, supposed riminality, identity or similarity of temperament, and the like, is impracticable, and would be useless if it were practicable.*

On this subject, commenting on an article in the Edinburgh Review, Captain Maconochie holds this language:

Like all other exercises of mere authority, authoritative classification, here recommended, will prove, I am convinced, a pure delusion; and, in fact, very few practical men, I believe, are not ready even now to pronounce it such. There is no rule by which to regulate it. If by offense, this is the mere accident of conviction; if by age, the youngest criminals, born and cradled in sin, are very often the most corrupt; if by supposed similarity of temper or antecedent character, no one can certainly pronounce on this, and men are as often and oftener improved by associating with their opposites as with those who resemble them. It is impossible to attain real benefit by such means. One general difference between prisoners, at the same time, does exist, which I think it would be important, on many occasions, to keep in view, but not with the aim of separating them—I mean the difference between men who have erred from having more than an average amount of physical energy, and men who have sinned from having less than an average amount of moral principle. The treatment of the two should very considerably differ, and it might not be impossible or unwise to subject this to regulation.

The classification which alone Maconochie approves is based on character, conduct, and merit, as shown in the daily routine of prison life,

---

* I must enter my emphatic dissent from the position taken by the committee on criminal law, that if all the rugs, nets, and mats in England were made in the prisons, *and none outside,* nothing but "unmixed good" would come of it; and for this reason, that in that case prisoners would learn a business during their incarceration which would be of no possible advantage to them on their return to free society, and they would be even less fitted to command an honest living after their discharge than they were before their committal. This would be a contradiction to the whole modern doctrine of a reformatory prison discipline, the very core and essence of which is that the prisoner, while undergoing his sentence, should have imparted to him the *power* as well as the *will* to earn honest bread after his release. The true policy is *to multiply trades in prisons,* and to give convicts some choice as to what trades they will learn, thus affording them an opportunity to consult, to a certain extent, their own tastes and aptitudes, as well as enabling them to calculate the chances of success that different trades would give them on their liberation. The error of the committee arises, no doubt, from confounding, in their thought, convicts and machinery, two elements or objects identical for certain purposes of their argument, but differing essentially in other respects.—E. C. W.

such as that which is found in the Crofton prison system, or, possibly, in some particular prisons managed on the same general principles.

XVII. *In a reformatory system of prison discipline, the employment of the prisoners themselves as sub-officers, and even as jurors in trying their fellow-prisoners, is attended with good effects.*

When the object of prison discipline is the moral amendment of the persons subjected to it, the employment of these as under-officers is excellent. Each prisoner, in this case, feels elevated by the elevation of his companion, and the self-respect of the whole body is thus cultivated. It is quite different if the object of the discipline is coercion. In this latter case, nothing can be worse, for the sub-officers uniformly abuse their petty power, and the individual prisoner is doubly crushed under the tyranny of merely another but favored slave.

When a system of prison discipline is mild, rational, and reformatory, nothing conduces more to its success than employing those under to it, even largely in conducting it. They serve both as examples and encouragement to all the others. But when, on the contrary, the system is arbitrary, despotic, coercive, nothing can be more injurious. They always exceed their recognized powers.

Captain Maconochie gives the following account of his management, in this particular, of the penal colony on Norfolk Island:

One of my earliest cares, after lauding and studying in some degree the details of the establishment, was in a certain measure to disperse and distribute the men. The barracks were very deficient in suitable accommodation, and were much overcrowded. Regard to decency was impossible in them, and the worst offenses had become common. I sought to combat these evils by lights, and by readings aloud each night for a time in the dormitories. But the main evil was not touched by these means. To abate this I selected, under the guidance of the officers, the best and most trustworthy men, camped them out in the bush, allowed them to choose others as their companions, for whom they agreed to be responsible, gave them huts and gardens close to their work, and ultimately derived the greatest benefit from the whole arrangement. This indulgence was naturally coveted. It became at once a *stimulus* and a reward for good conduct, its refusal a punishment for bad, and its abuse a most unpopular offense among all. The maxim that confidence begets fidelity was never more strikingly illustrated. This distribution of the men necessitated a greater employment of prisoner overseers and sub-overseers, and I was otherwise most favorable to this. In conducting a coercive system such employment often leads to tyranny and abuse, but in a reforming one it is most beneficial. It encourages the best men, increases their influence with the others, and makes these aspire to similar trusts. The very possession of such trusts is also itself a reformatory agent. I saw many instances of originally very different men thus, and thus alone, rendered trustworthy.

In another place he says:

I should never have got on at all on Norfolk Island had I not largely employed prisoners in my management; but by having a host of *persuaders*, for it was thus that I chiefly sought to use them, distributed constantly among the people, most of them taken from among their own "good men," the manly foundation of whose character recommended them to me, as to their companions, in spite of the crimes too often unnaturally superinduced on it by the circumstances in which they had been placed, I prevented much of the evil previously almost boasted of, and to a very considerable extent directed public opinion against what remained of it, even among the old prisoners, to whom no other portion of my own peculiar system was permitted to be applied than the spirit thus imported from it into the old forms of administration. I know that there is a strong prejudice among theoretical reasoners against the employment of prisoner sub-officers, and the instances of cruelty and corruption that may be cited of them in past times in our penal settlements are at once frightful and too true. This, however, has not been the fault of the prisoners themselves, but of those who, by their mistaken notions of discipline, have infused a wrong spirit into them. If they are properly controlled and directed, there is no one, I am certain, who has a practical knowledge of the management of prisoners but will testify to their extreme usefulness. They are like the petty and non-commissioned officers of a ship or regiment, who are, also, equally selected from the ranks sought to be controlled.

On the subject of employing prisoner jurors, in trials for prison offenses, Captain Maconochie says:

I could have wished to complete the resemblance to free life which I had established by interesting my overseers and other better men in the administration of justice on the island, making them eligible to act as jurors in our prison courts. I am certain that this would have had a great effect on all, but it was beyond my power to do it formally, and I knew that even an application for such power would be ill-received at Sydney. I did, however, make a near approach to it. I opened the doors of our courts, previously closed to prisoners, invited as many to attend them as could be spared from their stated labor, tried every case myself, on important occasions even in the barrack-yard after hours, amid them all; on questions of conflicting evidence would refer to them for suggestions; often received important hints from them, on which I acted; on grave occasions always postponed passing sentence for at least a day after finding a verdict, that I might maturely weigh all the concurring circumstances, and thus in every way sought to beget in them confidence in my desire to act right, and without passion, in regard to them. Nor is there any feeling that it is more desirable to impress on such a community. It is itself improving. As intimated, I would gladly have appointed a select few formally as jurors, but that I feared the innovation might be considered too great at Sydney. I am convinced that in administering summary justice it will be found always beneficial to engage persons of the same class with those subjected to it to co-operate therewith. As it was, besides the measures above detailed, I appointed one man, a very acute and intelligent prisoner, to act as counsel for all accused of offense. He was forbidden to tell me anything that he knew to be false, but, apart from this, his duty was to make the best case for each that the circumstances would admit. I gained two advantages from this: I was led to investigate more closely what he did not say; and the stupid and loutish among the prisoners, who are usually much run down by overseers, had an equal chance with the clever to have their stories fairly told. By the means above described I at length completely overcame what had originally given me much vexation—the sympathy of the prisoners with offense.

XVIII. *Undue restraint on the correspondence of prisoners, and too minute and rigid a surveillance, are both of evil tendency and effect in prison management.*

A prison rule, common to many different countries, is that prisoners shall not have any communication with their families till after they have been three months imprisoned, and only once every three months afterward—just as if it could be the wisdom or interest of society to screen them from the knowledge in detail of the sorrow and the suffering into which their crimes have plunged those dearest to them, or to weaken, almost to severance, those ties which, if maintained, would most facilitate their return to society and stimulate their exertions in it. The regulation is meant as an aggravation to suffering, but in most cases it operates rather as a relief; and it deeply injures the criminal by impairing, and sometimes almost obliterating, whatever good feeling still survives, when a wife and family, a mother, or sister, is thus bebarred from communicating their griefs and distresses to the author of them, and from directing to him whatever monitions, counsels, or exhortations may to them seem fit and necessary.

Captain Maconochie claims, not without reason, that the introduction of the mark system would enable the authorities to modify, most advantageously, the restriction mentioned in the preceding paragraph—often most injurious in its effect—viz, that on frequency of intercourse, by letter or visit, with friends and relations outside. This is prevented altogether, except at long intervals, generally three months, and, as stated above, when the privilege comes to all in their turn, as a right, and always without any special effort or sacrifice on the part of the prisoner to obtain it, and bearing, consequently, like a time sentence, lightly on the worst men, but pressing hard, and often with blighting effect, on the better and more promising. The heedless, the hardened, and the profligate care nothing for it; to many of them it is even a shield, guarding them from the knowledge of the tears and reproaches of those whom they have deeply injured, perhaps ruined, by their misconduct; while the father, the husband, the brother, still thoughtful and affectionate, is profoundly moved by it; and all are so far injured that they become partially forgotten by their more distant friends in these long intervals, and, as a consequence, on discharge, lose their active services to assist them in recovering the means of an honest living. In every way the arrangement is thus seen to be bad. But, under the mark system, it could be easily and most beneficially modified by imposing a charge on every prisoner receiving a letter or visit, the reception or non-reception of either being entirely in his own choice. Writing himself, he will have to pay in marks for paper and postage-stamps, his letters, as a matter of course, being always subject to examination. But beyond these checks, there should be none inside the prison, as regards the matter of letter-writing; and outside, on visits, only one, viz, a proper authentication as to the character and relationship of the visitor.

As regards the second branch of the maxim, which serves as heading to the present section, Captain Maconochie remarks:

Scarcely any point is more insisted on in modern codes of prison discipline than that of keeping prisoners under a constant and rigorous supervision, a practice which, however plausibly it may be advocated, both generates and fosters that habit of eye-service which so peculiarly unfits a discharged prisoner for the task of self-guidance after release

Again:

It seems to me impossible to avoid the conclusion that the minute supervision and regulation maintained in our best jails, relaxed necessarily in our inferior ones, impossible to be maintained in ordinary transportation, and for which I systematically substituted, where I could, a large measure of self-guidance, with a strong motive to direct it right, is, in strictness, unfavorable to the reform of prisoners. It may give the desire of amendment, but it takes away the power. It enfeebles character, makes it ever seek to lean upon direction, and delivers it up, bound hand and foot, to subsequent temptation.

XIX. *Individualization is an essential principle of a reformatory prison discipline.*

Prisoners, to insure their highest improvement, must be treated *individually*. While they are all alike placed under a general law, the conduct of each, as directed by it, should be specially and minutely noted. The improving effect of this would be found very great. It would be a first step toward restoring to each that feeling of self-respect without which no recovery will ever be found permanent. Each should be enabled to know, even from day to day, the light in which his conduct is viewed in all important particulars by those placed over him; for thus alone, as his good purpose strengthens, will he be enabled to correct that wherein he may be found deficient. To this end a card should be hung in his cell, with four rows of figures constantly kept upon it. The first should indicate the prisoner's general conduct; the second his degree of industry and exertion; the third his attention and improvement, as noted by the chaplain; and the fourth the same, as shown by the schoolmaster's record. By this means, whenever the governor, or chaplain, or a magistrate, or any other entitled to make such perquisition, goes round, the whole conduct—and thence the character—of the individual would be instantly patent, and censure, caution, advice, or exhortation could be addressed as each might be needed. These marks would also form the basis of those estimations of character according to which prisoners would be passed through the different stages of treatment, rising successively from grade to grade, until, beginning at the lowest, they should have at length reached the highest.

It will be found important that rewards for exertion and improvement, other than physical comforts, be progressively added; or even that they should, at the discretion of the prisoner, be substituted for such comforts. It is right and fair, and even improving, that consideration for the last should be used as a *stimulus* in the lower stages of reformatory treatment. Such, indeed, is the arrangement of Providence in human society, and we cannot copy a better type. But in proportion as the higher nature of the prisoner is developed and cultivated, higher objects of desire should be suggested and made similarly attainable, in order at once to keep the upward tendency active, and to raise the character of its aspirations. For this purpose a longer allowance of gas-light, a wider scope of books and instruction, and increased facilities of communication with families and respectable friends outside, these and other like indulgences will be found powerful and most improving encouragements. At no stage, however, should any remission be made of the call for continued active exertion. To reward a prisoner, in any part of his course, by permitted idleness, is to undo the improvement that may have been already effected in him by dissociating the ideas of sustained effort and success, which should, as much as possible, be kept inseparably together in his mind. Even when partially sick, employment of some kind should, wherever practicable, be thus given him. The surgeon should be constantly invited to suggest such. Not infrequently this will even promote recovery—if not otherwise, yet by making a state of sickness not entirely a state of exemption. If even light employment will impede recovery, the surgeon will, of course, interfere to forbid it.

XX. *Prison officers need a special education and training for their work.* On this subject Captain Maconochie holds the following language:

When prisons are made real peniteutiaries—schools of penitence and reform—the military type in which so many visiting justices and governors now so much rejoice, should bo sedulously excluded from them, and a clerical type rather substituted. A change in the classes of men from which their officers are usually selected would be also most desirable. The writer's opinion is that governors of prisons should even form a class by themselves, to be devoted to that service exclusively, in which they should, when young, be thoroughly trained in all their duties, which are various. They should serve first in the lower offices; then as deputy governors; then as governors of small prisons; thence, according to their ascertained merits, chiefly tested by the small proportion of reconvictions to them, transferred to large; and thence progressively become disposable for service in the same capacity in any part of the Queen's dominions. Thus alone would the details of prison discipline be gradually perfected, and uniformity in its administration be also attained. Only when the administration of punishment is thus made a profession will it become scientific, uniform, and *successful*. Promotion in the department thus formed should be much influenced by success in keeping down reconvictions. When these are numerous, there are almost always faults in the officers as well as in the men.

XXI. *The essential complement of a reformatory system of prison discipline is such provision for discharged prisoners as will most effectually hold them to their honest intents and prevent their falling back into crime.*

After adverting to the duty, and even necessity, on the part of society, of taking an interest in liberated prisoners, Captain Maconochie thus adverts to his experience as governor of the prison at Birmingham:

Since the Birmingham jail opened an effort has been made to realize this portion of the anticipation founded on the whole system. Aided by a small fund raised by voluntary subscription, more than forty women have been assisted over the first difficulties of their return to society, at an expense not exceeding from twelve to fifteen shillings each. The chief expense has been for sending to a distance such as had friends out of Birmingham willing to receive them, and for giving to others decent clothing in which to seek for service, and to all a few shillings, by the aid of which to get over creditably the first few days. Very few of these women have been returned to prison, and a fair proportion are known to be doing well. Similar efforts have been also made to assist the men and boys again into service, and with much the same results.

Again :

When a prisoner has completed his training under this [the mark] system—in other words, after he has completed his *minimum* time and fulfilled his entire task—it would be very desirable that he should have, at his own option exclusively, the power of remaining, up to a given time, in precisely the same circumstances as before, subject to the same rules, and in no respect differing in external appearance from what they were, but with the privilege of leaving when they please, and of receiving, when discharged, a money payment (say a penny for each mark) for whatever surplus they may, within this time, have accumulated. Many plans have been lately suggested for the relief of discharged prisoners, but none, I am convinced, would be so effective as a small fund thus obtained, the fruit of their own voluntary diligence and self-denial, and bearing its own testimony, with probably a concurring one from the governor and chaplain whom they leave that they really possess these virtues, and have exhibited them through the course of, perhaps, a long previous sentence.

Still again :

An observation may be appropriately submitted here on the essential difference that exists between the mark system and all others that have ever preceded it. *Their* elementary principle has been, without exception, the *subjugation* of prisoners ; the reducing them, by whatever means, to implicit, immediate obedience ; the regulating their every act, almost their every thought, by an arbitrary standard ; the making them thus what are called good prisoners, too much, if not altogether, overlooking the injury so done to their power of acting worthily afterward as freemen. Crushed and degraded as they thus are while in prison into mere machines, they inspire, and can inspire, no confidence on their discharge. Even when they then *profess good resolutions, the sincerity of these is doubted. Too often their expression really is hypocritical ; and morally weak as their treatment has made them, the stability of their resolutions cannot be confided in, even when they are most sincere. They have so long acted under the influence of mere obedience to external direction that when this is removed or replaced by some evil influence, like children deprived of the support of leading-strings, they totter and almost inevitably fall, for their powers, as well as their purposes, have been thus enfeebled. * * * * * *

Every shade in this picture would be reversed if the mark system were introduced, in its whole length and breadth, into our systems of public punishment. So necessarily reformatory, so industrially, morally, intellectually, and religiously *educational* is it in its whole structure that it would be scarcely possible for even the worst to pass through an extended course of it without being sensibly improved ; while, as the mass of discharged prisoners would be found well-purposed and useful, the present unfavorable impression of them would abate ; they would more easily find honest bread ; their difficulties would diminish in proportion as their power of overcoming them increased ; and at length even an *esprit de corps* might be expected to arise among them, impelling them to consider it manly, as well as right, to overcome temptation and pusillanimity. Their long previous aspiration of improvement, and their habit of voluntary self-denial in prison, would strongly conduce to this, and would be one of the most beneficial results that could be obtained from the plan.

I have now completed the design with which I commenced this paper, namely, that of presenting, in outline, the views and reasonings of Alexander Maconochie on the subject of prison discipline. The exhibition, though as far as it goes a faithful reflection of his teachings, has little of the warmth and intensity that glow on every page of the writings of this great social philosopher ; and especially does it lack those living illustrations from his own experience which impart such animation and power to his productions ; for it must not be forgotten that this great thinker was equally great as a worker. Maconochie was not a mere theorist, sending forth his speculations from the cabinet of an amiable recluse. He was, as well, a man of action, who applied the principles which he developed, with reformatory results as precious as they were remarkable ; first on Norfolk Island, and afterward in the jail of Birmingham, though in neither up to the limit of his wishes or his convictions; for in both he was in a thousand ways hampered and repressed by the prejudices and the pusillanimity of "the higher powers." To John Howard belongs the higher honor of having awakened mankind to thought upon this vital question ; to Alexander Maconochie will yet be assigned the highest honor of having guided that thought to enlightened, wise, and fruitful action. I leave off, then, as I began, with the expression of my belief that among prison reformers Maconochie holds the most conspicuous place; that he stands pre-eminent in the "goodly company." In him head and heart, judgment and sympathy, the intellect and the emotional element, were developed in harmonious proportions; were equally vigorous and equally active; and all consecrated to the noble work of lifting the fallen, reclaiming the vicious, and saving the lost.

C.—REPORTS OF STANDING COMMITTEES OF THE NATIONAL PRISON ASSOCIATION OF THE UNITED STATES.*

1. REPORT OF THE EXECUTIVE COMMITTEE.

The first annual report of the executive committee of necessity can embrace little more than the record of the organization of the association, which was not perfected until the year had considerably advanced. The chief work accomplished (which was one of no ordinary import to the cause of penal reform and the cure of crime) has been the successful preparation, in European kingdoms and on our own continent, for an international prison congress in London during the ensuing summer. The labor of this vast undertaking has fallen wholly upon the able corresponding secretary of the association, and his wisdom, perseverance, and executive ability are fully illustrated in the wide and remarkable results of his endeavors, which are set forth in his interesting report, as commissioner of the United States, made to the President of the Republic.

The national association for the United States became a necessary incident of the movement to secure an international congress. From a very extended correspondence with leading writers upon penal science, and with prominent magistrates and heads of penitentiaries in this country and Europe, the expediency of a great central public convention for a comparison of views among thinkers, and of a discussion of the vital questions still unsolved, was clearly justified, as promising the best results to the cause of penal reform. Such a gathering could not be arranged without long and laborious preparation, and it was adjudged advisable to hold a preliminary congress in this country, at which definite measures could be taken for the calling of the larger and more august body to represent all the civilized nations of the earth.

The congress which met at Cincinnati, Ohio, commencing October 12, 1870, and continuing for a full week, was one remarkable for the number of its representative men and women, the high official and social position of many of its members, the ability and variety of the papers read, and the valuable practical discussions which followed the reading of the essays. One of the chief topics of consideration, suggested in the printed call for the convention, was the question of the expediency of the proposed international congress, and the inauguration of preliminary measures to secure it if its convocation should be deemed desirable. The proposition for the congress being unanimously accepted, it became evident that a national association, as an organ of communication with foreign bodies, would be indispensable to secure unity and efficiency of action; and that, as a permanent corporation, it would bring about a

---

* These reports were presented and read at the first annual meeting of the association, held in the city of New York, January 27, 1871.

harmony of operation among the various prison and reformatory societies, effect a system of home and foreign exchange of documents, and serve in many ways, quite apparent, the cause of penal reform.

Upon a motion, therefore, of Governor Baker, of Indiana, a committee of twelve gentlemen of well-known intelligence and interest in the questions involved, from different portions of the country, was appointed to prepare a charter for such an association, to secure an act of incorporation in either of the States of New York, Pennsylvania, or Ohio, and to complete the organization by the election of additional members, in accordance with the requisitions of such an act.

At the session of the legislature of New York, in 1871, a very liberal and satisfactory charter was secured, which was formally accepted by the incorporators under the act on the 26th of April, 1871. At this, and a succeeding meeting in May, the association was fully organized, a form of constitution and by-laws was prepared and accepted, a list of officers were appointed, and a number of foreign corresponding members were elected. The full details, with the names of officers and members, will be found in another portion of the report. The name of Dr. E. C. Wines, as the American commissioner to represent this country in the preliminary measures for the inauguration of the national congress, was the unanimous nomination of the Cincinnati convention, and was the one name thought of for the position of corresponding secretary, when the new organization was completed. How well this unanimous sentiment has been already justified will be made to appear in the work which the secretary has so successfully prosecuted during the portion of the year that has elapsed since the association had an existence.

On the very important matter of finance, the executive committee have not an entirely satisfactory report to make. In addition to the heavy labors of his office, with the innumerable details incident to the arrangements for the prospective congress, entailing an absence of nearly five months from the country, the secretary has been obliged to be the collector of all the funds received into the treasury of the association. This, added to the other labors of his office, is obviously too much for the strength of any one man; and it will be indispensable that a financial agent, or assistant secretary, be appointed, who shall devote himself, as far as may be necessary, to gathering the means required for the work of the association, which is likely to increase from year to year, until its dimensions assume a vastness and importance commensurate with the field which it proposes to occupy.

The field and objects of the association are thus exhibited in a circular prepared by the corresponding secretary, at the request of the board :

As set forth in the act of incorporation, it has the following objects in view: 1. The amelioration of the laws in relation to public offenses and offenders, and the modes of procedure by which such laws are enforced. 2. The improvement of the penal, correctional, and reformatory institutions throughout the country, and the government, management, and discipline thereof, including the appointment of boards of control, and of other officers. 3. The care of, and providing suitable and remunerative employment for, discharged prisoners, and especially such as may or shall have given evidence of a reformation of life.

As regards the first of these objects : There is scarcely a reform more necessary to-day than that of the criminal codes of our several States. Everywhere there is needed an administration of justice more prompt, more effective, more humane, more reformatory ; that is to say, more in harmony with the rational aim of all repressive legislation—the diminution of crime. It will be the work of the association to study and develop the reforms needed in this department of social science, and especially to seek to impress upon our criminal legislation the great principles of humanity and reformation, which alone will render repressive laws at once effective and popular.

As regards the second.of the objects named: The improvement of our penal and correctional institutions, by improving their discipline, is no less important than the reform of our criminal codes. The great aim here is, first, to arrest the increase of crime, which is at once a disgrace and a danger to our age, and then to diminish its volume. Two problems, especially, claim our study at this point—the first, a problem of prevention; the second, of cure. Preventive agencies need to be more widely and actively applied. The true field of promise, as regards the repression of crime, lies just here; and if the right methods of working it can but be ascertained and employed, there is reason to hope that the stream of crime may be thus, in great part, cut off in the fountain. But the second problem is, to reclaim and restore those who have fallen. A few experiments of a reformatory prison discipline—less, however, than can be counted on the fingers of a man's hands—have been made in different parts of the world; and the results have been such as to excite not only the hopes but the wonder of those who have been made acquainted with them. When reformation comes to be everywhere made the real aim of prison discipline, as it should be, and all prison officers work heartily and intelligently to that end, we believe that results will be accomplished of which the most sanguine scarcely dare dream at present. A formidable obstacle exists to the introduction and use of a truly reformatory discipline in our prisons, in the undue influence of party politics over their government and administration in nearly if not quite all our States. While this influence remains dominant, leading necessarily to instability in the tenure of office and a low grade of official qualification, all reforms must be partial, temporary, and uncertain; and we shall have made but little progress that will prove solid and lasting, until we have overcome this difficulty. It will be the office and work of the National Prison Association to study, with earnest and persistent application, all the problems here indicated; to unfold the results of such study in their annual reports and other publications; and to endeavor to reduce to practice the principles reached through their investigations, in improved prison systems and a better administration and discipline in the prisons of our several States.

As regards the third object mentioned in the charter: The problem how to dispose of discharged convicts, how to hold them to their honest intents, and prevent their relapse, is one of the most perplexed and difficult in the whole science of penology. Yet, to save the released criminal, especially when he has left the penitentiary with a determination to engage in a course of honorable industry, is an object of the highest importance to the community, as well as to himself. The effect of punishment, under the present state of public sentiment, destroys, in great measure, the convict's prospect on his discharge. The ignominy of his imprisonment clings to him in his freedom. Society does not trust, and therefore will not employ him. Thus a popular punishment, as unjust as it is cruel, follows the legal penalty he has undergone, and the liberated criminal is often driven to the hard necessity, whether he will or no, of returning to crime to avoid the horrors of starvation. It will be the high duty, as it will also be the self-imposed labor, of the association, whom we represent and in whose name we speak, to study, and, if possible, to solve the problem, as grave as it is intricate, which we have just stated.

Beyond the objects recited in our constitution, or rather included therein, will be that of visiting the penal and reformatory institutions of the country, especially in States where such institutions are in an unsettled or formative condition, and of aiding the authorities in charge by information, suggestion, counsel, &c., in the work of creating or improving their prisons and prison systems.

Still another duty of the association, clearly embraced within its scope, as declared in the constitution, will be that of offering an annual review of the progress and condition of penal affairs in the several States, as a knowledge thereof shall be obtained by personal visitation, or as the same may be exhibited in the messages of their governors, in the reports of their prisons and reformatories, in the reports of State committees and prison societies, and in the statements received in reply to circulars that may have been sent out in quest of information; which review will, as a matter of course, be accompanied with such criticisms, suggestions, and recommendations as may be judged suited to the exigencies of the case in hand, whatever it may be. Here also will, equally, as a matter of course, fall the most complete exhibition attainable of the penal and reformatory statistics of the States, which will, it is confidently believed, from year to year, improve in fullness and uniformity till they shall have approached, at least, the standard of perfection; and we shall thus have gathered a body of information in this form, of the highest value as a guide to just conclusions, and as a basis for wide and effective legislation.

The coming year will be one of great interest, and will doubtless form an era in the history of penal and reformatory discipline. The gathering of practical prison reformers, of writers upon this leading question of social science, and of representative men from the various nations of Europe and America, the collection of the gathered experience and wisdom of a century of thought and experiment, will render this one hundredth anniversary of Howard's first movement for the improvement of the condition of imprisoned men memorable in the annals of penitentiary reform. The condensed and sifted report of the discussions of the occasion, which will be, doubtless, embodied in the second report of the corresponding secretary, cannot fail to be a full compensation for, and justification of, the incident expense in the organization of the association, and of the efforts to secure the international reunion of a congress, and it may be hoped and believed that it will.

HORATIO SEYMOUR, Chairman.

NEW YORK, January 27, 1871.

---

2. REPORT OF THE COMMITTEE ON PRISON DISCIPLINE.

The subject intrusted to this committee is a large and rather indefinite one, embracing, as it apparently does, the discipline of prisons of all kinds, in all the States and Territories of the Union. To discuss it properly would demand a volume, rather than the few pages within which we must confine our remarks. Let us begin, then, by stating, as briefly as possible, what the problem of prison discipline is, as it presents itself in this country.

In seeking to measure, statistically, the prison population of the United States at any given time, the tables of the national census (even when made up, as they have recently been, under the direction of so diligent and enlightened a chief of the Census Bureau as General Walker) afford comparatively little help. So imperfect is the census law, and so unskilled are the enumerators employed, that, in the tables as made up, no proper discrimination is made between the different classes of prisoners in each State and Territory, and even the whole number in all the prisons is quite inadequately stated. For example, the enumerators for Illinois returned the "whole number in prison" in that State June 1, 1870, as only 430, which was less than the number at that date confined in the eighty county jails of Illinois. The 1,000 or 1,200 State prison convicts then confined in the great castle at Joliet were quite overlooked; and Illinois, with more than two and one-half millions of inhabitants, appeared to have less than one-third as many criminals as New Jersey, with less than a million people. Again, the New York enumerators reported the number then confined in this great State as only 4,142, although the city of New York alone, at that time, held under imprisonment 1,360 persons, while there were about 1,400 at Sing Sing, 1,000 at Auburn, 500 at Dannemora, 350 at the Albany penitentiary, and in the whole State not less than 6,500 prisoners in confinement. In many, perhaps most, of the States, the enumeration was more exact; and probably these defects of which we speak have been partially corrected in the revised census tables not yet published. From such data as we have we estimate the whole prison population of the country at any one time as varying from 35,000 in July to 40,000 in February. Of this whole number an average of some 16,000 are probably confined in the forty State prisons, while 12,000 more are held under sentence in houses of correction, work-houses, district penitentiaries, and jails, and 8,000 more are awaiting trial or are held as witnesses in the jails, station-houses, and other places of detention in the United States. Among these 40,000 prisoners are all grades of criminality and many grades of innocence; they are confined in some thousand or more prisons, of every style of architecture, and under every variety of discipline except the best; and in some of our prisons a close approximation is probably made to the best attainable, if not the best imaginable, system of discipline. The problem is to adapt this best system to the different grades of our prisons and to the almost infinite variety of circumstances that present themselves in a country so vast and heterogeneous as ours. To do this requires better graded prisons, a more thorough classification of prisoners, and an infinite patience and practical wisdom in applying the maxims of a sound theory to the daily management of these thousands of our fellow-beings, held in confinement under some forty different jurisdictions, and, if we include counties and great cities, not less than a thousand mutually independent prison authorities. The prison reformer, however sanguine, might well shrink from dealing with a subject so formidable in its breadth and the variety of its detail.

And yet, thanks to the patient labors of our corresponding secretary, Dr. Wines, and others, who in past years have given their thoughts to this problem of American prison discipline, it by no means offers those difficulties which are conceived at the first sight. A few great classes are found to include these hundreds of prisons, these tens of thousands of criminals; while the century now almost elapsed since Beccaria and Howard began to demand the improvement of prisons, has accomplished much, by many thoughtful heads, just and humane hearts, and laborious hands, toward the establishment of a wise and effectual system of prison discipline. The methods in use in our American prisons are reducible to three: the old congregate system which prevailed before the building of the Auburn prison, half a century ago, and still lingers in many places; the new congregate, or Auburn, or silent system; and the separate or Pennsylvania system, now in use, it is believed, only in that State, on this side of the Atlantic, though common enough in the states of Europe. Outside of Pennsylvania, the Auburn system, more or less modified, prevails in nearly all the State prisons, and in the better-managed city and county prisons. In Pennsylvania, the separate system prevails at the eastern penitentiary in Philadelphia, where it began at the Moyamensing prison in the same city, and at many of the other county prisons. The old congregate system, or lack of system, prevails in some few of the State prisons, and in many of the ill-managed county prisons. Indeed, the tendency of the Auburn system, when carelessly administered, is to revert to the old method of congregation, out of which it sprang.

From the best accounts we can obtain, a great majority of the county jails in the United States, estimated at nearly a thousand in number, are conducted virtually on the old congregate system. Within the past two years official reports have been made, more or less in detail, concerning the county jails of Maine, Massachusetts, New York, Pennsylvania, Ohio, Michigan, Illinois, and a few other States; and, except in Massachusetts, and a few of these jails in Maine, Pennsylvania, and New York, the rule is congregation and bad discipline at those periods when the jails are most crowded, and often all the rest of the year. In the States from which we have no reports on this subject, there is no reason to suppose that things are any better. An intelligent commission now engaged in examining the prison system of Connecticut, finds its county jails in a sad condition in many respects; and similar information comes to this committee from New Jersey, Missouri, and elsewhere. In New Hampshire, within the past five years, a great improvement has been made in the county prisons, but they are still

far from being model establishments. In Alabama we learn that the
sentenced prisoners in several of the county jails, to the number of
eighty in all, have recently been employed at open-air labor, at a
distance from their prisons, by a railroad contractor; the men work
like free laborers during the day, but sleep at night chained together
in gangs of ten. This practice may prevail in some of the other
Southern States, but we have not heard of it; we shall speak of this
more at length in another place.

We may illustrate the present condition and state of discipline in
hundreds of these county jails, by quoting from a few of the official
reports above mentioned. The special commissioners to examine the
penal, reformatory, and charitable institutions of Michican, through
their chairman, Judge C. J. Walker, of Detroit, thus reported early in
1871:

> Ours has been the experience of all who have undertaken to examine the actual con-
> dition of county jails, whether in this or other States. Their condition is wretched
> beyond all power of description, and beyond all conception of those who have not had
> the experience of their own senses in the matter. The defects in them are not owing
> so much to the manner in which they are kept, as to inherent defects in their construc-
> tion, their dilapidated condition, and a fatal vice in the common jail system. The
> jails are crowded to excess; two, and sometimes three, persons are put into a single
> cell, and a corridor not large enough to accommodate half a dozen is the living and
> eating room of a score of prisoners. As a rule, continued good health is impossible
> under such circumstances. The moral condition of our jails is infinitely worse than
> their sanitary condition, and after a full examination and careful consideration, we
> have come to the clear and painful conviction that they are the very hot-beds and
> nurseries of vice and crime, and that the State is directly responsible for a large share
> of the crime which it seeks to punish. If the wisdom of the State had been exercised
> to devise a school of crime, it would have been difficult to devise a more efficient one.
> Here are the competent teachers, the tractable pupils, the largest opportunities for in-
> struction, with nothing to distract attention from the lessons. (Pages 5, 6, and 7.)

These are the observations of Judge Walker, of Michigan, a clear-
headed and experienced lawyer, and they are fully sustained in the case
of Illinois, by the remarks of Rev. F. H. Wines, secretary of the Board
of Charities in that State, who says in his first report, made soon after
the adjournment of the Cincinnati prison congress:

> The greatest of all faults in the construction of our county prisons is the absence of
> any means of classifying prisoners. The sane are not separated from the insane; the
> guilty are not separated from the innocent; the suspected are not separated from the
> convicted. Hardened criminals and children are thrown together; the sexes are not
> always separated from each other. The effect of this promiscuous herding together is
> to make the county prison a school of vice. In such an atmosphere, purity itself could
> not escape contamination. The prisoners, in nearly every instance, are absolutely
> without employment for mind or body. There are no libraries in the jails; even a
> Bible is ordinarily wanting. Idleness is a fruitful source of vice; and enforced idle-
> ness has developed the most debasing passions and habits. No attempt at secular in-
> struction and education is made in any jail in Illinois. The efforts made at reforma-
> tion of criminals are unsystematic, unintelligent, fitful, and, in most of the counties,
> wholly wanting. (First biennial report of the board of State commissioners of public
> charities, December, 1870, pp. 213, 214.)

The Ohio board of charities take the same view of the county jails in
that great State. In their fourth biennial report made early in 1871,
(page 20,) they say:

> Our jails are and always must be, as now conducted, nurseries of crime; but with
> separate confinement for prisoners awaiting trial, and hard work elsewhere for those
> convicted and sentenced, it is believed that the jails may be much improved, while
> their expenses would not be materially increased, and might, perhaps, be diminished.
> It is not right that those who are simply accused of crime, both the innocent and the
> guilty, the young as well as those steeped in crime, should be doomed to an imprison-
> ment more demoralizing and brutal than confinement in the penitentiary; but such is
> the fact in reference to most of the jails of Ohio.

It is needless to multiply citations to show what is so evident to all

S. Ex. 39——14

who have any practical acquaintance with prisons managed on the old congregate system. There is no longer any excuse for ignorance on this point; the brutalizing, wasteful, and every way deplorable results of such prisons are well known; and it should be the first effort of our association to have them reformed. Along with this effort should go one for the like reformation in city prisons, station-houses, calabooses, lock-ups, or by whatever name are called those houses of detention where petty criminals, and sometimes those of high criminality, undergo their first few hours of confinement. These places are almost always municipal prisons, and are more numerous, perhaps, and contain more persons in a year, than all other prisons put together. But it must be understood that the period of confinement for each person arrested is very short, ranging from half an hour to a week, but usually less than a day. Hither are brought all persons arrested at night in cities and villages, and a great many of those arrested by day. From one-half to five-sixths of these persons are discharged without conviction, and a great number without trial; the rest are taken from court to the jail, the work-house, or the house of correction, according to the magnitude of their offense or the convenience of the parties. If the offense is gross, or the trial can be delayed, they are sent to jail to await trial; otherwise they are sentenced to some convict prison, or, if fined and unable to pay, are detained in jail. Numerous and important as these municipal prisons are, little is known of them by the general public; for they are seldom entered by any save prisoners, officers of police, criminal lawyers, or other persons whose business leads them there. But they are powerful auxiliaries in the work of corrupting the young, and making shameless the older culprits, while they often receive and contaminate persons guilty of no offense, and charged with none. They are the holes where petty official fraud and abuse hide and coquette with monstrous vice; they are the workshops of detectives, where felony is compounded and impunity is manufactured to order. It is time that some new Howard should enter upon the work of their exposure and purification; but each of our great cities would need a Howard of its own for an undertaking so serious.

A few of our county jails and most of those establishments known in different portions of the United States as houses of correction, workhouses, houses of industry, and penitentiaries, (other than States prisons,) are conducted on the new congregate or Auburn system, with various modifications, suited to the time, the place, and the character of the prison officers. A comparatively small number of this class of prisons are conducted, in Pennsylvania, on the separate system; but this does not include the new work-house of Allegheny County, at Pittsburgh. It is in this class of our prisons that the greatest improvements in penal and reformatory discipline have recently been made. Here, too, are found our most experienced and best prison officers—such men as Amos Pilsbury, at the Albany penitentiary; Z. R. Brockway, at the Detroit house of correction; Henry Cordier, of the Allegheny County workhouse; and others who might be named. The management of prisons of this class is, as a rule, more permanent than that of either State prisons or jails; and, as a natural consequence, the best officers are attracted to them. In some, as the Albany penitentiary, the Auburn system is maintained with much rigor; in others it is greatly relaxed, and there is an approach to the best features of the Irish system, as taught and practiced by Maconochie and Crofton. Were our criminal laws generally and judiciously amended, so as to allow longer sentences for the petty criminals who make up the great majority in these establishments, they would soon display results more gratifying, we believe, than those obtained in any of our State prisons, both as respects reformatory, industrial, and pecuniary success. With all the disadvantages of short sentences, the best four prisons of this grade are now self-supporting, and, to a considerable degree, preventive of crime. New prisons of this class are constantly appearing, especially in the older and more populous States, and always in or near large cities. The tendency is to make them practically district prisons, receiving convicts from a wide area or a great population, and to classify their inmates more and more thoroughly. The new prison commission of Massachusetts has been occupied for the last year or two in developing a working plan for such classified district prisons throughout the whole of that State, which now contains more prisons of this grade than any other State.

Coming now to those prisons which it has been customary to reckon as the most important of all the American prisons, because they receive persons convicted of the higher crimes and are managed directly by the State authorities, we find that the number of these State prisons is something more than forty. Many of them are known by the distinctive title of "the penitentiary" in the States where they are located. But this is a name given also to places where lesser criminals are confined, under county or municipal authority, and therefore it will be convenient to drop the word in this connection and speak of each establishment owned or managed by the State authorities as a State prison. In most of the States there is but one prison of this class; in Delaware, and perhaps one or two of the other States of small population, there is none; in New York there are three, and in Massachusetts, Pennsylvania, and Indiana there are two each. The second State prison in Massachusetts, however, (established at Bridgewater in 1866 under the name of a "State work-house,") receives only persons convicted of light offenses, and therefore belongs in grade rather with the houses of correction previously mentioned, and will not be considered in the remarks about to be made on the class here styled State prisons. This class includes establishments of the most diverse description, ranging in the number of prisoners which they contain from the huge structures at Sing Sing, Joliet, and Columbus, with more than a thousand convicts in each, down to the prison of Rhode Island, which combines with itself a county jail, and the diminutive prisons of Oregon and Nevada, with less than fifty convicts in each. At most of these establishments the prisoners are employed within the walls, but in some of the Southern States, notably in Virginia, Alabama, Mississippi, and Tennessee, some part of the convicts have been worked on railroads, mines, &c., at a distance from the prison establishment. We can see many advantages in this mode of employing the convicts, provided it were adopted, as at Lusk, in Ireland, in connection with a well-graded system of promoting them from one degree of freedom to another, until they should be prepared for their final discharge and restoration to society. But the experiment in open-air labor in the States named seems to be purely a business operation, by which the State is expected to gain or to save money, and we have heard that it is carried on with very little regard to any care for the reformation of the convict.

Just at present the number of State prison convicts seems to be slightly decreasing in the older Northern States, but increasing rapidly at the South and West. The number of colored convicts is much larger than before the civil war, and in many, probably most of the southern prisons, these make a majority of the inmates. We estimate the average number in all the State prisons as about sixteen thousand, and probably all these, except the six or seven hundred now confined in the Eastern penitentiary at Philadelphia, are governed by what is loosely called the Auburn system. In the establishment just named, the separate or cellular system is still in force, though the number of convicts is so much greater than that of cells that a considerable portion of them lodge two in a cell. In nearly all the States provision is made for shortening the sentence of convicts for good conduct, but, so far as we know, few or none of the prisons have adopted the simple and exact mark system for determining the record of a prisoner, which is in vogue in Ireland with such good results. Nor is opportunity given for classifying the convicts according to merit, and for promoting them from one grade to another, as is done in Ireland. School education also, which, in the Irish convict prisons, under the regulations established by Sir Walter Crofton, has played so important a part in the reformation of criminals, is greatly neglected in our forty-odd State prisons. In a few of them schools are maintained, but generally without teaching many of the prisoners or giving much instruction to the small number included in the classes. The number of these schools is increasing, however, and the demand for them is more urgently made each year. The same is true of measures for aiding and supervising discharged convicts, though in this work also our prisons fall very much behind those of Ireland.

A strong feature of the American State prisons has always been the amount of productive labor performed in them. Several of them, especially in New England, are self-sustaining, and even return a small revenue to the State in excess of the cost of maintaining the prison and paying all its expenses. None of the largest prisons, however, except that of Ohio, are thus self-sustaining; and it may be laid down as a rule that, beyond a maximum of five or six hundred prisoners, it is difficult to employ them so that their labor will repay the cost of their support. It has been found comparatively easy to make the small prisons of Maine, New Hampshire, and Connecticut pay their expenses by their earnings, with an average, for a period of years, of less than two hundred convicts; but almost impossible to make the great prisons of New York, Illinois, California, and Missouri do this, even for two years in succession. The Massachusetts prison at Charlestown, from which we have financial returns for a longer period than from any other prison in the country, is an evidence to the same effect. During the fifty-six years that these returns cover, the Charlestown prison has exhibited a profit above its expenses in eighteen years, a deficit in thirty-five years, and in the three remaining years a balance so small either way as to leave it in doubt whether its expenses were fully met by its earnings. But in the first thirty years, when its number of convicts averaged less than three hundred, the Charlestown prison made an aggregate deficit, during the whole period, of less than $60,000; while in the twenty-six years since, the average number having been nearly five hundred the greater part of that time, the aggregate deficit has been more than $120,000, or twice as much as when the prison was small. Although we do not regard the revenue derived from the labor of convicts as of much importance, compared with their judicious treatment and their moral improvement, it still seems proper to note the facts that prisons of moderate size can readily be made self-sustaining, while the larger ones cannot. At the same time all the influences of a prison of less than five hundred convicts are more favorable to the reformation of its inmates than the circumstances of the great establishments, like those of Sing Sing, Auburn, Joliet, and Columbus. We believe, therefore, that it would generally be better policy for a State to build a new prison when its convicts rise above an average of five hundred in number, than to enlarge the old establishment; unless, indeed, it chooses to adopt some method of conditional pardon, by which the increase in numbers can be kept down.

Were this committee to undertake a discussion of the general principles of prison discipline, it could do little more than repeat the admirable statements and arguments laid before the Cincinnati prison congress by Dr. Wines, and in substance adopted by that assembly. We cannot omit this opportunity to remark, however, that the lapse of another year, and the added testimony it has furnished to the excellence of the so-called Irish prison system, tends to confirm and deepen the impression that it is the duty of prison managers in the United States to adopt the main features of that system with as little delay as possible. We believe them to be as practicable in this country as they have proved themselves to be in Ireland; and while they would encounter here some peculiar difficulties, the circumstances of our community would offer some peculiar advantages for their introduction.

The first great want to be met in the United States, however, is something which preceded the establishment of Sir Walter Crofton's system in Ireland, and which is indispensable here to the adoption of any general improvement of our prisons as a whole. We need in every State an inspector or a commission of inspectors, who shall have access to the prisons of all grades, and some power of supervision over all. Such inspectors would bring to the notice of the legislatures and of prison officers the actual defects and necessities of the prison system of each State; they could take a comprehensive, practical view of the whole field of action, and recommend such changes as would correct the glaring anomalies and gross abuses of the existing prison system in nearly all our States. Some of this preliminary work has already been done, but much more remains to do. In the words of an earnest writer in one of our reviews,

Provision should be made in every State for such examinations by an impartial inspector or commission, not chosen by political intrigue or local partiality, but bringing to the work a knowledge of the subject and a spirit of intelligent humanity. We hazard nothing in predicting that the first recommendation of such inspectors would be a more strict separation and classification of prisoners, for that has always been the first result of careful examinations in congregate prisons. Probably they would next urge, as half the wardens in the country do, the importance of "commutation," or *conditional remission;* that is, the shortening of sentences for good behavior; and would insist on some effectual means of aiding discharged prisoners to find employment. They would then call for a better religious and secular instruction of the convicts while in prison, and a systematic organization of their labor. They would demand instruction in reading and writing for every prisoner in the land, and would cry out against that enforced idleness which is the curse of our jails. Along with these things, they would seek to regulate by wise rules and by frequent inspection the sanitary condition of the prisons. They would see that baths were regular, that the food was neither too good nor too bad, that cleanliness was made a religion, that the wardrobe of the prisoners was sufficient and properly changed, and that they should have an occasional holiday. They would demand that the contractor should not stand between justice and the convict; and that neither the convict nor the public should be defrauded in the payment of wages. They would point out faults in the prison officers, and specify what qualities and what experience are needful in such establishments. (North American Review, October, 1866, pp. 411-12.)

In the opinion of this committee the members of the National Prison Association should labor in all the States to secure such an inspection and supervision of the prisons, of all grades, and should make the reports of such inspectors the basis of future reforms in prison discipline. In this way, without giving up our investigation and discussion of the principles of prison administration, we may earlier reach what we all desire—a practical application of these principles, at least in part, to the present treatment of prisoners.

For the committee,

F. B. SANBORN,
Chairman.

NEW YORK, *January* 26, 1872.

---

3. REPORT OF THE COMMITTEE ON DISCHARGED PRISONERS.

The question, what can be done for discharged prisoners? is encompassed with difficulties, and yet it is a question which concerns society no less than it does himself. With tastes depraved, with habits bad, with moral powers originally weak and made feebler by vicious indulgence, they are sent forth from our prisons with scanty pecuniary means or none at all. But worse than this, they go out with the taint of the prison upon them. Few are willing to employ them; fewer still to receive them into their homes. Instances are not rare in which men, after years of confinement, have left the prison with an honest purpose, but they have either been refused all employment, or, if they have obtained work, they have been deprived of it as soon as their antecedents have become known. Mechanics outside spurn and insult them, and farmers are unwilling to take them into their families. They have formed acquaintance in the prison, if not previously, with the vile and the wicked. Such are always ready to welcome them, and the consequence is that they fall into their hands, and soon return to criminal courses.

The committee propose to consider, in the present report, the needs of discharged prisoners; what has been done for such; what can be done for them.

I.—WHAT DO DISCHARGED PRISONERS NEED?

The first and most urgent need of the liberated prisoner is human sympathy. Without sympathy life is miserable, even to those most favorably situated. But to one who has been long deprived of it, even though the fault may have been his own, it is like a cordial to meet with some one person who is willing to forget the past, who never alludes to it, and who accepts and treats him as a brother, a man of like feelings with himself, and having a heart from which all traces of tenderness and truth have not been obliterated. Perhaps no human being ever becomes so completely hardened as to have wholly lost all the better feelings of his nature. Even among the most hackneyed and abandoned of criminals, there is still about them a softer part, which will give way to the demonstrations of tenderness and sympathy. This one element of better character survives the dissipation of all the others. Fallen as a brother may be from the moralities which once adorned him, the manifested sympathy of his fellow-men still carries a charm and a power along with it; and therefore there lies in this an operation which, as no poverty can destroy, so no depravity can extinguish. These better feelings should, therefore, be developed and cultivated to the utmost degree possible. They furnish ground of hope that even the most abandoned may be reclaimed and regenerated. Christian men, and especially Christian women, will find an ample field for labor in this direction.

The second need of the discharged prisoner is pecuniary help. Some money he must have, or a life of crime becomes a necessity. A portion of the earnings of every convict should belong to him, and should be retained for his use after liberation. Until this provision is accorded, which is equally the dictate of justice and policy, some assistance should be provided by the benevolent, enough at least to enable him to "make a start in the world."

The third need of the discharged prisoner is employment. Such persons should, at the earliest practicable moment after their discharge; be placed in a position to help themselves. In this way only can a feeling of independence, which is essential to self-respect, be generated, and their own inward force of character be developed and strengthened.

The fourth need of the liberated convict is wise and affectionate counsel. This indeed will be of little value unless his other wants are supplied. It is useless to give a man advice while you leave him hungry and shivering, with nothing to do; but give him food, clothing, and work, and he will be in better condition to appreciate your counsels, and more willing to act upon them.

II.—WHAT HAS BEEN DONE FOR DISCHARGED PRISONERS?

The committee would here state that in 1869 the French government instituted a special commission to study the question how best to dispose of discharged prisoners. M. Demetz, founder and director of the agricultural colony of Mettray, one of the members of the imperial commission, addressed a letter of inquiry to the Prison Association of New York. This letter was answered by our corresponding secretary, at that time holding the same position in the New York association. In his communication to M. Demetz, the secretary reviewed at much length the provisions and efforts made in the several States of our own country for the relief and care of liberated prisoners, basing his review on information derived from answers to numerous circulars sent out to gentlemen best informed upon this subject in their respective States. In the following exhibit, the committee will not hesitate to draw freely from the paper addressed by the secretary to M. Demetz.

Massachusetts leads all the States of the Union in the care she takes for her liberated prisoners, and the efforts she puts forth to save them from falling back into crime. In this State there has long existed a society in aid of discharged prisoners, which, with an appropriation from the State, supports an agent to look after such convicts as are discharged from the State prison. He also does something for the men discharged from the minor prisons of the counties; but this is only incidental. His chief work is among the State prisoners, and for them he does much good in procuring employment, &c. This State agency for aiding discharged convicts has existed more than twenty years. It has proved the salvation of large numbers of the class for whom it was created. It is the practice of the agent to call often at the State prison to obtain information concerning the prisoners who are about to be discharged. He sees them personally, and confers with them concerning their wishes and intentions. In this way he gains a knowledge of their history, character, capabilities, and wants, which aid him essentially in finding the right employment for them, and adopting the best means to secure them against relapsing. The number aided during the years 1866 to 1869 was five hundred and sixty-two. Of these one hundred and seven were provided with places; eighty-nine were supplied with tools with which to start a little business of their own; and one hundred and sixty-seven were furnished with means to return to their friends, or to seek employment in other and more distant parts of the country. It is the policy of the agent to keep trace of the men aided as far as possible. In the majority of cases the results are gratifying. Letters are often received, full of gratitude, and ascribing their good resolutions, hopes, efforts, and success to the help given them by the agency. Employers, also, are generally satisfied with service rendered by these liberated prisoners. In proof of this, the agent mentions several firms in Boston, who have from a dozen to twenty discharged convicts, each, constantly at work for them, and cases occur in which these convicts are placed over large gangs of men as foremen, a trust to which they are found perfectly competent, and which they discharge in a satisfactory manner. Some of his men the agent reports as utterly incapable, except when under the constant and watchful care of judicious friends, of resisting the temptation to do wrong. Threats, entreaties, counsel, appeal, kindness, rewards, are all lost upon them. Happily such cases are comparatively few. He finds that the great majority, under proper treatment, can be made men among men, an honor to themselves and a blessing to the community.

There are two societies of ladies, one in Springfield and the other in Boston, which provide for a few of the discharged female prisoners. That at Springfield, however, is for friendless women and children in general; not specially for prisoners, of whom it receives only now and then one. It is different with the society at Boston, which is designed for the relief and reformation of discharged female prisoners only. Their establishment, called a Temporary Asylum for Discharged Female Prisoners, is at Dedham, one of the suburbs of the city. The society has had under treatment, during its six years of existence, two hundred and eighty-seven women, all of them outcasts from society, because they had been imprisoned criminals. But at the asylum they find a refuge and a home. They are neatly clothed, comfortably fed, and treated with a motherly love and kindness. They receive instruction in the common branches of learning, and careful training in the principles and duties of the Christian life. They are taught to work, that they may have the power as well as the will to earn an honest living. And what is the result? Some find the restraints of the place too irksome, and leave it in disgust. To others it proves a true Bethesda, in whose healing waters the sickness of the soul finds a perfect cure. Ninety-three families have had servants from the asylum. More applications are received than can be met, so that employers have greater difficulty in securing women than the women have in getting places. The ladies express the belief that but for their timely interposition, scarcely one of these two hundred and eighty-seven fallen sisters would have been arrested in her downward course; but all would have gone on sinning themselves and dragging others with them—a blot, a burden, and a curse to society. What a noble charity is that which has rescued and saved the major part of them! Surely these Christian women are treading in the very footprints of the Son of God, who came to seek the wanderer and to save the lost—the sinning, the lowly, the poor in spirit, the broken in heart; the very meanest of whom He named his brother, his sister, his friend!

Such are the provisions made in Massachusetts for liberated adults, male and female. Of late a new officer has been appointed by the State to look after the children who go out from the reformatories and schools for poor and truant children. He is called the visiting agent, and his duties are numerous and important. This is undoubtedly the most active and noteworthy of the means employed by Massachusetts to provide for aud shield her liberated juveniles. When the law creating this agency is completely carried out by a suitable and efficient machinery, it will, beyond a doubt, operate as a powerful check to juvenile delinquency in that State, and similar agencies established in all our States would constitute a more effective restraint upon youthful transgression than any system known to the committee in this country.

In the State of New York there are but two organized agencies which give attention to discharged prisoners of adult age—the Prison Association of New York and the Women's Prison Association and Home. The latter was originally organized as a department of the former, during the first year of its existence; but after a time it appears to have been judged that the work could be better carried on through distinct organizations, and a separation took place. Since the separation, as before, the ladies who constitute the women's association have cultivated their hard field with diligence, and a fair measure of success. They have had under treatment at their home, altogether, some three thousand women, the average daily number being about thirty. These have been mainly, though not wholly, persons discharged from prisons; more, however, from prisons of a lower than of a higher grade—misdemeanants rather than felons. One-sixth of those received have either left without permission, or been discharged as incorrigible. Of the remainder, the major part have been placed at service, and most of these favorably reported of by their employers. The entire annual cost of each has not exceeded one hundred dollars, and one-fourth of this sum has, on an average, been met by her earnings.

The object mainly contemplated in founding the New York Prison Association was to assist discharged convicts, and encourage them in their efforts to reform and live honestly. But other ends were intended as well, particularly the improvement of prison discipline and attention to persons under arrest who were held for trial or examination. The main strength of the association has been given to the last two objects, not from any undervaluation of the first, but from the want of means to prosecute it with due vigor. Still, in the aggregate, much has been accomplished. During the twenty-seven years of its existence, the association, besides relief to still greater numbers in the form of clothing, board, tools, traveling expenses, &c., has procured permanent situations at work for more than four thousand liberated prisoners; and, according to the best information attainable, not more than a tenth of these have relapsed into crime, while the remaining nine-tenths have become upright, industrious, useful members of society. But this is little when compared with the work to be done. The number annually discharged from the State prisons exceeds one thousand, while the number released from houses of correction, here called penitentiaries, can hardly be less. With adequate machinery, faithfully and skillfully worked, it is believed that no inconsiderable proportion of these unfortunate and criminal men might be saved. The time immediately following a prisoner's discharge is the critical moment with him. The great point is to bridge the gulf that lies between him and honest bread. That passed, if he really desire to reform, he is safe.

As regards those discharged from the juvenile reformatories: The sentences here are during minority, which means till reformed. There are four large reformatories in the State—three of them in the city of New York—besides a reform school-ship. They all have what are called "indenturing committees." The whole business of discharging inmates from the institutions is placed in the hands of these committees, who either return them to their parents, if their own homes are deemed suitable, or, if not, find homes for them elsewhere. The common way is to indenture the boys to farmers, mechanics, or tradesmen; while the girls are generally placed at domestic service in respectable families. Much pains is taken to find suitable homes for the liberated, where the good work of reformation, supposed to have been well advanced in the refuge, may be carried forward to completion. The customary contract with persons to whom the children are indentured is suitable support as to food and clothing, a certain number of months' schooling each year, and a hundred dollars, (500 francs,) with a good outfit of clothes, on reaching majority, to start in life with. The institutions keep watch and ward over their *élèves* after their departure from their precincts, never losing their grasp and guardianship of them, so long as they remain under age. The chaplain of the mother-reformatory of this country—the New York House of Refuge—visits each year, at their new homes, as many of the inmates thus placed as his time will permit; and particularly, when the parents of children, judged to be reformed, desire to have such children restored to themselves, he goes to their homes if they are in or near the city, to learn from personal inspection whether it would be safe and proper to return them there; and he reports to the indenturing committee, for their guidance, the result of his inquiries. More commonly than otherwise, the homes of the parents turn out to be unsuitable places for the reception and residence of the children, and other homes have to be sought for them.

Two of the reformatories of New York—the Juvenile Asylum and Catholic Protectory—have each an agency in the great West, whither large numbers of their inmates are sent, and by which they are distributed through the mighty valley of the Mississippi. These agencies maintain a constant and active supervision over the wards of their respective institutions, visiting them at their homes, adjusting difficulties between them and their employers, seeking new homes for those who have been improperly placed, and, in general, shielding them, as far as possible, from hurtful influences, and guarding their interests against the encroachments of injustice. A recent report of the agency of the Juvenile Asylum states that of twenty-eight boys and girls sent to Tazewell County, Illinois, in 1858, five had returned to New York, four had been killed in the late war for the Union, and the remaining nineteen, who had remained at the West, were all doing well; and the most of them were married and settled in life. The protectory has a farm connected with its agency on which the children work until they are provided with places.

New Hampshire, in imitation of Massachusetts, instituted, in 1867, a State agency to aid discharged convicts. It remained in existence for only two years. During its continuance, it appears to have been highly successful in promoting the object of its creation. The agent, in his last report, states that, of the prisoners discharged during the year covered by the report, nearly all had found employment at once; that quite a number had obtained work in the town where the prison is situated; that they are earning good wages; that their employers are satisfied with their service and their conduct; and that, of the forty-three discharged during the year, only one had been returned to prison; and of the remaining forty-two, but one had been charged with or even suspected of crime. Since the abolishment of the State agency, a prisoners' aid society has been organized which, the committee is informed, is doing a good work in caring for discharged prisoners.

In Rhode Island there has been, for many years, an efficient Sunday-school in the State prison, consisting of some twenty classes, which are taught by a devoted band of volunteer workers, male and female. These excellent ladies and gentlemen do much to aid, encourage, and reclaim the members of their several classes, not only while they continue under their instruction, but after their liberation. It has often happened that they take the released prisoner to their own homes, and care for him there till they have found employment for him. But these unorganized and isolated efforts, though useful and praiseworthy, are not found sufficient to meet the necessities of .the case. Steps have recently been taken looking to the formation of a prison association for the State.

Mr. Woodbury, superintendent of the State reform school of Maine, says that, in his institution, when boys have no suitable home of their own, they endeavor to find one for them; that henceforth they propose to safely invest for this class of boys a portion of their earnings, so that, when they reach ther majority, they may have a little capital to start with; and that he is of the opinion that the most effective way to save the liberated from a relapse is to impress upon our penal institutions a more distinctly reformatory character, by grading the prisons and classifying the prisoners, by establishing schools, creating libraries, instituting lectures, enlarging the religious agencies, giving a greater breadth and higher development to industrial, training, and, in general, to cite his own words, by "studying and imitating the life and character of Him who came to seek and save lost men." Then he would have "only those discharged who showed a fitness to return to society;" that is, he would have the sentences run till reformation is assured. Mr. Rice, warden of the Maine State prison, writes, that "this State has yet made no provision whatever for aiding discharged convicts." It is remarkable, that he then goes on to sketch a prison system substantially the same as that outlined by Mr. Woodbury, and closes with this declaration: "In my opinion, such a course of discipline and instruction would so well prepare convicts to meet and withstand the temptations of the outside world as to obviate, in a great measure at least, the necessity of any special provision for assisting them on their liberation."

The Rev. Mr. Butler, chaplain of the State prison of Vermont, says that in that State nothing has been done and nothing is proposed to be done, either by the State or by any philanthropic association, beyond the suit of clothes and the two dollars given by the State to every convict as he leaves, and occasionally a little private assistance, afforded in special cases. With this meager outfit of clothing, and this miserable dole of money, the released prisoner goes back to society to shift for himself among the people who, at first, will, for the most part, have as little to do with him as possible. Could a more effectual method be devised to obstruct his reformation, and to give effect to the principle, "once a criminal, always a criminal?" Mr. Butler marvels at the prevalent apathy on this subject, but says that it is as profound as it is inexplicable.

The committee are not informed what provision, if any, is made in Connecticut to save adult convicts who have been discharged from prison. Dr. Hatch, superintendent of the reform school for boys, says: "We return, at our expense, all boys to their homes; or, if they have no homes, we find places for them to work, and support them till able to support themselves."

What the committee has learned regarding the care, or, to speak more truly, the almost utter want of care, for discharged prisoners in New Jersey, is very sad. While a few excite the sympathy of friends and receive some aid, to the mass no word of counsel or cheer is spoken, no act of kindness done by any benevolent association; and neither State, county, òr municipality takes any thought of them, till they come again within the clutches of the law. It is a relief to know that, with respect to the boys sent out from the reform school, the case is different. When they attain the grade of "honor," which, by continuous good conduct, they may do in a year, they are considered eligible for a situation in society. The superintendent is careful to place them where they will be surrounded with good influences, and where they remain, till of age, wards of the institution.

In Pennsylvania, the Society for Alleviating the Miseries of Public Prisons, whose benevolent and useful labors date their commencement from the year 1787, has done and is doing much in aid of discharged convicts. In a late report the managers say : "Larger provision should be made for discharged convicts. They need pecuniary aid; they need advice; and they need protection and patronage. Our society has given much attention to this subject. But its plans and efforts have been restricted to its own sphere of action, and the results of its labors have been gratifying, though necessarily limited." One very interesting case is cited in the report—that of a man who received his entire education in the prison. On his liberation, aided by the society, he left Philadelphia, proceeded some distance into the country, rented a house and shop, and went to work as a mechanic. To-day he has, in the language of the report, "A flourishing business, a good run of customers, a two-story house, a spring-house, wash-house and garden, feed and pasture for a cow, and two acres of ground, and is doing well—working, of course, steadily and earnestly from morning till night." In one of his letters occurs this prayer: "My God bless you all for the kind treatment and instruction which I received," which, say the board, has surely been answered, since there is "an abundant blessing in the consciousness that the labors of love have been so fruitful."

A prisoners' aid association has been for some years in existence in western Pennsylvania, with its seat at Pittsburgh. The committee, though not informed of the details of its work, believes it to be an active and useful organization.

In Maryland, a prisoners' aid association was established in April, 1869. They employ an agent, the Rev: Mr. Doll, who gives his whole time to the work ; not, indeed, wholly to seeking employment and caring for discharged prisoners, but to that and other appropriate labors for their benefit. At the beginning of every month he goes to the State penitentiary and city jail, where he receives the names of all the prisoners who are to leave that month. With each he holds a personal interview, inquiring into their circumstances and purposes. They are given to understand, and, if possible, brought to feel, that they have friends who care for them, sympathize with them, and are ready; if they desire it, to hold out to them a helping hand. Procuring homes and employment is found the most difficult part of the work, owing to the distrust and prejudice generally felt toward this class of persons. Sending them out of the city to distant points, either to their own homes, or such others as may be found for them, proves to be the best service that can be rendered them, because the most efficacious in saving them. This society is very earnest and very active, and the good it accomplishes is proportional.

Ohio has no organized agency for the care and encouragement of released prisoners. The convict in the State prison gets, on his discharge, a suit of clothes and five dollars in money; that is all. The late worthy chaplain, Rev. Mr. Byers, gives some affecting instances of relapse from no other cause than the lack of the aid and sympathy needed on liberation. He says that he has known young men (who left the prison with good resolutions) to return within a few weeks, solely and indubitably because of the inadequate provision made for them by the State. He relates also the case of a reformed convict, who had been pardoned on account of his excellent conduct and the confidence it had inspired, to whom private aid had been given and good employment secured. This man, though laboring faithfully and behaving with the utmost propriety, was turned away from a respectable boarding-house, and driven by derision and ridicule from the shop in which he worked, simply because he had been a convict, "a jail-bird," as the word is.

The report is the same from Missouri—nothing done, nothing proposed to be done. A former warden of the State prison says: "During a residence in Missouri of more than the third of a century, I do not remember to have met a single man or woman whose Christian charity has been exercised to any extent in this particular field." A sorrowful testimony, this.

To the present time no organized effort has been made in Indiana for the relief and assistance of liberated prisoners; the consequence of which neglect, the committee have good authority for saying, is that a large proportion of those who are discharged from the State prisons go out to prey upon the community. The house of refuge, which has been in operation only two years, has discharged twenty-five boys, for all of whom good places have been found in private families; and this method of disposal is to be continued in the future. Earnest efforts are making in this State for a general improvement in the prison system, including an organized plan of aiding discharged convicts. Numerous relapses, arising from the want of such assistance, call loudly for improvement in this regard. With a good penitentiary system, in which the prisoners should be classified and enabled gradually to improve their condition, the intelligent friends of prison reform in that State are of the opinion that good places might be found in private families for all. In this way, they think, the liberated prisoners would be quietly absorbed into the community, and enabled to take their places therein as upright citizens.

California, a State far toward the sunset, being laved by the waters of the Pacific, has a prison commission which is full of zeal and energy, and also, like Dorcas of old, "full of good works and alms-deeds done by them." They have done much for the rescue of discharged convicts, yet far less than was needed, far less than they would have done if they had been blessed with an exchequer more amply provided. Owing to the intelligent and indefatigable exertions of this association, the State of California is among the foremost of those which are struggling for an improved prison system. There is now before her legislature two propositions of great interest and importance. One of these looks to such a change in the constitution of the State as will take the administration of prisons out of the arena of politics, and impress upon it a character of stability and permanence. The other is a bill to create a State reformatory, not for juvenile delinquents, but for young criminals not exceeding thirty years of age, who have committed a first offense, and who, in the proposed prison, shall be subjected to a treatment really reformatory.

The warden of the State penitentiary of Iowa, Mr. Heisey, has individually assisted numbers of worthy prisoners, on their release, in obtaining work. Recently a prisoners' aid society has been formed, with the same object in view, and it is not doubted that the good work will now be prosecuted more efficiently because more systematically. Application will be made to the legislature for pecuniary aid, which, it is believed, will be granted. Mr. Heisey avers that there is great need of such an agency, since "the discharged convict is not infrequently led to the commission of crime in' consequence of his inability to procure employment, through the prejudices which, on account of his incarceration in the penitentiary, and which he himself feels has forever disgraced him."

An aid society was, some years ago, formed in Joliĕt, the seat of the State prison of Illinois; but whether it is still in existence, or what it has accomplished in behalf of discharged prisoners, the committee is not informed.

Whether anything, and if anything, what, has been done in Michigan, in aid of discharged prisoners, the committee cannot say, having no information.

South Carolina is the only Southern State engaged in the late civil war from which information has been received upon this point. But what is true of this is substantially true of all the rest. Indeed, this is more than intimated in a letter of General Stolbrand, warden of the State penitentiary. "It is," he says, "with great regret that I must make the confession for my State that it has done nothing to help liberated convicts in their endeavors to sustain an honest life. Since my appointment, in January, 1869, to superintend this institution, I have, in some twenty or more instances, been instrumental in obtaining employment for discharged criminals; but, beyond that, I am not able to point to any steps, municipal or otherwise, in that direction. There has been no effort in this direction that I am aware of in this State, and I think not in any other Southern State; and, although only by adoption a southerner, I feel humiliated to make the statement."

Such, in substance, is the sum of the committee's knowledge of what has been done, or is now doing, in the United States for liberated prisoners. In the aggregate, it is considerable; but viewed in relation to the demands of either duty or policy, it is little.

III.—WHAT CAN BE AND OUGHT TO BE DONE FOR DISCHARGED PRISONERS.

It is evident, and cannot be successfully disputed, that society has not done its whole duty to the criminal when it has punished him, nor even when it has reformed him. Its obligation does not cease when it opens his prison door and bids him walk forth in freedom. Having lifted him up, it has the still further duty to aid in holding him up. Some systematic provision to this end is the essential complement of all effective reformatory punishment. In vain shall we have improved the convict in mind and heart, in vain shall we have given him a capacity and fondness for labor, if, on his discharge, he finds none to trust him, none to meet him kindly, none to offer him the opportunity of earning honest bread. Though willing to work, he can get no work to do. Though yearning to show himself worthy of association with the good and the pure, he is repelled as if contact with him were pestilential. His good purposes are defeated; his hope of redemption vanishes. What can such a one do, if he live at all, but live a criminal? What though his reformation be genuine, can it be permanent? Impossible! He will surely be clutched again by his old associates in sin, and drawn back into the abyss of crime, from which he had vainly striven to emerge. So it has been too often and too generally, and so it is still. It is, then, the clear duty of the State as such, or of the citizens in voluntary association, as it is no less clearly their true policy, after liberating their convicts, to estab-

lish some agency whereby they may be strengthened in their good resolutions, provided with work, and, in all suitable ways, encouraged and
aided in their efforts to reform and lead an honest life,

There are several ways in which the required aid may be made available ; not all, probably, equally good, but all having their special points
of merit, and all very much better than nothing.

There is, first, the plan of a State agency. This has been tried for
many years in Massachusetts, and has stood the test of experiment. It
was tried for two years in New Hampshire, where it appeared to yield
valuable results. Some other States, as Rhode Island and New Jersey,
have sought, but without success, to introduce the system. It does not,
therefore, appear to be a plan likely to take root very widely, and some
other, better adapted to the genius of our people, must be adopted
instead.

There is, then, secondly, the plan of voluntary associations, which seems
better to meet, if not the necessities of the case, at least the tastes and
proclivities of our citizens. The results of this system, so far as it has
been applied, have been excellent. The system, to a certain extent, has
been tried in New York, Pennsylvania, Maryland, and California.
Abroad, especially in England and France, it has been tested much more
extensively, and has, both in this country and others, proved the salvation of thousands of liberated prisoners. It is the wish and will be the
effort of the National Prison Association to secure efficient working organizations in all our States which will charge themselves with the
needful attention to this vast and vital interest of society.

There is, thirdly, the plan of a refuge or home for discharged prisoners, to be established by the State or by private citizens. In the code
of reform and prison discipline, prepared for Louisiana by Edward Livingston at the instance of the legislature of that State, he provided a
penal and reformatory system, embracing four classes of institutions,
which he named, severally, the house of detention, the penitentiary, the
school of reform, and the house of refuge and industry. This last was
intended as a home for liberated prisoners, where they should find temporary employment during the period intervening between their discharge and their complete absorption into the ranks of virtuous industry in free society. After expressing the hope and belief that the
discipline of the penitentiary would, in the case of the major part of the
prisoners, issue in effacing previous bad impressions, in creating lasting
habits of industry and virtuous pursuit, and in discharging the subject of
the discipline from the prison a better, wiser, and happier man, Mr. Livingston adds these solemn and weighty words: "But these happy
effects will be counteracted, the care, labor, and expense of your reformatory discipline will have been uselessly incurred, if your proselyte
to virtue and industry is to have the one exposed to the seduction of
his former associates and the other rendered useless by the want of
means to exert it. It will be in vain that you have given him the skill
necessary for his support if no one will afford him an opportunity of
using it, or that you have made him an honest man if all the world
avoids him as a villain. His relapse is certain, unavoidable, and his
depravity will be the greater, from the experience that reformation has
been productive only of distrust, want, and misery. 'Seven evil
spirits' will take possession of the mind that has been 'swept and
garnished' by your discipline, and the 'the last state of that man shall
be worse than the first.' To avoid this result, so destructive of the
whole system, an asylum is provided in the house of refuge and industry. Here the discharged convict may find employment and subsistence,

and receive such wages as will enable him to remove from the scenes of his past crimes, place him above temptation, confirm him in his newly acquired habits of industry, and cause him safely to pass the dangerous and trying period between the acquisition of his liberty and restoration to the confidence of society. Independently of this resource, the industrious convict receives at his discharge a proper proportion of his surplus earnings. He receives friendly advice as to his future pursuits, and a certificate (if he has merited it) of such conduct as will entitle him to confidence. The consequences of reconviction are solemnly represented to him, and his conduct, if he remain in the neighborhood of the prison, is carefully watched, so that if he return to habits of idleness and intemperance, his career to crime may be stopped by a commitment to the house of industry as a vagrant. The cause, the temptation, or the excuse for relapse being thus removed, it is hoped that instances of return to vicious pursuits will become more rare, and that many will become useful members of society, who, under the present system, either burden it by their poverty or prey upon it by their crimes. The house of refuge is rendered the more necessary because a man of prudence will no more receive or employ a convict discharged from one of our present penitentiaries than he would shut up with his flock a wild beast escaped from its keepers. But the reformatory plan, once fairly in operation, its principles studied, developed, steadily adhered to, improved by the light of experience, and its beneficial effects upon morals perceived, the man who has undergone its purifying operation will, in time, be no longer regarded with fear and contempt, and society, by confiding in his reformation, will permit him to be honest. The house of refuge will then become less necessary, and its expense of course diminished."[*]

After the lapse of half a century institutions of this kind are beginning to be established in this and other countries. Two industrial homes, one for male, the other for female discharged prisoners, have been in operation for a number of years in connection with the Wakefield prison, in England. Both are prosperous pecuniarily, and are doing much good. No prisoner who has been discharged from the Wakefield jail need or can ever return to it again, on the plea that he can get no work to do. The Female Refuge at Golden Bridge, near Dublin, has had a satisfactory, and, indeed, as Mr. Commissioner Hill, of England,

---

[*] In a paragraph immediately following the above-cited passage, Mr. Livingston disposes so neatly of a common objection to skilled labor in prisons that, although the argument does not belong strictly to the subject under consideration, the committee cannot resist the impulse to transfer it to their report in a note. He remarks: "Before I quit the consideration of this establishment, it may be necessary to dispose of an objection sometimes raised to it as well as to the penitentiary—that the products of mechanical operations which may be carried on there will be sold cheaper than they can be afforded by the regular mechanic, who is burdened with the support of a family, with rent, taxes, and other charges, and thus injure the innocent in order to find employment for the guilty. This objection could only have weight if all the convicts were employed in one business, and that in a country where there is a greater supply of labor than there is a demand for it. But here the very reverse of this is the fact. Again, if all the convicts should be employed in a single occupation it must be because there is an excess of demand for that species of labor over the supply, and while that continues there can be no injury. When that demand is reduced, the business will be abandoned, both within and without the prison. As respects the public interest, there can be no doubt, for the question reduces itself to this: whether the convicts are to be maintained in idleness, or suffered to contribute by labor to their own support? And even as regards particular classes of mechanics, the same reasoning that would prevent their trade being carried on in prison would go to show that it ought to be limited without. But the best answer to the objection is, that experience has never realized any of the evils that have been apprehended."

says, a triumphant history of twelve years, during which hundreds of liberated convicts have been saved by it from relapsing into crime. Indeed it is, we are informed, a rare thing for any female convict who has passed through it to be reconvicted and sent back to prison. Nearly all are saved. The Carlisle Memorial Refuge for Convict Women, at Winchester, corroborates the testimony of Golden Bridge. The Home for Discharged Female Prisoners, founded and managed by the New York Women's Prison Association, and the temporary asylum for the same class of persons at Dedham, Massachusetts, under the care of a society of Boston ladies, speak the same language. These facts would seem to prove, beyond dispute, the practicability and utility of such asylums, especially for women. But they should be made strictly transitional. Their whole intent and aim should be to bridge the gulf that lies between the prison and employment in general society, to provide a defense for the critical, and to the convict who desires to reform, momentous period which follows immediately on liberation.

The intermediate prison, at Lusk, near Dublin, is an institution of essentially the same character as Mr. Livingston's house of refuge; with this difference, that its inmates are still within the grasp of their sentence, while those of the refuge have passed out of the range of its power, and of their own free will have come to enjoy the benefits of a home which has invited them to its hospitable shelter. The advantages which Mr. Livingston hoped from his refuge are, at Lusk, matters of daily experience. The intermediate prison, it will be remembered, is an essential part of the Crofton prison system, constituting its third or probationary stage.

The fourth and most essential agency for saving discharged prisoners would be an improved prison discipline, a training while in prison, which would issue, wherever such a result is possible, in a genuine and radical reformation of the convict. The committee, without going into much detail, would offer an outline of such a system as, in their judgment, would be most likely to accomplish the result indicated.

1. The reformation and rehabilitation of criminals—not vindictive suffering—should be made the supreme aim of the system.

2. Progressive classification, based on character and merit, and not on any arbitrary principle, such as age, crime, &c., should be made a fundamental principle. No better method has yet been devised to this end than that offered in the Crofton prison system, where there is—I. A penal stage, with separate imprisonment, longer or shorter, according to conduct. II. A reformatory stage, worked on the mark system, where the prisoners are advanced from class to class, as they earn such advance, giving at each step increased comfort and privilege. III. A probationary stage, into which are admitted only such as are judged to be reformed, and where the object is to test their moral soundness—the reality of their reformation. IV. A stage of conditional liberty, (ticket of leave,) in which the *reformed convict* enjoys full freedom, subject, however, to a revocation thereof, and a return to the prison, for any misconduct.

3. A system of rewards for good conduct and industry should be instituted, whereby hope shall become an ever-present and ever-active force, more potent and controlling than fear in the minds of prisoners. Such rewards should consist of: *a*, a diminution of sentence; *b*, a share by the prisoners in their earnings; *c*, a gradual withdrawal of prison restraints, and a constant increase of privileges, as they shall be earned by good conduct.

4. Greater breadth should be given to moral and religious agencies.

5. There should be a stronger infusion of the educational element in our prison system.

6. Industrial training should have a higher development and a greater breadth.

7. Moral must be substituted for material forces in our prison discipline to the utmost extent possible.

8. Prison officers must receive a special education for their work, and prison-keeping be thus raised to the dignity of a regular calling, so that a scientific character may be given to it.

9. A probationary stage, already referred to in the second specification above, in which the training shall be more natural, and the moral cure of the delinquent can be adequately tested, must be introduced into our prison systems. This principle does not yet command universal concurrence, though the tendency of opinion sets strongly in that direction. It is singular, however, that while it has received a wide theoretical assent, the theory, so far as we are informed, has been reduced to practice nowhere except in the Irish convict prisons under the Crofton system. The reason for such a chasm, and that so generally existing, between principle and act, must be sought, no doubt, in the difficulty of bringing the two practically together, and in the further fact that a successful application of the principle requires an adjustment thereto of the other and antecedent stages of a prison system. The principle cannot possibly be incorporated, as an isolated element, into *any* prison system; but must, of necessity, come in as the complement of a system, all the parts of which are contrived and adjusted to reformation as the one great end in view. There is no prison system in our country, and probably not elsewhere, other than the one to which it originally belonged, on which this principle *could* be ingrafted, without changes so radical as to constitute a new system. Yet it is a principle so essential to a true and effective prison discipline, that, sooner or later, the changes *must* be made which will permit its introduction. There is a problem of the gravest importance, and as difficult as it is grave, on which the minds of prison reformers throughout the world are now bent with an interest that may be characterized as intense—the problem how to secure the re-absorption of released prisoners into society, without a relapse into crime. Thousands upon thousands, intent on a better life on their emergence from prison walls, fall back into transgression, simply because the ban of society is upon them; nobody trusts them, nobody will give them work, nobody will permit them to earn and eat honest bread. The solution of the problem stated above, so vital and yet so hidden, so important, and at the same time so perplexed, lies in the direction of this principle—lies, in fact, in a successful application of this principle, as a living and indispensable part of a prison system. The discharged convict, though reformed and resolved to live honestly, fails to get work; and he fails so generally that failure is the rule and success the exception. Why is this? It is not that society is hard-hearted; that it has no sympathy with misfortune; that it is vindictive and cruel; that it tramples upon a man merely because he is down. Far from it; but society *distrusts* the liberated prisoner; it has no *confidence* in him; and, what is yet more to the purpose, it has *no guarantee for its confidence*. It is this *want of a guarantee* that builds a wall of granite between the convict on his release and remunerative employment. Conquer the distrust of society, replace that distrust with confidence, furnish the needed guarantee that the man is trustworthy, and every difficulty will vanish; every shop, every factory, every farm, every avenue of honest toil will be open to his entrance. But the prob-

lem is *how* to abate the prejudice which society feels toward the liberated convict; *how* to overcome the dread which it has of him; *how* to allay its fears; *how* to win for him its confidence and conciliate its regard. There is but one way to accomplish this result. The convict must furnish *proof* during his incarceration that it is safe to confide in him; safe to put him at the work-bench; safe to place in his hands "the shovel and the hoe;" safe to admit him to the intimacy of the fireside and the home circle. In other words, he must be tried, his cure must be tested, before he is discharged. But this can *never* be done where the system of imprisonment is one of material isolation to the end; neither can it any more be done where the system of imprisonment is one of moral isolation to the end. There must be a field, an opportunity for the trial. But such a theater and such a chance the separate system can *never* furnish; nor any more can the congregate system, on its present basis. Both our existing systems must be in part retained, in part discarded, in part changed; and so changed that the passage from imprisonment to liberty shall not be, as now, *per saltum,* by a single bound; but the change must be such that the former shall gradually, almost imperceptibly, melt into the latter; such that the latter part of the imprisonment shall be little more than moral, in which, as far as may be, all the arrangements shall be those of ordinary life, with its trusts, its temptations, its responsibilities, its victories over self and sin, its toning up and strengthening of the character by the friction to which the man is in these various ways subjected. Or, to sum up all in one word, the *principle* of the Crofton "intermediate prison," in the form which it has in Ireland, or some other, must be impressed upon *our* system of imprisonment, where, doubtless, it will yield the same precious fruit that it does in the country in which the idea was first conceived and applied. "The same precious fruit." What fruit? The conquest of distrust, the implantation of confidence toward liberated prisoners. And has that result been achieved? Yes, to the fullest extent. What was thought to be an impossibility—what is yet so regarded by many—has become a living fact. In Ireland the labor of discharged convicts, which, fifteen years ago, was spurned as a gift, is to-day eagerly sought.

CHARLES COFFIN,
Chairman.

The committee believe that prisoners prepared for discharge under the influences of a prison system such as that sketched above would readily find employment, and be re-absorbed into free and virtuous society; and thus would be solved a problem which has been regarded as one of the most difficult and perplexing in penitentiary science.

---

4. REPORT OF THE COMMITTEE ON JUVENILE DELINQUENCY.

The subjects on which this committee are called upon to report are so vast and complicated, and the time of the convention is so limited, that we have felt it most advisable to present but one portion of the great work being performed in the country in behalf of our unfortunate or criminal youth, and that is, the *preventive measures*, which naturally often receive less attention in such assemblies than the more imposing labors of reformation.

Moreover, on this latter field, the National Prison Association, or, to speak more precisely, the national congress, which is the parent of the association, has already listened, on a previous occasion, to very lucid and able papers, and to no less clear and instructive discussions.

We shall confine ourselves in the present paper to an examination of certain sources of juvenile crime, not usually much considered, treating briefly of others which have been often and ably discussed; and then shall give a brief *résumé* of certain preventive measures in New York—which may be found of much value if adopted in other cities—and the results of these extended movements on the records and statistics of juvenile crime.

If certain aspects of our subject seem too briefly dealt with, the association will consider the brief time allowed for such important discussions.

THE CAUSES OF JUVENILE CRIME.

The great practical division of causes of crime may be made into preventable and non-preventable. Among the preventable, or those which can be in good part removed, may be placed : Ignorance, intemperance, overcrowding of population, want of work, idleness, vagrancy, the weakness of the marriage tie, and bad legislation.

Among those which cannot be entirely removed are inheritance, the effects of emigration, orphanage, accident, or misfortune, the strength of the sexual and other passions, and a natural weakness of moral or mental powers.

In treating these in this paper we shall pass over ignorance, orphanage, want of work, and the effects of emigration, and shall omit entirely the great and terrible source of crime, intemperance, as these have all been so exhaustively and ably discussed in previous sessions of the prison association. The principal consideration will be given in this paper to "the weakness of the marriage tie" as a cause of crime; to inheritance, and to overcrowding, especially in New York, as a prolific source of juvenile crimes.

WEAKNESS OF THE MARRIAGE TIE.

It is extraordinary among the lower classes in how large a number of cases a second marriage, or the breaking of marriage, is the immediate cause of crime or vagrancy among the children. When questioning a homeless boy or street-wandering girl as to their former home, it is extremely common to hear either, "I couldn't get on with my step-mother," or, "My step-father treated me badly," or, "My father left, and we just took care of ourselves." These apparently exceptional events are so common in these classes as to fairly constitute them an important cause of juvenile crime. When one remembers the number of happy second marriages within one's acquaintance, and how many children have never felt the difference between their step-mother and their own mother, and what love, and patience, and self-sacrifice are shown by parents to their step-children, we may be surprised at the contrast in another class of the community; but the virtues of the poor spring very much from their affections and instincts; they have comparatively little self-control; the high lessons of duty and consideration for others are seldom stamped on them; and religion does not much influence their more delicate relations with those associated with them. They might shelter a strange orphan for years with the greatest kindness, but the bearing and forbearing with the faults of another person's child year after year, merely from motives of duty or affection to its parent, belong to a higher range of Christian virtues, to which they seldom attain. Their own want of self-control and their tendency to jealousy, and little understanding of true self-sacrifice, combine to weaken and embitter these relations with step-children. The children themselves have plenty of faults, and have doubtless been little governed, so that soon both parties jar and rub against one another, and, as neither have instincts or affections to fall back upon, mere principle or sense of duty is not enough to restrain them. What would be simply slights or jars in more controlled persons become collisions with this class.

Bitter quarrels spring up between step-son and mother or step-daughter and father; the other parent sometimes sides with the child, sometimes with his partner, but the result is similar. The house becomes a kind of pandemonium, and the girls rush desperately forth to the wild life of the streets, or the boys gradually prefer the roaming existence of the little city Arab to such a quarrelsome home. Thus it happens that step-children among the poor are so often criminals or outcasts.

It needs a number of years among the lowest working classes to understand what a force public opinion is, in all classes, in keeping the marriage bond sacred, and what sweeping misfortunes follow its viola-tion. Many of the Irish peasants who have landed here have married from pure affection. Their marriage has been consecrated by the most solemn ceremonies of their church. They come of a people peculiarly faithful to the marriage tie, and whose religion has especially guarded female purity and the fidelity of husband and wife. At home, in their native villages, they would have died sooner than break the bond or leave their wives. The social atmosphere about them, and the influence of their priests, make such an act almost impossible. And yet, in this distant country, away from their neighbors and their religious instruct-ors, they are continually making a practical test of "free-love" doc-trines. As the wife grows old or ugly, as children increase and weigh the parents down, as the homes become more noisy and less pleasant, the man begins to forget the vows made at the altar and the blooming girl he then took, and perhaps meeting some prettier woman or hearing of some chance for work at a distance, he slips quietly away, and the deserted wife, who seems to love him the more the more false he is, is left alone. For a time she has faith in him and seeks him far and near, but, at length, she abandons hope and begins the heavy struggle of maintaining her little family herself. The boys gradually get beyond her control; they are kept in the street to earn something for their sup-port; they become wild and vagrant, and soon end with being street-rovers, or petty thieves, or young criminals. The girls are trained in beggary or peddling, and, meeting with bold company, they gradually learn the manners and morals of the streets, and after a while abandon the wretched home and break what was left of the poor mother's hope and courage by beginning a life of shame. This sad history is lived out every day in New York. If any theorists desire to see what fruits "free-love" or a weak marriage bond can bear among the lowest working classes, they have only to trace the histories of great numbers of the young thieves and outcasts and prostitutes in this city. With the dan-gerous classes "elective affinities" are most honestly followed. The results are suffering, crime, want, and degradation to those who are innocent.

INHERITANCE.

A most powerful and continual source of crime with the young is inheritance, the transmitted tendencies and qualities of their parents,

or of several generations of ancestors. It is well known to those familiar with the criminal classes that certain appetites or habits, if indulged
abnormally and excessively through two or more generations, come to
have an almost irrisistible force, and no doubt do modify the brain so
as to constitute almost an insane condition. This is especially true of
the appetite for liquor, and of sexual passion, and sometimes of the
peculiar weakness, dependence, and laziness, which make confirmed
paupers. The writer knows of one instance, in an alms-house in western
New York, where four generations of females were paupers and prostitutes. Almost every reader who is familiar with village life will recall
poor families which have had dissolute or criminal members beyond the
memory of the oldest inhabitant, and who still continue to breed such
characters. I have known a child of nine or ten given up, apparently
beyond control, to licentious habits and desires, and who in all different
circumstances seemed to show the same tendencies; her mother had
been of similar character, and quite likely her grandmother. The
"gemmules," or latent tendencies, or forces, or cells, of her immediate
ancestors were in her system and working in her blood, producing irrisistible effects on her brain, nerves, and mental emotions, and finally, not
being met early enough by other moral, mental, and physical influences,
they have modified her organization until her will is scarcely able to
control them, and she gives herself up to them. All those who instruct
in or govern houses of refuge, or reform schools, or asylums for
criminal children and youth, will recall many such instances. They are
much better known in the Old World than in this; they are far more
common here in the country than the city. My own experience during
twenty years has been in this regard singularly hopeful. I have
watched great numbers of degraded families in New York, and exceedingly few of them have transmitted new generations of paupers, criminals, or vagrants. The causes of this encouraging state
of things are not obscure. The action of the great law of "natural
selection," in regard to the human race, is always toward temperance
and virtue. That is, vice and extreme indulgence weaken the physical powers and undermine the constitution. They impair the faculties by which man struggles with adverse conditions, and gets beyond
the reach of poverty and want. The vicious, and sensual, and
drunken die earlier, or they have fewer children, or their children are
carried off by diseases more frequently, or they themselves are unable
to resist or prevent poverty and suffering. As a consequence, in the
lowest class, the more self-controlled and virtuous tend constantly to
survive, and to prevail in "the struggle for existence" over the vicious
and ungoverned, and to transmit their progeny. The natural drift
among the poor is toward virtue. Probably no vicious organization
with very extreme and abnormal tendencies is transmitted beyond the
fourth generation; it ends in insanity, or *crétinism*, or the wildest crime.
The result is then, with the worst endowed families, that the "gemmules,"
or latent forces of hundreds of virtuous, or at least not vicious generations, lie hid in their constitution. The immediate influences of
parents or grand-parents are of course the strongest in inheritance;
but these may be overcome, and the latent tendencies to good, coming
down from remote ancestors, be aroused and developed.
  Thus is explained the extraordinary improvement of the children of
crime and poverty in our industrial schools, and the reforms and happy
changes seen in the boys and girls of our dangerous classes, when placed
in kind western homes. The change of circumstances, the improved
food, the daily moral and mental influences, the effect of regular labor

and discipline, and, above all, the power of religion, awaken these hidden tendencies to good, both those coming from many generations of comparative virtue and those inherent in the soul, while they control and weaken, and cause to be forgotten, those diseased appetites or extreme passions which these unfortunate creatures inherit directly, and substitute a higher moral sense for the low moral instincts which they obtained from their parents. So it happens, also, that American life, as compared with European, and city life as compared with country, produces similar results. In the United States a boundless hope pervades all classes; it reaches down to the outcast and vagrant. There is no fixity, as is so often the fact in Europe, from the sense of despair. Every individual, at least till he is old, hopes and expects to rise out of his condition.

The daughter of the rag-picker or vagrant sees the children she knows continually dressing better or associating with more decent people; she beholds them attending the public schools and improving in education and manners; she comes in contact with the greatest force the poor know—public opinion, which requires a certain decency and respectability among themselves; she becomes ashamed of her squalid, ragged, or drunken mother; she enters an industrial school, or creeps into a ward school, or "goes out" as a servant. In every place she feels the profound forces of American life; the desire of equality; ambition to rise; the sense of self-respect, and the passion for education.

These new desires overcome the low appetites in her blood, and she continually rises and improves. If religion in any form reach her, she attains a still greater height over the sensual and filthy ways of her parents. She is in no danger of sexual degradation or any extreme vice. The poison in her blood has found an antidote. When she marries, it will inevitably be with a class above her own. This process goes on continually throughout the country and breaks up criminal inheritance. Moreover, the incessant change of our people, especially in cities; the separation of children from parents, of brothers from sisters, and of all from their former localities, destroy that continuity of influence which bad parents and grandparents exert, and does away with those neighborhoods of crime and pauperism where vice concentrates and transmits itself with ever-increasing power. The fact that tenants must forever be "moving" in New York is a preventive of some of the worst evils among the lower poor.

The mill of American life, which grinds up so many delicate and fragile things, has its uses, when it is turned on the vicious fragments of the lowest strata of society.

Villages, which are more stable and conservative, and tend to keep families together more, and in the same neighborhoods, show more instances of inherited and concentrated wickedness and idleness. I think we have, in New York, comparatively little of successive generations of paupers, criminals, and vagrants. The families are constantly broken up; some members improve; some die out, but they do not transmit a progeny of crime.

Among those public influences on the young, it has been often a question with some whether the public schools did not educate the daughters of the poor too much, and thus make them discontented with their condition and exposed to temptation.

It is said that these working-girls, seeing such fine dresses about them, and learning many useless accomplishments, have become indifferent to steady hard labor, and have sought in vice for the luxuries which they first learned to know in the public schools. My own observations, however, lead me to doubt whether this occurs unless as an exceptional fact. The influence of discipline and regular instruction is against the style of character which makes the prostitute. Where there is a habit of work, there is seldom the laziness and shiftlessness which especially cause or stimulate sexual vice. Some working-girls do, no doubt, become discontented with their former condition, and some rise to a much higher, while some fail; but this happens everywhere in the United States, and is not to be traced especially to the influence of our free schools.

We have spoken of the greater tendency of large cities, as compared with villages, in breaking up vicious families. There is another advantage of cities in this matter. The especial virtue of a village community is the self-respect and personal independence of its members. No benefits of charity or benevolent assistance and dependence could ever outweigh this. But this very virtue tends to keep a wicked or idle family in its present condition. The neighbors are not in the habit of interfering with it; no one advises or warns it; the children grow up as other people's children do, in the way the parents prefer; there is no machinery of charity to lift them out of the slime; and if any of their wealthier neighbors, from motives of benevolence, visited the house and attempted to improve or educate the family, the effort would be resented or misconstrued. The whole family become a kind of *pariahs;* they are morally tabooed, and grow up in a vicious atmosphere of their own, and really come out much worse than a similar family in the city. This phenomenon is only a natural effect of the best virtues of the worst community.

In a large town, on the other hand, there exist machinery and organization through which benevolent and religious persons can approach such families, and their good intentions not be suspected or resented. The poor people themselves are not so independent, and accept advice or warning more readily. They are not stamped in public repute with a bad name; less is known of them; and the children under new influences break off from the vicious career of their parents and grow up as honest and industrious persons. Moreover, the existence of so much charitable organization in the cities brings the best talent and character of the fortunate classes to bear directly on the unfortunate, far more than is the fact in villages.

OVERCROWDING.

The source of juvenile crime and misery in New York which is the most formidable, and at the same time the most difficult to remove, is the overcrowding of our population. The form of the city site is such—the majority of the dwellings being crowded into a narrow island between two water-fronts—that space near the business portions of the city becomes of great value. These districts are necessarily sought for by the laboring and mechanic classes, as they are near the places of employment. They are avoided by the wealthy on account of the population which has already occupied so much of them. The result is that the poor must live in certain wards, and as space is costly the landlords supply them with (comparatively) cheap dwellings, by building very high and large houses, in which great numbers of people rent only rooms instead of dwellings.

Were New York a city radiating from a center over an almost unlimited space, as Philadelphia, for instance, the laborers or the mechanics might take up their abode anywhere, and land would be comparatively cheap, so that that blessing of the laboring class would be attainable, of separate homes for each family.

But on this narrow island business is so peculiarly constructed, and population is so much forced to one exit—toward the north—and the poor have such a singular objection to living beyond a ferry, that space will inevitably continue very dear in New York, and the laboring classes will be compelled to occupy it.

To add to the unavoidable costliness of ground-room on this island, has come in the effect of bad government.

It is one of the most unpleasant experiences of the student of political economy that the axioms of his science can so seldom be understood by the masses, though their interests be vitally affected by them.

Thus every thoughtful man knows that each "new job" among city officials, each act of plunder of public property by members of the municipal government, every loss of income or mal-appropriation or extravagance in the city's funds, must be paid for by taxation, and that taxation always falls heaviest on labor.

The laboring classes of this city rule it, and through their especial leaders are the great public losses and wastefulness occasioned. Yet they never know that they themselves pay for these continually in increased rents. Every landlord charges his advanced taxation in rent, and probably a profit on that. The tenant pays more for his room; the grocer more for his shop; the butcher and tailor and shoemaker and every retailer has heavier expenses from the advance in rents, and each and all charge it on their customers. The poor feel the final pressure. The painful effect has been that the expense for rent has risen enormously with the laboring classes of this city during the last five years, while many others of the living expenses have nearly returned to the standard before the war.

The influence of high rents is to force more people into a given space, in order to economize and divide expense.

The latest trustworthy statistics on this important subject are from the excellent reports of the Metropolitan Board of Health for 1866. From these it appears that the First ward of this city, with a population of 58,953, has a rate of population of 196,510 to the square mile, or 16.1 square yards to each person; the —— ward, with 31,537 population, has a rate of 185,512 to the square mile, or 17.2 yards to each; the Seventeenth ward, with 79,563, has the rate of 153,006; the Fourteenth ward, with 23,382, has a rate of 155,880; the Thirteenth ward, with 26,388, has 155,224; and so on with others, though in less proportion. The worst districts in London do not at all equal this crowding of population.

Thus East London shows the rate of 175,816 to the square mile; the Strand, 161,556; Saint Luke's, 151,104; Holborn, 148,705, and Saint James, Westminster, 144,008,

If particular districts of our city be taken, they present an even greater massing of human beings than the above averages have shown. Thus, according to the report of the council of hygiene in 1865, the tenant-house and cellar population of the Fifteenth ward numbered 17,611, packed in buildings over a space less than thirty acres, exclusive of streets, which would make the fearful rate of 290,000 to the square mile. In the Seventeenth ward, the board of health reports that in 1868 4,120 houses contained 95,091 inhabitants, of whom 14,016 were children under five years. In the same report, the number of tenement houses for the whole city is given at 18,582, with an estimate of one-half the whole population dwelling in them, say 500,000. We quote an extract from a report of a visitor of the Children's Aid Society of the First ward describing the condition of a tenement house:

What do you think of the moral atmosphere of the home I am about to describe below?

To such a home two of our boys return nightly. / In a dark cellar, filled with smoke, there sleep, all in one room, with no kind of partition dividing them, two men and their wives, a girl of thirteen or fourteen, two men and a large boy of about seventeen years of age, a mother with two more boys, one about ten years old and one large boy of fifteen; another woman with two boys, nine and eleven years of age—in all, *fourteen persons.*

This room I have often visited, and the number enumerated probably falls below rather than above the average that sleep there.

It need not be said that with overcrowding such as this there is always disease, and as naturally crime. The privacy of a home is undoubtedly one of the most favorable conditions to virtue—especially in a girl. If a female child be born and brought up in a room of one of these tenement houses, she loses very early the modesty which is the great shield of purity. Personal delicacy becomes almost unknown to her. Living, sleeping, and doing her work in the same apartment with men and boys of various ages, it is well-nigh impossible for her to retain any feminine reserve, and she passes, almost unconsciously, the line of purity at a very early age. In these dens of crowded humanity, too, other and more unnatural crimes are committed among those of the same blood and family.

Here, too, congregate some of the worst of the destitute population of the city—vagrants, beggars, unsuccessful thieves, broken-down drunken vagabonds who manage as yet to keep out of the station-houses, and the lowest and most bungling of the "sharpers."

Naturally the boys, growing up in such places, become, as by a law of nature, petty thieves, pick-pockets, street-rovers, beggars, and burglars. Their only salvation is that these dens become so filthy and haunted with vermin that the lads themselves leave them in disgust, preferring the barges on the breezy docks or the boxes on the sidewalk, from which eventually they are drawn into the neat and comfortable boys' lodging-houses, and there find themselves imperceptibly changed into honest and decent boys. This is the story of thousands every year. The cellar population alone of the city is a source of incessant disease and crime. And with the more respectable class of poor who occupy the better kind of tenement houses, the packing of human beings in these great caravansaries is one of the worst evils of this city.

It sows pestilence and breeds every species of criminal habits. From the eighteen thousand tenement-houses comes 73 per cent. of the mortality of our population, and we have little doubt as much as 90 per cent. of the offenses against property and person.

Overcrowding is the one great misfortune of New York. Without it we should be the healthiest large city in the world, and a great proportion of the crimes which disgrace our civilization be nipped in the bud. While this continues as it does now, there is no possibility of a thorough sanitary, moral, or religious reform in our worst wards.

Few girls can grow up to majority in such dens as exist in the First, Sixth, Eleventh, and Seventeenth wards and be virtuous; few boys can have such places as homes and not be thieves and vagabonds. In such pens, typhus and cholera will always be rife, and the death-rate reach its most terrible maximum.

While the poorest population dwell in these cellars and crowded attics, neither Sunday-schools, nor churches, nor missions, nor charities can accomplish a thorough reform.

What, then, is to be done to remedy this terrible evil? Experience has proved that our remedial agencies can, in individual cases, cure even the evils resulting from this unnatural condensing of population. That is, we can point to hundreds of lads and young girls who were born and reared in such crowded dens of humanity, but who have been transformed into virtuous, well-behaved, and industrious young men and women, by the quiet daily influence of our industrial schools and lodging-houses.

Still these cases of reform are in truth exceptions. The natural and legitimate influence of such massing of population is all in the direction of immorality and degeneracy. Whatever would lessen that would at once, as by a necessary law, diminish crime, and poverty, and disease. The great remedies are to be looked for in broad general provisions for distributing population.

Thus far the means of communication between business New York and the suburbs have been singularly defective. An underground railway, with cheap workmen's trains, or elevated railways, with similar conveniences, connecting Westchester County and the lower part of the city, or suburbs laid out in New Jersey or on Long Island, expressly for working people, with cheap connections with New York and Brooklyn, would soon make a vast difference in the concentration of population in our lower wards. It is true that English experience would show that laboring men, after a dreary day's work, cannot bear the jar of railway traveling. There must be, however, many varieties of labor—such as work in factories and the like, where a little movement in a railroad train at the close of a day would be a refreshment. Then as the laboring class was concentrated in suburban districts, the various occupations which attend them—such as grocers, shoemakers, tailors, and others—would follow, and be established near them.

Many nationalities among our working class have an especial fondness for gardens and patches of land about their houses. This would be an additional attraction to such settlements; and with easy and cheap communication we might soon have tens of thousands of our laborers and mechanics settled in pleasant and healthy little suburban villages, each perhaps having his own small house and garden; and the children growing up under far better influences, moral and physical, than they could possibly enjoy in tenement houses.

There are many districts within half an hour of New York where such plots could be laid out at $500 each, which would pay a handsome profit to the owner, or where a cottage could be let with advantage for the present rent of a tenement attic. Improved communications have already removed hundreds of thousands of the middle class from the city, to all the surrounding neighborhood, to the immense relief of themselves and families. Equal conveniences, suited to the wants of the laboring class, will soon cause multitudes of these to live in the suburban districts. The obstacle, however, as in all efforts at improvement for the working people, is in their own ignorance and timidity, and their love of the crowd and bustle of a city.

More remote even than relief by improved communications is a possible check to high rents by a better government. A cheap and honest government of the masses in New York would at once lower taxation and bring down rents. The enormous prices demanded for one or two small rooms in a tenement house are a measure (in part) of the cost of our city government.

Another alleviation to our overcrowding has often been proposed, but never vigorously acted upon, as we are persuaded it might be, and that is the making the link between the demand for labor in our country districts and the supply in New York closer. The success of the Children's Aid Society in the transfer of destitute and homeless children to homes in the West, and of the commissioners of emigration in their "Labor Exchange," indicate what might be accomplished by a grand organized movement for transferring our unemployed labor to the fields of the West. It is true they would not carry away our poorest class, yet it would relieve the pressure of population here on space, and thus give more room and occupation for all.

But admitting that we cannot entirely prevent the enormous massing of people, such as prevails in our Eleventh and Seventeenth wards, we can certainly control it by legislation.

The recent sanitary acts of New York attempt to hold in check the mode of building tenement houses, requiring certain means of ventilation and exit, forbidding the filling up the entire space between the houses with dwellings, and otherwise seeking to improve the condition of such tenement houses. There only need two steps further, in imitation of the British lodging-house acts, removing altogether the cellar population when under certain unhealthy conditions, and the other limiting by law the number who can occupy a given space in a tenement room. The British acts assign 240 cubic feet as the lowest space admissible for each tenant or lodger, and if the inspector find less space than that occupied he at once enters a complaint, and the owner or landlord is obliged to reduce the number of his occupants under strict penalties. A provision of this nature in our New York laws would break up our worst dens and scatter their tenants or lodgers.

The removal of the cellar population from a large proportion of their dwellings should also be made. Liverpool removed 20,000 cellar occupants in one year—1847—to the immense gain, both moral and sanitary, of the city. New York needs the reform quite as much. There need be no real hardship in such a measure, as the tenants could find accommodations in other parts of the city or the suburbs; and some would perhaps emigrate to the country.

One often proposed remedy for ills of our tenant-house system—the "model lodging-house," has never been fairly tried here. The theory of this agency of reform is, that if a tenement-house can be constructed on the best sanitary principles, with good ventilation, with a limited number of tenants, no overcrowding, and certain important conveniences to the lodgers, all under moral supervision, (so that tenants of notoriously bad character are excluded,) and such a house can be shown to pay, say 7 per cent. net, this will become a "model" to the builders of tenement-houses; some building after the same style because public opinion and their own conscience require it, others because competition compels it. Thus, in time, the mode of structure and occupancy of all the new tenement-houses would be changed by the "model-houses."

But to attain this desirable end, the "model houses" must first pay a profit, and a fair one. So long as they do not succeed in this they are a failure, however benevolent their object and comfortable their arrangements. In this point of view the "Wakelow houses" in London are a success, and do undoubtedly influence the mode, building, and management of private tenement-houses; in this, also, the "Peabody houses" are not a success and will have no permanent influence.

The model-houses in London for lodging single men have, as the writer witnessed, changed and elevated the whole class of similar private lodging-houses. The experiment ought to be tried here, on a purely business basis, by some of our wealthy men. The evil of crowded tenement-houses might be immensely alleviated by such a remedy.

THE GREAT PREVENTIVE MEASURES OF NEW YORK.

The extended movements for the prevention of youthful poverty and crime which I am about very briefly to note originated in 1853 with the writer and a few other gentlemen, of whom only three or four are now living, our first treasurer, Mr. J. E. Williams, being our main-stay through all these years.

We had all been deeply moved by the terrible suffering and crime among the neglected children of this city, and resolved to form an organization devoted entirely to this subject. We took an office on the corner of Amity street and Broadway, the whole force being at first the writer and an office-boy. We organized as the Children's Aid Society of New York and were subsequently incorporated, in 1855.

From the beginning we aimed at four different objects: First and foremost, at removing, after a short probation, the floating and homeless boys and girls of the city to *places and homes in the country ;* second, at opening *industrial schools and workshops* for the children of the poor, especially for little girls who had homes, but who were too ragged, dirty, irregular in attendance, or too much in want of food and clothing to attend the public schools, and who were growing up as petty thieves and little vagabonds ; third, we proposed to found *lodging-houses* for the homeless children, where they could be sheltered, partly fed, instructed, brought under moral influences, and at length provided with *homes ;* and fourth, to open *free reading-rooms,* as a means of improving and elevating the youth of the lowest wards.

For nearly twenty years we have steadily aimed at these various objects, through opposition, under persecution, amid the financial bankruptcy of the mercantile community on whom we depend, and during the great war for the life of the Union. The plan as it was first formed, we can modestly say, has been justified by events and blessed by Providence.

Our annual income has increased from $4,732.77 to about $175,000. We have now about seventy teachers employed, and various other agents. We have transplanted to country homes over 20,000 poor boys and girls ; during the past year, 3,386. We have now nineteen industrial schools and twelve night-schools, with an aggregate attendance of 9,500 and an average of about 2,900.

We have five lodging-houses—four for boys and one for girls—with an aggregate attendance through the year of 11,928 different children, and an average of over 400 each night.

In one lodging-house alone—the newsboys'—there have been over 50,000 different boys since its opening.

There are also five reading-rooms for lads and young men under charge of the society.

For all these movements there have been expended since the foundation of the society $1,093,923.48.

From our industrial schools but the smallest proportion ever turn out criminals or paupers ; probably not five out of one thousand.

Of the children sent to the country, comparatively few return to the city, and, so far as we can ascertain, a very hopefully small percentage are ever chargeable on the community or commit criminal offenses. Great numbers are now filling places of trust and usefulness throughout the country. Some are possessed of large properties, and others are thriving as teachers or in professions.

All these various branches of our preventive charity have attracted to them the most humane and enlightened men and women of the city, who have devoted a vast deal of labor and time and means to this work of " saving the children " from crime and pauperism.

It is to their co-operation and generous assistance, under Providence, that its success is due.

So far as is known, no other large city has founded so extensive an organization for the prevention of juvenile crime. Since our opening, a similar society was founded, at our suggestion, in Brooklyn, which has now several lodging-houses. Newsboys' lodging-houses have also been founded, in imitation of ours, in Toronto, New Orleans, Philadelphia, Washington, Chicago, and other cities. Some of them, however, have not succeeded. A new one has recently been opened in London, in Gray's Inn Court, in imitation of the New York house.

At present about one half of the income of the Childrens' Aid Society is derived from public sources and one half from private subscription.

Besides these preventive measures should be mentioned the excellent work of the Home of the Friendless, the well-known labors of the Five Points' Missions, the Howard Mission, Wilson School, and the various church and mission schools for the children of the poor.

THE RESULTS

of all these preventive and educational movements are best shown by the following statistics of juvenile crime, taken from the reports of the city prisons and the police.

CRIME CHECKED AMONG GIRLS.

We have compared especially those offenses of which children or youth are usually guilty—such as " vagrancy," which includes, undoubtedly, open prostitution, as well as homelessness and general vagabondism, " petty larceny," and " pocket-picking." The date of the year, it should be noticed, is always twelve months in advance, owing to the time of issue of the reports, so that the statistics for 1871, for instance, apply to 1870.

Of female vagrants there were imprisoned, in all our city prisons in—

1857	3,449	1863	1,756
1859	5,778	1864	1,342
1860	5,830	1869	785
1861	3,172	1870	671
1862	2,243	1871	548

We have omitted some of the years on account of want of space ; they do not, however, change the steady rate of decrease in this offense.

Thus, in eleven years, the imprisonments of female vagrants have fallen off from 5,880 to 548. This surely is a good show ; and yet in that period our population increased about 13½ per cent., so that, according to the usual law, the commitments should have been this year over 6,673.*

* The population of New York increased from 814,224, in 1860, to 915,520, in 1870, or only about 12½ per cent.

The increase in the previous decade was about 50 per cent. There can be no doubt that the falling off is entirely in the middle classes, who have removed to the neighboring rural districts. The classes from which most of the criminals come have undoubtedly increased, as before, at least 50 per cent.

I have retained for ten years, however, the ratio of the census, 12½ per cent.

If we turn now to the reports of the commissioners of police, the returns are almost equally encouraging, though the classification of arrests does not exactly correspond with that of imprisonments; that is, a person may be arrested for vagrancy, and sentenced for some other offense, and *vice versa.*

The reports of arrests of female vagrants run thus:

1861	2,161	1869	1,078
1862	2,008	1870	701
1863	1,728	1871	914
1867	1,591		

We have not, unfortunately, statistics further back than 1861.

Another crime of young girls is thieving or petty larceny. The rate of commitments runs thus for females:

1859	944	1865	977
1860	890	1869	989
1861	880	1870	746
1863	1,133	1871	572
1864	1,131		

The increase of this crime during the war, in the years 1863 and 1864, is very marked; but in twelve years it has fallen from 944 to 572, though, according to the increase of the population, it would have been naturally 1,076.

The classification of commitments of those under fifteen years only runs back a few years. The number of little girls imprisoned the past few years is as follows:

1863	403	1868	289
1864	295	1870	281
1865	275	1871	212

CRIME CHECKED AMONG THE BOYS.

The imprisonments of males for offenses which boys are likely to commit, though not so encouraging as with the girls, shows that juvenile crime is fairly under control in this city. Thus "vagrancy" must include many of the crimes of boys; under this head we find the following commitments of males:

1859	2,829	1865	1,350
1860	2,708	1870	1,140
1862	1,203	1871	994
1864	1,147		

In twelve years a reduction from 2,829 to 994, when the natural increase should have been up to 3,225.

Petty larceny is a boy's crime; the record stands thus for males:

1857	2,450	1869	2,338
1859	2,626	1870	2,168
1860	2,575	1871	1,978
1865	2,347		

A decrease in fourteen years of 502, when the natural increase should have brought the number to 2,861.

Of boys under fifteen imprisoned, the record stands thus since the new classification:

1864	1,965	1870	1,625
1865	1,934	1871	1,017
1869	1,872		

Of males between fifteen and twenty, in our city prisons, the following is the record:

1857	2,592	1868	2,927
1859	2,636	1870	2,876
1860	2,207	1871	2,936
1861	2,408		

It often happens that youthful criminals are arrested who are not imprisoned. The reports of the board of police will give us other indications that, even here, juvenile crime has at length been diminished in its sources.

ARRESTS.

The arrests of pickpockets run thus since 1861, the limit of returns accessible:

1861	466	1868	348
1862	300	1869	303
1865	275	1870	274
1867	345	1871	313

In ten years a reduction of 153 in the arrests of pickpockets.
In petty larceny the returns stand thus in brief:

1862	4,107	1870	4,909
1865	5,240	1871	3,912
1867	5,269		

A decrease in nine years of 195.
Arrests of girls alone under twenty:

1863	3,132	1870	1,993
1867	2,588	1871	1,820

When we consider the enormous destruction of property, the cost to the public of their prosecution and support, and the loss of productive energy which all these youthful criminals occasioned to society by their offenses and imprisonment, we can approximate the immense saving, even in a pecuniary respect, to the city, of labors which thus reduce the number of vagrants, thieves, and convicts.

There can be no question that no outlay of public money or of private charity is so productive, or pays so well, as that for educational and charitable enterprises like our own.

D.—REVIEW OF THE STATE AND CONDITION OF PENAL AND REFORMATORY INSTITUTIONS IN THE UNITED STATES.

NOTE.—An extended paper on the county jails, State prisons, houses of correction, houses of refuge, and reform schools of the United States has been prepared for publication as a part of the present report, but such an avalanche of work was precipitated upon the Public Printer, taxing the resources of his office to its utmost capacity for weeks, and even months, that, it was found absolutely impossible to get the Commissioner's report out in time for the meeting of the congress of London on any other condition than that of curtailing the document by the suppression of that portion of it. This suppression had to be assented to, however reluctantly, upon the principle expressed in the homely adage that "half a loaf is better than no bread."

CHARLES L. BRACE,
Chairman.

NEW YORK, *January* 27, 1871.

APPENDIX.

THE NATIONAL PRISON ASSOCIATION OF THE UNITED STATES OF AMERICA.*

I.—OFFICERS OF THE ASSOCIATION FOR 1872.

President.—Hon. Horatio Seymonr, Utica, New York.

Vice-Presidents.—Hon. James G. Blaine, Speaker United States House of Representatives, Augusta, Maine; Hou. Daniel Haines, Hamburgh, New Jersey; Hon. Francis Lieber, LL. D., 48 East Thirty-fourth street, New York; General Amos Pilsbury, superintendent Albany Penitentiary, Albany, New York; Hon. Conrad Baker, governor of Indiana, Indianapolis, Indiana.

Treasurer.—Salem H. Wales, esq., 520 Fifth avenue, New York.

Corresponding Secretary.—E. C. Wines, D.D., LL.D.; office, 194 Broadway; residence, Irvington, New York.

Recording Secretary.—Bradford K. Peirce, D. D., chaplain House of Refuge, Randall's Island, New York.

II.—BOARD OF DIRECTORS.

Samuel Allinson, Yardville, New Jersey.

William H. Aspinwall, esq., 33 University Place, New York.

Hon. Conrad Baker, governor of Indiana, Indianapolis, Indiana.

Henry W. Bellows, D. D., 232 East Fifteenth street, New York.

Hon. James G. Blaine, Speaker United States House of Representatives, Augusta, Maine.

Rev. Charles L. Brace, secretary Children's Aid Society, 19 Fourth street, New York.

Z. R. Brockway, esq., superintendent Detroit House of Correction, Detroit, Michigan.

James Brown, esq., 38 East Thirty-seventh street, New York.

Charles F. Coffin, president board of directors, House of Refuge, Richmond, Indiana.

Hon. Theodore W. Dwight, LL. D., president Columbia College Law School, 37 Lafayette Place, New York.

G. S. Griffith, esq., Baltimore, Maryland.

Hon. Daniel Haines, Hamburgh, New Jersey.

E. W. Hatch, M. D., superintendent State Reform School, West Meriden, Connecticut.

Hon. R. B. Hayes, Cincinnati, Ohio.

Morris K. Jesup, esq., 59 Liberty street, New York.

John Taylor Johnston, esq., 119 Liberty street, New York.

Hon. Francis Lieber, LL. D., 48 East Thirty-fourth street, New York.

A. J. Ourt, M. D., corresponding secretary board of public charities, 737 Walnut street, Philadelphia, Pennsylvania.

---

* It was by this association that the international penitentiary congress was first formally proposed, and by it the work of preparation has been mainly conducted, through its corresponding secretary, who was also clothed with an official character by a commission from the President of the United States to represent the Government in the congress.

S. Ex. 39——16

B. K. Peirce, D. D., chaplain House of Refuge, Randall's Island, New York.

General Amos Pilsbury, superintendent Albany penitentiary, Albany, New York.

F. B. Sanborn, esq., editor, Springfield, Massachusetts.

Hon. Horatio Seymour, Utica, New York.

Hon. L. Stanford, Sacramento, California.

Oliver S. Strong, esq., president board of managers New York House of Refuge, 61 Bible House, New York.

Salem H. Wales, 520 Fifth avenue.

Hon. and Rev. G. William Welker, Goldsborough, North Carolina.

A. R. Wetmore, president board of managers New York Juvenile Asylum, 365 Greenwich street, New York.

Hon. R. K. White, Louisville, Kentucky.

John E. Williams, esq., president Metropolitan National Bank, 108 Broadway, New York.

E. C. Wines, D. D., LL. D., 194 Broadway, New York.

III.—STANDING COMMITTEES.

1. *Executive committee.*—The president, treasurer, corresponding secretary, and recording secretary, *ex officio ;* H. W. Bellows, D. D., Rev. Charles L. Brace, and O. S. Strong.

2. *Committee on criminal law reform.*—H. Seymour, F. Lieber, Daniel Haines, Conrad Baker, James G. Blaine, Theodore W. Dwight, R. B. Hayes.

3. *Committee on prison discipline.*—F. B. Sanborn, Z. R. Brockway, Amos Pilsbury, A. J. Ourt, G. William Welker.

4. *Committee on juvenile delinquency.*—C. L. Brace, B. K. Peirce, O. S. Strong, E. W. Hatch, A. R. Wetmore.

5. *Committee on discharged prisoners.*—Samuel Allinson, Daniel Haines, Charles Coffin, R. K. White, G. S. Griffith.

IV.—CORRESPONDING MEMBERS.

John Stewart Mill, esq., Blackheath Park, Kent, England.

Mr. Commissioner M. D. Hill, Heath House, Stapleton, near Bristol, England.

Miss Mary Carpenter, Red Lodge Reformatory, Bristol, England.

Miss Florence Nightingale, South street, London, England.

Right Hon. Sir Walter Crofton, C. B., Hillingdon, Uxbridge, England.

Sir John Bowring, Claremont, Exeter, England.

Frederic Hill, esq., 27 Thurlow Road, Hampstead, London, England.

Edwin Hill, esq., No. 1 Saint Mark's Square, Regent's Park, London, England.

Miss Florence Hill, Heath House, Stapleton, near Bristol, England.

Miss Joanna Margaret Hill, Birmingham, England.

Alfred Aspland, esq., Dukenfield, Ashton-under-Lyne, England.

William Tallack, esq., No. 5 Bishopsgate street, Without, London, England.

Charles Ford, esq., 24 New street, Spring Gardens, London, England.

Rev. Sydney Turner, inspector of reformatories, 15 Parliament street, London, England.

W. L. Sargant, esq., Birmingham, England.

Edwin Chadwick, esq., Montlake, England.

A. Augus Croll, esq., Putney, England.

Miss Francis Power Cobbe, 26 Hereford Square, London, England.

George W. Hastings, esq., 1 Adam street, Adelphi, London, England.

T. B. Ll. Baker, Hardwicke Court, Gloucester, England.

T. L. Murray Browne, esq., No. 4 Old Square, Lincolu's Inn, London, England.

Edwin Pears, esq., Secretary of British Social Science Association, No. 1 Adam street, Adelphi, London, England.

Captain E. F. Du Cane, surveyor general of prisons, No. 44 Parliament street, London, England.

John Lentaigue, esq., inspector of county and borough jails, Dublin, Ireland.

Patrick Joseph Murray, esq., director of convict prisons, Dublin, Ireland.

Captain J. Barlow, director of convict prisons, Dublin, Ireland.

M. Bonneville de Marsaugy, 7 rue Penthiévre, Paris, France.

M. Victor Bournat, 20 rue Jacob, Paris, France.

M. E. Robin, (pasteur,) 21 rue Piat, Belleville, Paris, France.

M. J. Jaillant, director of prisons, ministry of the interior, Paris, France.

M. Jules de Lamarque, chief of bureau, direction of prisons, Paris, France.

Dr. Prosper Despine, 12 rue du Loisor, Marseilles, France.

M. Charles Lucas, member of the Institute, Paris, France.

M. le Vicompt d'Haussonville, member of the national assembly, rue St. Dominique, Paris, France.

M. Auguste Demetz, 92 rue de la Victoire, Paris, France.

M. A. Corne, sous-prefect, St. Omer, France.

M. Berden, administrator of prisons, Brusseles, Belgium.

M. J. Stevens, inspector general of prisons, Brusseles, Belgium.

M. Auguste Visschers 106, rue Royale, Brusseles, Belgium.

Mr. Alstorphius Grovelink, inspector of prisons, the Hague, Netherlands.

Mr. W. H. Suringar, president of the Netherlands Society for the Moral Reform of Prisoners, Amsterdam, Netherlands.

Rev. Dr. Laurillard, secretary of same, Amsterdam, Netherlands.

Mr. B. J. Ploos Von Amstel, Amsterdam, Netherlands.

Dr. Guillaume, director of the Penitentiary, Neuchâtel, Switzerland.

Mr. Max Wirth, chief of the statistical bureau, Berne, Switzerland.

Signor F. Cardon, director general of prisons, Rome, Italy.

Signor M. Bettrani-Scalia, inspector general of prisons, Rome, Italy.

Baron Franz Von Holtzendorff, professor of law in the University of Berlin, Charlottenburg, near Berlin, Prussia.

Rev. Dr. Wichern, director of the Rauhe Haus, Horn, near Hamburg, Germany.

Mr. Fr. Bruün, director of prisons, Copenhagen, Denmark.

V.—LIFE DIRECTORS BY THE CONTRIBUTION OF TWO HUNDRED DOL-
LARS OR UPWARD, AT ONE TIME, TO THE FUNDS OF THE ASSOCIA-
TION.

Timothy M. Allyn, Hartford, Connecticut.

James Brown, New York.

Morris K. Jesup, New York.

W. Soldatenkoff, St. Petersburg, Russia.

VI.—Life Members by the Contribution of One Hundred Dollars or Upward at One Time.

William H. Aspinwall, New York.
W. Amory, Boston, Massachusetts.
H. K. Corning, New York.
Erastus Corning, Albany, New York.
D. Denny, Boston, Massachusetts.
Edward Earle, Worcester, Massachusetts.
George B. Emerson, Boston, Massachusetts.
Mrs. Mary A. Holden, Providence, Rhode Island.
Joseph Howland, Matteawan, New York.
John Taylor Johnston, New York.
Amos Pilsbury, Albany, New York.
Jonathan Sturges, New York.
N. Thayer, Boston, Massachusetts.
E. C. Wines, New York.
John David Wolfe, New York.

VII.—Contributions to the National Prison Association from May, 1871, to May, 1872.

California.

Mrs. L. Hutchison, Bishop Creek.................................... $10

Connecticut.

Timothy M. Allyn, Hartford....................................	$500	
James E. English, New Haven................................	25	
R. S. Fellowes, New Haven....................................	10	
Rev. Thos. K. Fessenden, Farmington	10	
Miss M. W. Wells, Hartford..................................	25	
		570

Illinois.

Geo. W. Perkins, Pontiac.. 10

Indiana.

Charles F. Coffin, Richmond 10

Kentucky.

P. Caldwell, Louisville 10

Maryland.

W. R. Lincoln, Baltimore 10

Massachusetts.

W. Amory, Boston....................................	100
William J. Bowditch, Boston	10
Gridley J. F. Bryant, Boston........................	10
John W. Candler, Boston	50
Cash, Boston..	10
D. Denny, Boston	100
Mrs. Henry F. Durant, Boston	50
Edward Earle, Worcester............................	100
Geo. B. Emerson, Boston............................	100
Charles O. Foster, Boston...........................	25
A. Hardy, Boston	25
S. G. Howe, Boston..................................	10
Mrs. Julia Ward Howe, Boston	10
Samuel Johnson, Boston	10
H. P. Kidder, Boston	50
O. W. Peabody, Boston..............................	50
Avory Plumer, Boston...............................	10

M. S. Scudder, Boston $20
E. S. Tobey, Boston 50
Nathaniel Thayer, Boston 100
J. C. Tyler, Boston 10
Samuel D. Warren, Boston 50
$950

Michigan.

O. Goldsmith, Detroit 10
H. V. N. Lothrop, Detroit 10
R. McLelland, Detroit 10
James McMillen, Detroit 10
John S. Newberry, Detroit 10
C. J. Walker, Detroit 10
60

New Hampshire.

Rev. William Clark, Andover 10

New York.

William H. Aspinwall, New York 200
James Brown, New York 400
Stewart Brown, New York 100
H. K. Corning, New York 150
Erastus Corning, Albany 200
Winthrop S. Gilman, New York 100
Joseph Howland, Matteawan 150
James Hunter, New York 20
Morris K. Jesup, New York 200
John Taylor Johnston, New York 100
Henry T. Morgan, New York 50
Amos Pilsbury, Albany 100
H. F. Phinney, Cooperstown 25
Guy Richards, New York 45
Jonathan Sturges, New York 150
E. C. Wines, New York 200
John David Wolfe, New York 200
Weston & Gray, New York 100
Salem H. Wales, New York 100
John E. Williams, New York 50
2,640

Ohio.

G. E. Howe, Lancaster 10
Mrs. R. A. S. Janney, Columbus 10
20

Pennsylvania.

Henry Cordier, Claremont, Allegheny County 50
T. H. Nevin, Allegheny 10
60

Rhode Island.

A. E. Burnside, Providence 10
A. C. Barstow, Providence 20
Jacob Dunnell, Pawtucket 10
W. W. Hoppin, Providence 10
Mrs. Mary A. Holden, Providence 100
Robert H. Ives, Providence 60
William J. King, Providence 40
Mrs. Henry Lippitt, Providence 20
Jesse Metcalf, Providence 10
Seth Padelford, Providence 10
Mrs. G. M. Richmond, Providence 30
Miss Caroline Richmond, Providence 20
A. & W. Sprague, Providence 100
James Y. Smith & Nichol, Providence 40
Amos D. Smith, Providence 10
H. J. Steere, Providence 10
James Tillinghast, Providence 20
Royal C. Taft, Providence 20
Rev. Augustus Woodbury, Providence 20
560

Russia.

W. Soldatenkoff, St. Petersburg $200

Total contributions for the year 5,120

VIII.—ACT OF INCORPORATION.

The people of the State of New York, represented in senate and assembly, do enact as follows:

SECTION 1. Horatio Seymour, Theodore W. Dwight, Francis Lieber, Amos Pilsbury, James Brown, William H. Aspinwall, John Taylor Johnston, John E. Williams, Theodore Roosevelt, Morris K. Jesup, Isaac Bell, James G. Blaine, Conrad Baker, Rutherford B. Hayes, Daniel Haines, Enoch C. Wines, Oliver S. Strong, Bradford K. Peirce, Charles L. Brace, Charles F. Coffin, Howard Potter, Henry S. Terbell, Z. R. Brockway, Frank B. Sanborn, Edward W. Hatch, and their associates and successors in office, are hereby constituted a body corporate and politic, by the name of "The National Prison Association of the United States of America," whose duty it shall be to consider and recommend plans for the promotion of the objects following; that is to say—

1. The amelioration of the laws in relation to public offenses and offenders, and the modes of procedure by which such laws are enforced.

2. The improvement of the penal, correctional, and reformatory institutions throughout the country, and the government, management, and discipline thereof, including the appointment of boards of control and of other officers.

3. The care of, and providing suitable and remunerative employment for, discharged prisoners, and especially such as may or shall have given evidence of a reformation of life.

SEC. 2. The principal place of business of the said corporation shall be in the city of New York; and the management and disposition of its affairs, property, and funds shall be vested in the persons named in the first section of this act, and their associates and their successors in office, who shall remain in office for such period, and be displaced and succeeded by others to be elected at the times and in the manner prescribed by the by-laws. The number of members to constitute a quorum shall be fixed by the by-laws.

SEC. 3. The said corporation shall have power to purchase or take by gift, grant, devise, or bequest, real and personal property to an amount not exceeding three hundred thousand dollars, subject to the provisions of chapter three hundred and sixty of the laws of eighteen hundred and sixty.

SEC. 4. The said corporation shall have and possess all the general powers, and be subject to all the liabilities, contained in the third title of chapter eighteen of the first part of the Revised Statutes.

SEC. 5. This act shall take effect immediately.

STATE OF NEW YORK,
   Office of the Secretary of State, ss:

I have compared the preceding with the original law on file in this office, and do hereby certify that the same is a correct transcript therefrom, and of the whole of said original law.

Given under my hand and seal of office at the city of Albany, this twenty-ninth day of April, in the year one thousand eight hundred and seventy-one.

DEIDRICH WILLERS,
Deputy Secretary of State.

IX.—CONSTITUTION.

ARTICLE I. This association shall be called the National Prison Association of the United States of America, and its objects shall be—

1. The amelioration of the laws in relation to public offenses and offenders, and the modes of procedure by which such laws are enforced.

2. The improvement of the penal, correctional, and reformatory institutions throughout the country, and of the government, management, and discipline thereof, including the appointment of boards of control and of other officers.

3. The care of, and providing suitable and remunerative employment for, discharged prisoners, and especially such as may or shall have given evidence of a reformation of life.

ART. II. The officers of the association shall be a president, five vice-presidents, a corresponding secretary, a recording secretary, a treasurer, and a board of directors, not exceeding thirty in number, of which the officers above named shall be *ex officio* members.

ART. III. There shall be the following standing committees, namely: An executive committee, of which the president shall be *ex officio* chairman, the recording secretary *ex officio* secretary, and the corresponding secretary and treasurer *ex officio* members; a committee on criminal law reform; a committee on prison discipline; a committee on juvenile delinquency; and a committee on discharged prisoners.

ART. IV. The board of directors, of whom any five members shall constitute a quorum—two of said members being officers of the association—shall meet semi-annually, and in the interval of its meetings its powers shall be exercised by the executive committee, which shall fix its own times of meeting.

ART. V. Committees of correspondence shall be organized in the several States, as may be found practicable; and the formation of State associations shall be encouraged.

ART. VI. Any person contributing annually to the funds of the association not less than ten dollars shall be a member thereof; a contribution of one hundred dollars at any one time shall constitute the contributor a life member; and a contribution of two hundred dollars at any one time shall entitle the contributor to be a life director. Corresponding members may be appointed by the board of directors or by the executive committee. The power of electing officers shall be confined to the corporate members of the association.

ART. VII. The association shall hold an annual meeting at such time and place as the executive committee shall appoint, on which occasion the several standing committees, the corresponding secretary, and the treasurer shall submit annual reports. Special meetings may be called by the president in his discretion, and shall be called by him whenever he is requested to do so by any three members of the board.

ART. VIII. All officers of the association shall be elected at the annual meeting or some adjournment thereof; but vacancies occurring after the annual meeting may be filled by the board of directors, who shall also appoint all committees not chosen at the annual meeting; and all officers shall hold over till their successors are chosen.

ART. IX. The executive committee shall consist of seven members of the board of directors—the president, the recording secretary, the corresponding secretary, and the treasurer being *ex officio* members—any three of whom shall constitute a quorum for the transaction of business.

ART. X. This constitution may be amended by vote of a majority of tbe members of the association at any meeting thereof : *Provided*, That notice of the proposed amendment shall have been given at the next preceding meeting.

X.—BY-LAWS.

I. The order of business at each stated meeting of the board shall be as follows:
1. Reading of the minutes.
2. Report of the treasurer.
3. Report of the corresponding secretary.
4. Reports from standing committees.
5. Reports from special committees.
6. Miscellaneous business.

II. The president, corresponding secretary, recording secretary, and treasurer shall perform the customary duties of their respective offices.

III. The president shall appoint the committees, unless otherwise ordered by the association.

IV. The president shall decide questions of order, subject to an appeal; and the rules of order shall be those in Cushing's Manual, so far as they may be applicable.

V. No bills shall be paid by the treasurer unless approved and signed by the chairman of the executive committee, or by some other member of said committee designated by him.

VI. No alteration shall be made in these by-laws, except on notice of the proposed amendment given at a previous meeting of the board.